The Medieval Mind

Contents of *A History of Western Philosophy*, SECOND EDITION

I. The Classical Mind

1 Pre-Socratic Philosophy / **2** Education Through Violence / **3** Atomism / **4** Plato: The Theory of Forms / **5** Plato: The Special Sciences / **6** Aristotle: Metaphysics, Natural Science, Logic / **7** Aristotle: Ethics, Politics, Art / **8** The Late Classical Period

II. The Medieval Mind

1 The New Religious Orientation / **2** Christianity: The Formative Years / **3** Augustine: God the Creator / **4** Augustine: The Created Universe / **5** The Medieval Interval / **6** Thomas: Metaphysics / **7** Thomas: Psychology, Ethics, Politics / **8** The End of the Middle Ages

III. Hobbes to Hume

1 Renaissance / **2** Reformation / **3** Science and Scientific Method / **4** Hobbes / **5** Descartes / **6** Spinoza / **7** Leibniz / **8** Locke / **9** Berkeley / **10** Hume

IV. Kant to Wittgenstein and Sartre

1 The Age of Reason / **2** Kant: Theory of Knowledge / **3** Kant: Theory of Value / **4** Reactions Against Kantianism: Hegel and Schopenhauer / **5** Science, Scientism, and Social Philosophy / **6** Kierkegaard and Nietzsche / **7** Three Philosophies of Process: Bergson, Dewey, and Whitehead / **8** The Analytical Tradition: Russell and Wittgenstein / **9** The Phenomenological Tradition: Husserl and Sartre

W. T. JONES
California Institute of Technology

The
Medieval Mind

A History of Western Philosophy
SECOND EDITION

Harcourt Brace Jovanovich, Inc.

NEW YORK   CHICAGO   SAN FRANCISCO   ATLANTA

LIST OF COPYRIGHTS AND ACKNOWLEDGMENTS

The author records his thanks for the use of the selections reprinted in this book by permission of the following publishers and copyright holders:

BURNS & OATES LTD. for excerpts from *Summa Contra Gentiles* by Thomas Aquinas, translated by the English Dominican Fathers.

CHATTO AND WINDUS LTD. for excerpts from *Medieval Lore from Bartholomew Anglecus*, Kings Classics, edited by R. Steele.

JOHN CIARDI for an excerpt from *The Purgatorio* by Dante, translated by John Ciardi.

J. M. DENT & SONS LTD. for excerpts from *The Romance of the Rose*, translated by F. S. Ellis.

LIVERIGHT PUBLISHING CORPORATION for excerpts from *The Confessions of Saint Augustine*, translated and annotated by J. G. Pilkington, M.A. Reprinted by permission of Liveright, Publishers, New York.

THE NEW AMERICAN LIBRARY, INC., for excerpts from *The Purgatorio* by Dante, translated by John Ciardi. Copyright © 1957, 1959, 1960, and 1961 by John Ciardi. Reprinted by arrangement with The New American Library, Inc., New York.

RANDOM HOUSE, INC., for excerpts from *Basic Writings of St. Thomas Aquinas*, Vols. I and II, edited by A. C. Pegis. Copyright 1945 by Random House, Inc. Reprinted by permission of the publisher.

SAINT JOHN'S COLLEGE BOOKSTORE for excerpts from *On the Division of Nature* by John Scotus Erigena, translated by C. Schwartz.

CHARLES SCRIBNER'S SONS for excerpts from *The History of Christian Thought*, pp. 75–229, by Arthur C. McGiffert. Copyright 1933 by Charles Scribner's Sons; renewal copyright © 1961 by Gertrude H. Boyce McGiffert. And for excerpts from *Selections of Medieval Philosophers*, Vol. I, pp. 91–254, and Vol. II, pp. 313–30, edited and translated by R. McKeon. Copyright 1929 by Charles Scribner's Sons; renewal copyright © 1957. Reprinted with the permission of Charles Scribner's Sons.

THE SOCIETY OF AUTHORS for an excerpt from *The Divine Comedy* by Dante, translated by Laurence Binyon. Reprinted by permission of Mrs. Nicolete Gray and The Society of Authors, on behalf of the Laurence Binyon Estate.

GRACE H. TURNBULL for excerpts from the *Enneads* by Plotinus, translated by Stephen MacKenna, from *The Essence of Plotinus*, edited by Grace H. Turnbull.

Preface

The changes incorporated into this revision of A *History of Western Philosophy* reflect what I have learned, in the seventeen years since the book was first published, about the history of philosophy, the nature of the philosophical enterprise itself, and the role that philosophy plays in the general culture. They also reflect a good deal of thought about what characteristics make a textbook useful.

The most noticeable innovation is the division of the book into four separate volumes: *I. The Classical Mind; II. The Medieval Mind; III. Hobbes to Hume;* and *IV. Kant to Wittgenstein and Sartre.* This division has provided space for expansion of the text, especially in the fourth volume. It also conforms to the way in which courses in the history of philosophy are now organized and enables the reader to choose the periods on which he wishes to concentrate.

In my revision I have been able to condense and at the same time clarify the exposition materially. In addition, I have greatly simplified the elaborate

system of subheadings used in the first edition, for I believe that today's generation of students no longer needs such a complex set of guideposts. The conden-
sation of material and the elimination of superfluous heads have allowed me to
expand the discussions of a number of thinkers and to add discussions of many
others who were omitted from the earlier edition. For instance, in Volume I,
I have added a short section on axiomatic geometry and a longer section on Greek
Scepticism, with extracts from the writings of Sextus Empiricus. In Volume II,
I have added a discussion of Gnosticism and have balanced this with a section on
physical theory in the late Middle Ages, illustrated by quotations from John
Buridan. It is Volume IV, however, that contains the most extensive additions.
The sections on Hegel, Marx, and Nietzsche have been completely rewritten and
greatly expanded; there are entirely new chapters on Kierkegaard, Wittgenstein,
Husserl, and Sartre.

There are also a great many changes—some of them major—in my interpretation and evaluation of individual thinkers and their theories. For instance, I have
softened my criticisms of Greek Atomism and of Augustine, and in the sections on
St. Paul and on the author of the Fourth Gospel I have taken account of recent
scholarship. There is, indeed, hardly a page that has not undergone extensive
revision. This edition is a thoroughgoing and rigorous updating of the first
version.

Despite all these alterations, my point of view remains basically the same.
In revising, as in originally writing, this history, I have been guided by four
principles—concentration, selectivity, contextualism, and the use of original
sources.

An historian of philosophy can either say something, however brief, about
everyone who philosophized, or he can limit himself to giving a reasonably con-
secutive account of a number of representative thinkers, omitting discussion of
many second- and third-flight philosophers. I have chosen the latter approach,
for two reasons. First, many works based on the first approach are already
available, and I see no good reason for adding to their number. Second, such
works are likely to be unintelligible to the beginning student. I still recall my
own bewilderment as an undergraduate in seeking to understand a complicated
theory that some expositor had "boiled down" to a summary. The principle of
concentration rests on the thesis that it is better to understand a few theories
than to be superficially acquainted with a great many.

But concentration implies selectivity, and I can hardly hope that even those
who accept the principle of concentration will approve all my selections. There
will probably be no difference of opinion about the great figures of the remote
past. Everyone will surely agree that Plato and Aristotle are the masters of
their age. And perhaps there will be general agreement that Augustine and
Thomas occupy similar positions in the Middle Ages—that Augustine demands
more attention than, say, Boethius, and Thomas more attention than Duns
Scotus. But how is one to choose among philosophers of more recent times?
Here one must try to anticipate the judgment of time. To some extent, I have

simply avoided the issue by dealing with more philosophers in the modern period. The result is that, whereas the first two volumes cover more than two millenia, the last two focus on hardly more than four hundred years.

Even so, I have been forced to be selective by my determination that here, as in the earlier periods, I would not mention a philosopher unless I could deal with his views in some detail. Thus I have repressed a natural desire at least to mention Fichte and Schelling, in order to provide extended analyses of Hegel and Schopenhauer. All these thinkers represent reactions to Kantianism, and although they differ among themselves in many ways, it is better, I believe, to select and concentrate on a few than to attempt to give a complete enumeration.

Also underlying the writing of this history is the generally recognized but seldom adopted principle that philosophers are men, not disembodied spirits. Some histories of philosophy treat theories as if they were isolated from everything except other philosophical theories. But all the great philosophers have actually been concerned with what may be called "local" problems. To be understood, their theories must be seen as expressions—doubtless at a highly conceptualized level—of the same currents of thought and feeling that were moving the poets and the statesmen, the theologians and the playwrights, and the ordinary men, of the age. Otherwise, how could their philosophies ever have been accepted? These philosophers furnished satisfactory answers only because they were alert to the problems that were exercising their contemporaries and because they were harassed by the same doubts. The cultural milieu in which a given philosophy emerges can be ignored only at the risk of making the philosophy seem a detached (and so meaningless and inconsequential) affair.

In carrying out this principle I have begun my account of Greek philosophy by describing the state of affairs in Athens at the end of the Peloponnesian War, and I have drawn on the plays of Euripides and Aristophanes to illustrate the mood of the times. This, I believe, is a necessary setting for Plato, because his central thesis—the theory of forms—was an attempt to answer the scepticism and cynicism of his age. Plato's insistence on the existence of "absolute" standards for conduct and for knowledge is understandable only as a reflection of the social, economic, and political chaos and the moral and religious collapse that occurred at the end of the fifth century.

Similarly, my discussion of medieval philosophy is prefaced with an account of the dissolving Roman Empire, and I have tried to indicate the rich and diversified cultural background within which Christian philosophy developed. In discussing the theories of Augustine and Thomas I have kept in mind that, whereas Augustine expressed the eschatological fervor of a new sect fighting for its life, Thomas embodied the serenity of an imperial and universal religion whose piety had been softened by a new sense of responsibility for "that which is Caesar's."

Finally, in discussing the development of early modern philosophy I have tried to show the many factors—exploration and discovery, the rise of money

power, Humanism, the Reformation, and above all the new scientific method—
that combined to overthrow the medieval synthesis and to create new problems
that philosophy even today is struggling to resolve. In a word, I have conceived
the history of philosophy to be a part of the general history of culture and hence
to be intelligible only in its cultural context.

The fourth principle is my conviction that in philosophy—or in any discipline, for that matter—nothing takes the place of a direct, patient, and pains-
taking study of a great and subtle mind. For this reason there is much to be
said for the use of a source book. But a source book alone has serious limitations, because its selections are apt to be discontinuous and difficult to follow.
The advantage of a text is that it can explicate obscure passages and draw
comparisons. Even so, explication and interpretation are not substitutes for the
documents themselves. Therefore, each of the volumes in this series stands
halfway between textbook and source book and tries to combine the advantages
of both: I have set out a philosopher's thought in his own words by a careful
selection of key passages and have bound these together with my own comment and criticism. The quoted passages constitute about one third of the contents.

To undertake to give an account of the history of philosophy in its cultural
context is a formidable and perhaps presumptuous task for a single expositor.
In this undertaking I have received help from a wide variety of sources. In
addition to those who have read and commented on the first edition, whose names
I shall not repeat here, I wish to thank many friends and colleagues who have
called my attention to points that needed correction: Stanley M. Daugert,
Stewart C. Easton, Robert L. Ferm, John H. Gleason, Douglas Greenlee, Ray-
mond Lindquist, Edwin L. Marvin, James A. McGilvray, Philip Merlan, John E.
Smith, Robert T. Voelkel, Culver G. Warner, Rev. S. Y. Watson, S.J., and R. M.
Yost, Jr. I am much indebted to Robert J. Fogelin, from whom I learned a great
deal during the years we taught a joint course on nineteenth-century philosophy,
and to Clark Glymour, who has sent me extensive notes, especially on the history
of science. My greatest appreciation is due to Cynthia A. Schuster, who read the
revised version of Volumes I, II, and III and commented in immense—and
immensely helpful—detail, and to Stephen A. Erickson, on whom I have constantly leaned for advice about matters small as well as great and whose detailed
comments both on the first edition and on successive drafts of the revision have
been invaluable. These readers have saved me from many errors of fact and interpretation; for errors that remain I must be responsible, and I shall be grateful if
any that come to notice are pointed out to me.

I am obliged to the many publishers and copyright holders (listed on pages
iv–v) through whose cooperation the quotations used in these volumes appear.
Since I have followed the style of the various writers and translators I have
quoted, there is some variation in spelling, capitalization, and punctuation in
the reprinted passages. Full bibliographical notes, keyed to the text by letters
rather than numbers, appear at the end of each volume.

For the secretarial work on the manuscript I am chiefly indebted to Helen Armstrong, Dorothy Overaker, Catherine Tramz, and Judith Strombotne, who divided the typing. I am also grateful to Paul Cabbell, who checked all references in the first three volumes and made many helpful suggestions, to Joan McGilvray, who performed a similar function for the last volume, and to my good friend Margaret L. Mulhauser, who generously allowed me to impose on her the onerous task of proofreading.

W. T. Jones

Contents

6

7

8

Introduction

Because the first Christians were only a very small minority in an indifferent and even hostile empire, and because they alone anticipated the imminent arrival of the day of judgment, they lacked the social, political, and cultural interests of the ancient world. They were intent upon their own salvation, and they believed that this salvation would be assured by faith in Christ, the risen Lord. Medieval philosophy was born when these Christians discovered that simple piety no longer satisfied them, and when the desire to *understand* revived. Unfortunately for the smooth development of a Christian philosophy, the Christians' beliefs actually stemmed from a variety of sources—the Judaic inheritance, the teachings of Jesus, the experiences of the first disciples, the mystery cults, and an overlay of late Hellenistic speculation. (Chapter 1.) It was extremely difficult to organize these disparate notions into a coherent body of doctrine, and the formative centuries of Christianity were dominated by a series of struggles to eliminate heresy and to establish orthodoxy. (Chapter 2.)

Augustine played an important role in this work. He wrote the *City of God* to explain why God had allowed Rome to fall victim to the barbarians, but he was far more than a clever publicist and apologist. Augustine's attempts to justify God's ways led him to make a thorough analysis of both the divine nature and human nature. His conception of God was greatly influenced—always within the framework of the canonical writings—by profound personal experiences: his sense of sin, his feeling of utter inability to save himself, his appreciation of the redeeming grace that flowed to him from outside. (Chapter 3.) But Augustine was never able to reconcile his convictions about God's infinitude (and man's corresponding finitude) with the necessity for attributing free will to man in order to absolve God from responsibility for man's sin. (Chapter 4.)

For centuries after the death of Augustine there was little philosophical activity—these were dark ages indeed. Gradually, however, learning and culture revived, and universities were founded. Meanwhile, the Church, too, was changing. Despite a nostalgia for the simplicity and otherworldliness displayed by the early Christians, the Church acquired social and political power in becoming a great this-worldly institution, with the responsibilities—and the temptations—that this power entailed. (Chapter 5.)

Philosophical speculation during the latter part of the Middle Ages was chiefly concentrated on ascertaining the status of universals (a problem that had theological as well as epistemological implications) and on defining and delimiting the respective spheres of faith and reason. In the course of these investigations, the instruments of logical analysis were greatly refined and the Scholastic method was devised. All this prepared the way for Aquinas' synthesis of classical learning with Christian insights. Aquinas reinterpreted the traditional Christian view of the divine nature in terms of the basic Aristotelian concepts of form and matter, actuality and potentiality. This synthesis was a much more consistent and formally complete metaphysics than Augustine had been able to work out. (Chapter 6.) Furthermore, Aquinas' theories of psychology, ethics, and politics reflected both his own interest in this world and its affairs and the changed position and functions of the Roman Church. (Chapter 7.)

After Aquinas, philosophers turned from large-scale synthesis to analysis of relatively small-scale, "technical" problems. Whereas Roger Bacon was an empirically oriented, and even pragmatic, thinker, Duns Scotus and William of Occam were subtle logicians who undertook to refine and correct Aquinas' theory of knowledge. But their thinking, like that of all their predecessors, was limited by the concept of orthodoxy. However rational and acute philosophical analysis might have become, it still had to operate within the strict limits set for it by transcendental truths, truths that were above reason and immune to analysis. The ultimate criterion for all knowledge and the ultimate sanction for all conduct was not the concurrence of human minds guided by the light of reason but the authority of a divinely inspired text and a divinely established institution. Given this ideal of orthodoxy, a major development in philosophy could hardly occur until Western men were prepared to break radically with the whole Christian world view. (Chapter 8.)

Perhaps the principal element of this world view was its sacramental out-look. What made Augustine, Aquinas, and the other medieval thinkers so funda-mentally alike was this outlook they shared. What distinguishes the modern mind so sharply from the medieval mind is that modern men have largely lost that out-look and now share the basically secular point of view of the Greeks. To say that medieval men looked on this world as a sacrament means, first, that they con-ceived this world to be but the visible sign of an invisible reality, a world thor-oughly impregnated with the energy, purpose, and love of its Creator, who dwells in it as He dwells in the bread and wine on the altar. Second, it means that medieval men conceived of this world as a sacrifice to be freely and grate-fully dedicated to the all-good, all-true Giver. Thus, whereas for us (and for the Greeks) the world by and large means just what it seems to be, for men of the Middle Ages it meant something beyond itself and immeasurably better. Whereas for us (and for the Greeks) life on earth is its own end, for medieval men life's true end was beyond this world.

It can hardly be denied that this sacramental point of view was a block to progress—progress in knowledge of how to control the environment and utilize it for this-worldly purposes. To many it seems equally obvious, now that this viewpoint has disappeared, that men have rid themselves of much that was a liability—ignorance, superstition, intolerance. What is not so obvious is that the modern world has also lost something of value. If the sacramental outlook of the Middle Ages manifested itself here and there in what a modern clinician would describe as acute psychopathology, it also manifested itself in serenity and confidence, in a sense of purpose, meaningfulness, and fulfillment—qualities that the modern clinician looks for in vain among his contemporaries.

Order these my loves, O Thou who lovest me!

JACOPONE DA TODI

O Light Eternal, who in thyself alone
  Dwell'st and thyself know'st, and self-understood,
  Self-understanding, smilest on thine own! . . .
  Like to a wheel whose circling nothing jars
  Already on my desire and will prevailed
The Love that moves the sun and the other stars.

DANTE

CHAPTER 1

The New Religious Orientation

Secularism was perhaps the most pervasive characteristic of the classical mind. Man's leading problem, it held, is the achievement of well-being in this world. It believed men have the intellectual and moral capacities to solve this problem and to fashion a good life for themselves by their own efforts. The Middle Ages were, by contrast, a period during which philosophy was dominated by other-worldly interests. The problems not of this life but of the next seemed of primary importance. Instead of a social, there was now a supernal ideal. Ethics and politics as the leading sciences gave way to the science of theology, which, for the Greeks, had been merely an appendix to physics. And science itself (conceived of as rational inquiry) declined in importance in an age in which man's natural powers were regarded as severely limited. The medieval mind, acutely conscious of its inability to achieve the supernatural good for which it now hoped, put its trust in an Infinite Being held to be supremely good and powerful and the creator of everything that is. Man's proper relation with this being became the primary concern of the Western world for some twelve centuries.

Though this profound change in orientation did not, of course, occur overnight, the thought of Marcus Aurelius (121–180 A.D.) can be regarded as a turning point. The spirit of the future was plainly visible in his *Meditations* and in Stoic doctrine generally, seen in such characteristics as otherworldliness, deprecation of this life and its transitory affairs, religious fervor, emphasis on duty, a sense of sin, and the notion of a universal society. Nevertheless, these ideas were still tempered by a basically classical outlook because of an insistence that man is a social, and a civic, being.

During the course of the next century the emphasis markedly shifted—not, of course, that classical attitudes disappeared altogether, but rather that the newer ideas now tended to dominate.

The Mystery Cults

Among the earliest manifestations of this new spirit were the so-called mystery cults. Of these, three are important and representative.

THE GREAT MOTHER

The worship of the Great Mother concerned the myth of the goddess Cybele. When her lover, Attis, died, the goddess mourned, and death came upon the world. When Attis was brought back to life, the goddess rejoiced and nature put on a garment of green. To rehearse the myth was doubtless at first simply a way to assure a good crop. Later, when it became a way for the worshipers to share in the immortality of Attis, the old vegetation rites were retained. In the spring of the year the adherents of the cult indulged in a period of mourning for the dead Attis. They fasted and flagellated themselves; more passionate devotees castrated themselves in a frenzy of excitement. These latter worshipers, exalted by their sacrifice, became priests of the cult.

Another rite of the Great Mother, which shows again how a very primitive ceremony gradually evolved into a religion of redemption, was the "taurobolium." In this ceremony the initiate stood in a pit below a platform on which a bull was butchered. "Through the thousand crevices in the wood," wrote a fourth-century observer, "the bloody dew runs down into the pit. The neophyte receives the falling drops on his head, clothes and body. He leans backward to have his cheeks, his ears, his lips and his nostrils wetted; he pours the liquid over his eyes, and does not even spare his palate, for he moistens his tongue with the blood and drinks it eagerly."[a] Stemming from an ancient magical belief that a man takes on the characteristics of the animal of whose body he partakes, this rite became a kind of baptism in which the initiate was purged of his sins. "Reborn into eternity" was a favorite motto of the worshipers of the Great Mother.

ISIS AND OSIRIS

Like the myth of the Great Mother, the myth of Isis involved the death and resurrection of a god, Osiris, and guaranteed the salvation of the devout. As with Attis, the ritual simulated first the death of Osiris, then the lamentation of Isis, and finally the joy of Osiris' resurrection. This ritual was, however, more restrained than that of the Great Mother. It involved two daily services—a morning ceremony at which the priest drew aside the covering that during the night had veiled the statue of the goddess and an evening ceremony at which the statue was again concealed.

MITHRA

Mithraism, too, was concerned with a savior god whose worship held the promise of eternal life. But in Mithraism this now familiar redemptionist belief was connected with a complex theology whose central tenets were derived from a dualistic metaphysics. Mithraism held it impossible to explain the universe as the product of a single principle, as Greek science on the whole had sought to do. According to Mithraism, two principles are at work in the world. One of these is responsible for all the good that occurs, the elements of order in the universe; the other, for all the evil and disorder. But instead of treating these principles as natural forces, Mithraism deified them as good and evil powers. The universe is merely the battleground on which these powers contend, and men, like loyal soldiers, should take their place on the side of the good power.

But support of the cause of goodness is handicapped by the soul's history. From its original home in heaven every soul has traveled down toward the earth through the spheres of the seven planets. As it has passed through each sphere it has acquired some of the disabilities that mark this life of the flesh. Its time here on earth in the prison house of the body is a testing ground for the soul. If the soul does well—if it is continent, loyal, and devout—it will be reunited with god in that region of beauty and light whence it came. Otherwise, it will suffer eternally in hell with the demons who are the agents of the evil principle in the universe.

In this scheme, Mithra was both judge and savior. He presided over the trial at which, after a man's death, the merits and demerits of his soul were weighed; he supported his worshipers in the never ending struggle against evil, and he promised the faithful final victory.

The rites of Mithra elaborately symbolized this theological doctrine. Full membership in the sect could only be won gradually. The prospective worshiper had to pass through seven stages, corresponding to the seven phases of the soul's descent to earth, by which he was gradually lifted from the impurity of his former life to the level of full communion. Admission to each new grade was preceded by ordeals that tested the soul's worthiness.

Since Mithra was associated with the sun (for the sun, bringer of light, was also the god of purity and goodness, in contrast with the powers of evil, which were identified with darkness), many of his rites were tied to events in the solar year. He was worshiped thrice daily—at dawn, noon, and sunset; the seventh day of the week was especially sacred to him; and the greatest of all his festivals fell on December 25, the day of the sun's nativity, when he was reborn after the winter solstice.

RECEPTION OF THE CULTS AT ROME

These mystery cults met with a varying reception in Rome. But generally they were officially opposed during Republican times and welcomed under the Empire. Thus, despite the fact that the Great Mother, introduced from Phrygia in 205 B.C., when the Carthaginian War was going badly, was given credit for the victories that soon followed, the Senate strictly limited her worship. In imperial days, however, Roman citizens were permitted to serve as her priests and to participate openly in her rites, and imperial princes were included among her devotees.

Similarly, during the closing years of the Republic repeated attempts were made to break up the worship of Isis. In 59, 58, 53, and 48 B.C. orders were issued to destroy the altars of Isis, and in 21 B.C. her worship was forbidden in the city. But such was the hold the cult already had on the populace that none of these measures—not even a severe persecution ordered by the emperor Tiberius in 19 A.D.—was successful, and gradually the emperors themselves came first to tolerate and eventually to support the sect.

The worship of Mithra, which originated in Persia, reached Rome about the middle of the first century B.C. For one hundred years or so it met with little success, and then suddenly, under the Antonines, it swept over the West with astonishing rapidity. It was especially popular with the army, which carried it to every outpost of the Empire.

Why was there a marked change from opposition during the Republic to encouragement during the Empire? The answer to this question will throw a good deal of light upon the changes in the cultural milieu that occurred during the first three centuries A.D.—changes that prepared the way for the coming of Christianity. Doubtless the early hostility to some extent simply reflected the conservatism of Roman officialdom. But as a matter of fact the beliefs and practices—indeed the whole spirit—of the cults and those of the traditional Roman religion were quite incompatible. The Roman religion was not especially otherworldly, and there was certainly nothing redemptionist about it. It was a formal, somewhat cold worship of local dieties regarded by the Romans as the protectors and supporters of the regime. Its motivation was almost wholly practical and civic. Thus, one of the most important functions of the Roman priests was to supervise the auguries by which the future could be foretold and the policies of the state determined.

By the first century B.C., it is true, the upper classes had largely lost belief in these gods. Julius Caesar, for instance, felt free to assert publicly in the Senate the Epicurean view that the soul is not immortal and that death ends all. But whatever the leaders themselves believed or did not believe, they were assiduous in supporting the old religion as an important means of maintaining the discipline and loyalty of the people. It was natural, therefore, for them to oppose cults whose adoption by the populace might disrupt the social and political cohesion of the Roman community.

But the very characteristics of the sects that caused this antagonism were later on, in the Empire, the source both of their immense popularity with the masses and of the official approval that was eventually accorded them. It was in the third century A.D. that they all experienced an astonishing growth. What, then, was there about the third century that induced that growth?

After the death of Marcus Aurelius in 180 A.D., the Roman throne was occupied by a succession of weak and incompetent rulers. Every army set up its own "emperor," central authority virtually disappeared, and the barbarians breached the Rhenish and Danubian frontiers. In Gaul, only the major walled cities escaped pillage; in Greece, Athens, Corinth, and Sparta were sacked. A revived Persian monarchy threatened the Eastern provinces. For eighty years not a single emperor died peacefully, and in one fourteen-year period (235–249 A.D.) there were no less than seven emperors.

At the end of the century another line of strong rulers appeared, but by this time the Empire had lost its vitality, the countryside had been laid waste, commerce had been disrupted, cities had been deserted. Only the strongest measures could halt the ruin. Therefore Diocletian, who came to the throne in 284, radically altered the character of the Principate. All surviving traces of Republican forms were abandoned, and the emperor became a despot, surrounded with all the ceremonial of an Oriental monarch. He was now called "Lord and Master," and his subjects, even those of highest rank, were obliged to prostrate themselves before him. These visible signs of absolutism were accompanied by corresponding constitutional changes. Local distinctions and privileges were wiped out, and a completely centralized bureaucracy was installed, so that there was a continuous chain of command from the emperor to the most insignificant official in the most obscure province of the Empire.

Nor was the third century a wasteland politically and economically only. Literature and the arts experienced a corresponding decay. The mood of the times was, naturally, despondent. One observer of the scene wrote,

> You must know that the world has grown old, and does not remain in its former vigour. It bears witness to its own decline. The rainfall and the sun's warmth are both diminishing; the metals are nearly exhausted; the husbandman is failing in the fields, the sailor on the seas, the soldier in the camp, honesty in the market, justice in the courts, concord in friendships, skill in the arts, discipline in morals. This is the sentence passed upon the world, that everything which has a beginning should perish, that things which have reached maturity should grow old, the strong weak, the great small, and that after weakness and shrinkage should come dissolution.[b]

This sense of helplessness and defeat was produced, doubtless, not only by the pressure of external events—the visible crumbling of the Empire, the barbarian raids, and the civil strife—but also by the internal reorganization of the Empire effected at the end of the century. As government became more remote and more despotic, and as social and political organizations grew larger, men lost the sense of controlling their destinies. An edict issued by a faraway and inaccessible emperor might affect one's fortunes drastically, but one had no way of influencing it or even of understanding why it happened; one knew only that a great power was loose and operating in one's world.

It was natural that the religions by means of which the men of this new era sought satisfaction were very different from those that had served the needs of the old Greeks and Romans. When men had lived in a small city-state, when they had ruled themselves, their gods reflected the worshipers' sense of independence. But now, in a vast empire that was going to pieces before their eyes despite all that a despotic ruler could do, men found comfort in belief in an omniscient, omnipotent, and all-good deity, strong enough and wise enough to guide the affairs that human personalities, however exalted, could no longer control. So the new-style emperor, called "Dominus" and worshiped as an absolute despot, became at once the model and the visible symbol of a still greater god who held the whole universe in his hand and whose commands were imperial edicts requiring instant obedience.

Neoplatonism

Philosophy was naturally not immune to these changes in outlook. The tone of religiosity already evident in Stoicism appeared even more strongly in an important school of philosophy developed in the third century and known as Neoplatonism. Unlike Mithraism and the other cults, Neoplatonism was a philosophical theory; as such, it was concerned with epistemological and metaphysical problems to which the cults were indifferent. For instance, the Neoplatonists were aware of the ambiguities in Plato's theory of forms; they made a genuine effort to deal with these difficulties—and at a far more sophisticated level, philosophically speaking, than had the Stoics. In the process of attempting to solve the technical philosophical problems on which Platonism broke and to which Aristotle had provided at best only a partial answer, Neoplatonism developed a philosophy of religion that was to have a long career in Western thought. Indeed, the Neoplatonic version of Platonism proved to be one of the chief modes of Plato's continuing influence on philosophical thought.

The two aspects of Platonism that chiefly appealed to the Neoplatonists were its tendency toward transcendence and its antirationalism, or rather—since that is perhaps too strong a term—its insistence that none of the really important truths can be communicated by conceptual means. In both respects the Neoplatonists simply emphasized those passages in Plato's writing that suited their own biases and ignored those in which Plato himself had sought to correct his more extreme statements. Thus the Neoplatonic reworking of Platonism plainly showed the mood of the new age.

As regards transcendence, Plato's insistence on the inferior status of the sense world and on the superior reality of the transcendent forms complemented the otherworldliness and world-weariness of the third century. The antirationalist side of Plato's thought had already been taken up in the last centuries of the old era by the so-called Academic sceptics, who had concentrated on those passages in which Plato had argued that physics can never be more than a "likely story."

But there is a significant difference between the ways in which the Neoplatonists and the Academic sceptics reacted to this antirationalist strain of thought. The latter had been content to remain sceptical about metaphysics and to fall back for guidance in the affairs of daily life upon an essentially pragmatic attitude. Since we can never know the absolute truth about anything, we should, they held, operate on the basis of probability. This has a very modern sound. Today we like to think that we do not lust after certainty. If a theory or a line of action "works," that is, produces satisfactory results, most people do not worry about whether it is "true." This pragmatic attitude seems also to have satisfied the Academic sceptics. But by the third century the conditions of life had changed. Men now sought certainty—through the mysteries of the Great Mother, through the worship of Isis, through the support of Mithra, through faith in Jesus of Nazareth. The same overwhelming desire for certainty affected the Neoplatonists, and since, like the sceptics, they had abandoned the old Greek conviction that truth can be reached by reason, they tried to find it by some suprarational method.

The trend toward otherworldliness reinforced this desire to find a new and better mode of knowledge. As the conditions of their life worsened, as men saw the world around them collapsing, they naturally turned away from it and found solace in the vision of another and a better world—perfect as this one is imperfect, beautiful as this is ugly, wholly good as this is corrupt and evil. These two considerations have an obvious affinity: The better world, about which ordinary experience can tell us nothing whatever, is experienced in the inner certainty of a suprarational vision. The central problem of philosophy for Neoplatonism, then, was how to achieve this vision, how to reach that better world. Neoplatonism shared this orientation with the Eastern cults. Its interest, like theirs, was in man's relation, not to other men and to nature, but to the other world. Hence, whereas the dominant interest of classical philosophy as represented by Plato and Aristotle, and even by the Stoics, had been ethical, the dominant interest of the new philosophy was religious. This signaled that the classical world was at an end.

Plotinus

Little is known about the origins of Neoplatonism or about the life of Plotinus (about 204–270 A.D.), the principal representative of the early period of the school. Plotinus was so completely uninterested in the things of this life (he seemed ashamed, his disciple Porphyry wrote, of being "in the body" at all) that his friends could find out from him little concerning his early years. It appears, however, that he grew up in Alexandria, one of those cities in which the West (as represented by Greco-Roman culture) and the East (as represented by the mystery cults and the new savior-religions) met and fused. Plotinus was obviously well trained in the classical schools. In an effort to learn more about the lore of the East he is said to have accompanied the army of the emperor Gordian on an expedition against the Persians. On his return Plotinus went to Rome, where his teachings soon became fashionable. Plotinus taught orally and seems to have written nothing until his fiftieth year, when he began to put down the notes of his lectures. After his death these were carefully edited by Porphyry, but they remain some of the most obscure of all philosophical writings, not only because of the manner of their composition but even more because of their intrinsic difficulty.

PLOTINUS' VERSION OF PLATONISM

It has already been noted that Neoplatonism was a philosophy of religion— "of religion" because of its emphasis on getting into a right relation with a suprarational reality; "philosophy" because it based this program, not (as with the cults) on the rituals and legends of vegetation gods, but on a reinterpretation of Plato's metaphysics. One of the key passages for this reinterpretation was Plato's account of the Form of the Good. In the *Republic*, he likened it to the sun, which renders physical things visible and is at the same time the cause of their generation and growth. So the Form of the Good operates in the realm of forms: It "not only infuses the power of being known into all things known, but also bestows upon them their being and existence, and yet the good is not existence, but lies far beyond it in dignity and in power."

This suggestion that reality is beyond being was not carried any further by Plato. On the contrary, it was followed immediately by the claim that reality is *not* beyond being, that we *can* attain a knowledge of the most real world, even of the Form of the Good, by dialectic—that is, by logical and rational methods.

This is an example of Plato's usual ambivalence toward the nature of reality and its relation to the world of ordinary experience. He held in suspension, without finally choosing between them, quite different points of view. And just as Aristotle opted for the world of ordinary experience, Plotinus opted for the suprarational. Acting on the hint given in the *Republic* and on similar suggestions in other dialogues (in the *Symposium*, for instance), Plotinus developed the notion of a reality that is beyond being and beyond knowledge:

> The One, as transcending intellect, transcends knowing.
>
> The One is, in truth, beyond all statement; whatever you say would limit It; the All-Transcending, transcending even the most august Mind, which alone of all things has true being, has no name. We can but try to indicate, if possible, something concerning It. If we do not grasp It by knowledge, that does not mean that we do not seize It at all. We can state what It is not while we are silent as to what It is. . . .
>
> The All-Transcendent, utterly void of multiplicity, is unity's self, independent of all else. That from which all the rest take their degree of unity in their standing, near or far, towards It. It is the great Beginning and the Beginning must be a really Existent One, wholly and truly One. All life belongs to It, life brilliant and perfect. It is therefore more than self-sufficing, Author at once of Being and self-sufficiency. . . .
>
> Only by a leap can we reach this One which is to be pure of all else, halting sharp in fear of slipping ever so little aside and impinging on the dual; for the One does not bear to be numbered with anything else; It is measure and not the measured. The First cannot be thought of as having definition and limit. It can be described only as transcending all things produced, transcending Being. To seek to throw a line about that illimitable Nature would be folly, and anyone thinking to do so cuts himself off from the most momentary approach to Its least vestige.
>
> As one wishing to contemplate the Intellectual Nature will lay aside all representations of the senses and so may see what transcends the realm of sense, so one wishing to contemplate what transcends the Intellectual attains by putting away all that is of the intellect, taught by the intellect, no doubt, that the Transcendent exists, but never seeking to define It. Its definition could only be "the Indefinable," for This is a Principle not to be conveyed by any sound; It cannot be known on any hearing, but if at all, by vision.
>
> We ought not to question whence It comes; there is no whence, no coming or going in place; It either appears (to us) or does not appear. We must not run after It, but we must fit ourselves for the vision and then wait tranquilly for it as the eye waits on the rising of the sun which in its own time appears above the horizon and gives itself to our sight. . . .
>
> The Source, having no prior, cannot be contained by any other form of

being; It is orbed around all; possessing, but not possessed, holding all, Itself nowhere held. It is omnipresent; at the same time, It is not present, not being circumscribed by anything; yet, as utterly unattached, not inhibited from presence at any point.

God is present through all,—not something of God here and something else there, nor all of God gathered at some one spot; there is an instantaneous presence everywhere, nothing containing, nothing left void, everything therefore fully held by Him. . . .

That awesome Prior, the Unity, is not a being, for so Its unity would be vested in something else; strictly no name is apt to It, but there is a certain rough fitness in designating It as Unity with the understanding that It is not the unity of some other thing such as point or monad. Nor is Its impartibility that of extreme minuteness; on the contrary It is great beyond anything, infinite not in measureless extension or numerable quantity but in fathomless depths of power. It is wholly self-existent. Something there must be supremely adequate, autonomous, all-transcending, most utterly without need. All need is effort towards a first principle; the First, Principle to all, must be without need of anything.[d]

These conclusions about the transcendence and the utter unity of ultimate reality follow, Plotinus thought, from the inevitably conditioned character of knowledge. Plato had of course held that most of our so-called knowledge (he had termed it "opinion" on this account) is conditioned. It is limited, that is, by premises of which we are often quite unconscious. "I shall vote for X," we conclude, after an investigation of the qualifications of the various candidates. But this conclusion presupposes (what we may never have considered at all) that representative government is desirable. Hence our conclusion is only provisional and hypothetical. We are in fact concluding, "If representative government is desirable, and if . . . , and if . . . , then I ought to vote for X."

But Plato had set beside this conditioned sort of thinking another and a better kind of thinking (dialectic) that, being unconditioned, is capable of reaching absolute truth. Now it is the case that Plotinus also *talked* about dialectic, and what he said faintly echoes Plato's account in the *Sophist* and the *Parmenides*. Dialectic, according to Plotinus,

> . . . is the method or discipline that brings with it the power of pronouncing upon the nature and relation of things—what each is, to what kind it belongs and in what rank it stands in its kind, and whether its being is Real Being. Dialectic treats also of the good and the not-good, and of what is eternal and what is not eternal, and of these not by seeming knowledge but with authentic science. Finally it settles down in the Intellectual Cosmos and there plies its own peculiar Act; it has abandoned all the realm of deceit and falsity and pastures the Soul in the "Meadows of Truth." It distinguishes the Forms and Authentic Existence and primary genera and follows in thought their intercommunications, until it has traversed the entire Intellectual Realm and returned in analysis to the first principle. Now it rests; at

peace while there, it is no longer busy about many things; it has arrived at Unity and it contemplates; it leaves to another science all that coil of premises and conclusions called the art of reasoning. The Divine Mind furnishes its standards, the most certain for any soul that is able to apply them. What else is necessary, Dialectic puts together for itself, combining and dividing, until it has reached perfect Intellection. For it is the purest perfection of Intellection and Wisdom. And being the noblest of our endowments, it must needs deal with Authentic Existence, the highest there is; as Wisdom it deals with Being, as Intellection with what transcends Being. . . .

Dialectic is the most precious part of Philosophy. It does not consist of bare rules and theories; it deals with verities. It knows the Truth, knows above all the operation of the Soul. All that is submitted to it it attacks with the directness of sense-perception and it leaves petty precisions of process to what other sciences may care for such exercises. . . .[e]

It is not easy to extract any clear conception from this rhapsodical account. But whatever Plotinus meant by dialectic, it can at least be said that he thought it radically different from systematic, rational thought—that "coil of premises and conclusions" that Plato seems to have held dialectic to be. For Plotinus, dialectic was a kind of mystic vision in which truth is grasped completely and all at once. Thus, though Plotinus may have adopted Plato's terminology, and though he certainly started from a Platonic thesis, his metaphysics is quite different from that of Plato. Whereas Plato held that there is a kind of rational thought that can reach an unconditioned truth, for Plotinus reality was unknowable by rational means.

Paradoxically, Plotinus used rational arguments to support this antirationalist position. Ultimate reality, he argued, must not be limited in any way. Suppose that it is limited; then there is an other beyond it that does the limiting. Are the so-called real and this other in relation? Obviously they must be. Then they are parts of a larger whole, and the alleged real is not the whole, but a part. Hence ultimate reality can have no other. But if reality is unconditioned and if thought is conditioned, it seems to follow that reality is unknowable, at least by rationalistic thinking.

Moreover, we cannot, according to this line of reasoning, attribute *any* specific properties, or attributes, to reality. For instance, many philosophers, including many Christian theologians, have held that we can attribute personality and volition to ultimate reality. But if Plotinus was correct, this is a mistake. For every person we know anything about is limited. My ego has meaning only as contrasted with other selves that I am not. But reality has no other and so cannot be a self in any sense of the word that we can understand. Similarly, it is impossible to attribute will, desire, or any other mode of conation to the real, since these—even more obviously than thought—imply an other, in this case an object aimed at.

Having reached this conclusion we may seem to have reached the end. Yet Plotinus proceeded to use a great many fine names to designate the unnamable and the unknowable. Thus he called it God, the First, the Good, the Absolute, the Infinite, even though he also insisted that no positive description of it is possible. How can this be? These epithets cannot be positive descriptions, that is, they cannot attribute any definite characteristics to the One, for any definite characteristic would limit it.

Rational argument, it is clear, can tell us only what the One is *not*. This is something, but not much. Suppose, for instance, that you do not know anything at all about the author of the *Enneads* except that he is not Plato, nor Aristotle, nor Kant. It is true that you have a bit of knowledge about him, but it must be allowed that your knowledge is inadequate.[1]

PLOTINUS' MYSTICISM

This limitation on reason and rational argument would not have distressed Plotinus himself because he had (or so he believed) a totally different and altogether better way of getting into communication with the real. In fact, his attack on rational thinking was part and parcel of his affirmation of an extrarational vision. He *wanted* reason to be incompetent, for its incompetence would emphasize the value and the significance of mystical experience.

That Plotinus had a mystical experience and that it gave him an inner conviction of certainty about the nature and the meaning of the universe throws a great deal of light on why he held such-and-such metaphysical and epistemological views. But mystical experiences, however real and vivid they may be to the person who experiences them, are hardly a very satisfactory basis for a philosophical theory. To begin with, such experiences are essentially private and are limited to a relatively few people.[2] Those who have not had this experience can hardly form any clear idea of what Neoplatonism is about. Suppose, for instance, that the experience of red were taken as fundamental and all-important and that a whole philosophy were constructed around this experience. Anyone suffering from red-green color blindness would be severely handicapped. Most of us, however, *have* experienced red, and though our difficulties with the "red" philosophy might still be serious, they would not be basic. But with Neoplatonism, the situation is reversed: The experience that is the basis of the theory is itself exclusive.

And there is another difficulty, which can be illustrated by Faust's reply to Gretchen. When she asks, "Do you believe in God?" he answers, "Who can name Him? I have no name for Him! Feeling is everything. Name is sound

---

1 Later in the Middle Ages John Scotus used this line of argument explicitly to interpret the Christian doctrine of divine transcendence. See pp. 174–80.
2 Plotinus claimed that this intuitive knowledge is "a power which all possess," but he admitted that "few use it." According to Porphyry, his biographer, Plotinus achieved the mystic state four times in six years.

and smoke." This is an intelligible position for a poet to adopt; what the poet objects to, and asserts the inadequacy of, is not words as such but the precise, rigidly defined terminology of science.[3] The poet himself uses words, but he uses words of a special kind, in a special way. His art is designed to capture and communicate the ineffable, to give to airy nothing a local habitation and a name.

This position may or may not be correct; it is at least consistent. The same thing, however, cannot be said for the *philosophical* mystic. He wants to give a theory about the universe as it is revealed in his mystical experience; but a theory is a rational account, and the experience is ineffable. Hence the experience inevitably transcends the conceptual scheme that must be employed if it is a *theory* that is being presented.[4]

THE NATURE OF REALITY

So far the discussion has centered on the Neoplatonic interpretation of Plato's dictum that reality (the One, the Absolute, the First) is beyond being.[5] But in the passage in question Plato also says that reality is the "author of the being of all things known"—like the sun, the good is a cause. So Plotinus, following this hint, maintained that the Absolute is a power or force or energy. The whole universe, visible and invisible, is a product of this activity, which overflows to create a succession of types of existence. These decrease in reality as their distance from their source increases, until at the extremity of the creative process they disappear into bare nothingness, just as the light given off by some source of illumination gradually fades away into darkness. The first emanation, as Plotinus termed it, is *nous* (variously translated as Spirit, Divine Mind, Intelligence, Intellectual Principle). From *nous* emanates Soul, which contains in itself all particular souls, including human souls. Soul in its turn creates, in accordance with the archetypal Platonic forms, nature, that is, the phenomenal world. In this way the whole universe is the result of a succession of creative acts in which each principle, beginning with the Absolute, produces the next lower principle, each lower principle being, insofar as its lower nature permits, the imitation of the higher. These doctrines may be illustrated with a few passages from the *Enneads*.

---

3 On the subject of terminological precision, one of Plotinus' most sympathetic interpreters writes that his "classifications . . . are not intended to be rigorous and exclusive. In his philosophy there are no hard boundary lines drawn across the field of experience. . . . Neoplatonism deals throughout with spiritual, nonquantitative relations, which cannot be . . . treated as logical counters"—Inge, *The Philosophy of Plotinus*, Vol. I, pp. 122–23.

4 Plotinus occasionally seems to have recognized the ultimate frustration of his position. Thus, "the vision baffles telling. . . . It is not to be told, not to be revealed to any that has not himself had the happiness to see"—*Enneads* (Turnbull), VI, ix, 10–11.

5 See p. 8.

The entire Intellectual Order may be figured as a kind of light with the One in repose at its summit as its King. We may think of the One as a light before the light, an eternal irradiation resting upon the Intellectual; This, not identical with its source, is yet not so remote from It as to be less than Real-Being; It is the primal Knower. But the One, as transcending intellect, transcends knowing.

. . . .

It is the Good, for It is the power from which Life and Intelligence proceed; these grow from It as from the source of essence and existence. Its being is not limited, nor, on the other hand, is It infinite in the sense of magnitude; Its infinitude lies in Its power; It does not change and will not fail, and in It all that is unfailing finds duration. Having no constituent parts It accepts no pattern, forms no shape. . . .

In this way the Supreme may be understood to be the cause at once of essential reality and of the knowing of reality. The sun, cause of the existence of sense-things and of their being seen, is indirectly the cause of sight, without being either the faculty or the object; similarly this Principle, the Good, cause of Being and Divine Mind, is a light appropriate to what is to be seen There and to their seer. . . . Imagine a spring that has no source outside itself; it gives itself to all the rivers, yet never is exhausted by what they take, but remains quietly at rest; the tides that proceed from it are at one within it before they run their several ways. . . .

This Absolute is none of the things of which It is the source; Its nature is that nothing can be affirmed of It—not existence, not essence, not life—It transcends all these. But possess yourself of It by the very elimination of being, and you hold a marvel! Thrusting forward to This, attaining, and resting in Its content, seek to grasp It more and more, understanding It by that intuitive thrust alone, but knowing Its greatness by the beings that follow upon It and exist by Its power. . . .

The huge illumination of the Supreme pouring outwards comes at last to the extreme bourne of its light and dwindles to darkness; this darkness, lying there beneath, the Soul sees and by seeing brings to shape; since it must go forth, it will generate a place for itself; at once body exists. . . .

Side by side exist the Authentic All and its counterpart, the visible universe. . . . What we know as Nature is a soul, offspring of a yet earlier Soul of more powerful life, and . . . it possesses in its repose a vision within itself. The vision on which Nature broods is a spectacle born of it by virtue of its abiding in and with itself and being itself an object of contemplation. It is a vision somewhat blurred, for there exists another, a clearer, of which Nature is the image; hence what Nature produces is weak; the weaker contemplation produces the weaker object.

In the same way human beings, when weak on the side of contemplation, find in action their trace of vision and reason; their spiritual feebleness unfits them for contemplation; they are hurried into action as their way to the vision which they cannot attain by intellection.[f]

These passages also illustrate the difficulty of constructing a theory on the basis of a mystical experience. To many, "emanation" is an almost meaningless word; "overflow" is a spatial phenomenon that is obviously inapplicable to an alleged nonspatial event; and the metaphor about light is, unfortunately, merely a metaphor. Indeed, though Plotinus certainly seems to have attributed causal activity to his Absolute, it would seem that to do so is just as contradictory as to attribute to it thought or will, for, like thought or will, causality involves an other, namely, the effect that the cause produces. Thus it is impossible to determine the relation supposed to exist between the Absolute and the world. Do Absolute and world face each other as cause and product? Or is the world somehow included in its cause? That is to say, was Plotinus a dualist or a pantheist? Passages supporting both interpretations can be found. Probably the answer is that he was both—and neither.

This problem can be put another way: What is the ontological status of the Absolute's emanations? Though Plotinus insisted that his Real is an indivisible unity, the Real seems to separate into a variety of entities, and the same difficulty holds with respect to these subordinate reals. Thus, Soul, which is an emanation of the Absolute, divides into various individual souls. If they are real, Soul's unity is lost; if unreal, are they mere appearance? And, if so, to whom? Plotinus avoided having to face these questions by identifying value with reality. Now it is fairly obvious that there are degrees of value (that is, that some things are better than others). Hence, if value and reality are identical, it would seem that there are degrees of reality—that some things have more "being" than other things. And if there are degrees of reality we have a way of escaping the dilemma about the Absolute's unity. When we want to insist on its unity we can remind ourselves that its emanations are not actually real; when the emanations threaten to disappear altogether we can hasten to assure ourselves that, after all, they are partly real.

But is Plotinus' identification of value and reality acceptable? Many people today are probably out of sympathy with the frame of mind that underlies this equation—so much so that they will have difficulty even understanding what it means, let alone accepting it. It is important, therefore, to remind ourselves that over the centuries there have been many who have regarded this identification as a basic truth. Again and again philosophers have divided on this issue, and their differences reflect profound differences in Western culture. Accordingly, though we cannot—at least not here—resolve the issue, we can take these differences as a clue to the currents of thought and feeling that animate society.

One more puzzle may be mentioned in connection with the notion of the Absolute as a cause. This concerns the status of the phenomenal world and is a further complication of the general problem concerning the reality and the otherness of the Absolute's emanations. What about the objects of the phenomenal world—the earth, the stars, and the planets of ordinary experience? Are they, like the various individual souls, somehow emanations of the Absolute, or are they merely appearances for souls with sense organs like ours? If the latter, of what are they appearances? These and similar difficulties might cause an unfriendly critic to reject the very idea of a reality-beyond-being as hopelessly confused. If we cannot say what reality is, what is the good of talking about it? To this, Plotinus could have replied only that it is simply the inadequacy of the terminology that is to blame. He had had the experience of the ultimate reality, and in it all difficulties and contradictions are reconciled and harmonized. He *knew* what this reality is, even though he could not *say* what it is.

Let us therefore turn from Plotinus' account of reality to his description of how it is experienced.

THE WAY OF ASCENT

According to Plotinus, the life of the universe is a double movement, first of egress from, and then of return to, god. Man, of course, shares in this life: He is an exile who thirsts to return to god, his home. Plotinus gave no reason why this double movement should occur, that is, no account of why god should create a universe only to reabsorb it. Characteristically, he was less interested in the reasons for the human predicament than in mapping the way back to god.

Generally speaking, he held that there are two ways for man to reach god: One may be called the long way home; the other is shorter but, unfortunately, much less within man's power. Of the former little need be said. Plotinus accepted a doctrine of reincarnation like that of Plato and the Pythagoreans. In a series of lives a man might be reborn in successively higher forms and eventually pass altogether out of the cycle of birth and death. Or if, instead of living virtuously, one gives oneself up to sensual gratification and lust of the flesh, one will be reborn into lower and lower forms.

> In the immaterial Heaven every member is unchangeably itself forever; in the heavens of our universe, while the whole has life eternally and so too all the nobler and lordlier components, the souls pass from body to body entering into varied forms, and, when it may, a soul will rise outside the realm of birth and dwell with the soul of all. . . .
>
> Our souls must have their provinces according to their different powers; released, each will inhabit a star consonant with the temperament and faculty within constituting the principle of the life. Emancipated souls have transcended the spirit-nature and the entire fatality of birth and all that belongs to this visible world. . . .
>
> Those that have lived wholly to sense become animals; according to the particular temper of life, ferocious or gluttonous animals. Those who in their pleasures have not even lived by sensation, but have gone their way in a torpid grossness, become mere growing things, for this lethargy is the entire act of the vegetative, and such men have been busy betreeing themselves. . . .
>
> The evil-liver loses grade because during his life the active principle of his being took the tilt towards the brute by force of affinity. If, on the

contrary, the man is able to follow the leading of his higher spirit, he rises; he lives that spirit; that noblest part of himself to which he is being led becomes sovereign in his life; this made his own, he works for the next above until he has attained the height.g

So much for the long way home. The short way home is the moment of intuition in which the mystic actually experiences union with god. There is little we can do to help ourselves here. The vision is simply something that happens to us, if we are fortunate. What, then, can we do to fit ourselves to receive the vision? Though Plotinus never treated this question formally, he did, in the course of the *Enneads*, suggest several different lines of preparation. For one thing, he advocated the contemplation of nature:

> Admiring this world of sense as we look upon its vastness and beauty and the order of its eternal march, thinking of the gods within it, the celestial spirits and all the life of animal and plant, let us mount to its Archetype, to the yet more authentic sphere: There we are to contemplate all things as members of the Intellectual—eternal in their own right, vested with perfect knowledge and life—and presiding over these, pure Mind and unapproachable Wisdom.h

The contemplation Plotinus had in mind was not, of course, a busy, scientific, or inquiring attitude, but a deep, quiet, and meditative mood: "So let the soul that is not unworthy of the vision contemplate the Great Soul; freed from deceit and every witchery and collected into calm. Calmed be the body for it in that hour and the tumult of the flesh, ay, all that is about it calm; calm be the earth, the sea, the air, and let heaven itself be still. Then let it feel how into that silent heaven the Great Soul floweth in!"i Beauty in any form, Plotinus thought, is a road to the divine. A sense of beauty lifts us gradually from the enjoyment of beautiful objects to an appreciation of the in-dwelling form that is the source of the physical object's beauty, and, finally, to that which is the source of the form itself.

Besides this outer way to the mystical vision, Plotinus believed there is an inner path. After all, like nature, each of us has "something of the divine" in him. The divine's creatures are not only products of its activity but also imitations, each in its own way, of its nature. This is, of course, why we can find our way back to god through nature. Similarly, by shutting out everything external, by concentrating exclusively on our inmost self, we can find god.

> By what direct intuition, then, can It be brought within our grasp?[6]
> The answer is that we can know It only in the degree of human faculty; we indicate It by virtue of what in ourselves is like It. For in us also there

---

6 [The insertion in the text of a series of questions and answers suggests that the *Enneads* were, in part at least, a record of Plotinus' conversations with his pupils—AUTHOR.]

is something of that Being. Wherever you be you have only to range over against this omnipresent Being that in you which is capable of drawing from It and you have your share in It; imagine a voice sounding over a waste of land; wherever you be in that great space you have but to listen. . . .

In order to know what Divine Mind is you must observe Soul and especially its most God-like phase. One certain way to this knowledge is to separate yourself from your body and very earnestly to put aside the system of sense with desires and impulses and every such futility, all setting definitely towards the mortal; what is left is the phase of Soul which we have declared to be an image of the Divine Intellect, retaining some light from that Sun, just as the region about the sun . . . is radiant with solar light.[j]

Plotinus expressed this thought elsewhere by instructing us to "purify" our souls:

What is meant by purification of the Soul is simply to allow it to be alone; (it is pure) when it keeps no company, entertains no alien thoughts; when it no longer sees images, much less elaborates them into veritable affections. Is it not a true purification to turn away towards the exact contrary of earthly things? Separation too is the condition of a soul no longer entering the body to lie at its mercy; it is to stand as a light set in the midst of trouble but unperturbed through all. Purification is the awakening of the soul from the baseless visions, the refusal to see them; its separation consists in limiting its descent towards the lower, accepting no picture thence, in banning utterly the things from which it is separated, when, risen above the turbid exhalations of sensuality and superabundance, though not free of the flesh, it has so reduced the body that it may be tranquilly carried.[k]

This *via negativa*, as it is called, is the path many mystics have taken. What distinguishes Plotinus from the standard type of Christian mystic is that for him there was no preliminary period of remorse and grief. Not all, certainly, but perhaps most Christian mystics seem to pass through what St. John of the Cross called "the dark night of the soul"—an overwhelming sense of sinfulness and helplessness. This, as we shall see, was true of Augustine. But Plotinus was never burdened in this way, for in his view evil was not real. He was, as Dean Inge says, "serene and cheerful, confident that the ultimate truth of the world is on his side"[l] and that sooner or later he would return to god.

In this we can, perhaps, see a last faint trace of the old assured, poised, and self-confident spirit of the classical world. But it is only a trace. Like the other men of his time, Plotinus found this world a sea of troubles and a vale of tears; like them he sought to leave it; and like them he found perfect peace only in otherworldliness. "He labored strenuously," according to Porphyry, "to free himself and rise above the bitter waves of this blood-drenched life." Confidence survived in Plotinus only in his optimism about the possibility of achieving blessedness.

The Coming of Christianity

So far some of the movements that were contemporary with the rise of Christianity have been examined in order to understand the climate of opinion in which it developed and which is reflected in its doctrine. Though some of these movements employed the language of old vegetation myths, some the language of crude Oriental dualisms, and some the technical language of Greek philosophy, they all rejected the old humanistic-naturalistic ideal in favor of a suprahuman excellence that can be achieved only by the aid of some supernatural agency. It is easy to see that in this respect they were but varying responses to the frustration and despair of the time of troubles that men were then experiencing.

In the days of the Antonines, the Empire must have seemed a permanent solution to the problems created by the collapse of city-state culture. Thus disappointment was even greater when it became evident that the Empire was incapable of coping with economic crisis and barbarian invasion. The popularity of the mystery cults, which brought hope to the masses, reflected this widespread uneasiness. But the masses had doubtless always been ignorant and superstitious, ready to put their trust in occult powers.

The rise of Neoplatonism is therefore even more striking evidence of the change in mood, for this was a view that appealed not to the uneducated proletarian but to the upper-class intellectual. The transformation it effected in Platonism is a good index of the alteration that had occurred in men's basic attitude toward life and its problems. Instead of a natural, or at any rate an intelligible, reality, we now find a beyond-being and a beyond-knowledge reality. The primary intellectual problem is not so much to understand this natural world as to grasp the reason why a transcendent and creative "One" should have chosen to produce it. The primary practical problem is to find a way of returning to that One from which we have sprung. Instead of the old view that the good life consists in self-culture through community living, there is now the belief that this world is evil, that man's good consists in release from it, and that this is beyond man's own power.

Because Neoplatonism was the outstanding contemporary philosophical theory, Christianity eventually had to take account of it. The earliest versions of Christianity were, it is true, like the mystery cults, directed largely toward the uneducated and illiterate. Later, when Christianity became socially respectable and aspired to a philosophical rationale, Neoplatonism proved both a model and a threat. Its bias toward transcendence, its asceticism, its deprecation of reason, and its emphasis on the centrality of mystical experience naturally held a strong appeal. But at the same time Christians had to steer clear of its pantheism and its denial of the reality of evil.

But this is to anticipate. First the process by which a specifically Christian view of life gradually emerged must be sketched. In this undertaking the point of view followed elsewhere will be adopted—that is, it will be assumed that Christianity was a part of the great shift in values that has been described and that it is in terms of this common cultural background that both its gradual emergence and its final triumph are to be understood. It has been relatively easy to adopt an objective, historical attitude toward the views thus far studied, for none of us, presumably, is a worshiper of Mithra or Osiris or the Great Mother. But many of us have been brought up in the Christian tradition, and for many centuries the insights of Christianity have been held (by Christians) to be divinely inspired. It is especially important, therefore, to see that, like all other systems of belief, Christianity had a temporal and a cultural locus. This locus was, of course, the crumbling Empire.

To its contemporaries Christianity was just another mystery cult, an obscure and inconsequential Jewish sect, far less significant, even in the third century, than many of the rivals it was shortly to supplant. The early Christians themselves did not understand the cultural relativity of their beliefs and practices. When they observed the parallels[7] between their practices and beliefs and those of the other cults, they concluded that the latter were deliberate caricatures of the "true" religion. But from the perspective of two thousand years we can see that the times called for belief in a heavenly father, in a savior god, in a promise of immortality, and in rites of purgation and renewal. It is impossible today, when most of the surviving descriptions of Mithraism are Christian in origin and bitterly prejudiced, to say how much Mithraism borrowed from Christianity and how much Christianity borrowed from Mithraism. That Christianity should have survived, whereas the other cults gradually disappeared, is not so much evidence of the objective truth or moral superiority of the Christian beliefs, as it is testimony to the energy, the ingenuity, the polemical ability, and the administrative skill—not to mention the good luck—of the early Christian fathers. It is also testimony to the fact that Christianity filled an important social need, and that, while holding out hopes for a happier future beyond the grave, it was not unmindful of the need for improving the miserable present of the urban masses.

Christians are naturally disposed to attribute the triumph of Christianity to divine plan, but they admit that divine causality flowed (in this case at least) through natural channels whose operations can be traced and recorded. Hence there need be no dispute between Christians and historians of philosophy. The important point is that the beliefs offered by all these sects met a social need. And it is interesting to see how a change in the Western mind called forth these beliefs, and how these beliefs, in their turn, produced a new type of mind in the West. The real triumph of Christianity was not so much its defeat of paganism as the way it permanently marked the history of the West.

---

7 Some of these parallels have been noted on pp. 3–4.

Jesus: The Jewish Heritage

PAGAN VIEW OF THE CHRISTIANS

Jesus was born about 4 B.C., during the reign of Augustus. He was crucified in 29 A.D., during the reign of Tiberius. For nearly three centuries after his death the religion that bears his name spread, but its growth was slow. It has been estimated that even in the fourth century, after it had become the state religion, its adherents numbered not more than one-tenth of the population of the Empire. This slow growth cannot be attributed to official hostility. For, though there were persecutions, they were hardly on the scale that the early Christian fathers reported. As a matter of fact, for a long time after the death of Jesus, Christianity made little impression one way or another on the outside world, and it was not so much on religious as on political grounds that the Christians were suspect. Indeed, the attitude toward them that led to the "persecutions" by Diocletian and Decius cannot have been very different from the attitude of many Americans today toward the Communist Party in the United States—that is, the Christians seemed a menace to the unity and solidarity of the state. Although they were few in number, they were a virtually independent group within the Empire, owing their allegiance not to the divine emperor but to their own God. Technically, therefore, they were traitors, and it is surprising that they were not treated much more severely.

Moreover, very little was demanded of the Christians. The authorities were quite indifferent to what a man believed, as long as he conformed outwardly to the rites of the state religion. They could not understand, therefore, why the Christians refused to conform, and to Roman officialdom the Christians seemed ignorant as well as dangerous. Even well-educated pagans concluded that the Christians were atheists and "enemies and haters of the human race." They were generally regarded as madmen, hopelessly immersed in the blackest superstition. Thus Lucian, a second-century satirist, wrote with contempt that "these wretches persuade themselves that they are going to be altogether immortal, and to live for ever, wherefore they despise death, and many of their own accord give themselves up to be slain."[m]

What were the actual beliefs of these Christians, who were hated by the few who knew something of them and ignored by the rest of the population? Jesus thought of himself as a Jew (which he was) and conceived his mission to be to reform, not to destroy, the Jewish worship.[8] For these reasons, if we want to understand Christianity, we must know something of its Jewish background.

---

8 Jesus preached in the synagogues (see Matt. 4:23), and after his death his disciples attended the ceremonies in the Temple (see Acts 3:1), worshiping as Jews and differing from their fellows only in their belief that Jesus was that Messiah whom the whole nation awaited.

YAHWEH

Although in historic times the Jews were monotheists who called their god Yahweh, surviving traces in the Old Testament show that this monotheism evolved from sources in which there appeared fetish, tabu, totem, and other characteristics of primitive religions everywhere. Yahweh himself seems originally to have been a war god, associated with clouds and other meteorological phenomena. It was perhaps Moses[9] who, as he fused the several tribes into a single nation, made Yahweh the national god. At any rate, according to subsequent traditions, Yahweh chose the Israelites to be his people, led them into Palestine, which he had selected for their habitation, and watched over them like a very short-tempered father. Yahweh was conceived of as father both in the sense of being the administrator of stern justice and in the sense of being the source of his children's life. But Yahweh was not merely a Jewish god. He was the father and creator of the whole universe, and, what is more, he had created it out of nothing. Why should such a great creator god trouble himself especially about one particular group? The Jews seem not to have asked themselves this question. A supreme national egoism made it easy for them to believe that this universal creator had chosen them above all other peoples.

Despite Yahweh's concern for them, his people had a singularly unfortunate career. After the death of Solomon (922 B.C.) the Israelite kingdom split into two weaker monarchies, both of which had succumbed to foreign domination by the beginning of the sixth century B.C. As a result of the rise of Assyria, Babylonia, and Persia, these Hebrew kingdoms, along with the Greek cities further north in Asia Minor, lost their independence. This is not surprising since the Jewish state was quite insignificant, compared with the great empires of the East. Though from this time on, except for one brief interval, the Jews were ruled by a succession of foreigners, they never gave up hope of reviving their independence, and this intense nationalism deeply marked their religious thinking.

It was inevitable that the Jews, surrounded as they were in Palestine by ardent polytheists, should gradually adopt some of the beliefs of their culturally more developed neighbors. This was probably especially true after they came under the suzerainty of Assyria, when at least external conformity to the worship of the conquerors was prudent.

It is testimony to the extraordinary religiosity of the Jews that this weakening of their former single-minded devotion to Yahweh offered them a natural explanation of the otherwise incomprehensible misfortunes that burdened his chosen people: Yahweh was a jealous god who had repeatedly told the Jews to have no other god before him. Isaiah actually maintained that the great Assyrian

---

9 Moses is thought to have lived in the thirteenth century B.C., but the earliest written "histories" of his career (which, much edited by still later hands, appear in the Old Testament) date from not earlier than the middle of the ninth century B.C. Hence it is quite impossible to distinguish the facts of his life from subsequent mythologizing and hero worship.

empire was merely a tool used by Yahweh to inflict merited punishment on the Jews.

> O Assyria, rod of my anger,
> And staff of my fury!
> Against a godless nation I send him,
> And against the people of my wrath I charge him,
> To despoil them, and to prey on them,
> And to trample them down like mire of the streets.
> But not so does he think,
> And not so does he plan;
> For destruction is in his mind,
> And to cut off nations not a few. . . .
> But when the Lord has finished all his work on Mount Zion and Jerusalem,
> he will punish the arrogant boasting of the king of Assyria, and his
> vainglorious pride. . . .
> Shall an ax boast over the man that hews with it,
> Or a saw lord itself over the man that plies it?
> As though a rod were to sway the man that wields it,
> Or a staff were to wield what is not wood![n]

The problem for the Jews was how to get back into Yahweh's good graces. The most obvious solution was to return to the traditional ritual that Yahweh had decreed for his people when they were still wandering in the desert. As a result the Jewish religion in these earliest days tended, like all primitive religions, to emphasize an exact and punctilious performance of its god's rites. Only later did the Jews come to feel that Yahweh was less interested in the merely external performance of ceremonies than in the frame of mind of the worshiper—what Yahweh demanded, it came to be said, was righteousness and purity of heart. Naturally, it was a long time before this insight emerged as a fully articulate doctrine. Its gradual development can be traced in the writings of the various Hebrew "prophets."

One of the earliest of these prophets was Elijah. He lived in the middle of the ninth century B.C., during the reign of King Ahab, who had been induced by his foreign-born wife, Jezebel, to worship idols and to commit all manner of other "abominations." It appears that the Yahweh whose worship Elijah sought to defend against these wicked foreign practices was still, in many respects, the old Mosaic god of wrath. Thus, in Elijah's view, what angered Yahweh was Ahab's disobedience and frowardness. As soon as Ahab showed proper respect for his superior, Elijah's Yahweh was content.

> Then the word of the Lord came to Elijah the Tishbite, saying,
> "Have you seen how Ahab has humbled himself before me? Because he has humbled himself before me, I will not bring the evil in his days; in his son's days I will bring the evil upon his house."[o]

On the other hand, the Yahweh who spoke to this visionary did not address him, as he had addressed Moses, from cloud or thunder:

> Now behold, the Lord was passing by, and a great and mighty wind was rending the mountain and shattering the rocks before the Lord; but the Lord was not in the wind. After the wind came an earthquake, but the Lord was not in the earthquake. After the earthquake a fire; but the Lord was not in the fire, and after the fire the sound of a gentle whisper. Now as soon as Elijah perceived it, he wrapped his face in his mantle. . . .[p]

For the prophet Amos, who lived perhaps one hundred years after Elijah, Yahweh was still a god of wrath, but he was no longer a vain monarch, insisting on his prerogatives but capable of being won over by flattery. According to Amos, what angered Yahweh was not disobedience so much as luxury and vice.

> Woe to them who are at ease in Zion, . . .
> Who lie upon ivory couches,
> And stretch themselves out upon divans;
> And eat lambs from the flock. . . .[q]

The Hebrews were to be punished

> Because they have sold the innocent for silver,
> And the needy in exchange for a pair of sandals;
> [Because] they . . . trample upon the heads of the poor,
> And thrust aside the humble from the way.[r]

They were to be punished, that is, for injustice, not for ritualistic impurity. Nor could they hope to conciliate Yahweh by merely external acts of propitiation. According to Amos, Yahweh declared:

> I hate, I spurn your feasts,
> And take no pleasure in your festal gatherings.
> Even though you offer me burnt-offerings,
> And your cereal-offerings, I will not accept them;
> And the thank-offerings of your fatted beasts I will not look upon.
> Take away from me the noise of your songs,
> And to the melody of your lyres I will not listen.
> But let justice roll down like waters,
> And righteousness like a perennial stream.[s]

Again and again during the eighth century B.C. prophets arose to sound this note. Thus, for instance, Yahweh explained to Hosea:

> . . . I delight in piety, not sacrifice;
> And in the knowledge of God, rather than burnt-offerings.[t]

And so, Micah:

> With what shall I come before the Lord,
> And bow myself before God most high?
> Shall I come before him with burnt-offerings,
> With calves a year old?
> Will the Lord be pleased with thousands of rams,
> With myriads of streams of oil?
> Shall I give my first-born for my transgression,
> The fruit of my body for the sin of my soul?[10]
> You have been told, O man, what is good,
> And what the Lord requires of you:
> Only to do justice, and to love kindness,
> And to walk humbly with your God.[u]

These prophets of the eighth century B.C. came a long way from the earliest conception of Yahweh. And later thinkers who attempted to combine the two Yahwehs faced the same problem that was to confront the Greek tragic poets of the fifth century B.C.—the problem of harmonizing a set of primitive beliefs with a later, more enlightened moral insight. The result, for the Hebrews as for the Greek poets, was a certain tension that was never wholly resolved; the old beliefs refused either to die out or to take on the new coloration.

One of the Hebrews who attempted to effect this reconciliation was the author of the book of Deuteronomy. Writing toward the end of the seventh century B.C., he invented an ingenious formula for fusing together the old external, ritualistic emphasis and the new inner, spiritual emphasis. The traditional rites, he held, were important, but only as expressions of gratitude to Yahweh for his loving-kindness. Thus, while insisting on ceremony, the author of Deuteronomy recognized that the motive of the worshiper was relevant. For the truly religious man, strict adherence to Yahweh's commands was not an external compulsion, for the worshiper who loved Yahweh gladly did what would please him, just as in an (ideal) human family the children obey their parents not because of fear but because of love experienced and returned. The Psalms are full of this sense of happy obedience: "Oh, how I love thy law," sang the Psalmist. "The law of thy mouth is worth more to me than thousands in gold and silver." And again, "I walk at large, because I have sought thy precepts," for the delight of the righteous man is "in the law of the Lord, and in his law does he study day and night."[v]

---

10 [R. H. Pfeiffer, in *Introduction to the Old Testament* (Harper & Row, New York, 1941), p. 179, notes that "Since ordinary sacrifices had not brought about desired results [that is, liberation from the Assyrian yoke], many Judeans . . . revived the long obsolete sacrifice of the first-born, believing that, by giving to the deity the most precious thing on earth, its wrath would be allayed. Accordingly, the first-born of both sexes were sacrificially slain and cremated . . . in a shrine called Tophet, just outside Jerusalem"—AUTHOR.]

With the intention of updating and harmonizing all existing traditions and practices, the author of Deuteronomy and other priestly lawyers drew up a systematic and inclusive code. This naturally covered a wide variety of fields, including what would now be called civil and criminal procedures, as well as religious matters.[11]

In the course of time this code unfortunately became frozen into an unalterable body of law. The result, in the long run, was what may be called an antilegalistic reaction. For one thing, since it was impossible to bring the Law up to date, it became more and more difficult to apply it without obviously strained and artificial interpretations. Again, constant harping on the Law caused men to drift back into the older ritualistic attitude, in which worship consisted in punctilious conformity. Impatience with this overemphasis on the Law and with the legal hair-splitting that accompanied it naturally reinforced the old sentiment, going back to the prophets, that insisted on the spirit, not the letter.

JESUS' ATTITUDE TOWARD THE LAW

This antilegalistic point of view was shared by Jesus.[12] For example, Jesus pointed out that literal-minded Jews and pedantic lawyers assumed the injunction about keeping the Sabbath holy to mean that men should not work on that day. When his disciples husked a handful of corn to eat during a journey, the owners of the corn claimed that husking was "work" and so was wrong. Jesus surmised, however, that their real motive was less a desire to protect the Sabbath against sacrilege than a desire to protect their property against trespass.

Or again, though the Law said only, "Thou shalt not commit adultery," Jesus cautioned that we should not assume virtue to consist simply in abstaining from intercourse with a married woman. This misses the inner meaning of Yahweh's prohibition, for "Anyone who looks at a woman with desire has already committed adultery with her in his heart."[w] Similarly, though the Law said only, "Thou shalt not kill," Jesus held that one has already committed murder when one is angry with one's brother in one's heart.

Jesus also had great contempt for the numerous petty regulations that a rich

---

11 The code covered everything from how to plant seeds to how to treat slaves, from the punishment for rape to a warning against pagan mourning customs, from a law of contracts to regulations governing the investiture of hostile cities.

12 Jesus' indictment of the current overemphasis on the Law was part of a widespread climate of opinion in Judea. The Essenes, for instance, a Jewish monastic sect, held that the only way to be faithful to the Law was by withdrawing altogether from the complexities of the "modern" world. Living simple and rigidly abstemious lives in the desert, they emphasized the virtues of piety, justice, humility, and self-discipline. So, too, the most famous rabbi of the time, Hillel, held that the strict interpretation of the Law should be "tempered by kindness, gentleness and consideration of others." He taught, as Jesus did, in maxims given a paradoxical form in order to emphasize their message. Some of these maxims—"My abasement is my exaltation"; "Judge not thy neighbor until thou art in his place"; "He who wishes to make a name for himself loses his name"; "What is hateful to thee do not to another"—are strikingly similar to the teachings of Jesus.

man could easily obey but that imposed considerable hardship on the ordinary workingman: "To eat with unwashed hands does not defile a man," he said. In general, his position was that what matters is not so much what we actually do as the thoughts that issue from our hearts.

> And the Pharisees and the scribes asked him, "Why do your disciples not observe the rules handed down by our ancestors, but eat food without purifying their hands?" . . .
> "How skillful you are," he said to them, "in nullifying what God has commanded in order to observe what has been handed down to you. . . . Do you not see that nothing that goes into a man from outside can pollute him? . . . It is what comes out of a man that pollutes him. For it is from inside, from men's hearts, that designs of evil come; immorality, stealing, murder, adultery, greed, malice, deceit, indecency, envy, abusiveness, arrogance, folly—all these evils come from inside, and they pollute a man."[x]

Though Jesus sometimes carried this point of view to such an extreme that he seemed to say the overt act has no significance whatever, he was too good a Jew to reject the Law altogether. But he believed that Hebrew jurists were using the Law to "justify" unjustifiable conduct, that they were callous and inhumane, intent simply on the letter of the Law and deaf to the human motives and values involved. Therefore, as he said, he did not want to do away with the Law but to complete it—to explain what it really meant. Since its real value was being frittered away in the multiplication of trivial rules, he tried to condense it into a few simple precepts. It is significant of his attitude that the two commandments that seemed to him to sum up a man's duty—love thy God with all thy heart, and love thy neighbor as thyself—were drawn from the Law itself, the one from Leviticus, the other from Deuteronomy.

FATHERHOOD OF GOD

Another major point in Jesus' teaching was the fatherhood of God. "If you . . . know enough to give your children what is good, how much more surely will your Father in heaven give what is good to those who ask him for it!"[y] "In my Father's house," he said, "are many mansions," and his hope was that we should live so that we might be children of our Father who is in heaven. This emphasis on the filial relationship of man to God was not, of course, a discovery of Jesus'. It was central in many of the other Eastern cults popular in the Empire and doubtless contributed to their success. Also, long before Jesus' day the Jews had generally come to think of God as a father—as they might think of a human father, though on an exalted scale, of course. That is, just as it was held that a human father had complete sovereignty over his children, so God was conceived to be absolutely powerful; and just as a human father hopefully tempered this power with loving-kindness, so God was the merciful and providential Father of his children. Later on, Gentile Christians, who did not know the Hebrew traditions and who came across this doctrine for the first time upon their conversion, naturally made much of it. But what is important about Jesus' notion of God the Father is not its novelty (or lack of it) but the fact that through Jesus it was transferred from the Hebrews to the West.

For Jesus, God was by no means simply sweetness and light. The Hebrew tradition of a wrathful Yahweh was too deep-seated for Jesus not to have been touched by it. Like the prophets before him, Jesus was wroth with the "unfaithful and sinful age" in which he lived:

> Then he began to reproach the towns in which most of his wonders had been done, because they did not repent.
> "Alas for you, Chorazin! Alas for you, Bethsaida! . . . And you, Capernaum! Are you to be exalted to the skies? You will go down among the dead! For if the wonders that have been done in you had been done in Sodom, it would have stood until today.[13] But I tell you that the land of Sodom will fare better on the Day of Judgment than you will!"[z]

JESUS' BELIEF IN IMMINENT JUDGMENT DAY

Moreover, Jesus was dominated by a conviction that the end of the world was near—was, indeed, so imminent that he believed "some of them that stand here will see its coming." "Repent ye, for the Kingdom of God is at hand" was therefore his reiterated thesis. He thought the generation about him lived in wickedness and corruption, hovering on the brink of a chasm, careless of the fate in store for it. It behooved him, therefore, like the prophets of old, to urge his fellows to repent, to prepare themselves for the day of judgment. In comparison with the urgency and immediacy of this need, nothing else seemed to him of consequence. For this reason the moral teachings of Jesus have sometimes been interpreted as "interim morality." The extremes to which he urged his contemporaries seem most comprehensible in terms of his sense of crisis and his expectation that the world was about to end and that a wrathful Father would soon judge his erring children.

Since the world was soon to end, it was, from his point of view, the sheerest common sense to urge his fellows to give away all their goods to feed the poor. Under such circumstances, what could it matter that another strike one?—"Turn the other cheek." In similar fashion we must understand Jesus' otherwise harsh saying, "Let the dead bury their dead." He cannot have been urging the neglect of ordinary duties of this kind;[14] he must simply have been expressing in a dramatic fashion his conviction of the imminence of the end for us all, both living and dead.

---

13 [Sodom had long ago been destroyed by Yahweh because of its wickedness—AUTHOR.]
14 Taken literally, this dictum conflicts, for instance, with the commandment, "Honor thy father and mother," on which Jesus insisted (Matt. 19:19).

THE TEACHINGS OF JESUS

So far some of Jesus' leading ideas have been mentioned, but if we look for a formal ethical theory—even a doctrine of virtues—in Jesus' teachings, we shall be disappointed. There is certainly nothing in the gospels like Aristotle's *Ethics*, nothing even like Cicero's *De Officiis*. Jesus' teachings were not systematic; he taught in paradoxes and by means of parable and example. Nevertheless, because all the ethical theories subsequently developed in the West have been deeply marked by his views, it is necessary to try to summarize them.

To begin with, then, what about "pleasure"? To fix the place and the role of pleasure had been one of the primary concerns of all the classical moralists. Though Jesus did not take up this question specifically, it is clear that he was totally uninterested not only in what may be called "sensual" pleasures but also in the cultivation of the talents, that is, those "higher" esthetic satisfactions that loomed so large in the thought of Plato and Aristotle. In this respect, Jesus' view was like that of the Greek Cynics, but the background of thought that led him to this conclusion was quite different.

Thus Jesus himself did not insist on that absolute chastity some of his followers were to take as their ideal, and he was so convivial a comrade that his enemies called him a glutton and a winebibber and criticized him for liking "low" company too well. Yet, though Jesus was not himself an ascetic, his sense of the imminence of the Kingdom led him habitually to ignore everything but righteousness. Hence it was possible, later on, for ascetic-minded Christians to find authority for their views in his teachings. As a result Christianity developed a markedly ascetic bias.

Jesus' own position was simple: In the first place, we need take no thought for the morrow, for there will be no morrow; in the second place, the more we concern ourselves with property and possessions, the more likely we are to neglect readying ourselves for the last judgment:

> Do not store up your riches on earth, where moths and rust destroy them, and where thieves break in and steal them, but store up your riches in heaven, where moths and rust cannot destroy them, and where thieves cannot break in and steal them. For wherever your treasure is, your heart will be also. . . .
>
> Whoever wants to preserve his own life will lose it. . . . For what good does it do a man to gain the whole world and yet part with his life?[a]

Similarly, Jesus was inclined to be critical of the wealthy—partly because he believed, as do the poor in every generation, that they got their riches unjustly, and partly because, having possessions, they were naturally inclined to "take thought for them." From Jesus' point of view the poor had a great advantage, the rich a great disadvantage, in preparing themselves for the day of judgment.[15]

---

15 This is what Jesus meant when he said that it is harder for a rich man to enter the Kingdom of God than for a camel to go through the eye of a needle (Matt. 19:24).

Later, when Christianity came into contact with the impoverished populations of the Empire, this attitude lent it tremendous sales value. It was reassuring, when one had nothing, to be told that the less one had, the better were one's chances for immortality and eternal bliss.

Beyond this negative injunction to put away the things of this world, what can a man do, positively, to "seek the Kingdom of God and His righteousness"? Jesus' answer was that we should obey the Law—not just its letter, of course, but its spirit. And this means, as can be inferred from numerous scattered sayings of Jesus, cultivating a certain disposition, or frame of mind. This disposition includes *humility* ("The son of man came not to be ministered unto but to minister"—"I am among you as he that serveth"—"Judge not that ye be not judged"); *forgiveness* ("Love your enemies, bless them that curse you, do good to them that hate you, and pray for them which despitefully use you and persecute you"); *charity* ("Love thy neighbor as thyself"); *faith* ("Have faith in God. . . . What things soever ye desire, when ye pray, believe that ye receive them, and ye shall have them"); and *acceptance* ("Thy will be done").

JESUS' ETHICS COMPARED WITH GREEK ETHICS

The most striking thing about this list of virtues, as compared with Greek ethical thought, is the absence of any social ethic. Almost the only political statement made by Jesus was in reply to the question, "Is it lawful to pay tribute to Caesar?" By this inquiry his enemies hoped to present him with an embarrassing dilemma. If he denied that it was right to pay tribute, he would go on record as a rebel against his country's overlords; if he answered affirmatively, he would antagonize all those who hoped for independence and, in addition, would seem to put pagan law above the law of Yahweh. The question was, therefore, an example of the legal hair-splitting Jesus detested, and his answer to it—"Render to Caesar the things that are Caesar's, and to God the things that are God's"—was a masterpiece of diplomatic equivocation, which subsequent generations have interpreted to suit their various requirements. At best it is only a negative injunction, and, taken by itself, it cannot serve as the basis for a political or social system.

There are several reasons for this omission in Jesus' teachings. In the first place, social philosophy was prominent in Greek thought because the Greeks held man to be a social animal whose good could be attained only in communal give-and-take with his fellows, and it therefore seemed essential to solve the problems of communal living. But, whereas the Greeks had been concerned with working out man's destiny in this world, Jesus was otherworldly: God's Kingdom, he held, was so imminent that it was profitless to worry about techniques of government. In the second place, because of his emphasis on "inwardness," his concentration on motivation, Jesus was uninterested in overt behavior or in the social and political devices used to control it. And, finally, the fact that Jesus was a member of a subject race ruled by foreigners meant that politics could not have had the same primacy for him that it had had for the free elite of a Greek city-state.

As long as the Christians were a minority group living in, but not an organic part of, the Roman Empire, as long as they momentarily expected the last judgment, they could afford to follow Jesus in his neglect of politics. But later on, when the eschatological hope faded, when the coming of the Kingdom receded into the distant future, and when Christianity, now the state religion, was obliged to assume responsibility for a crumbling empire, the Christians found it necessary to study politics. And later generations of Christian thinkers, who had to construct political and social systems on the basis they had inherited from Jesus, faced a difficult problem. This concern with politics was, as we shall see, but one of the changes forced on Christianity by its emergence as a world religion.

But lack of a political or social interest is not the only, or even the chief, difference between Jesus' point of view and that of Greek ethical theorists. There is nothing in Jesus' list of virtues that corresponds to Aristotle's "intellectual virtues"—science, art, philosophic wisdom, and so on. One reason for this, doubtless, was Jesus' sense of crisis, which left no time for scholarship; another may have been that, coming from "plain people," he had not experienced the delights of scholarship.[16]

When we turn to Aristotle's moral, or practical, virtues, we enter an area in which Jesus *was* vitally interested—but even here his point of view was quite different from that of Aristotle. Jesus himself had nothing, for instance, to say about courage, an important Aristotelian virtue. And later Christians who reintroduced it as a virtue interpreted it narrowly as the heroism of the martyr prepared to die for his faith—a courage very different from that of Aristotle's citizen who faced death because it would be disgraceful to flee. Again, whereas for Aristotle pride was the crown of the virtues, for Jesus it was a grievous sin, and meekness, humility, and willing acceptance of Yahweh's commands were virtues.

The difference in point of view is enormous. For Aristotle the good life consisted in realizing the full potentialities of human nature. To the questions, "Why be courageous? Why be just?" Aristotle in effect answered, "Because courage and justice are aspects of human nature rightly understood (the ideal, that is, that reason discovers; not necessarily the actual), and the coward or the unjust man, who is thus denying one of his essential functions as man, cannot possibly be happy." And as for pride, Aristotle held that since it is a very fine thing to be a man, it would be ridiculous not to act the part.

But Jesus began with God, not with man. For him the good life consisted

---

16 This is possibly one point that distinguished Jesus from his older contemporary, Hillel (see p. 26, n. 12). Hillel, like Aristotle, was a learned man.

in pleasing God, not in developing to its full the form "man." This is why Jesus felt that pride was such a grievous sin—to be proud was to be self-centered when one ought to be God-centered.

Thus the fact that Jesus concentrated his attention on God meant that his ethics had a completely different sanction for moral living. It might be barely possible, by stretching the meaning of words, to say that what Jesus wanted was happiness, but for him happiness consisted in obeying a stern but loving Father, not in living up to one's ideal of manhood. But it is better not to use the word "happiness" at all in connection with Jesus' ethics. The word suggests that the Christian sanction is the reward that an omnipotent Father bestows on his compliant children. This indeed *is* the sense in which some of his disciples understood Jesus, but the reward Jesus himself envisaged was the sense of having conformed to God's will. God's approving, "Well done, thou good and faithful servant," was the best reward he could conceive of. This contrasts sharply with Aristotle's sense of self-congratulation; nothing in his thought corresponds to Jesus' "Thy will be done."

Another difference created by the primacy of God in Jesus' thought is his altruism, as compared with Aristotle's egoism. According to Aristotle the ultimate sanction for socially oriented conduct is the agent's own happiness. His treatment of friendship is a case in point. Aristotle advised us to cooperate with our neighbor; Jesus urged us to love him and, what is more, to do so, not merely for mutual profit and enjoyment, but because we are all children of the same Father. This sense of the common fatherhood of God led Jesus to emphasize the essential equality of all men—or rather, of all Jews, for there is little evidence that Jesus thought of teaching or having a message for any but his fellow Jews.[17]

Plato and Aristotle would not have understood this point of view. The ideal of the Greek moralists was exceptionally rich—the full and all-round development of a complete personality. But they thought this possible only for a small elite, even among Greeks. The basic moral problem for them was therefore a problem of selection: how, out of the mass of humanity, to find those capable of this kind of development.

In comparison with the Greek ideal, Jesus' view was, qualitatively speaking, narrow and limited—but it had two great advantages: It was genuinely altruistic and outgoing, and it was truly democratic. The good it envisaged was equally open to all. Once the violent reaction against paganism subsided, even the Christians realized there was much of value in Greek ethics. Accordingly, the problem became how to combine the Greek insight into quality with the Christian emphasis on equality—how to create opportunity for all, rather than how to select the fortunate few.

---

17 There is thus in Jesus' teaching a provincialism parallel to that which caused Plato and Aristotle to distinguish sharply between Greeks and barbarians.

THE MESSIAHSHIP OF JESUS

So far discussion has centered on Jesus' conception of God and of the relation in which men ought to stand to Him. But what did Jesus conceive to be his own relation to God? It is easy to say that he thought himself the Messiah sent to announce the coming of the Kingdom. But in what sense, exactly, did Jesus understand this mission? This is a question of great difficulty that we cannot hope to settle here and that, happily, is not especially relevant to a purely philosophical discussion. In fact, from the point of view of historians, the opinions of Jesus' contemporaries are more important than those of Jesus himself. It is not what Jesus meant but what they thought he meant that had an impact on the course of events.

Jesus repeatedly preached the imminent coming of the Kingdom, but so did many another Jew of that day, and not everyone understood this vague expression in the same way. Whatever moral and eschatological meaning it had for Jesus, the ordinary man in the street understood it in a political sense. Longing for independence from foreign rule, he took the promised Kingdom to be a revival of an autonomous Hebrew monarchy. From this point of view the Messiah was a second Moses, a military leader who would throw out the Romans and establish peace, freedom, and prosperity. For the Romans themselves this Messianic hope naturally created a serious political problem, especially since there was a vigorous underground party—the Zealots—agitating for rebellion who were only too happy to make political use of this naïve belief about the coming of the Messiah.

It is against this background that we must understand the events leading up to Jesus' death. As long as Jesus and the prophet John the Baptist (who had designated him as the Messiah) remained in the desert and confined themselves to talk, the Roman authorities could afford to overlook the matter. But when they came down to the urban centers and tried to inflame the mob, it was obviously a serious business. First, John was eliminated—conveniently, by one of the Romans' local puppets who had been antagonized by his violent language and gratuitous insults. Then, when Jesus entered Jerusalem in accordance with an ancient tradition foretelling the coming of the Messiah, and when the people received him as such, he was arrested quietly at night and despatched so promptly that no one outside his immediate circle knew what was happening. It was not necessary to deal with any but the ringleader, for his disciples fled with ignominious haste.

The Jewish leaders who operated under the Roman officials were in the position of modern quislings. They could not protect Jesus, nor did they wish to. Why, indeed, should they have sympathized with this "madman" from the provinces? Even those who may have secretly shared Jesus' supposed goal of independence knew the time was not ripe; they can only have regarded Jesus as an unmitigated nuisance who stirred up trouble to no avail. Hence one can hardly blame them or hold them responsible for Jesus' death. Certainly Jesus did not, for he had known what was going to happen to him.

Why, then, did Jesus deliberately choose to die? This is one of the many puzzles Jesus' disciples had to face after his death. The solution they worked out was largely determined by their understanding of his Messiahship, just as their understanding of his Messiahship was deeply marked by the events on the hill of Calvary. The impression Jesus made on the Romans and on the Jews at large has been noted. But the opinion Jesus' own disciples formed of his Messiahship remains to be seen. If the impression made on the Romans and Jews decided the tragic outcome of Jesus' expedition to Jerusalem, the impression made on the disciples decided the future of the Church.

The Jesus Movement

It is anachronistic, of course, to talk about "Christianity" as existing during Jesus' life—or even for many years after his death. What must now be traced, indeed, is the gradual development of Christianity—a body of theological beliefs and complicated dogmas—out of the simple teachings of Jesus, Judaism, Oriental mystery cultism, and late Greek philosophy. These miscellaneous beliefs had to be harmonized and organized into one body of doctrine. Doctrine itself had to be accommodated to the administrative needs of a growing institution. Neither of these closely associated enterprises was in any sense planned. Doctrines and institutions grew—the work of many hands; and as they grew they created problems with which future generations had to contend.

HOW THE MOVEMENT SURVIVED

Let us begin by asking how the little movement that Jesus had started managed to survive. That the crucifixion caused a crisis that might well have destroyed it at its birth is surely obvious. For, whatever Jesus' own view of his role in the coming Kingdom, there is little doubt that his disciples interpreted his Messiahship literally and believed, up to the final catastrophe on the hill of Calvary, that Jesus was to reign as an earthly monarch, with themselves as his chief advisers.[18] His execution was, therefore, a tremendous shock. It is not surprising that the disciples scattered and that the authorities did not feel it necessary to take measures against them. What *is* surprising is that their belief in the Messiahship of Jesus revived. It revived because they became convinced that after his death Jesus appeared to them and talked with them. This restored their belief that Jesus was, after all, a supernatural being. It also restored their faith in the coming of the Kingdom. And, indeed, as they looked back on Jesus'

---

18 Because the disciples expected a great future for themselves, a certain amount of rivalry developed among them: Who was to sit on King Jesus' right hand? Who on his left? (Mark 10:37 ff.)

life, it was not the purity or nobility of his ethical insights but his miraculous powers that chiefly impressed them.

In this way the disciples found the confidence to resume preaching the coming of the Kingdom. What exactly this Kingdom meant to them is difficult, indeed impossible, to determine. But until the Messiah's return brought the Kingdom, they made their lot more bearable by organizing a communal life of mutual self-help. In the early days, we are told, "the believers all shared everything they had with one another, and sold their property and belongings, and divided the money with all the rest, according to their special needs."[b] It seems likely that the earliest Christian congregations performed for their members many of the functions of a modern trade union or fraternal organization—providing medical care, suitable burial, relief for widows and orphans.

Whereas some were content to define religion largely in economic terms,[19] others emphasized a spiritual and otherworldly element. In this connection the contrast between the two versions of the Beatitudes is significant. Luke's simple "Blessed are you who are poor" becomes, in Matthew's version, "Blessed are those who feel their spiritual need," that is, the poor in spirit, not the poor in fact. And Luke's assurance that the hungry will be fed becomes Matthew's assurance that those who hunger and thirst after righteousness will be satisfied. Similarly, Luke's drastic "Sell what belongs to you, and give away the money!" is softened in Matthew with a significant qualification: "If you want to be perfect, go! Sell your property and give the money to the poor . . . ."[c]

It is hard not to see in these emendations a recognition that the coming of the Kingdom had been postponed and that believers therefore needed to find a *modus vivendi* for life in this world. It seems also that the disciples were now reaching beyond the poor and downtrodden to a well-to-do class, to which health and burial insurance would not have had strong appeal.

SHIFT OF EMPHASIS TO JESUS

In other words, as time passed and the movement spread, the emphasis of the Christian "message" shifted to the promise of immortality; and with the change in the message there was a change in the conception of its author. Jesus was becoming the central figure of a new religion. In Jesus' own mind the focus of attention had been Yahweh, father and creator. For the disciples, increasingly, it became Jesus himself. And whereas Jesus had taught that salvation lay in cheerful obedience to Yahweh's law, the disciples taught that it lay in accepting their belief that Jesus was indeed the long-awaited Messiah.

But if Jesus was divine, what was his relation to the Father? Originally the disciples had thought of Jesus simply as "anointed by God," that is, designated by Yahweh to perform a certain mission, just as in the past Amos and Elijah

---

19 "A religious observance . . . is this: to look after orphans and widows in their trouble, and keep one's self unstained by the world" (James 1:27).

and Isaiah and David and other of Yahweh's children had been designated by him. But with the increasing concentration on the divinity of Jesus, this could no longer suffice. Various formulas were put forward that were the source of bitter quarrel in the growing Church and that have survived to this day to divide the Christian community.

The divinity of Jesus created further difficulties. Why had the coming of the Kingdom (whatever this was conceived to mean) been postponed? Why had the divine Jesus allowed himself to be killed by the Romans? As regards the first question, the disciples decided that the time was not yet ripe, that the Jews were too wicked and that their refusal to accept Jesus' teaching and his crucifixion were signs of this. Accordingly, since the disciples wanted to hasten Jesus' return and the fulfillment of his mission, they saw their duty clearly: They could best hasten the coming of the Kingdom by bringing their fellow Jews to see the light. As for the second question, they recalled that Jesus had said he came to give his life as a ransom for many.[20] It must somehow be that his suffering on the cross was designed to help pay for these sins of the Jews. Unfortunately, these answers created still more puzzles. To whom was the ransom paid? To the devil? But this seemed to imply a rival to Yahweh's power, who had to be bought off. And could not the creator God, the loving Father, have found a less terrible way of redeeming His erring children?

If these were desperate puzzles for the disciples, they presented even greater difficulties for the fellow Jews to whom the disciples preached the new gospel. To these determined monotheists, any suggestion of the divinity of Jesus (whom they recalled as a plain man, the son of a carpenter, who died as a common criminal) must have seemed blasphemous. Thus, though the opposition to Jesus himself had been largely political in origin, the antagonism to his disciples had a religious animus. Though the disciples originally thought of themselves as Jews, with a mission to preach to Jews, the increasing antagonism they experienced caused them to turn their attention toward others.[21] As has been seen, conditions in the Empire were such as to assure a ready reception for a savior god who promised immortality to his worshipers. Moreover, there were special circumstances that favored a savior god with a Jewish background.

THE JEWS OF THE DISPERSION

As it happened, only a small fraction of the Jewish population lived in Palestine.[22] The great majority of the Jews, called the Diaspora (Dispersion)

20 Of course, the saying (Mark 10:45) may be a later attribution to justify the belief, but the annual sacrifice of a scapegoat that was supposed to absorb the sins of the people was an ancient part of the Jewish religion (Lev. 16:8 ff.) and similar rites have appeared in many primitive religions.

21 The final break occurred in 70 A.D. when the Christian Jews (as those who adhered to the Jesus movement while remaining faithful to Judaism and the Law may be called for convenience) refused to join the rest of the Jewish nation in a rebellion.

22 According to one estimate there were 4,500,000 Jews in the Empire (7 per cent of the population), of whom not more than 70,000 lived in Palestine.

because they were scattered through the Empire, were perhaps less severely orthodox than the Jews of Palestine. Living in Alexandria, in Rome, in Antioch, and in other imperial cities, they were in frequent contact with pagans and with the liberalizing influences of Greek thought. At the same time, the worship of Yahweh had a certain appeal for the Jews' neighbors, and throughout the Empire considerable numbers were converted. It appears that these converts were not always required to follow the Law in all its rigor, nor to submit to the rite of circumcision.[23] In this way there came to be a fairly large segment of the imperial population that can fairly be described as a fertile field for the ministry of the disciples: men and women familiar with, and sympathetic to, the general point of view of Judaism but not bound by rigorous orthodoxy.

THE GENTILE MISSION

Gradually, then, as the disciples found opposition to their activities in Jerusalem and Palestine, they shifted their attention to other communities in the eastern Mediterranean and to Rome itself, where they sought to convert Gentiles as well as Hellenized Jews. These encounters naturally brought about further changes in the teachings of the Jesus movement. It was not so much that concessions were deliberately made to win Gentile converts, though this doubtless occurred. More important by far was the fact that the new audience, being unacquainted with the finer points of Judaism, understood the teachings of the disciples in a very different fashion. Soon these new interpretations became, to the confusion of later theologians, a part of Christian doctrine. Moreover, the converts themselves began to spread the good word, and among these new teachers were men whose backgrounds and temperaments were very different from those of the simple Galileans who had formed the nucleus of the movement. Of these newer teachers the greatest by far was St. Paul. He was not only the leader of the Gentile mission; it may be said that he, more than any other individual, was responsible for the development of Christianity, as a distinct religion, out of what has been called here the Jesus movement.

---

23 The stricter Jews maintained that full submission to this rite was necessary. There was also a struggle over circumcision within the Jesus movement itself—a struggle between those who insisted that all Gentile converts must submit to it and those (like St. Paul) who held it to be unnecessary. See p. 45.

CHAPTER 2

Christianity: The Formative Years

The Mysticism of Paul

Perhaps the most significant thing about Paul's background is the fact that he was a Jew of the Diaspora, with the advantage of contact with Greek culture. He was born in Tarsus, a Greek city in Cilicia, about the beginning of the Christian era. His family, who were well-to-do and had the distinction of being Roman citizens, saw to it that he received an excellent education. In due course he was sent to Jerusalem to study under the most distinguished rabbis of the day, and it is a sign of how much he had been exposed to non-Jewish influences, and so of how much he had to learn from his Jewish teachers, that he first read the Law in Greek translation, not in the original Hebrew.

Paul was proud of his Jewish heritage. He was, he said, of the stock of Israel of the tribe of Benjamin, a Hebrew of Hebrews.[a] Perhaps just because of his less rigorous background (like the parvenu noble who is more royal than the king), Paul became exceedingly zealous in "the traditions of my fathers." When he found a stubborn little group preaching the blasphemous and idolatrous doctrine that Jesus was the Messiah, he eagerly joined in the effort the stricter Jews were making to destroy this wicked heresy. Indeed, if we are to believe his own later estimate, he surpassed most of his contemporaries in the fury with which he persecuted and ravaged the Jesus movement.[b]

PAUL'S VISION

Then one day, as he traveled to Damascus on this very business, he experienced a vision and was converted to the Jesus movement, whose message he straightway began to preach. The accounts in the Acts of this momentous occasion are full of picturesque detail, but Paul's own version is extraordinarily abbreviated: He said simply, "It pleased God to reveal His Son in me."

There have been countless attempts to explain Paul's vision.[1] Pious Christians have attributed it to the direct intervention of the Lord; equally fervent Freudians have said that Paul was a psychotic, suffering from sexual repression and a father fixation. Others have tried to account for the vision on the basis of some permanent physical abnormality, like epilepsy, or some temporary disability, like fatigue so extreme as to result in hallucination. Still others have regarded the vision as a mirage. There is not enough evidence to decide among these alternatives. But even if we knew more concerning the circumstances surrounding it, it would seem more profitable to concentrate our attention on the results of Paul's experience than to speculate about its causes. The results of the vision were momentous—not only in Paul's own life but in the history of the Western mind. For Paul understood his vision of Jesus, the anointed of the Lord, not in the narrowly Jewish sense of Jesus' disciples, but in the light of the wider Hellenistic culture into which he had been born and which he had put aside when he went to Jerusalem to study under the rabbis. That is to say, Paul naturally interpreted his mystical experience in the light of his knowledge of the mystery cults already popular and widespread in the East. Thus, though there seems to have been nothing mystical in the teachings of Jesus nor in the earliest interpretation of them, Paul understood the Jesus movement as a mystery religion. For him Jesus was less a Jewish Messiah than a resurrected God. Though he believed that the coming of the Kingdom was imminent, he envisaged it less as that final accounting on the day of judgment that Jesus had preached than as a spiritual state—the individual's union with his savior.

Paul, then, shared that deep need for immortality, that sense of dependence

1 To Paul the important point was that he had *seen* the Lord. Compare I Corin. 9:1, "Have I not seen Jesus Christ our Lord?" and I Corin. 15:8, "And last of all he was seen of me, as one born out of due time."

in an uncertain world, that was sweeping the imperial population and had already resulted in the enormous popularity of such cults as those of Attis, Osiris, and Mithra. But because of his upbringing—perhaps (who can say?) because he had been engaged in an attempt to eradicate the Jesus movement—the vision that appeared to him was not Attis or Mithra; it was Jesus. This meant that the actual teachings of Jesus, the Judaic background on which these teachings rested, and the opinions and attitudes of the disciples all underwent a radical transformation in Paul's hands. By making the Jesus movement understandable and acceptable to the Gentile world, by accommodating it to the basic cultural needs of the time (which he could do precisely because those needs were also his own), Paul made it possible for an obscure Jewish Messiah-cult to become a world religion.

THE LETTER TO THE ROMANS

Paul's letter to the Christian community at Rome contains a compact statement of his message.

> I want you to understand, brothers, that I have often intended to come to see you . . . to preach the good news to you at Rome also. For I am not ashamed of the good news, for it is God's power for the salvation of everyone who has faith, of the Jew first and then of the Greek. . . .
>
> Suppose you call yourself a Jew, and rely on law, and boast about God . . . . Circumcision will help you only if you observe the Law; but if you are a lawbreaker, you might as well be uncircumcised. So if people who are uncircumcised observe the requirements of the Law, will they not be treated as though they were circumcised? And if, although they are physically uncircumcised, they obey the Law, they will condemn you, who break the Law, although you . . . are circumcised. For the real Jew is not the man who is one outwardly, and the real circumcision is not something physical and external. The real Jew is the man who is one inwardly, and real circumcision is a matter of the heart, a spiritual, not a literal, thing. . . .
>
> What does this mean? Are we Jews at a disadvantage? Not at all. We have already charged Jews and Greeks all alike with being under the control of sin. As the Scripture says,
>
>> "There is not a single man who is upright,
>> No one understands, no one searches for God." . . .
>
> For no human being can be made upright in the sight of God by observing the Law. All that the Law can do is to make man conscious of sin. But now God's way of uprightness has been disclosed without any reference to law, though the Law and the Prophets bear witness to it. It is God's way of uprightness and comes through having faith in Jesus Christ,[2] and it is for

---

2 [It is significant of the transformation taking place that Paul speaks not simply of "Jesus" but of "Jesus Christ." *Christos* is but the Greek translation of "Messiah," which originally meant (as we have seen) merely "anointed" or "designated." However, in calling Jesus "Messiah" the disciples gradually came to mean more than that he had been designated by Yahweh to lead

all who have faith, without distinction. For all men sin and come short of the glory of God, but by his mercy they are made upright for nothing, by the deliverance secured through Christ Jesus. For God showed him publicly dying as a sacrifice of reconciliation to be taken advantage of through faith. . . .

A man is made upright by faith; the observance of the Law has nothing to do with it. Does God belong to the Jews alone? Does he not belong to the heathen too? Of course he belongs to the heathen too; there is but one God, and he will make the circumcised upright on the ground of their faith and the uncircumcised upright because of theirs. . . .

So as we have been made upright by faith, let us live in peace with God through our Lord Jesus Christ, by whom we have been introduced through faith to the favor of God that we now enjoy, and let us glory in our hope of sharing the glory of God. . . . For, through the holy Spirit that has been given us, God's love has flooded our hearts. For when we were still helpless, at the decisive moment Christ died for us godless men.[c]

It will be seen that Paul first made the historical Jesus into a savior god and then built up a mythical setting for this god out of the Jewish legends and stories that he and Jesus, as Jews, knew in common. How, for instance, did we come to sin and so to require the services of Christ the Savior? For answer Paul fell back on the old Jewish myth of the creation. God created Adam, the first man, free from sin. But Adam disobeyed his Maker, and we, his descendants, have inherited his sins. Just as the sin of one man (Adam) brought death and all our woe into the world, so the virtue of one man (Jesus) saves us; and just as Adam's sin was disobedience, so the virtue by which Jesus redeems the many is obedience.

It is just like the way in which through one man sin came into the world, and death followed sin, and so death spread to all men, because all men sinned. . . . So Adam foreshadowed the one who was to come. . . .

So as one offense meant condemnation for all men, just so one righteous act means acquittal and life for all men. For just as that one man's disobedience made the mass of mankind sinners, so this one's obedience will make the mass of them upright.[d]

Because of our inheritance from Adam we are all corrupt, and so doomed, but for God's mercy in sending His Son to be a sacrifice for us. But though Paul associated this corruption with "our sinful body," he meant more than may be suggested by his reference to "the lusts of the flesh." It is true that he seems to have had an especially strong aversion to the sexual aspect of life, and that

the Jews to freedom. And when the Gentiles called Jesus "Christ" the word meant more to them than it did to the disciples: To the Gentiles, with their background in paganism and Eastern mysticism and their lack of interest in Hebrew nationalism, it meant "savior god"— AUTHOR.]

he regarded all the various processes by which the body lives—digestion, elimination, and so on—as either bad or low.

> When we were living mere physical lives the sinful passions, awakened by the Law, operated through the organs of our bodies to make us bear fruit for death. But now the Law no longer applies to us; we have died to what once controlled us, so that we can now serve in the new Spirit, not under the old letter.[e]

Though it is easy to see how Paul—and other ascetics too, of course—could find a sanction for any bias against the "organs of the body" in Jesus' teachings (for, as we have seen, Jesus' sense of the imminence of the Kingdom caused him to give scant value to bodily activities), neither Judaism nor Jesus had connected sin specifically with the "flesh." And Paul was too good a Jew to condemn the body wholly—after all, it had been fashioned by an all-good creator god. Hence, for Paul, sin had a more complex meaning and a wider reference than mere incontinence. Whereas conventional Judaism thought of sin as deviation from the letter of the Law and Jesus had thought of it as deviation from the spirit of the Law, Paul interpreted it in terms of a divided will. For Paul, the contrast between the flesh and the spirit was the contrast between a will that is torn and divided because it pursues conflicting ends and a will that is unified and free because it is wholly dedicated to a higher end.

Thus Paul adopted a metaphysical dualism not dissimilar to the dualism that was central to many of the mystery religions. Further, Paul believed that the will remains divided, that is, corrupt, unless man is aided by outside powers. No matter how much unaided man may see, and in a sense want to do, the good, his lower nature wins out and he chooses the bad. Without God, man is thus the helpless spectator of his own destruction.

> I am physical, sold into slavery to sin. I do not understand what I am doing, for I do not do what I want to do; I do things that I hate. But if I do what I do not want to do, I acknowledge that the Law is right. In reality, it is not I that do these things; it is sin, which has possession of me. For I know that nothing good resides in me, that is, in my physical self; I can will, but I cannot do what is right. I do not do the good things that I want to do; I do the wrong things that I do not want to do. But if I do the things that I do not want to do, it is not I that am acting, it is sin, which has possession of me. I find the law to be that I who want to do right am dogged by what is wrong. My inner nature agrees with the divine law, but all through my body I see another principle in conflict with the law of my reason, which makes me a prisoner to that law of sin that runs through my body. What a wretched man I am! Who can save me from this doomed body? Thank God! it is done through Jesus Christ our Lord! So mentally I am a slave to God's law, but physically to the law of sin.[f]

All this differs markedly from Jesus' teachings, not only in its extreme asceticism and dualism, but also in its sense of man's frustration and helplessness. Insofar as Jesus thought about this point at all, he seems to have taken for granted that the normal man, whom Paul held to be utterly helpless, is quite capable of working out his own problems. Jesus seems to have believed that for salvation it is only necessary that man take as good care of his inner life as law-abiding Jews habitually took of their outer life—and he seems to have thought that any man is capable of this.

By contrast, Paul—in accordance with the sentiment of all the mystery religions—felt the need of transcendental help. "What a wretched man I am! Who can save me from this doomed body?" Paul, of course, found his answer on the road to Damascus, in the risen Christ. Jesus, as Paul understood him, was a kind of parallel, or model, of man. Just as man is a dualism of body and spirit, so Jesus, the God-become-man, was a dualism of the human and the divine. In both there is a tension between a lower and a higher principle, but in Jesus, unlike the unaided man, the higher principle won out. His resurrection was testimony to this. And this explains the overwhelming importance for Paul of the crucifixion and the resurrection, as compared with the other events of Jesus' life. The miracles and healings and castings out of demons that so stirred the original disciples interested him little. But the crucifixion showed that Jesus was truly a man, a man who died; the resurrection, that he was a God with life eternal.

But not only did Jesus suffer *as* we suffer; he suffered *for* us, and Paul held his resurrection to be a promise to us of our delivery from the body of this death. How can this be? Here we enter the heart of Paul's mystery. Just as the devotee of Attis or Osiris was afforded immortality by identification with his god, so Paul felt that he, in that experience on the road to Damascus, had been united with his Christ.

> So there is no condemnation any more for those who are in union with Christ Jesus. For the life-giving law of the Spirit through Christ Jesus has freed you from the Law of sin and death. For though it was impossible for the Law to do it, hampered as it was by our physical limitations, God, by sending his own Son in our sinful physical form, as a sin-offering put his condemnation upon sin through his physical nature, so that the requirement of the Law might be fully met in our case, since we live not on the physical but on the spiritual plane. People who are controlled by the physical think of what is physical, and people who are controlled by the spiritual think of what is spiritual. For to be physically minded means death, but to be spiritually minded means life and peace. For to be physically minded means hostility to God, for it refuses to obey God's law, indeed it cannot obey it. Those who are physical cannot please God. But you are not physical but spiritual, if God's Spirit has really taken possession of you; for unless a man has Christ's spirit, he does not belong to Christ. But if Christ is in your hearts,

though your bodies are dead in consequence of sin, your spirits have life in consequence of uprightness. . . .

We know that in everything God works with those who love him, whom he has called in accordance with his purpose, to bring about what is good. For those whom he had marked out from the first he predestined to be made like his Son, so that he should be the eldest of many brothers; and those whom he has predestined he calls, and those whom he calls he makes upright, and those whom he makes upright he glorifies.

Then what shall we conclude from this? If God is for us, who can be against us? Will not he who did not spare his own Son, but gave him up for us all, with that gift give us everything? Who can bring any accusation against those whom God has chosen? God pronounces them upright; who can condemn them? Christ Jesus who died, or rather who was raised from the dead, is at God's right hand, and actually pleads for us. Who can separate us from Christ's love? Can trouble or misfortune or persecution or hunger or destitution or danger or the sword? . . .

For I am convinced that neither death nor life nor angels nor their hierarchies nor the present nor the future nor any supernatural forces either of height or depth nor anything else in creation will be able to separate us from the love God has shown in Christ Jesus our Lord![g]

Thus, for Paul, to be saved was to be united with Christ, and salvation was not something that occurred in the future, after one's physical death. It could take place during this life, for the believer was made over into a new man. Just as Jesus "was raised from the dead through the Father's glory, we too may live a new life. . . . For when he died, he became once for all dead to sin; the life he now lives is a life in relation to God. So you also must think of yourselves as dead to sin but alive to God, through union with Christ Jesus."[h]

That one could indeed be saved was not just a promise, according to Paul. It had actually happened—suddenly and dramatically—in his own life. The death from which he had been saved was the sinful life he had been living. Before the great event that occurred on the road to Damascus, he was a slave to his body and its lusts. After this event, he experienced a marvelous freedom from bodily desires. These were psychological facts that Paul accounted for by saying that Christ now lived in him: "It is not I that live, but Christ that liveth in me."

THE MYSTICAL UNION WITH CHRIST

Paul's focus on mystical union with Christ was a radical departure from the old worship of Yahweh, with its emphasis on obedience to the Law. The true believer, according to the Jews, was grateful to Yahweh and followed his commands. The true believer, according to Paul, is identical with his crucified Lord, dies with him, and is resurrected with him. What dies in the believer who through faith shares Jesus' death on the cross is the flesh and the lusts thereof—the sense of restriction and failure and compulsion. What is born in the believer's identification with the resurrected Christ is a new freedom that transforms this earthly existence. Paul expressed this in his statement that "Christ ransomed us from the Law's curse." The Law, Paul argued, had been given men as a rule to follow *before* the coming of Jesus. And, like a schoolmaster whose stern and rigorous discipline only causes his pupils to become more stubborn, the Law failed to reform mankind. Men either simply ignored it or, if they followed it, did so in a grudging and resentful spirit. But what the Law could not do, God accomplished by sending His Son to die for us on the cross.

> But now that faith has come, we are no longer in the charge of the attendant. For in Christ Jesus you are all sons of God through your faith. For all of you who have been baptized into union with Christ have clothed yourselves with Christ. There is no room for "Jew" and "Greek"; there is no room for "slave" and "freeman"; there is no room for "male" and "female"; for in union with Christ Jesus you are all one.[i]

This view was naturally attacked by the strict Judaizing branch of the Jesus movement—those who, adhering strictly to Jesus' own conception of the scope of his mission, insisted that salvation was limited to Jews and to those Gentiles who submitted to the rite of circumcision and followed the other ceremonial demands of the Law.[3] Had the stricter sect won out, Christianity would have been closed to the great majority of men. Did Paul take his position against circumcision deliberately, because he saw that only by relaxing the requirement could the Jesus movement become a world religion? This may well be the case. Certainly, he was a missionary, imbued with a missionary fervor to spread the gospel.

Of course, there were religious considerations, as well as possible propagandistic ones, that led Paul to abrogate the Law. It was not his observance of the Law that had saved him; it was the vision vouchsafed on the road to Damascus. It was nothing he had done; it was something that happened to him. What is important, he naturally concluded, is not what one does or leaves undone but the faith that unites one to Jesus. Hence the character of his mystical experience committed him to a position that made the Gentile mission possible.

If the strict constructionalists opposed Paul's teaching on this point, some of his converts actually abused it. It is obviously a view that is easy to abuse. If faith means a new birth, and new birth means perfect freedom, why should the reborn not do as they please? Moreover, if faith means salvation, the faithful need no longer fear the consequences of their acts.

The purpose of Paul's letter to the Galatians seems to have been not only to silence the strict constructionalists but also to condemn those who went to the other extreme.

---

3 This was a matter of heated debate in the young Christian communities. See, for instance, Acts 11:2, in which the disciple Peter is obliged to defend himself against the charge of those who may be called the strict constructionalists that he has eaten with uncircumcised persons.

> For you, brothers, have been called to freedom; only do not make your
> freedom an excuse for the physical. . . .
>
> I mean this: Live by the Spirit, and then you will not indulge your physical
> cravings. For the physical cravings are against the Spirit, and the cravings
> of the Spirit are against the physical; the two are in opposition, so that you
> cannot do anything you please. . . . The things our physical nature does are
> clear enough—immorality, impurity, licentiousness, idolatry, sorcery, enmity,
> quarreling, jealousy, anger, selfishness, dissension, party-spirit, envy, drunken-
> ness, carousing, and the like. I warn you as I did before that people who
> do such things will have no share in the Kingdom of God. But what the Spirit
> produces is love, joy, peace, patience, kindness, goodness, faithfulness, gentle-
> ness, self-control. . . .
>
> If we live by the Spirit, let us be guided by the Spirit.[j]

In other words, a man who lives in the spirit—who has real faith, who has
been truly converted—can no longer do, or even want to do, evil deeds. For
if he *really* lives in the spirit, he will also walk in the spirit. To walk in the
spirit, to be united with Christ, means to love God. Love of God so fills the
heart of this "new man"[4] that it crowds out every other motive and gives even
his most ordinary acts new meaning.

> For just as there are many parts united in our human bodies, and the parts
> do not all have the same function, so, many as we are, we form one body
> through union with Christ, and we are individually parts of one another. We
> have gifts that differ with the favor that God has shown us, whether it is
> that of preaching, . . . or of practical service, . . . or [that of] the teacher
> who exercises his gift in teaching, the speaker, in his exhortation, the giver
> of charity, with generosity, the office-holder, with devotion, the one who does
> acts of mercy, with cheerfulness. Your love must be genuine. . . .[k]

And so we come to the thirteenth chapter of the first letter to the Corinthians,
with its poem of love: No matter what knowledge, beauty, strength, or wisdom
we may have, it is nothing without love. "Though I speak with the tongues of
men and of angels and have not love I am become as sounding brass, or a tinkling
cymbal. And though I have . . . all knowledge and though I have all faith, so
that I could remove mountains, and have not love I am nothing. And though
I bestow all my goods to feed the poor and though I give my body to be burned,
and have not love it profiteth me nothing." Love is the source of all the other
virtues: "it envieth not, vaunteth not itself, is not puffed up, doth not behave
itself unseemly, . . . thinketh no evil, . . . beareth all things, believeth all things,
hopeth all things, endureth all things."

This emphasis on inner morality is Jesus'. But the love of which Paul speaks
is not Jesus' love of Yahweh, nor yet his love of his neighbor; it is a mystic

4 See p. 41.

love of the crucified Christ. And to love, Paul added faith and hope—faith in Jesus, hope and expectation of the promised salvation. "Now abideth faith, hope, love, these three, but the greatest of these is love."

PAUL'S MARTYRDOM

This is eloquent preaching, and Paul was a great missionary. His was not the mysticism of ecstatic contemplation; it overflowed in energetic action. Up and down the land he went, teaching and preaching, and when he could not go, he wrote. He had constantly to meet bitter attacks from enemies and, what was perhaps worse, to correct the backsliding of newly won converts. He was mobbed, imprisoned, persecuted—"I bear on my body the marks of the Lord Jesus." Finally, in Jerusalem, things came to a head. "The high priest and the chief of the Jews" haled him, as they had earlier haled Jesus, before the Roman governor, charging that he was "a pestilent fellow, a mover of sedition among all the Jews throughout the world; a ringleader of the sect of the Nazarenes, who also hath gone about to profane the temple." The Jews would have preferred to deal with the case themselves, but Paul was a Roman citizen and it was impossible, however much his Jewish enemies desired it, to deal with him quickly. He was imprisoned first at Caesarea and then, after shipwreck and divers other adventures, at Rome. There, after a long period of imprisonment, he was tried, sentenced, and executed, probably in 62 A.D.

PAULINE CHRISTIANITY

Paul was a mystic and a missionary, not a philosopher. Why, then, devote so much attention, in a history of philosophy, to his views? The answer is that his views became a part of the subject matter of philosophy, not only in the Middle Ages but even in modern times. Both the specific problems philosophers have dealt with and their ways of dealing with them have been deeply influenced by Paul. Such was the intensity of his vision on the road to Damascus, and such the strength of his personality, that his version of Jesus survived. Of course, it should not be inferred that it occurred to Paul that what he preached was a "version" of Jesus. We can see, however, that Paul's temperament and his particular cultural background were largely responsible for his understanding of the vision. If he had not lived, or if he had been a Jew of Jerusalem, it is doubtful that Christianity would have developed into a world religion. If he had been a Greek, not a Jew, the religion he fathered would probably have been just another Eastern mystery cult—an ethical and metaphysical dualism to which was attached the notion of a savior god dying for his worshipers. Because he was a Jew, and a Jew of the Diaspora, he superimposed a mystery cult on a Judaic base. It is precisely because his understanding of Jesus' message was compounded of so many elements—traditional Judaism, the Messiah cult, the mystery of a resurrected god—that his teaching of the message had so universal an appeal. On the other hand, since these diverse elements did not perfectly fuse, the problem of synthesizing them into a consistent view was a formidable legacy that Paul left to subsequent generations.

For instance, later Christians were forced to examine the question of the relative importance of faith and of works in effecting salvation. Though Paul repeatedly affirmed faith as the means to mystic identification with Christ, he also emphasized the importance of works—of the sacramental rites, specifically baptism and the Eucharist. Whatever these ceremonies may have meant to other first-generation Christians,[5] to Paul, influenced as he was by the Eastern mysteries, their significance was obvious. In many of the mystery sects, as we have seen, there was a baptism either in blood or in water by which the initiate's sins were purged away and a sacrificial meal in which the body of the slain god was eaten and by means of which his eternal life was communicated to the worshiper.[6] Thus there are side by side in Paul's teaching two quite contradictory theses: one that salvation is magical (that is, follows automatically from the performance of certain rites), the other that it is spiritual (that is, more a matter of internal change than of merely external rituals).

Christian apologists have tried to minimize the magical element in Paul's view and have even held that it was precisely the absence of this element that distinguished his mystic Christianity from the mystery cults of the East. No one would deny that Paul had a much clearer insight into the meaning of salvation than the cultists had. On the other hand, it must ,be allowed both that he occasionally lapsed into magic and that they occasionally rose above it and saw (as he usually did) that salvation lies in an attitude of mind rather than in magic rites. The difference between Paul and the cultists on this point is one of degree, not one of kind. It is not that Paul brought something new into the world, but rather that, though his Christian mysticism and the Oriental mysticisms alike had their higher and lower moments, in Paul's view the higher moments tended to predominate.

But even taking Paul at his higher moments, there is a conflict in his teaching between faith and works: If, as Paul said, "A man is not justified by the works of the Law but by the faith of Jesus Christ," what is the role of the various sacraments the Church administers? It is easy to see why this became a vital question of Church doctrine. Salvation by faith is an individual matter; mystical identification with Christ is a private relationship between the believer and his God, and the Church, seen from this vantage point, is simply a spiritual commu-

---

5 The ceremony of the Last Supper, for instance, probably originated as a commemorative meal and only gradually took on a sacramental character.

6 Naturally, this parallelism did not disturb Paul; but one hundred years later, when Christianity was making claims to uniqueness and coming to view the other Eastern mysteries as dangerous rivals, it caused the Church intense embarrassment. Of the many explanations offered by the Church fathers, perhaps the most ingenious was that of Tertullian, who claimed that the devil, foreseeing that these Christian rites were to be instituted, deliberately imitated them in order that confusion might ensue.

nity of believers united by the common relation in which they stand to their savior. This point of view, obviously, is an expression of religious individualism. But those who thought of the Church as an organization and an institution naturally had to insist both on formal requirements for membership and on a proper sense of subordination to ecclesiastical authority. From this point of view the sacraments have an essential function. Eventually this conflict over salvation by faith or by works, first adumbrated by Paul, became a fundamental issue on which, at the time of the Reformation in the sixteenth century, Catholic Christendom splintered.

Another point in Paul's teaching that was to cause grave dispute was his doctrine of "original sin," as it was later called. Paul probably did not recognize this aspect of his thought as a "doctrine," for he did not think in such terms. But his letter to the Romans was laden with trouble for future theologians. Before his conversion, Paul was acutely conscious of his sin, that is, of his inability to choose to do those things that he believed he ought to choose. He did not believe that he was unique in this respect. On the contrary, he held that "All alike [are] under the control of sin." This conception of the innate sinfulness of man was not only an outgrowth of personal experience; it allowed Paul to magnify Christ's role. The less capable men are of saving themselves, the more essential Christ's death and resurrection become.

Paul, for his part, was content to attribute this universal sinfulness and helplessness of man to Adam's disobedience.[7] But though Adam's sin was doubtless "original," both in the sense of being the first ever committed and in the sense of being the source of all subsequent sinning, later theologians could hardly avoid the questions Paul's formula raised: How did men inherit Adam's sin? And why did God inflict them with this terrible inheritance? And, even allowing that Adam's sin somehow explains that of all men, why did an all-knowing and all-powerful God permit him to sin in the first place and so to cause all the suffering humanity has experienced in its long history?

Moreover, if men are truly helpless because of Adam's disobedience, how can they be held responsible for the sins they commit? And why, if those who are saved contribute nothing to their salvation, should they be chosen and others be left to their fate? In his letter to the Romans Paul wrote that God has "marked out" and "predestined" some for salvation. Is it not unjust first to condemn all future generations for something their first parents did and then to exempt from this condemnation a few who are indistinguishable morally or otherwise from all the rest? In this way the problem of free will emerged as one of the central themes of subsequent philosophizing.

Finally, Paul held that Christ the Savior is the son of that monotheistic Yahweh in whom he also believed. But what exactly does this mean? Paul was not very explicit on this point. In one place he said that "though he possessed the nature of God," Christ Jesus "did not grasp at equality with God. . . . That

7 See p. 41.

is why God has so greatly exalted him, and given him the name above all others . . . ."[1] Another passage suggests that Paul thought of Christ as a kind of viceroy or agent who will disappear when his work is done: "After that will come the end, when [Christ] will turn over the kingdom to God his Father. . . . And when everything is reduced to subjection to him, then the Son himself will also become subject to him who has reduced everything to subjection to him, so that God may be everything to everyone."[m]

The question of the nature of this filial relation did not trouble Paul himself because of the perfect clarity of his vision. But it was the source of trouble later on when philosophers and theologians attempted to rationalize the Christian mystery and to find a logical formula to reconcile the divine Son with the monotheistic Father.

John and the Logos Mystery

THE PROBLEM OF THE INCARNATION

So far we have considered only one of several problems resulting from the new claim that Jesus was divine—the problem of how to reconcile his Godhead with the monotheistic Yahweh. But, assuming this puzzle to be somehow solved, there is still a question about how and why divinity came to reside in a particular human being, the man Jesus, son of Joseph the carpenter of Nazareth. With this puzzle Paul, as usual, was blissfully unconcerned. It was enough for him that Christ the Savior, "though he possessed the nature of God, . . . laid it aside to take on the nature of a slave and become like other men."[n] Others, however, tried to go behind Paul's certainty about the *fact* of the incarnation, asking how and when it occurred. Some maintained that the divine spark entered the man Jesus at his birth; some pushed the moment further back and held that Jesus had no human father but was conceived of the Holy Ghost. In all these accounts, however, the crucial problem of the incarnation—the in-dwelling of divinity in human form—remained.

To this problem the unknown author of the Gospel according to John[8] turned his attention.

> In the beginning the Word[9] existed. The Word was with God, and the Word was divine.
> It was he that was with God in the beginning. Everything came into existence through him, and apart from him nothing came to be. It was by

---

8 For a discussion of the complex question of the authorship and date of this gospel, see A. Richard-son, *The Gospel According to St. John* (Collier, New York, 1962), pp. 15–28.

9 [The term translated as "Word" is the Greek *logos*—AUTHOR.]

him that life came into existence, and that life was the light of mankind. The light is still shining in the darkness, for the darkness has never put it out.

There appeared a man by the name of John,[10] with a message from God. He came to give testimony, to testify to the light, so that everyone might come to believe in it through him. He was not the light; he came to testify to the light.

The real light, which sheds light upon everyone, was just coming into the world. He came into the world, and though the world came into existence through him, the world did not recognize him. He came to his home, and his own family did not welcome him. But to all who did receive him and believe in him he gave the right to become children of God, owing their birth not to nature nor to any human or physical impulse, but to God.

So the Word became flesh and blood and lived for a while among us, abounding in blessing and truth, and we saw the honor God had given him, such honor as an only son receives from his father. . . .

No one has ever seen God; it is the divine Only Son, who leans upon his Father's breast, that has made him known.°

JOHN'S AND PAUL'S VIEWS COMPARED

John, as this author has been named by tradition, moved in a different world from that of Paul. "Word," or logos, is a technical term drawn from Greek philosophy, and the concept it signifies was foreign both to the mystery cults and to ancient Judaism. Yet in some respects, it is clear, the views of John and Paul were very similar. To begin with, though neither had had the advantage of knowing Jesus personally, each had had an intense mystical experience that he regarded as an adequate substitute for personal acquaintance and that strongly colored his conception of the Christian message. In the second place, they agreed in some important respects about the content of this message. Both were Jews, and based their religion on the old Judaic conception of Yahweh, yet both held that the salvation promised to man is open to all, Jew and Gentile alike, who have faith in Jesus as their savior.[11] They agreed, too, that this promised salvation is not continued existence in time; it is a rebirth in which the weight of sin, frustration, and defeat is lifted and the believer feels himself a new man:

> Anything you ask for as followers of mine [John has Jesus say] I will grant, so that the Father may be honored through the Son. I will grant anything you ask me for as my followers.
>
> If you really love me, you will observe my commands. And I will ask the Father and he will give you another Helper to be with you always. It is the Spirit of Truth. The world cannot obtain it, because it does not

10 [This is, of course, a reference to John the Baptist—AUTHOR.]

11 Compare, "For while the Law was given through Moses, blessing and truth came to us through Jesus Christ" (John 1:17).

see it or recognize it; you recognize it because it stays with you and is within you. . . .

Anyone who loves me will observe my teaching, and my Father will love him and we will come to him and live with him.[P]

John rose above the provincialism of the original Jesus movement because, like Paul, he interpreted the message and the personality of Jesus from the broader perspective of non-Jewish thought. But John's background was different from that of Paul: His mysticism was not the mysticism of the Eastern religious cults but that of Hellenistic Alexandria. John, that is to say, was more philosophically oriented than the apostle of the Gentiles and brought to the developing Jesus movement his understanding of current philosophical concepts. For him, Christ Jesus was not Paul's resurrected God; he was at once more exalted and more abstract—the logos of Hellenistic philosophy.

ORIGINS OF THE LOGOS DOCTRINE

The logos conception had faint beginnings in Heraclitus and a further development in Stoicism. Along with their universal materialism the Stoics had affirmed the existence of a creative and generative force, which they had called the logos and had conceived to be in some fashion divine. Two thousand years later, what the Stoics wrote about their logos sounds very vague. But it had a great appeal for late antiquity and in one way or another powerfully influenced much of the philosophical and religious thought of that time, including that of some Jewish sects.

Typical of this Hellenistic strain in Judaism is the theory of Philo, still another Jew of the Diaspora. Philo, who may be taken as a distinguished example of the cosmopolitan Jews of the Empire, was a member of the Jewish colony of Alexandria, one of the centers of logos-thinking.[12] Although a younger contemporary of Jesus, he appears never to have heard of him. Philo's aim, therefore, was not to bring the Jesus movement up to date but to harmonize Judaism with current intellectual trends. Yet, in making Yahweh philosophically respectable in Alexandria, he unknowingly provided the basis for a further development of Christianity.

In early times, when Yahweh was conceived of anthropomorphically, he seemed close to his people: He walked with Adam in the cool of the day and discoursed with his prophets in human fashion. Later on, however, anthropomorphism faded out and Yahweh became so majestic and cosmic a god that it was difficult to conceive of him in any intimate relation with man. Then the need was felt to bring him back, somehow, into relation with man, but without destroying his new transcendence. This was, of course, not a problem

---

12 Neoplatonism, which has already been discussed (pp. 6–18), was, of course, a later development in the same philosophical milieu.

peculiar to the Hebrew religion. As has already been noted, all over the Mediter-ranean world in the closing centuries of the classical period men sought to get closer to their gods.[13] Indeed, this desire was one of the signs that an era was ending; like the demand for a savior, it showed that the old classical culture, with its emphasis on self-respect, autonomy, and independence, was disappearing. Aristotle's completely transcendent god, perfect and removed—who contem-plates only his own nature and has no pity, love, or even hatred for the world—did not satisfy the new man who emerged in late classical times.

For many Jews the solution was to introduce intermediary beings between the transcendent Yahweh and his created world, and the later Hebrew scriptures are full of angelic agents of Yahweh's will. But the angelic hosts with which imaginative and poetic minds bridged the chasm between the divine and the human hardly satisfied Philo's more abstract intellect. He therefore adapted the currently popular notion of the logos to serve the same purpose.[14] To oversimplify a complex matter, it may be said that though Philo, as a Jew, naturally had to reject the Stoics' claim that the logos is material and divine, he clung to their notion of it as dynamic. He held it, in fact, to be the agency by which the creative Yahweh operates and by which this transcendent god reveals himself to the world.[15]

JOHN'S ACCOUNT OF THE LOGOS

So much for Philo and his version of the logos doctrine. It was easy for John to interpret the logos to the advantage of Christianity, thus making the new religion philosophically respectable among the learned of the day. For John, Jesus was simply the eternal and divine logos, which took on human shape—which acquired local habitation, as it were—at a particular point in space and time: in Palestine during the reigns of Augustus and Tiberius Caesar. *How* did this come about? This is a mystery about which, simply, we must have faith. *Why* did it come about? Here John had an answer, expressed in terms

13 See pp. 2–6.
14 The Neoplatonists' solution to this problem was similar: the affirmation of a whole series of emanations that serve as mediations between the purity and majesty of the One and the unreal sensible world. See p. 15.
15 For both these functions of Philo's logos there is support in the Jewish scriptures, providing one is prepared to interpret them loosely. In numerous passages the old Hebrew writers speak, for instance, of God's word (or, in Greek, *logos*): "By the word of the Lord were the heavens made . . ." (Ps. 33:6); "The Lord sent his word and healed them . . ." (Ps. 107:20); "I have slain them by the word of my mouth" (Hos. 6:5). Or again, in Gen. 1:3 it is written that Yahweh *said*, "Let there be . . ."—that is, he did not perform his creative act with his hands, like a potter works on clay, but with his *word* alone. Philo also found it possible to identify the frequent references to the wisdom of the Lord, for example, "The Lord by his wisdom hath founded the earth" (Prov. 3:19), or "Oh Lord how manifold are thy works, in wisdom thou hath made them" (Ps. 104:24), with his logos. That these writers meant by their statements nothing remotely like Philo's subtle doctrine was, from Philo's point of view, quite irrelevant: These old writers were wiser than they knew; the logos was speaking through them in ways they did not understand! By this method, of course, it is possible to make anything mean everything.

of his own acute need of salvation: God so loved the world that He sent His only begotten Son (the logos, that is; itself divine but dependent on God) into the world that through him the world might be saved.

Here John gave his own twist to the logos doctrine. What had interested Philo about the logos was its metaphysical and epistemological functions. It not only creates the world; it also illumines our minds so that we can understand the world.[16] For John, however, the redemptive activity of the logos was primary. The sense of personal inadequacy and the corresponding need of external support that John shared with so many men of his time explains this shift of emphasis. Though the Stoics had emphasized divine providence, they had thought of it in a highly abstract way: For them it was a principle, not a person. But as a Jew, John had behind him the Judaic Yahweh, a personal god and a father. His sense of the fatherhood of God and the sonship of the logos dominates the whole of the Fourth Gospel. What is more, this interpretation enabled him to see the motive for the incarnation as paternal love: "God so loved the world . . ." is one of the most treasured, because it is one of the most reassuring, lines of the New Testament. The logos became flesh not to judge us but to redeem us, not to punish us but to save us.

In emphasizing the loving-kindness and tender mercy of God the Father, John actually added nothing new to the old Hebraic conception of the deity.[17] What is unique about John's position is that Yahweh's sternness and wrath, which were also prominent features of the Jewish view, are altogether missing from the picture. In the first place, this was doubtless simply the individual interpretation of one who needed a God of mercy and forgiveness. But because of the canonical authority of John's name[18]—and because, too, his God of love found an echo in many another heart—this personal interpretation, along with the logos doctrine with which it was fused in John's mind, passed into the future Church.

The Effects of Institutionalism

Thus far in the study of the formative influences at work in the development of Christianity the impact of two inspired and highly original personalities whose chief influence was in the sphere of doctrine has been considered. Now a different kind of influence must be considered—the influence that institutional growth had on Christian doctrine and practice.

16 Compare the Neoplatonists' interpretation of Plato's Form of the Good, pp. 8–9.
17 See pp. 27–28.
18 For the early Christians, of course, the author of the Fourth Gospel was the apostle John, "the beloved disciple."

The effects of institutionalism are not, of course, confined to Christianity; they occur whenever an informal movement loses its first spontaneity and settles down to an organizational existence. But, as will be seen,[19] the concept of orthodoxy aggravated all the normal institutional pressures in the case of Christianity and made them even more important factors in its development than they are in that of most organizations.

A movement often starts with a few dedicated individuals whose enthusiasm and fervor attract others to their cause—whether this be political, economic, social, or religious. But the success of the movement in attracting members causes it to undergo a transformation. For instance, the "message" of the founders, which gives the movement its initial impetus, is often misunderstood and always altered by their successors. Yet this process of vulgarization and simplification at the hands of lesser men makes institutional existence and acceptance by the many possible.

WHAT THE MESSAGE GAINED AND LOST

Thus it was inevitable that the esoteric messages taught by Paul and John, and even the simpler but equally spiritual message of Jesus, would undergo modification as the Jesus movement became institutionalized. Only a mystic could comprehend the notion of salvation as identity with the resurrected God or with the divine logos. Men who were not mystics had to find ways of explaining the miracle of redemption—and ways, too, of securing it for themselves. Men who did not themselves experience Paul's sense of release from bondage to the Law had to find rules to live by. Men who did not share John's sense of the Father's overflowing love had to find sterner sanctions for the life of Christian piety they believed God wished them to lead.

Paul's conception of salvation as an *inner* change effected in this life through identification with Christ Jesus became the notion of something that is going to happen in the distant future. And his otherworldliness, which was essentially spiritual (the believer continues to live in this world, though he is no longer of it), degenerated into the belief that the Christian ought to separate himself from this world physically. The net result of all this—of the pressures of institutionalization—was that there gradually developed, beside mysticism and the logos doctrine, which the Church did not and could not repudiate, quite a different set of beliefs. They included an appeal to the magic of the sacraments (from which, as we have seen, Paul himself was not wholly free), a new and rigorously ascetic law (an attempt to put Jesus' radical interim ethics literally into practice), and a worship based on fear of God and of hell fire instead of on love and identification with the divine.

Movements tend to be radical and extreme. As they are institutionalized, they become conservative and resist the very excitement and ferment that gave

19 See pp. 60–69.

them birth.[20] This is almost inevitable. An institution constitutes a lot of men; rules are needed to reduce the number of separate decisions that are made and so to minimize the chances of contradictory policies' being initiated in different parts of the organization. But rules are perforce designed for the general case, and since all actual cases are particular, the rule never exactly fits. Hence an institution is generally insensitive to nuances, slow to move, loath to adjust itself to changing circumstances.

There is, therefore, always a tension between an institution and that rare creature, a genuine individual. That is, there will always be conflict between a mature institution and the kind of man who founds the movements out of which institutions develop. He has ideas, but the institution fears ideas; he proposes novelties, but the institution dreads change. Most of us probably sympathize with the institutions. As T. S. Eliot observed, we fear a real individual because he exposes our little life of dried tubers to the pains and hazards of spring and birth.

THE CHURCH AND ITS MYSTICS

It is not surprising, therefore, that the Christian Church and the Christian mystics have had some trouble achieving Christian unity. To the mystic the Church is unnecessary and dangerous—unnecessary because he has already experienced salvation in his vision, dangerous because the Church's hierarchical forms, its discipline and its bureaucracy, kill the spirit and elevate the letter and stultify the inner meaning of his religion.

To the Church as an institution, the mystic is a maverick. He is a nonconformist and a troublemaker; he upsets efficiently functioning procedures; he rejects the authority of the institution whenever it conflicts with his private vision. The weight of numbers and of persons, traditions, convenience, decency, and respectability count for him as nothing in comparison with his inner conviction. Indeed, too large a dose of mysticism can destroy even the most efficient of institutions.

Under the circumstances, what is surprising is the Church's remarkable capacity for keeping the Christian mystics within its fold, and not only keeping them there but using them to revitalize itself.[21] It is to them that the Church owes its astonishing resiliency and longevity. When its twenty centuries are

---

20 Compare the attitudes of the Republican Party at its inception with its attitudes one hundred years later, or look at the unrevolutionary Daughters of the American Revolution.

21 The Church's one outstanding mistake was made with regard to Martin Luther. The Church forced him to effect his reforms outside, which resulted in the establishment of rival institutions. Instead, it should have clasped him to its bosom and allowed him to reform it, as it had done with Francis of Assisi and other earlier reformers. In general, with such individualists the Church has a simple alternative: It can either canonize them or expel them as heretics. It cannot ignore them.

compared with the much shorter life span of even such a tough institutional specimen as the Roman imperium, it is not surprising that its adherents claim for it a divine establishment.

THE INSTITUTIONALIZATION OF THE JESUS MOVEMENT

So much, then, for institutions in general. Now it is necessary, first, to trace some of the major steps by which the Jesus movement, as interpreted by Paul and John and the other early leaders, became institutionalized and, second, to note some of the effects that this process had on doctrine.

One of the first problems that confronted the young Church was what to do about those who "spoke with tongues." Though some New Testament passages suggest that speaking with tongues was a sudden fluency in foreign languages, it is more reasonable to regard it as the utterance, often gibberish, of men in ecstatic trances. Since it was held that in these moments something of ineffable importance was communicated, speaking with tongues soon came to be a prized capacity, a sign of divine sanction, and a proof positive of the Messiahship of Jesus. Thus the original disciples spoke with tongues, and so, apparently, did Paul. But Paul, at least, was aware that there was a latent danger in this practice.

> Anyone who speaks ecstatically is speaking not to men but to God, for no one can understand him, though by the Spirit he is uttering secret truths. . . . I want you all to speak ecstatically, but I especially want you to be inspired to preach. The man who is inspired to preach is more useful than the one who speaks ecstatically—unless he can explain what he says so that it may do the church some good. . . .
>
> Thank God, I speak in ecstasy more than any of you. But in public worship I would rather say five words with my understanding so as to instruct others also than ten thousand words in an ecstasy. . . .
>
> If the whole church assembles and they all speak ecstatically, and ordinary people or unbelievers come in, will they not say that you are mad? . . .
>
> If there is any ecstatic speaking, let it be limited to two or three people at the most, and have one speak at a time and someone explain what he says. But if there is no one to explain it, have him keep quiet in church, and talk to himself and to God. And let two or three who are inspired to preach speak, while the rest weigh what is said; and if anything is revealed to another who is seated, the one who is speaking must stop. For in this way you can all preach one after another, as you are inspired to, so that everyone may be instructed and stimulated. . . .
>
> Let everything be done in a proper and orderly way.[q]

That last phrase—"in a proper and orderly way"—shows that the process of institutionalization was already beginning. The earliest Christian communities, as Paul's letter plainly shows, were free societies of equals who met together to exchange the good tidings.[22] These little groups were held together by spirit and fellowship. The apostles, who had known Jesus personally, had great authority. If a major controversy arose, they simply got together and argued things out, like Jewish rabbis, on the basis of the Law and the prophets—to which, of course, they added their memory of the sayings of Jesus.

But as time passed and the movement spread over the Mediterranean world, a great variety of doctrines flourished; many different kinds of people called themselves Christians and hoped for salvation through Jesus. Some developed dualisms far more explicit than that of Paul and, repudiating the Jewish heritage of an omnipotent Yahweh who created the world out of nothing, held that matter is real, self-subsistent, and evil. Others, following Paul (or so they thought), repudiated the Law altogether and with it threw out the whole of the Old Testament. Also, of course, through the years those who had had direct contact with Jesus gradually disappeared, until eventually no one was left who could speak with clear-cut authority. It was all very well to say that the final authority was the body of writings the disciples had left behind them. But who was to determine the meaning of these writings? Interpretation was clearly required since each of the divisive groups claimed that it had apostolic sanction for its views.

THE IDEAL OF ORTHODOXY

Now it is precisely this emphasis on the "sanction of the apostolic writings" that distinguishes the Christian Church's struggle to achieve institutional status from that of other organizations. So far, the problems discussed have been those any movement might face. Every institution—even a private club—has to enforce some modicum of conformity in conduct and secure some basis, however tenuous, of "ideological" agreement. For these purposes, in every institution there must be some generally recognized authority provided with an adequate technique for controlling or expelling dissidents. But institutional status is obviously compatible with considerable diversity of opinion and practice.

The special feature of Christian institutionalism can best be seen if the young Church is compared with the mystery cults. Though each of the cults claimed to provide the exclusive key to salvation, they were tolerant of one another in the way that Rotarians and Kiwanians, while holding firm to the superiority of their own organizations, nevertheless acknowledge the right of that of their rivals to exist and prosper if it can. But because Yahweh refused to allow the Jews any other gods before him, the Christians could not tolerate any rival to

---

22 Perhaps the nearest modern equivalent to these communities is the Society of Friends, whose individual "meetings" lack regularly appointed priests and whose members speak in public as the spirit moves them.

God the Father and His only begotten Son. And the same attitude of intolerance applied to differences of opinion within the movement itself. Whereas the mystery religions permitted wide differences of ritual and belief within their own worship, the Christians insisted on orthodoxy. They might differ passionately about *what* was orthodox, but from a very early stage in the development of the Church they all agreed on the principle of orthodoxy itself—that there is a particular set of beliefs that is absolutely *right* and that anything deviating from these beliefs by even a hair's breadth is absolutely wrong. Persons who accept the "right" beliefs are saved; persons who mistakenly accept the "wrong" beliefs are damned. But, once again, which *were* the right beliefs and which the wrong?

No wonder there was pressure to find a single, unambiguous, final source to which all essential beliefs could be traced. A formal solution, which is still basically the Church's doctrine, was worked out by Irenaeus, a Christian bishop who lived in the latter part of the second century. According to him, the truths necessary for salvation were conveyed by Christ to his twelve apostles. These truths every Christian must accept; persons who refuse to accept them are heretics, damned and outside the fold. As regards Church organization, Irenaeus held that bishops were originally appointed by the apostles, who transferred to the bishops their own authority. Since, by a laying on of hands, this authority was subsequently passed on to *new* bishops, every priest and every communicant should faithfully obey his bishop in all things. Bishops, then, are literally the heirs and representatives on earth of Christ. Conflicts between bishops, Irenaeus held, should be resolved by the vote of the collective episcopate, which is infallible.

In theory, and providing that one accepts Irenaeus' presuppositions, this is a logically watertight arrangement. In actual practice, however, since early councils were not well attended, those who found themselves in a minority could argue that the councils were not truly ecumenical. Moreover, when one is convinced that one's very salvation depends on the exact nuance with which belief is formulated, the ordinary drive, so often present in institutions, to make compromises in the interests of organizational harmony is no longer operative.

There was ample reason, certainly, for real differences of opinion. When we think of all the various and often radically different views that were regarded as equally apostolic—the Law and the prophets, Jesus the Messiah and his interim ethics, the mystery religion of Paul, the logos doctrine of John, and many others not even mentioned here—and that had therefore somehow or other to be reconciled with one another, fused into one body of doctrine, and reduced to a few simple canonical beliefs; when we consider the vast task of synthesis and interpretation that this early group of theologians had thus innocently set for themselves, we cannot be surprised that their early councils failed to settle exactly which beliefs were orthodox and which heretical.

Heresy and Orthodoxy

GRADUAL EMERGENCE OF ORTHODOXY

Some of the major formative influences, including the idea of orthodoxy, have now been surveyed. These influences worked to fashion the Jesus movement into a world religion: holy, apostolic, and catholic. But the idea of orthodoxy was present in Christians' minds as a motive and was operative in the repression of heresy long before it was filled out with a specific dogmatic content. It is a mistake to look at the formative centuries from the point of view of the centuries of maturity—to look at the third and fourth centuries as if they were the twelfth and thirteenth—and to assume that orthodoxy in those early times already existed as a firm basis from which a full-scale attack against heresy on all fronts was developed. It was in the course of piecemeal attacks on individual positions that the precise content of orthodoxy emerged, and what was eventually settled on as the orthodox view was much more the result of the dialectical skill and the forensic abilities of individual fathers than it was the result of the merits of the doctrines they advocated.

Nevertheless, in this somewhat hit-or-miss fashion the general lines of orthodoxy gradually came to be pretty firmly established, and by the beginning of the fourth century, though no overall, general Christian synthesis had yet been worked out, the lines within which such a synthesis would have to be produced had been laid down. Before a study of Augustine's attempt to effect such a synthesis is undertaken and an effort is made to give a rational account of Christian beliefs and attitudes, the process by which, in the course of attacks on individual heresies, the general outlines of orthodoxy were established should be shown.

For this purpose a brief account of four major heresies—the Gnostic, the Arian, the Pelagian, and the Manichean—will be given. These are major heresies not only in the sense that the struggle with them shook the young Church to its very foundation but also in the more important sense that each of the positions eventually declared heretical by the Church represents a basic and recurring attitude of mind.

These attitudes correspond to traditions lying outside Christian heritage, and their frequent revival throughout our history shows the failure of the Christian view of life, armed with the ideal of orthodoxy, either to assimilate or to extirpate all non-Christian elements in Western culture. They could not be extirpated because they are very deep-seated elements in our cultural heritage; they could not be assimilated because they contradict one or the other of the divers doctrines that came to be grouped together as Christian orthodoxy. Let us postpone for the present any consideration of Christianity's answer to the challenge presented by the four major heresies and consider the heretical views themselves.

THE GNOSTIC HERESY

It is easy to give a formal definition of Gnosticism: It is the view that knowledge (*gnosis*), rather than faith (*pistis*), is the means to salvation. But it is impossible to give any detailed account of Gnosticism. In the first place, there were many different sects; in the second place, though a number of Gnostic documents have come to light recently, the surviving traces of Gnostic teaching are fragmentary. But the chief difficulty is simply that Gnosticism was a melange, a farrago, of superstitious mumbo jumbo. However, from the fact that this mumbo jumbo was once taken seriously one can infer something important about the period: that it was a time when intellectual standards were relaxed, when the criteria by which men tested an assertion were emotion, feeling, and fancy, not logical consistency or empirical evidence.

The Gnostics held that there is a supreme being (called by various names—for instance, the One Father, the Power above all, Absolute Sovereignty) and that there are other lesser powers, angels and archangels, generated by this supreme being. The world and everything in it was made by seven of these angels, among whom at least some of the Gnostics included Yahweh, the god of the Jews. Man, too, was created by these angels, not by the supreme god. The angels are in rebellion against their creator and hold man prisoner. To save man, Christ (in some versions, Holy Spirit) descended. Not all men are saved—only those who have a divine spark that enables them to understand the knowledge given them.

But this bald summary hardly does justice to the rich imaginative detail of Gnostic teaching. According to a contemporary account by Irenaeus,[23] Simon the Samaritan, one of the Gnostics, actually claimed to be the Absolute Sovereignty and was worshiped by many as such. Simon taught

> . . . that he was the Absolute Sovereignty, i.e., the Father above all, and was willing to be called whatever men call him. . . . He led about with him a certain Helen, after he had redeemed her from a life of prostitution in Tyre, a city of Phenicia. He said she was the first conception of his mind, the Mother of all, through whom in the beginning he had the idea of making angels and archangels. This Thought, leaping forth from him and knowing what her father willed, descended to the lower regions and generated angels and powers by whom this world was made. But after she generated them, she was held captive by them because of envy, for they did not want to be considered the offspring of anyone else. For Simon was entirely unknown to them; his Thought was held captive by the powers and angels emitted by her. She suffered all kinds of humiliation from them, so that she did not run back upwards to her Father but was even enclosed in a human body, and through the ages transmigrated as from one vessel to another, into other female bodies.

---

23 Irenaeus, being a Christian bishop, was naturally hostile to Simon, from whom he thought "all heresies originated."

She was in that Helen because of whom the Trojan War was undertaken. . . .

Transmigrating from body to body, and always enduring humiliation from the body, she finally became a prostitute; she was the "lost sheep" [Luke 15 : 6]. For this reason he came, in order to rescue her first and free her from her bonds, then to offer men salvation through his "knowledge."

For when the angels misgoverned the world, since each of them desired the primacy, he came for the reformation of affairs; he descended, transformed and made like the powers and authorities and angels, so that among men he appeared as a man, though he was not a man, and he seemed to suffer in Judaea, though he did not suffer.

The prophets spoke their prophecies under the inspiration of the angels who made the world. Therefore those who have set their hope on Simon and Helen pay no further attention to them and do what they wish as free agents. For "by his grace men are saved, not by just works" [Eph. 2 : 8]. For actions are just not by nature but by convention, in accordance with the decrees of the angels who made the world and intended to lead men into slavery through precepts of this kind. Therefore he announced that the world would be destroyed and that those who were his would be freed from the rule of those who made the world.[r]

The fact that teachings like these had a widespread popularity in the second and third centuries and that they posed a formidable threat to Catholic orthodoxy provides valuable clues for understanding the drives that were animating the culture. For instance, Gnosticism's central idea is that of a special knowledge, a revelation, a message, conveyed to suffering mankind from on high. As has been mentioned, "gnosis" itself is a good Greek term meaning "knowledge." Plato, for example, had used it when he discussed knowledge of the forms. For him it denoted a public and objective knowledge, certifiable by rational means and available to anyone possessing native intelligence and sufficient education. In contrast, the "gnosis" of the Gnostics was a special, transrational knowledge, limited to a select few and largely incommunicable once acquired. Thus the Gnostics did to "gnosis" something similar to what the Neoplatonists did to "dialectic."[24]

The orthodox Christians did not reject this idea of a message from on high. Indeed, it was in many respects congenial to them, for they too claimed to be recipients of inside information about the mystery of the cosmos. What they objected to was the content of the Gnostic message, for they insisted on the uniqueness of the Christian message. The Gnostic message, far from being exclusive, was inclusive. Confronted with the bewildering variety of mystery religions and savior gods that the culture had spawned, the Gnostics aimed at synthesizing and combining them, bringing the Jewish Yahweh, the Christian Jesus, and many other deities into their fold by multiplying gods, angels, and

24 See pp. 10–11.

archangels. To effect this fusion the Gnostics had to read all their texts symbolically; this, too, was offensive to the orthodox Christians, who held that the story of Jesus was literally, not merely allegorically, true.

As many commentators have remarked, syncretism was one of the leading characteristics of Gnosticism. The age was seeking unity, and unity could be achieved either by exclusion or by inclusion—either by rejecting and destroying all messages save one or by synthesizing all the various messages into one. The Gnostics inclined toward the latter procedure, but the former—the way of the orthodox Christians—proved to be the wave of the future.

THE ARIAN HERESY

The second major heresy, the Arian, reflects the paradox inherent in the notion of a god who is both three and one. As we have seen, the monotheistic founders of Christianity had sought to resolve the puzzle about the divinity of Jesus by speaking vaguely of Father and Son. Moreover, a third element, the Holy Spirit, had been introduced, so that—like many other ancient religions—Christianity affirmed a trinitarian godhead. This was no problem, of course, for the other Eastern mystery cults, which rested easily in their polytheism; but it was an *embarras de richesse* for monotheistic Christianity. How could three gods be one? Various solutions were offered. According to some, Jesus was not God at all but mere man.[25] According to others, Jesus was indeed God, but not a separate divinity.[26] Hence, these thinkers concluded, it was God the Father who was crucified at Calvary. Still others, utilizing the logos doctrine, allowed that Jesus was both divine and separate from the Father but asserted that he was subordinate to, and created by, the Father.[27] All these views, and many others, were at one time or another defended by scriptural exegesis. Although a case could be made for each of them on the basis of apostolic authority, each view contradicted at least one other cardinal teaching of the Church.

Gradually the debate grew more acrimonious, and finally, shortly after the beginning of the fourth century, the whole matter came to a head. In accordance with the practice based on Irenaeus' theory, a Church council was called. It met in 325 at Nicaea, in Bithynia, which was chosen because of its mild climate. In spite of this inducement, only a few Western bishops attended. The council's final position, promulgated in a Nicene creed,[28] was reached only after prolonged and heated debate, and the minority refused to accept its defeat. The adherents of the rival views soon took to arms, and the imperial government lent its support first to this side, then to that, as a succession of emperors with varying theological

---

25 "Adoptionism," "Dynamic monarchianism."
26 "Patripassianism."
27 "Subordinationism."
28 The present Nicene creed is a somewhat later revision of this document.

convictions came to the throne. This struggle, in which thousands of persons lost their lives, continued throughout the century; even in Augustine's day it was still necessary to defend the orthodox position. Despite this indecisive history, the Council of Nicaea has been regarded as ecumenical and its findings have been, in their essential orientation, accepted as correct doctrine.

What was the view that aroused such passions? Since its principal advocate was Arius, a presbyter of the church in Alexandria, the heresy has been called by his name. Arius seems not to have balked at the logos doctrine itself; he held Christ to be, as the orthodox claimed, the logos of God—but he denied that Christ shares God's nature. Christ, he held, is not, like the Father, eternal and perfect. On the contrary, like everything else, he was created by the Father out of nothing, and he subsequently became incarnate in the body of Jesus of Nazareth.

In a word, Arius took monotheism seriously, as a good Christian must. Thus he held that Christ could not be God; he must have his own nature and an essence different from God's. Indeed, Arius seems to have been a rationalist, or at least a logician: His aim was apparently to make the Christian position consistent. But this brought him into conflict with the feeling of mysticism that, stemming from Paul, insisted that the human Jesus was in very truth a resurrected God and that redemption is an act of real union between man and the divine.

The orthodox position was quite simple. If one had to choose between logical consistency and the salvation through faith in Jesus that Paul and John had taught, it was far better to be saved than to be logical. Athanasius, the leader of the anti-Arian group, held that God is one, that Christ the Son is divine, and that God the Father and God the Son are distinct. Elaborate formulas were drawn up to express this complex relationship: God the Father and God the Son are of identical substance (this to protect and reaffirm the divinity of Christ), but they are two "persons" (this to avoid the position of the Patripassians, who held that God the Father suffered on the cross). How then do we salvage monotheism? The orthodox answer was that this is a mystery we are obliged to accept for the sake of our faith and our salvation.

Though Arius has been called a rationalist, one should guard against exaggerating his rationalism: He was certainly no eighteenth-century *philosophe.* For instance, though he boggled at a one god who is also three, he allowed that much about the relation among Father, Son, and Holy Spirit is "beyond the understanding of man."[29] Nevertheless, as compared with Tertullian, Arius and his difficulties with the Trinity will evoke a certain sympathy from most modern readers. Tertullian,[30] for his part, wanted to rule out as impious any attempt whatever to understand Christian doctrine. The very desire to understand implies

29 This statement was made in 357 in a decree of the Council of Sirmium, which, unlike the Council of Nicaea, was controlled by the Arians.
30 Tertullian, who lived in the second half of the second century, had a distinguished career as a jurist before he was converted to Christianity.

a lack of faith, he thought; a man who becomes a Christian as a result of having concluded, after an examination of evidence, that Christianity is true is far less meritorious than a man who becomes a Christian in spite of the evidence that seems to him *against* the truth of Christianity. Thus Tertullian wrote that Christian claims about the resurrection are to be believed precisely because they are "senseless." "The fact is certain, because it is impossible."[8]

As compared with Tertullian, then, Arius was a descendant—if only a remote one—of the classical rationalists. In the last analysis, the issue underlying the Arian controversy was anything but a narrow or technical theological question. For the dispute between Arius and his opponents turned on the question of whether the universe is a rational cosmos, complete in itself (as the Greeks had on the whole maintained), or whether ultimate reality lies outside the universe in the realms of a creator god, ineffable, exalted, and infinite, essentially different from his creation and incapable therefore of being understood by it. If the former—if the real is rational and the rational real—man as a rational animal is the master of his own destiny. If the latter, man's only hope is in the generosity of higher powers; his best attitude is one of humility and pious respect; and the key to his whole future is unquestioning faith in the extrarational, supernatural revelations of the ultimately incomprehensible divine. Since this is an absolutely fundamental parting of the ways, it is not surprising that it aroused passions or that it could not be settled by rational discussion but only by the sword.

Thus the Arian controversy points up important differences in method and approach, as well as in basic outlook, between the Greek and Christian mentalities. And it is these differences, not the details of disputes over the divinity of Jesus, that give this heresy lasting historical significance. The solution that won out—that became orthodox—was a sign that, for better or for worse, the Church had assigned reason a subordinate place in its scheme of things. It could therefore escape controversy only so long as men continued to be willing to accept this depreciation of their natural powers.

THE PELAGIAN HERESY

If the Arian controversy resulted from the Judaic inheritance of monotheism, the Pelagian controversy, the third major heresy, resulted from the Judaic inheritance of divine omnipotence and omniscience. This heresy derived its name from Pelagius, a monk of British birth who lived in Rome in the early years of the fifth century. Like Arius, Pelagius believed himself to be teaching true Christian doctrine—in other words, orthodoxy; like Arius, again, he could make a good case for his claim. He was doubtless more interested in morality than in theology, but, after all, in this he had the example of Jesus himself. At any rate, instead of beginning with the properties of God, Pelagius began with man's moral needs. In particular, he insisted on man's freedom of choice, for it seemed to him that the doctrine of inevitable human incompetence, which had its source in Paul's mystical experience of redemption through Christ,[31] led men to be slothful in Christian living and made it much too easy for them to excuse giving way to those very lusts of the flesh that Paul himself had condemned. Pelagius' practical attitude is expressed very clearly in a letter he wrote to a friend:

> Whenever I have to speak concerning moral instruction and holy living I am accustomed to point out first the force and quality of human nature and what it is able to accomplish and then to incite the mind of the hearer to many kinds of virtue, since it is not without profit to be summoned to those things which perhaps he has assumed are impossible to him. For we are by no means able to tread the way of virtue unless we have hope as a companion.[t]

To modern ears this may sound innocent enough, but to theologians who took seriously the part of Paul's teaching that emphasized man's helplessness (which Paul, as a mystic and a missionary, had not troubled to reconcile with his practical interests), this had serious implications. To begin with, it was agreed on all sides, certainly by Paul and doubtless also by Pelagius, that God is an absolutely infinite being. This means that God is omniscient—He knows everything. It follows that God has known, and known from eternity, that you would be reading this sentence at just this moment. Now you may feel that you could have put this book aside at the end of the last paragraph. That is, you may believe that a minute ago you could have chosen to stop reading—that this choice was "within your power." But obviously, if God has known (not just guessed or surmised, but *known*) that you would be reading now, you could not have chosen, a minute ago, to stop reading. Your feeling that you had an option is an illusion. You could not be not reading now, for this would contradict God's omniscience. Thus divine omniscience seems to rule out human free will.

In the second place, it was an article of faith that God is, ultimately, the cause of everything that happens. God not only knows what is going to happen; He is also the agent who brings it about. But a given act cannot have two different causes: If God is the cause, I am not. If, therefore, God does everything, man does nothing, and his sense of having at least some control over his environment and his destiny is an illusion.

Though it thus seemed fairly clear that orthodoxy required the rejection of human freedom, this involved grave difficulties. In the first place, since belief in freedom is one of the deepest and least eradicable of human convictions, it is hard to persuade men that they are suffering from a gigantic illusion. Moreover, since responsibility and free will seem to be connected, rejection of the latter seems to take the former with it. If a man has no control over what he does, how can he be held responsible for his acts? How, for instance, can he be blamed when he finds himself spending the day at the beach instead of

31 See p. 39.

reading about the Pelagian heresy? Since it appears that God is the only agent in the world, is He not responsible for our sins? This means, first, that God must be the producer of all evil and wickedness (which we mistakenly attribute to ourselves), thus raising the problem of explaining why an all-good and all-powerful God would run the universe so incompetently. It also means that God is manifestly unjust since, according to a cardinal Christian thesis, He both blames us and punishes us for those sinful acts of which, as it now turns out, He is the sole author.

These are certainly serious problems,[32] but the fundamental issue in the Pelagian heresy goes even deeper. The orthodox determination to exalt God led inevitably to the conclusion that man is worthless, for to allow *any* value or significance to humanity was to derogate by just that amount from the majesty, perfection, and supreme value of God. For the orthodox Christian, because all men are wicked and corrupt, they are all doomed to eternal torture; because they are fundamentally helpless, there is no exit from their predicament without God's merciful assistance. This drastic judgment on man's worth and capacity seemed to the early Christians the only means by which they could exalt God as they chose to. Their views were, as we have seen, part of a much broader climate of opinion that everywhere tended to reduce man's stature and to increase his sense of dependence and finitude. The Christians simply carried this tendency to an extreme. It is not surprising, therefore, that in the history of the West the Pelagian heresy—which has appeared in many guises but may be stated in generalized form as the belief that, however small, man is after all *something!*—has recurred again and again. Here, then, is another example of the Church's incapacity either to destroy or to assimilate a part of Western man's Greek heritage.

THE MANICHEAN HERESY

The fourth major heresy, the Manichean, resulted from a dilemma that was brought into prominence by orthodoxy's answer to Pelagius. In silencing Pelagianism, orthodoxy committed itself to the seemingly intolerable assertion that God is responsible for human wrongdoing. Indeed, if God does everything, He is responsible not only for our acts but for everything that happens in the world, including the plagues, famines, and wars from which we suffer. How are we to reconcile this conclusion with God's supposed goodness? If God were not omniscient, He might not know about all this evil; if He were not omnipotent, He might not be able to do anything about it; if He were not supremely good, He might not care about it. But as long as we insist that God is omniscient *and* omnipotent *and* all-good, are we not faced with an insoluble problem?

The Manichees, a sect named after Mani, its founder, tried to resolve this

---

32 The problem of free will still exists today, though a theoretically omniscient scientist has replaced an actually omniscient deity.

dilemma. Like the Arians and the Pelagians, they regarded themselves as good Christians; in fact, they held their position to be orthodox and that of their opponents to be heretical. But, according to orthodoxy, the Manichees made the mistake of trusting reason rather than authority,[33] and their reason told them that the problem of evil could not be solved without abandoning the notion of the infinity of God. Hence, authority to the contrary, they adopted a kind of metaphysical dualism and argued that, though God is indeed good, He is finite and limited by the evil power of Satan. It was Satan (such was the gloomy judgment the Manichees passed on this life) who created the material world and who captured our free spirits and imprisoned them in our bodies, there to suffer for sins committed in a previous existence. Christ, along with their founder Mani, they conceived to be a prophet sent by God to bring the good tidings of such salvation as men could hope for. This, since matter and the body are intrinsically and irremediably evil, could only be attained through the severest ascetic discipline. Manicheism was thus an amalgam of the beliefs of the mystery cults, transmigration theories like those of the Pythagoreans, and, even more obviously, Mithraism.[34]

This is, logically speaking, a reasonable account of the existence of evil. There is even, as the Manichees could point out, some support for their dualism in Christian teaching—in the writings of Paul, for instance, and in the teachings of all those who, with an ascetic bent, saw the flesh as evil and sought to mortify it. But orthodox Christianity had firmly turned its back on these dualistic elements in the apostolic and authoritative writings in the interests of the monotheistic and infinite God it had inherited from Judaism. Hence the orthodox Christians reacted violently against this new formulation of ancient wickedness.[35]

Though it appears that Manicheism won considerable popular support in the second half of the fourth century, its suppression about a century later cost fewer lives than the life-and-death struggle of orthodoxy and Arianism. This was not so much because people did not feel strongly about the problem of evil as it was because the secular arm, in the case of Manicheism, supported orthodoxy, or at least did not give aid and comfort to its opponents.

The fact is that Manicheism is a tough and recurring view that, refusing to stay defeated, has cropped up again and again in the history of the West.

---

33 According to Augustine, a critic who was the more severe because as a young man he had been seduced into the Manichee fold by the plausibility of their arguments, the Manichees claimed that "the terrors of authority being removed they would lead to God by pure and simple reason . . ."—*De Utilitate Credendi*, 2, quoted in McGiffert, *A History of Christian Thought*, Vol. II, p. 75.

34 It has been held with some reason that Manicheism was an attempt to effect a reconciliation between Christianity and Mithraism.

35 One of the orthodox complaints against Manicheism was precisely the one that the Pelagians brought against orthodoxy, namely, that the view stultified man's drive toward morality by allowing him to excuse and explain away his sinful acts. Augustine, for instance, pointed out that the Manichees held that it is not we ourselves who sin but some other, unknown nature in us.

During the later Middle Ages, for instance, it reappeared in so popular and plausible a form that it was deemed necessary to put it down in a particularly severe and bloody fashion. An account of the suppression of the Albigensian heresy, as Manicheism was called during this particular recrudescence, makes painful reading for those who value tolerance more than they value orthodoxy.

RELATION OF FAITH TO REASON

However effectively the Church might silence heretics, it still had to face the problems about the existence of evil and the fact of human responsibility that the heretics had tried to solve. It was one thing to condemn the wrong answers of heretics and another to find the right answers for oneself. Athanasius, a saint and bishop of Alexandria who lived during the fourth century, took the short way out of this difficulty: The unity of the Trinity is a mystery; it cannot be understood but must be accepted on authority and as an act of faith, on danger of suffering eternal torment in hell, the fate of sceptics and mistaken theorists alike. But it was difficult to suppress altogether the drive to find rational solutions, for the West never altogether lost its taste—a part of its classical heritage—for reasoning. And the Christians themselves wanted, as far as might be, to give a rational account of their views—not only for their own edification but to persuade the pagans (who were often philosophically inclined) and to confound the heretics. Finally, though the Church was prepared, at critical points, to take its stand on faith in a mystery, it was loath to adopt this last-ditch strategy. And rightly so: Since a mystery is an essentially private and incommunicable experience, a too facile multiplication of mysteries was incompatible with the growth of the Church as an institution. Orthodoxy and authority are clearly impossible without theology. For all these reasons, it was highly desirable that a systematic philosophy of Christianity be worked out.

We can see, then, that an adequate Christian philosophy must somehow include a compromise between a faith that claims to transcend explanation and a reason that takes for its goal a rational explanation of all experience. The earliest Christian thinkers were, however, far from being clearly aware of this need. They were for the most part content simply to prove what could be proved and to retire rapidly to authoritarian faith at the first suspicion of heresy. It was only slowly that men began to realize that the construction of a specifically Christian philosophical system required them to study explicitly the relative roles of faith and reason.

GREEK AND CHRISTIAN VIEWS CONTRASTED

Even apart from this complication, it is clear that a Christian philosophy must differ radically from any of the classical philosophies we have considered. This is obvious from the basically different orientation of Christian thought. In Christian thought, God is the primary—indeed, almost the exclusive—object of concern. Whereas the Greeks conceived it their chief task to give an account of man's relation to nature, the Christians considered that what alone matters is man's relation to a transcendent, infinite, absolutely perfect being. This changed the whole preoccupation of philosophy. For the Greeks, natural science and the social sciences were significant both in their own right and as instruments of the good life; for the Christians, they were irrelevant and even dangerous. For the Greeks, morality was essentially a social ethics and its aim was happiness. For the Christians, morality was a department of religious practice. Conduct was judged not by the end it achieves but by the degree of its conformity to God's commands, and since the perfection of the Deity gave the Christian an absolutely exalted ideal to aim at, the Christian always felt a sense of failure: No matter how good he was, he was not as good as he ought to be.

In contrast with this pessimism, Greek ethics was predominantly optimistic: Men, some men at least, could look forward to being as good (that is, as happy) as anyone can conceive of being. Whereas the Greeks identified falling away from the ideal with ignorance, the Christians conceived of it as sin, a willful rejection of the commands and wishes of a loving and all-powerful father. Whereas the Greeks held that the problem of conduct is essentially a problem of knowledge, the Christians (because they set themselves a supernatural goal) held that the problem of conduct is insoluble by human means and that man requires outside assistance in order to act virtuously. Whereas the Greeks felt that will and reason are identical because will is essentially rational, the Christians conceived will and reason to be contrary faculties, pulling man in opposite directions—Socrates' sturdy and optimistic "Virtue is knowledge of the good" is to be contrasted with Paul's despairing "I know the better but I choose the worse." The pathos, frustration, and helplessness of Paul's cry explain as nothing else can the Christian yearning for a divine father and savior.

The Greeks lived in a universe that was basically one, and they believed themselves to be, as it were, in step with it. That is, their world was a cosmos of which they were a part. The central problem for them was to understand this world, which, just because it was a cosmos, they held to be in essence understandable. By contrast, the Christians lived in a universe in which something was profoundly amiss. On the one hand there was a transcendent creator god; on the other, a corrupt and erratic world. The central problem for them, therefore, was not scientific but practical: how to get back into step, how to return to the creator from whom men have wandered.

The basic features of Greek thought were set by the high value put on man and his achievements; those of Christian thought, by the high value put on God and His perfection. From the point of view of many people today Greek thought may appear too optimistic, too complacent, too convinced of the essential rationality of man and his universe—in a word, rather naïvely anthropocentric. Similarly, from this point of view Christian thought may appear too pessimistic, too humble, too convinced of the irrationality of the universe and of man's helplessness and incapacity, too dominated by a sense of sin and a need of salvation—in a word, too otherworldly. If (as the Greeks would not have been disposed to admit) man is in truth lower than the angels, many people feel that he is, after all, only a *little* lower—he is not altogether vile and corrupt. The feeling that Christian thought and Greek thought both tend to go to extremes and the wish somehow to find a mean between them have been characteristic of Western culture since the Renaissance. The fact that both Christian and Greek insights are part of our Western heritage and that we are unwilling to repudiate either has determined one of the major tasks of philosophy since the sixteenth century.

But it is not merely in their presuppositions and starting points that the Greek and Christian philosophies of life differ. It is clear that they must also differ radically in method. A Christian philosophy is committed to the task of exegesis: It aims at formulating an orthodox and definitive statement by reconciling various texts, all of which have been accepted at the outset as authoritative. One of the most striking characteristics of early Christian thought, indeed, is that it required philosophers to become textual critics. The same phenomenon occurred in the Academy in the generations after Plato's death—and in the Lyceum after Aristotle's death. But it was a new spectacle, and a sign of the change in the West, for intellects of the first order, like Augustine, to be content to perform what was fundamentally a work of exegesis.

CHAPTER 3

Augustine: God the Creator

His Life and Times

Augustine, the first great Christian philosopher, was born in 354. The half-century before his birth had been marked by a considerable spread of Christian teaching and by a corresponding increase in the power of the Church as an institution. While the internal struggle to purge the Church of heresy and to work out the orthodox position continued, Christianity had constantly to do battle with paganism and occasionally to contend with suspicious or hostile governments. The greatest threat of the latter kind occurred just at the beginning of the fourth century. In 303 the emperor Diocletian ordered that the Christians' churches and sacred books be destroyed. Fires that broke out in the imperial palace shortly afterward were said to be the work of Christian incendiaries acting in retaliation;

as a result, even sterner measures were inaugurated.[1] Fortunately for the Christians, Diocletian abdicated in 305 and the succession to the throne was disputed. In 312 Constantine established himself as emperor, and the next year an edict of toleration[2] was issued:

> We judge it consonant to right reason that no man should be denied leave of attaching himself to the rites of the Christians, or to whatever other religion his mind direct him. . . . Accordingly the open and free exercise of their respective religions is granted to all others as well as to Christians; for it befits the well-ordered state and tranquillity of our times that each individual be allowed, according to his own choice, to worship the Divinity.[a]

The Christians, who claimed Constantine as their own and lavished praises upon him, believed that he had been converted at the battle that won him his throne, when the cross appeared to him in a vision with the helpful slogan, "In this sign conquer!" Constantine probably found it useful to pray to all sorts of gods for assistance, and if he thought that the Christian God had helped him gain the crown, he may have felt a certain gratitude toward Him. But his decision to encourage Christianity almost certainly stemmed from political considerations. It was to his advantage to be allied with this tough, fast-growing sect, which had by his time built up an extensive organization. In any case, whatever the returns Constantine expected from Christianity, imperial favor greatly assisted the rise of orthodoxy. For the emperors did not like ecclesiastical squabbling and found it desirable to encourage "uniformity." Indeed, it was Constantine who convoked the Council of Nicaea, lent it the prestige of his presence, and, though he must have been indifferent to the theological issues being debated, gave his invaluable support to the Athanasian party.

From Constantine's time on, with one exception,[3] the emperors were Christians and came increasingly under the thumb of the bishops, who soon learned how to make use of the divine power they claimed to represent. For instance, when a Christian mob burned down a Jewish synagogue, the emperor Theodosius ordered the synagogue rebuilt at the Christians' expense. Ambrose, Bishop of Milan at the time, held this to be an intolerable attack on Christian prerogatives and obliged the emperor to rescind his order. On another occasion, when Theodosius ordered the massacre of a whole city because of a riot in which the commander of the garrison had been killed, Ambrose again intervened, this

---

1 Every inhabitant of the Empire was required to show his reliability by sacrificing to the ancestral gods at the official altars. Those who could not show certificates to the effect that they had done so were to be put to death. This was neatly designed to entrap the Christians, since to sacrifice to the pagan gods was from their point of view the worst form of apostasy.

2 This extremely liberal document was, unhappily, far ahead of its times. Only a short time later the Christians, at last secure in their authority, began persecuting the pagans in violation of both the letter and the spirit of this edict.

3 Julian, maliciously called "the apostate" by the outraged Christians, but actually a noble and well-meaning man, ineffectually tried to return to the old gods.

time in a more worthy cause. On the emperor's refusal to yield, Ambrose excommunicated him and locked him out of the church. For eight months the stalemate continued, until finally, on Christmas Day, Theodosius surrendered and did public penance for having opposed ecclesiastical authority.

It was the same Theodosius who made Christianity (and Catholic Christianity at that) the official state religion and gave religious orthodoxy political status:

> It is our pleasure that all nations which are governed by our Clemency and Moderation should steadfastly adhere to the religion which was taught by St. Peter to the Romans, which faithful tradition has preserved, which is now professed by the Pontiff Damasus and by Peter, Bishop of Alexandria. We authorize the followers of this doctrine to assume the title of Catholic Christians, and we brand all others with the infamous name of heretics. They must expect to suffer the severe penalties which our Authority, guided by the heavenly Wisdom, shall think proper to inflict upon them.[b]

What a change! In a few short years Christianity had transformed itself from a sect of outcasts into the state religion. And this was more than merely the triumph of a certain dogmatic point of view, for, as the old Empire was losing its grip, the way was being paved for the emergence of a new kind of sovereignty. As weak emperors gave way to self-assured bishops, precedents were established that were eventually to permit the Church to assume control and to replace the dissolving political sanctions with new sacerdotal ones.

But the sudden success of Christianity must not be allowed to obscure the fact that paganism died slowly. Augustine's mother, for instance, was a Christian; his father, a pagan. He himself went through almost every one of the contemporary religious movements before he finally found peace in the religion of his mother. In Augustine's day, then, despite all that Christianity had gained during the first half of the fourth century, the situation was still fluid, and Augustine's work is understandable only as a part of the Christians' struggle for supremacy and for orthodoxy.

Augustine's parents lived in Tagaste, in North Africa, and, despite lack of means, they gave their son the best education North Africa could provide. He was sent to Carthage, the great town of the province, to study rhetoric, the study then regarded as providing the best preparation for a career in the civil service. And precisely as any bright and ambitious Australian or Canadian of the nineteenth century sooner or later ended up in London, so Augustine, in 383, when he was just short of thirty, found his way to Rome. Later he went to Milan, which for some years had been the imperial capital. Here, in 386, he was converted to Christianity. Two years later he returned to Africa, where he hoped to lead a life of retirement and pious reflection. But his abilities soon won him a high place in the Church. He became Bishop of Hippo and devoted the remainder of his long life to administrative duties and to a prolonged polemic against heresy, in the course of which his own positive doctrine gradually emerged. He died in 430, as the barbarians were closing in on the Empire and at a moment when, symbolically enough, the Vandals had Hippo itself under siege.

Such are the prosaic, external facts of his life. Augustine's significance lies not in them but in his internal life and in his writings—in his writings because, as has been said, Augustine fashioned the first philosophical exposition of Christianity, and in his personality because he can be taken to represent the new type of man born out of the dissolution of the classical world and destined to dominate the West for centuries.

The Inner Struggle

ACUTE SENSE OF SIN

Like Paul, Augustine experienced a momentous conversion; unlike Paul, he fully documented this experience in his *Confessions*. Yet, since the events he described took place many years before he wrote them down, his account may tell less how they appeared to him as they occurred than how he viewed them long after his conversion. Even with this reservation in mind, the first thing that strikes the modern reader of the *Confessions* is Augustine's extraordinary (or, as we might be inclined to say, "abnormal") sense of sin. By our standards, certainly, his childhood was remarkably blameless; yet to Augustine the escapades that we think of as normal products of youthful exuberance were signs of a diseased soul: "I will now call to mind my past foulness, and the carnal corruptions of my soul, not because I love them, but that I may love Thee, O my God. For love of Thy love do I it, recalling, in the very bitterness of my remembrance, my most vicious ways, that Thou mayest grow sweet to me. . . ."

This opening prepares us for the revelation of hideous crimes, but what, actually, did Augustine's sins amount to? To begin with, he was a bright boy, proud of doing well at school and eager to do still better. "I, unhappy boy, . . . was more fearful of perpetrating a [grammatical] barbarism than, having done so, of envying those who had not. These things I declare and confess unto Thee, my God, for which I was applauded by them whom I then thought it my whole duty to please, for I did not perceive the gulf of infamy wherein I was cast away from Thine eyes." For the rest, he deceived his teachers and his parents "with innumerable lies," he experienced a "love of play, a desire to see frivolous spectacles, and a stage-struck restlessness . . . ," in play he sometimes "sought dishonest victories, . . . being conquered by the vain desire of pre-eminence . . . ," and he was "enslaved by gluttony" and "committed pilferings from my parents' cellar and table."

> There was a pear-tree close to our vineyard, heavily laden with fruit. . . .
> To shake and rob this some of us wanton young fellows went, late one night

(having, according to our disgraceful habit, prolonged our games in the streets until then), and carried away great loads, not to eat ourselves, but to fling to the very swine, . . . and to do this pleased us all the more because it was not permitted. Behold my heart, O my God; behold my heart, which Thou hadst pity upon when in the bottomless pit.[c]

ATTITUDE TOWARD SEX

As he grew older, of course, Augustine had even greater worries. When he reached the age of puberty, he experienced those desires that are our "common inheritance from Adam," and these, too, seemed to him, at least in later perspective, evidences of his corruption. Moreover, when he was seventeen, his family found the funds to send him to the provincial metropolis to continue his education:

> To Carthage [then] I came, where a cauldron of unholy loves bubbled up all around me. I loved not as yet, yet I loved to love; and, with a hidden want, I abhorred myself that I wanted not. I searched about for something to love, in love with loving, and hating security, and a way not beset with snares. . . . My soul was . . . full of ulcers [and] miserably cast itself forth, craving to be excited by contact with objects of sense. . . . To love and to be loved was sweet to me, and all the more when I succeeded in enjoying the person I loved. I befouled, therefore, the spring of friendship with the filth of concupiscence, and I dimmed its lustre with the hell of lustfulness; and yet, foul and dishonorable as I was, I craved, through an excess of vanity, to be thought elegant and urbane. . . .
> Stage-plays also drew me. . . .
> During this space [I] went on seduced and seducing, deceived and deceiving, in divers lusts. . . . Here proud, there superstitious, everywhere vain![d]

Here again, most people today probably find it difficult to understand Augustine's sense of the enormity of his guilt. Compared with the sexual morality of most of his contemporaries, his conduct was a model of sobriety and virtue. Although, as he said, he "knew not lawful wedlock," he remained faithful to one woman for years and only discarded her[4] when his mother insisted that he find and marry a rich wife. In general, like Paul and many other early Christians, Augustine had a particular horror of the sexual aspect of life—perhaps because he had a strong sexual drive. Even so, like Paul, and unlike members of the more ascetic school of Christianity, Augustine allowed "lawful wedlock" for the

---

4 Augustine's desertion of this woman, who had followed him devotedly to Italy, may strike us as more wicked than his long extramarital relation with her. They had a son, Adeodatus, who seems to have been a promising youth but died when he was sixteen. Augustine appears to have been fond of the boy, but, characteristically, he felt guilty about his affection, which he characterized as "a lustful love, where children are born against the parents' will, although, being born, they compel love"—*Confessions* (Pilkington), IV, ii, 2.

purpose of procreation. He felt, however, that the sexual relation should be rigidly limited to this purpose and that even at that it should not be enjoyed.

INTELLECTUAL PRIDE

Moreover, as he looked back on his youth, Augustine felt that he had committed the sin of "intellectual arrogance." By this he meant that he had once believed he could fathom the mysteries of the universe and discover for himself the nature of reality. His mother had brought him up as a Christian, but he soon came to doubt the faith that she accepted unthinkingly. The young Augustine was not only disturbed by the difficulty of explaining, on orthodox Christian lines, the existence of evil; he was also troubled by the naïve anthropomorphism of many members of his mother's sect. It was easy for this bright young man to see that, when the Christian Scriptures were taken literally (which was the only way it occurred to these simple-minded Christians to take them), they were a tissue of absurdities and contradictions.

> For I was ignorant as to that which really is, and was, as it were, violently moved to give my support to foolish deceivers, when they asked me, "Whence is evil?"—and "Is God limited by a bodily shape, and has He hairs and nails?"—and, "Are they to be esteemed righteous who had many wives at once, and did kill men, and sacrificed living creatures?" . . .
>
> I, unfortunate one, imagined there was I know not what substance of irrational life. . . .
>
> And I used to ask Thy faithful little ones, my fellow-citizens,—from whom I unconsciously stood exiled,—I used flippantly and foolishly to ask, "Why, then, doth the soul which God created err?" . . .
>
> For it . . . seemed to me "that it was not we that sin, but that I know not what other nature sinned in us." And it gratified my pride to be free from blame, and, after I had committed any fault, not to acknowledge that I had done any, . . . but I loved to excuse it, and to accuse something else (I wot not what) which was with me, but was not I. . . . And because a piety—such as it was—compelled me to believe that the good God never created any evil nature, I conceived two masses, the one opposed to the other, both infinite, but the evil the more contracted, the good the more expansive. And from this mischievous commencement the other profanities followed on me. For when my mind tried to revert to the Catholic faith, I was cast back. . . . And it appeared to me more devout . . . to confess Thee finite, than . . . to believe that anything could emanate from Thee of such a kind as I considered the nature of evil to be.[e]

AUGUSTINE'S MANICHEISM

In other words, difficulties over the problem of evil led Augustine to become a Manichee.[5] And he remained a Manichee, though with increasing doubts, for

5 See pp. 67–69.

nine years. The characteristics of Manicheism that had attracted him in the first place—its appeals to rational proof in contrast with the orthodox view's appeals to authority and faith—were precisely the characteristics that finally induced him to abandon it. What Augustine wanted above all was certainty. The quest for certainty was a major motive of his life, as it was for his whole generation and for many generations to come. As he puzzled over evil and attempted to reconcile its existence with that of an omnipotent God, innumerable questions filled his mind. "Whence is evil? . . . Was [God] powerless to change [it] . . . seeing that He is omnipotent? . . . Could it indeed exist contrary to His will? . . . Such like things did I revolve in my miserable breast, overwhelmed with the most gnawing cares lest I should die ere I discovered the truth." So also, "I inquired, 'Whence is evil?' and found no result. . . . What torments did my travailing heart then endure! What sighs, O my God! . . . No man knoweth, but only Thou, what I endured."[f] According to Augustine's doctrine, to die in error meant eternal damnation. Hence the motive that led Augustine to seek the truth was neither intellectual curiosity nor anticipation of the pleasures of contemplation, as it had been for the Greek philosophers. It was a desperate need for salvation.

But years of intellectual effort convinced Augustine that the truth could not be reached by reason, and eventually he came to regard the Manichean period in his life as one of sin through intellectual pride, through overconfidence in his own mental powers. It appeared to him that the miserable doubts he had experienced during those years had been just punishment for his presumption. "I sought 'whence is evil?' . . . Nor saw I the evil in my very search." Thus he completely reversed himself. He claimed to have realized that the Manichees only mocked man's credulity "by audacious promise of knowledge" and that "it was with more moderation and honesty that [Catholic doctrine] commanded things to be believed that were not demonstrated (whether it was that they could be demonstrated, but not to any one, or could not be demonstrated at all)."[g]

AUGUSTINE'S NEOPLATONISM

But Augustine was a long time reaching this position. His early life, up to about the age of thirty, was dominated, as we have seen, by a search for rational truth and by a profound and disturbing sense of sin and guilt. He took these feelings with him from Africa to Italy, and the not inconsiderable success he soon won in his profession did nothing to relieve his unrest. The broader intellectual life of Italy, however, opened new horizons to him. He made the acquaintance of Ambrose, the bishop who disciplined Theodosius,[6] and learned from him that by interpreting the Bible allegorically one could make its naïveté and

6 See pp. 73–74.

its inconsistencies vanish. This was helpful; but even more valuable were insights Augustine gained through reading Neoplatonic metaphysics.

In the first place, he found in Neoplatonism a notion of the deity as a creative force, or energy, rather than as a crudely anthropomorphic architect or a handicraft worker. Coupled with what Ambrose taught him about allegory, this provided a plausible way of understanding the scriptural traditions about a creative Yahweh. In the second place, and even more important, Neoplatonism seemed to him to provide a solution for the problem of evil. Although the Neoplatonists were actually anything but clear about the status of matter, Augustine concluded from their writings that, if the whole world is a product of the Father's creativity, none of it can be bad. What we call evil is simply an incompleteness and a finitude resulting from the creature's inevitable separation from its maker. If evil were indeed something positive, as the Manichees held, we would have to ask how an omnipotent and all-good God could either create it or tolerate its existence. But if, as Neoplatonism seemed to show, evil is merely negative, merely the absence of good, Augustine held that there is no problem to solve. Hence the great stumbling block to his acceptance of orthodoxy was removed and his intellectual doubts were set at rest. He had found the truth.[7]

But, to his consternation, something was still lacking—the will to accept the truth that he had found. He experienced the terrible frustration that Paul had described in his letter to the Romans: "I can will, but I cannot do what is right. I do not do the good things that I want to do; I do the wrong things that I do not want to do. . . . What a wretched man I am! Who can save me from this doomed body?"[h] This was a period of black despair and frustration for Augustine. He had convinced himself of the truth of orthodox teaching, but nothing happened. He knew no inner light, no inner peace; his old life of sin, corruption, lust, and pride continued as before.

> I no longer doubted that there was an incorruptible substance, from which was derived all other substance; nor did I now desire to be more certain of Thee, but more stedfast in Thee. As for my temporal life, all things were uncertain, and my heart had to be purged from the old leaven. . . .
>
> Still very tenaciously was I held by the love of women. . . . I had now found the goodly pearl, which, selling all that I had, I ought to have bought; and I hesitated.[i]

He felt his will to be divided. There was something in him that prevented him from taking the step he most deeply desired. He was helpless,

---

7 Or so it then seemed to Augustine. Actually, as he later came to realize, much in this Neoplatonic solution did not square with Catholicism.

. . . bound, not with the irons of another, but my own iron will. . . . Because of a perverse will was lust made; and lust indulged in became custom; and custom not resisted became necessity. . . . But that new will which had begun to develope in me, freely to worship Thee, and to wish to enjoy Thee, O God, the only sure enjoyment, was not able as yet to overcome my former wilfulness, made strong by long indulgence. Thus did my two wills, one old and the other new, one carnal, the other spiritual, contend within me; and by their discord they unstrung my soul. . . .

Thus with the baggage of the world was I sweetly burdened, as when in slumber; and the thoughts wherein I meditated upon Thee were like unto the efforts of those desiring to awake, who, still overpowered with a heavy drowsiness, are again steeped therein. . . . Nor had I aught to answer Thee calling to me, "Awake, thou that sleepest, and arise from the dead, and Christ shall give thee light." And to Thee showing me on every side, that what Thou saidst was true, I, convicted by the truth, had nothing at all to reply, but the drawling and drowsy words: "Presently, lo, presently"; "leave me a little while." But "presently, presently," had no present; and my "leave me a little while" went on for a long while.ʲ

AUGUSTINE'S CONVERSION

Augustine's account of his conversion and of the struggle that led up to it is a fascinating—and a revealing—psychological document. While Augustine was still struggling vainly against his stubborn will, he was visited by Pontitianus, a Christian friend from Africa, who told Augustine the story of a conversion he had witnessed. Pontitianus

. . . related . . . how on a certain afternoon, at Triers, when the emperor was taken up with seeing the Circensian games, he and three others, his comrades, went out for a walk in the gardens close to the city walls, and there, as they chanced to walk two and two, one strolled away with him, while the other two went by themselves; and these, in their rambling, came upon a certain cottage . . . where they found a book in which was written the life of Antony.[8] This one of them began to read, marvel at, and be inflamed by it; and in the reading, to meditate on embracing such a life, and giving up his worldly employments to serve Thee. . . . And in the pangs of the travail of the new life, he turned his eyes again upon the page and continued reading, and was inwardly changed where Thou sawest, and his mind was divested of the world, as soon became evident; for as he read, and the surging of his heart rolled along, he raged awhile, discerned and resolved on a better course, and now, having become Thine, he said to his friend, "Now have I broken loose from those hopes of ours, and am determined to serve God; and this, from this hour, in this place, I enter upon. If thou art reluctant to imitate me, hinder me not." The other replied that he would cleave to him, to share in so great

8 [This is the St. Anthony who founded monasticism—AUTHOR.]

a reward and so great a service. . . . Then Pontitianus, and he that had walked with him through the other parts of the garden, came in search of them to the same place, and having found them, reminded them to return as the day had declined. But they, making known to him their resolution and purpose, and how such a resolve had sprung up and become confirmed in them, entreated them not to molest them, if they refused to join themselves unto them. But the others, no whit changed from their former selves, . . . returned to the palace. But the other two, setting their affections upon heavenly things, remained in the cottage. And both of them had affianced brides, who, when they heard of this, dedicated also their virginity unto God.

Such was the story of Pontitianus. But Thou, O Lord, whilst he was speaking, didst turn me towards myself, taking me from behind my back, where I had placed myself while unwilling to exercise self-scrutiny; and Thou didst set me face to face with myself, that I might behold how foul I was, and how crooked and sordid, bespotted and ulcerous. And I beheld and loathed myself; and whither to fly from myself I discovered not. And if I sought to turn my gaze away from myself, . . . Thou again opposedst me unto myself and thrustedst me before my own eyes, that I might discover my iniquity, and hate it. I had known it, but acted as though I knew it not,— winked at it, and forgot it. . . .

I, miserable young man, supremely miserable even in the very outset of my youth, had entreated chastity of Thee, and said, "Grant me chastity and continency, but not yet." For I was afraid lest Thou shouldst hear me soon, and soon deliver me from the disease of concupiscence, which I desired to have satisfied rather than extinguished.

· ·

Thus was I sick and tormented, . . . tossing and turning me in my chain till that was utterly broken, whereby I now was but slightly, but still was held. And Thou, O Lord, pressedst upon me in my inward parts by a severe mercy, redoubling the lashes of fear and shame, lest I should again give way, and that same slender remaining tie not being broken off, it should recover strength, and enchain me the faster. For I said mentally, "Lo, let it be done now, let it be done now." And as I spoke, I all but came to a resolve. I all but did it, yet I did it not. Yet fell I not back to my old condition, but took up my position hard by, and drew breath. And I tried again, and wanted but very little of reaching it, and somewhat less, and then all but touched and grasped it; and yet came not at it, nor touched, nor grasped it, hesitating to die unto death, and to live unto life; and the worse, whereto I had been habituated, prevailed more with me than the better, which I had not tried. And the very moment in which I was to become another man, the nearer it approached me, the greater horror did it strike into me; but it did not strike me back, nor turn me aside, but kept me in suspense.

The very toys of toys, and vanities of vanities, my old mistresses, still enthralled me; they shook my fleshly garment, and whispered softly, "Dost thou part with us?" . . .

From the secret depths of my soul, drawn together and heaped up all my misery before the sight of my heart, there arose a mighty storm, accompanied by as mighty a shower of tears. . . . I flung myself down, how, I know not, under a certain fig-tree, giving free course to my tears, and the streams of mine eyes gushed out, an acceptable sacrifice unto Thee. And, not indeed in these words, yet to this effect, spake I much unto Thee,—"But Thou, O Lord, how long?" "How long, Lord? Wilt Thou be angry for ever? Oh, remember not against us former iniquities"; for I felt that I was enthralled by them. I sent up these sorrowful cries,—"How long, how long? To-morrow, and to-morrow? Why not now? Why is there not this hour an end to my uncleanness?"

I was saying these things and weeping in the most bitter contrition of my heart, when, lo, I heard the voice as of a boy or girl, I know not which, coming from a neighbouring house, chanting, and oft repeating, "Take up and read; take up and read." Immediately my countenance was changed, and I began most earnestly to consider whether it was usual for children in any kind of game to sing such words; nor could I remember ever to have heard the like. So, restraining the torrent of my tears, I rose up, interpreting it no other way than as a command to me from Heaven to open the book, and to read the first chapter I should light upon. . . . So quickly I returned to the place where . . . I had put down the volume of the apostles, I grasped, opened, and in silence read that paragraph on which my eyes first fell,—"Not in rioting and drunkenness, not in chambering and wantonness, not in strife and envying; but put ye on the Lord Jesus Christ, and make not provision for the flesh, to fulfil the lusts thereof." No further would I read, nor did I need; for instantly, as the sentence ended,—by a light, as it were, of security into my heart,—all the gloom of doubt vanished away.[k]

AUGUSTINE'S MISSION

The year was 386—a momentous date in the history of the West, as well as in Augustine's own life. For him, from then to the end, there was never a doubt. Though he might again be tempted by the flesh, his complete conviction of the certainty of the Christian revelation never left him. What remained for him was to bring others, if he could, to a similar peace. He had been lost in outer darkness, "ignorant what way led back to Thee." God in His mercy had shown him the way home. Augustine was sure that the dramatic circumstances of his salvation had been intended to serve as a lesson to others. He therefore resolved to combat heresy wherever he found it, especially the insidious doctrine of the Manichees that had so long ensnared him. And since there were many others who suffered from intellectual doubts, he thought it desirable, so far as might be, to present a reasoned case for orthodoxy. But remembering his own years of failure, he recognized that he could not work out a rational synthesis without God's help. The intellectual arrogance of heretics and pagans was to be answered with intellectual humility. He would trust God to find the proper arguments for him, which God of course *could* do, if He but chose to.

Thus Augustine conceived it his duty to show other wayward sinners the truth of the Christian revelation. What *was* the Christian revelation? On its general nature all orthodox Christians had by now, of course, agreed: that God is an omniscient, omnipotent, and all-good creator; that man is his erring child; that Christ is the Son of God sent by the Father as mediator and savior. But doctrine was still sufficiently loose for its future development to have taken any one of a number of different paths. Such was the force of Augustine's personality, such his philosophical and rhetorical skills, that his personal interpretation of the Christian revelation deeply marked the course of that development and became a pervasive influence on Christian thought.

What, then, were the elements that entered into his understanding of Christian truth? To begin with, of course, there were the canonical writings, which Augustine held to be divinely inspired and which were themselves a mixture of Jewish, Pauline, and Johannine materials. Then there were Augustine's Neoplatonism and the Manichean dualism from which, in spite of everything, he never wholly freed himself. Finally there were his vivid personal experiences: the sense of sin and utter worthlessness; the sense, just before his conversion, of helplessness and diseased will; the sense, in the moment of conversion, of God's infinite grace; the sense, during the remaining years of his life, of God's constant providential care.

In the discussion of his philosophy that follows, it will be seen how Augustine struggled to reconcile these various elements and how their conflict prevented the achievement of a satisfactory synthesis. Augustine's view divides easily into two main parts—one concerning God the Creator, the other concerning His creature, the universe. Accordingly, the remainder of this chapter will examine Augustine's conception of God and his attempt to fuse together Greek metaphysics and Christian piety. The next chapter will treat, first, Augustine's conception of human nature and the ethical and political views he derived from it; second, his conception of the physical universe; and, third, his philosophy of history.

Augustine's Concept of God

As a mystic, Augustine wrote about God in the language of fervent piety.

> Great art Thou, O Lord, and greatly to be praised; great is Thy power, and of Thy wisdom there is no end. And man, being a part of Thy creation, desires to praise Thee. . . . Thou movest us to delight in praising Thee; for Thou hast formed us for Thyself, and our hearts are restless till they find rest in Thee. Lord, teach me to know and understand which of these should be first, to call on Thee, or to praise Thee; and likewise to know Thee, or to call upon Thee. . . .
> And how shall I call upon my God—my God and my Lord? For when I call on Him I ask him to come into me. And what place is there in me into which my God can come—into which God can come, even He who made heaven and earth? Is there anything in me, O Lord my God, that can contain

Thee? Do indeed the very heaven and the earth, which Thou hast made, and in which Thou hast made me, contain Thee? Or, as nothing could exist without Thee, doth whatever exists contain Thee? Why, then, do I ask Thee to come into me, since I indeed exist, and could not exist if Thou wert not in me? . . . Or should I not rather say, that I could not exist unless I were in Thee from whom are all things, by whom are all things, in whom are all things? Even so, Lord; even so. . . .

What, then, art Thou, O my God—what, I ask, but the Lord God? For who is Lord but the Lord? or who is God save our God? Most high, most excellent, most potent, most omnipotent; most piteous and most just; most hidden and most near; most beauteous and most strong; stable, yet contained of none; unchangeable, yet changing all things; never new, never old; making all things new, yet bringing old age upon the proud and they know it not; always working, yet ever at rest; gathering, yet needing nothing; sustaining, pervading, and protecting; creating, nourishing, and developing; seeking, and yet possessing all things. . . . Yet, O my God, my life, my holy joy, what is this that I have said? And what saith any man when he speaks of Thee? Yet woe to them that keep silence, seeing that even they who say most are as the dumb.[1]

But Augustine was not merely a devout Christian; he was also a philosopher. And from a philosophical point of view, what is most striking about the brief homily just quoted is the way in which it is dominated by God, rather than by Jesus. Augustine's mind, although much like Paul's in many other respects, fastened on the Father rather than on the Son. This is perhaps explained by the fact that, whereas Paul was a missionary who taught a religious mystery, Augustine was a philosopher with a strong metaphysical interest. Anyone with a philosophical mind, even one who is deeply religious, is primarily interested in the nature of reality. Thus Augustine belongs, in this respect at least, to the same tradition as Plato and Aristotle and Democritus, but with the important difference that, whereas their interest in the nature of reality was mainly secular, his was primarily religious. It was not, for instance, a desire to solve the problem of knowledge that led him to investigate the nature of reality, nor was it the hope of providing a firm basis for social ethics. His motive was the will to find a satisfactory object of religious faith. What he found, therefore, was naturally a different kind of reality from theirs. Whereas Plato or Democritus employed either a relatively neutral term, like "form" or "atom," or an ethically colored term, like "the Good," to designate what they held to be ultimate reality, Augustine used a purely religious term, "God."

Nevertheless, it would be easy to exaggerate the differences between a metaphysics that is primarily secular and one that has a religious orientation. Many philosophers have held that at their furthest bounds religion and metaphysics touch. As F. H. Bradley wrote,

All of us, I presume, more or less, are led beyond the region of ordinary facts. Some in one way and some in others, we seem to touch and have communion with what is beyond the visible world. In various manners we find something higher, which both supports and humbles, both chastens and transports us. And, with certain persons, the intellectual effort to understand the universe is a principal way of thus experiencing the Deity. No one, probably, who has not felt this, however differently he might describe it, has ever cared much for metaphysics. And, wherever it has been felt strongly, it has been its own justification.[m]

Plato would certainly have agreed with Bradley that "the intellectual effort to understand the universe is a principal way of experiencing the Deity," for Plato held that the ultimate reality we finally come to experience by means of dialectic is not an abstract "truth," remote from human aspirations. Because its nature is such that it satisfies our deepest desires, he argued, it is beautiful and good. Since this was also Augustine's conviction, and since, as it happens, Augustine's deepest aspirations were very much like Plato's, there are marked similarities between their two metaphysical theories.

Properties of God-Reality

GOD-REALITY IS IMMUTABLE

Both Augustine and Plato profoundly disliked change, and both held that, whatever other properties ultimate reality may have, it must be immutable and impervious to change and decay. Since one of the most striking features of the sense world is the fact that it changes, both concluded that this world cannot be wholly real. The notion that ultimate reality is unchanging fitted in well with the conception of God as the perfect being. If God is perfect, there is no reason for Him to want to change, for in a perfect being change would result in loss of perfection. As Plato pointed out in the *Republic*, since nothing can become more than perfect, a perfect being that changed could only become less than perfect.

Augustine could agree entirely with this line of argument. But the status of the changing sense world and its relation to unchanging reality were to cause him a great deal of trouble. These had been problems for Plato, too, but for a different reason. Since Plato was not willing to write the sense world off as wholly unreal, he had to try to explain its relation to immutable reality. This he was never able to do satisfactorily; his theory of forms foundered at this point. As for Augustine, we may suspect that he would have taken the easy way out but for dogmatic considerations, for he was even more otherworldly temperamentally than Plato. He might even have been willing to adopt the radical Parmenidean solution, according to which change is sheerly an illusion, and he certainly would have been satisfied with something like the ambiguous Neopla-

tonic doctrine of emanations. But Christian dogma forbade any such radical
treatment of the sense world.

The canonical writings said that God had created the world. If it is God's
creature, it must be *something*—it cannot be merely "appearance" or illusion.
It follows that, though both Augustine and Aristotle agreed that Plato had gone
too far toward denying reality to the sense world, they dealt with this situation
in totally different ways. Whereas Aristotle was impressed with the actuality
of the sense world, Augustine was impressed with the creativity of God. Hence,
whereas Aristotle ended up with a unified world, conceived of as a group of
individual substances, each an amalgam of form and matter, Augustine was left
with a divided world, an active God confronting a passive creature.

GOD-REALITY IS CREATIVE

It is fair to say, then, that Augustine did not so much solve Plato's problem
as substitute another and a more difficult one for it. Instead of the old puzzle
about the relation of appearance and reality, we have a new one about the
relation of creature and creator. And this is further complicated by the dogmatic
requirement that God produced this world "out of nothing." This follows not
only from the authority of Genesis but also from the consideration that if God,
like Plato's demiurge, had created the world by fashioning an already existing
material, the nature of this material would have been a limitation on God's free
act.

Plato, of course, could accept this consequence. Indeed, in the *Timaeus* he
used it to account for evil and the other deficiencies we find in the world: They
result from the intractability of the materials on which the demiurge worked.
But Augustine's God, unlike Plato's demiurge, was omnipotent. Hence Plato's
solution was not possible for Augustine. He had to hold that the world was created
out of nothing by a divine fiat. But is such an act intelligible? Augustine wrestled
long with this problem.

> But how didst Thou make the heaven and the earth, and what was the
> instrument of Thy so mighty work? For it was not as a human worker
> fashioning body from body, according to the fancy of his mind, in somewise
> able to assign a form which it perceives in itself by its inner eye. . . . How,
> O God, didst Thou make heaven and earth? Truly, neither in the heaven
> nor in the earth didst Thou make heaven and earth; nor in the air, nor in
> the waters, since these also belong to the heaven and the earth; nor in the
> whole world didst Thou make the whole world; because there was no place
> wherein it could be made before it was made, that it might be; nor didst
> Thou hold anything in Thy hand wherewith to make heaven and earth.[n]

We can easily agree with Augustine that the anthropomorphic language of
Genesis is not helpful in understanding creation. But when anthropomorphism
and metaphor are abandoned, what remains? It is not possible to explain creation

by extrapolating from human experience, that is, by arguing that God does on a larger scale the same sort of thing man does. We cannot hope to understand divine creativity by merely multiplying human creativity by infinity (whatever that would be!). Even when men are at their most "creative," they never do more than rearrange already existing materials. But creation out of nothing is not rearrangement, on however massive a scale. Because they are utterly different, not merely different in degree, God's creativity and man's have nothing in common but the name.

From the religious point of view, perhaps it is best simply to confess that creation is a mystery the human mind cannot fathom but must take on faith.[9] But from a secular point of view, creation is a concept that ought, as it were, to be intelligible. We can therefore both sympathize with Augustine's desire to give a reasoned account of it and understand the reasons for his failure. On the one hand, he had to hold that creature is not creator. To identify them, as the Neoplatonic doctrine of emanation tended to do, would have been to fall into the heresy of pantheism. On the other hand, to say too firmly that creature is not creator would have taken him dangerously close to another heresy. For if creature is separate and distinct, it must be in some way independent; and if creature is independent, creator cannot be all-powerful. It is obvious that, though the problem in which Augustine was enmeshed was perforce very difficult, he made it even more so by feeling obliged to approach it in terms of creator-creature instead of in the reality-appearance terms of secular philosophy.

Passing over these problems, what more can be said about reality than that it is itself immutable and the creator of the mutable world we live in? Like Plato, Augustine believed that ultimate reality (in Augustine's language, God) is the source of truth. Further, he agreed with Plato that even in our world of flux there must be some points of absolute certainty. Here again, a basic similarity of temperament led Augustine to a view close to Plato's, but dogmatic considerations required him to modify this view in a quite different direction. Whereas Plato found an absolutely certain starting point in mathematics, Augustine found it in the self. In a world of doubt there was, he thought, at least one thing he could not doubt—that he doubted. Indeed, the more he doubted, the more certain it was that he existed. A doubter must exist if doubts occur.

> I am not at all afraid of the arguments of the Academicians, who say, What if you are deceived? For if I am deceived I am. For he who is not, cannot be deceived; and if I am deceived, by this same token I am. And since I am if I am deceived, how am I deceived in believing that I am? for it is certain that I am if I am deceived. Since, therefore, I, the person deceived, should be, even if I were deceived, certainly I am not deceived in this knowledge that I am. And, consequently, neither am I deceived in knowing that I know. For, as I know that I am, so I know this also, that I know.°

9 This was the position Thomas was later to take. See pp. 229–31.

For Plato, one of the most important facts about reaility was that it is the source of truth. As soon as he had established, at least to his own satisfaction, that there is *some* absolutely certain knowledge (in mathematics), he went on to ask, "What does the existence of this absolutely certain mathematical knowledge imply about the nature of the real?" In other words, Plato moved from a consideration of what he took to be the nature of absolute knowledge to a consideration of what reality must be in order to be known.

Because Augustine was not greatly interested in the problem of knowledge, his thought moved in another way. There were several reasons for his lack of interest in the problem of knowledge. First, his consuming interest, in the light of which everything else paled, was "peace"—the desire for security. He was not much concerned with those social and political questions whose solution depends, Plato held, on the possibility of scientific knowledge. Second, as a believing Christian, he held that reason is an inadequate instrument for reaching the truth, which can be attained only through faith. Knowledge, he thought, is validated by faith in God's goodness and providence, not by logical reasoning or geometrical demonstration. It is thus characteristic of Augustine's whole point of view that the passage just quoted about the certainty of self-knowledge was merely incidental to his account of the nature of the Trinity. On the other hand, it is characteristic of the high quality of Augustine's philosophical insights that this thought—that we know our own existence directly and with certainty—became one of the basic premises from which, starting with Descartes, modern philosophy developed.

GOD-REALITY IS ETERNAL

Returning to Augustine's account of the divine nature, we find that God is eternal. Of course, Plato had held that ultimate reality is uncreated and unchanging, and this might seem to exhaust the idea of eternity. From a strictly philosophical point of view, this may be the case. The fact that the eternity of God meant much more to Augustine is therefore a good example of the influence of religion on metaphysics. Since this was a very important concept for Augustine, and since it is a very difficult one, a fairly long passage will be quoted here:

> Who shall . . . catch the glory of that ever-standing eternity, and compare it with the times which never stand, and see that it is incomparable; and that a long time cannot become long, save from the many motions that pass by, which cannot at the same instant be prolonged; but that in the Eternal nothing passeth away, but that the whole is present . . . ?
>
> Since . . . Thou art the Creator of all times, if any time was before Thou madest heaven and earth, why is it said that Thou didst refrain from working? For that very time Thou madest, nor could times pass by before Thou madest times. But if before heaven and earth there was no time, why is it asked, What didst Thou then? For there was no "then" when time was not.
>
> Nor dost Thou by time precede time; else wouldest not Thou precede all

times. But in the excellency of an ever-present eternity, Thou precedest all times past, and survivest all future times, because they are future, and when they have come they will be past; but "Thou art the same, and Thy years shall have no end." Thy years neither go nor come; but ours both go and come, that all may come. All Thy years stand at once, since they do stand. . . .

What is time? Who can easily and briefly explain it? Who even in thought can comprehend it, even to the pronouncing of a word concerning it? But what in speaking do we refer to more familiarly and knowingly than time? And certainly we understand when we speak of it; we understand also when we hear it spoken of by another. What, then, is time? If no one ask of me, I know; if I wish to explain to him who asks, I know not. . . .

Let us . . . see, O human soul, whether present time can be long; for to thee is it given to perceive and to measure periods of time. What wilt thou reply to me? Is a hundred years when present a long time? See, first, whether a hundred years can be present. For if the first year of these is current, that is present, but the other ninety and nine are future, and therefore they are not as yet. But if the second year is current, one is already past, the other present, the rest future. . . . See at least whether that year itself which is current can be present. For if its first month be current, the rest are future; if the second, the first hath already passed, and the remainder are not yet. Therefore neither is the year which is current as a whole present. [Nor] is that month which is current present, but one day only: if the first, the rest being to come, if the last, the rest being past; if any of the middle, then between past and future. . . .

But . . . there is not one day present as a whole. . . . If any portion of time be conceived which cannot now be divided into even the minutest particles of moments, this only is that which may be called present; which, however, flies so rapidly from future to past, that it cannot be extended by any delay. For if it be extended, it is divided into the past and future; but the present hath no space. . . .

And yet, O Lord, we perceive intervals of times, and we compare them with themselves, and we say some are longer, others shorter. We even measure by how much shorter or longer this time may be than that; and we answer, "That this is double or treble, while this is but once, or only as much as that." But we measure times passing when we measure them by perceiving them; but past times, which now are not, or future times, which as yet are not, who can measure them? Unless, perchance, any one will dare to say, that that can be measured which is not. When, therefore, time is passing, it can be perceived and measured; but when it has passed, it cannot, since it is not. . . .

What now is manifest and clear is, that neither are there future nor past things. Nor is it fitly said, "There are three times, past, present, and future"; but perchance it might be fitly said, "There are three times; a present of things past, a present of things present, and a present of things future." For these three do somehow exist in the soul, and otherwise I see them not: present of things past, memory; present of things present, sight; present of things future, expectation. . . .

I have just now said, then, that we measure times as they pass. . . . But how do we measure present time, since it hath not space? . . . For we say not single, and double, and triple and equal, or in any other way in which we speak of time, unless with respect to the spaces of times. In what space, then, do we measure passing time? . . .

My soul yearns to know this most entangled enigma. Forbear to shut up, O Lord my God, good Father,—through Christ I beseech Thee,—forbear to shut up these things, both usual and hidden, from my desire, that it may be hindered from penetrating them; but let them dawn through Thy enlightening mercy, O Lord. . . .

Dost Thou command that I should assent, if any one should say that time is "the motion of a body"? Thou dost not command me. For I hear that no body is moved but in time. This Thou sayest; but that the very motion of a body is time, I hear not; Thou sayest it not. . . . The motion of a body is one thing, that by which we measure how long it is another, who cannot see which of these is rather to be called time? For, although a body be sometimes moved, sometimes stand still, we measure not its motion only, but also its standing still, by time. . . . Time, therefore, is not the motion of a body.

· ·

Persevere, O my mind, and give earnest heed. God is our helper; He made us, and not we ourselves. Give heed, where truth dawns. Lo, suppose the voice of a body begins to sound, and does sound, and sounds on, and lo! it ceases,—it is now silence, and that voice is past and is no longer a voice. It was future before it sounded, and could not be measured, because as yet it was not; and now it cannot, because it no longer is. Then, therefore, while it was sounding, it might, because there was then that which might be measured. But even then it did not stand still, for it was going and passing away. . . . We, therefore, measure neither future times, nor past, nor present, nor those passing by; and yet we do measure times.

Deus Creator omnium; this verse of eight syllables alternates between short and long syllables. . . . By common sense . . . I measure a long by a short syllable. . . . Where is the short syllable by which I measure? Where is the long one which I measure? Both have sounded, have flown, have passed away, and are no longer; and still I measure, and I confidently answer (so far as is trusted to a practised sense), that as to space of time this syllable is single, that double. . . . Therefore do I not measure themselves, which now are not, but something in my memory, which remains fixed.

In thee, O my mind, I measure times. . . .

But how is that future diminished or consumed which as yet is not? Or how doth the past, which is no longer, increase, unless in the mind which enacteth this there are three things done? For it both expects, and considers, and remembers, that that which it expecteth, through that which it considereth, may pass into that which it remembereth. Who, therefore, denieth that future things as yet are not? But yet there is already in the mind the expectation of things future. And who denies that past things are now no longer? But, however, there is still in the mind the memory of things past. And who denies that time present wants space, because it passeth away in a moment? But yet our consideration endureth, through which that which may be present may proceed to become absent. Future time, which is not, is not therefore long; but a "long future" is "a long expectation of the future." Nor is time past, which is now no longer, long; but a long past is "a long memory of the past."

I am about to repeat a psalm that I know. Before I begin, my attention is extended to the whole; but when I have begun, as much of it as becomes past by my saying it is extended in my memory; and the life of this action of mine is divided between my memory, on account of what I have repeated, and my expectation, on account of what I am about to repeat; yet my consideration is present with me, through which that which was future may be carried over so that it may become past. . . .

Surely, if there be a mind, so greatly abounding in knowledge and fore-knowledge, to which all things past and future are so known as one psalm is well known to me, that mind exceedingly wonderful, and very astonishing; because whatever is so past, and whatever is to come of after ages, is no more concealed from Him than was it hidden from me when singing that psalm, what and how much of it had been sung from the beginning, what and how much remained unto the end. But far be it that Thou, the Creator of the universe, the Creator of souls and bodies,—far be it that Thou shouldest know all things future and past. Far, far more wonderfully, and far more mysteriously, Thou knowest them. For it is not as the feelings of one singing known things, or hearing a known song, are—through expectation of future words, and in remembrance of those that are past—varied, and his senses divided, that anything happeneth unto Thee, unchangeably eternal, that is, the truly eternal Creator of minds. As, then, Thou in the Beginning knewest the heaven and the earth without any change of Thy knowledge, so in the Beginning didst Thou make heaven and earth without any distraction of Thy action.[p]

This passage is interesting for a number of reasons. For one thing, it is a good example of Augustine's style. Even considerably reduced, as in this extract, the passage is exceedingly prolix—the effect, possibly, of Augustine's habit of dictating to a secretary and thinking things out as he went along. The way in which this really acute piece of psychological analysis is constantly interrupted by pious appeals for divine help is characteristic of Augustine's ambivalence toward reason and the constant danger he felt of falling into the sin of intellectual pride.

More important, of course, than such matters of style and form are the conclusions Augustine reached. The main steps of his argument, which may be a little difficult to distinguish in the original, are fairly straightforward. In the first place, time flows. In the second place, time is a continuum. No matter how short a duration (a year, a month, a day, an hour, a minute) I take as "present," it can be divided into parts that are earlier (and so past) and parts that are later (and so yet to come). Nevertheless, there is, in the third place, a sense in which past and future are both in my mind *now*, together with the present. If I recite the words, "Of man's first disobedience and the fruit of that forbidden tree,"

I recite them one after the other. When I get to "fruit," "disobedience" is past and "tree" is future. Yet somehow the line is in my mind *as a whole* as each successive word passes. Augustine proved this by appealing to our ability to measure time. Since we cannot measure a thing that is not, past and future must somehow, though past and though future, be also present when we measure them. As he said, "There are three times—a present of things past, a present of things present, and a present of things future."

Now what do these psychological facts about our experience of time have to do with eternity? The relation is simple. Even our finite minds can hold real pasts and real futures together in a true present. With us, of course, the span of this inclusive present is not great, but it gives us an inkling of what the span of God's infinite mind must be. God holds in one present *all* the past and *all* the future in the way in which I hold "disobedience," which is already gone, and "tree," which is yet to come, together with the present "fruit." God's eternity, in fact, is simply this holding together of a succession in a "now." It is just this power we are all aware of in ourselves, but carried, of course, to an infinite degree.

What are we to say of this argument? It would seem that Augustine is on sounder ground here than in his account of creation. There he could find nothing in human experience remotely like God's creative act, for all human production consists in the manipulation of previously existing material, whereas God's creativity is a fiat out of nothing. Here, however, he found something remotely analogous to the divine in human experience—the well-known phenomenon of "span." Of course, with God this human capacity to span a flow is supposedly carried to infinity, for in His eternity "nothing passes away; the whole is present"—not just the whole of a familiar poem, but the whole universe.

The question is, therefore, whether our minds can form any notion of the *infinite* expansion of a finite power. Or, rather, what sort of notion of infinity is going to satisfy us? Are we content to *feel* something—something at once exalting and humbling—when we think about infinity? Or do we want to be able to make a rational analysis of the concept? Because people differ so much about what constitutes a satisfactory criterion of explanation, two men who have roughly the same experience when "infinity" is mentioned may yet differ widely as to whether the word is meaningful, the one insisting that he understands it and the other maintaining that he hasn't the remotest idea of what it means. For Augustine and those with minds like his, the infinite is deeply moving; our inability to grasp it fully is precisely what appeals. In contrast, Aristotle disliked infinity and rejected the concept just because it seemed to him to elude analysis. Here, then, is another major parting of the ways in philosophy.

Of course, Augustine would not have viewed himself as facing the dichotomy that has been presented here. It is true that he insisted that God's knowledge of past and future is "far more wonderful, far more mysterious" than anything we can grasp. But he would have maintained that there is nevertheless empirical evidence of what infinity is like. There are, he would have said, many poets and mystics who not only experience those finite spans known to all of us but claim actually to have shared in God's eternity—or at least in something enough like it to have enabled them to know what God's experience itself must be.[10] Here we face another difficult question about which there will be many opinions. It would seem, however, that though such experiences are in some sense actual (not just extrapolations from the actual), they are not, as it were, in the public domain. They are not like the experience of seeing the earth from a satellite, which, though rare, is in the public domain in the sense of being available to anyone who can persuade NASA to launch him by rocket. Since they are in fact limited to a select few (who, moreover, have difficulty in reporting what they have experienced), those who have not had this privilege must take the resultant insight on the testimony of those who have.[11] The trouble with this is that philosophy, when it rests on evidence of this kind, abandons its claim to being a rational inquiry.

GOD-REALITY IS ALL-GOOD

Finally, according to Augustine, God is all-good. This, too, is a basically Platonic thesis, but, once again, because of Augustine's Christian orientation this general metaphysical position underwent a very different development in his hands. Though the concept of the goodness of God is the core of Augustine's account of ultimate reality, it would be difficult to find any formal arguments to support his thesis. That to exist is good, and that the most real thing of all will be most good, seemed to Augustine self-evident.

> Truly the very fact of existing is by some natural spell so pleasant, that even the wretched are, for no other reason, unwilling to perish; and, when they feel that they are wretched, wish not that they themselves be annihilated, but that their misery be so. . . . Is it not obvious . . . how nature shrinks from annihilation? . . . What! do not even all irrational animals . . . from the huge dragons down to the least worms, all testify that they wish to exist, and therefore shun death by every movement in their power? Nay, the very plants and shrubs . . . do not they all seek, in their own fashion, to conserve their existence, by rooting themselves more and more deeply in the earth, that so they may draw nourishment, and throw out healthy branches towards the sky?[q]

10 "It is a great and very rare thing for a man, after he has contemplated the whole creation, corporeal and incorporeal, and has discerned its mutability, to pass beyond it, and, by the continued soaring of his mind, to attain to the unchangeable substance of God, and, in that height of contemplation, to learn from God Himself. . . . But since the mind itself, though naturally capable of reason and intelligence, is disabled by besotting and inveterate vices . . . even from tolerating His unchangeable light, until it has been gradually healed, and renewed, and made capable of such felicity, it had, in the first place, to be impregnated with faith, and so purified"—*City of God* (Dods), xi, 2.

11 Of course, these privileged ones—poets, saints, and mystics—can always reply as Turner did to a lady who complained that she had never seen a sunset that looked like that in one of his paintings: "But don't you wish you had!"

That reality is supremely good has been held by many non-Christian meta-physicians, including Plato and Aristotle, who argued that the real is the end all things seek and in which they attain their final satisfaction. But to talk about the "goodness of God" is quite different from talking about the "goodness of reality." For one thing, since it was not knowledge but security that Augustine chiefly sought, the reality that satisfied his deepest desire was peace. God, he said,

> . . . is the fountain of our happiness, He the end of all our desires. . . . We tend towards Him by love, that we may rest in Him, and find out blessedness by attaining that end. For our good, about which philosophers have so keenly contended, is nothing else than to be united to God. . . .
>
> The blessedness which an intelligent being desires as its legitimate object results from a combination of these two things, namely, that it uninterruptedly enjoy the unchangeable good, which is God; and that it be delivered from all dubiety, and know certainly that it shall eternally abide in the same enjoyment. . . .
>
> And thus we may say of peace, as we have said of eternal life, that it is the end of our good.[r]

This is, of course, merely a reflection of Augustine's own deepest needs and those of his culture. If the "peace of God" did not dominate Plato's account of reality, it was because Plato was more interested in social and epistemological problems and felt more secure in his environment.

A more fundamental difference results from the fact that Augustine was not content to say merely that reality is good *for* men; it is good *to* them. This addition distinguishes the Christian and religious world view from the classical and fundamentally secular world view. Aristotle, for instance, explicitly argued that a perfect being would not be concerned about man: God would not be perfect if He cared about us. And clearly Aristotle himself felt no need for God's love. Augustine, for his part, rested both on Scripture—"for God so loved the world . . ."—and on his own felt need for a loving Father's care and protection.

Providence, Evil, and Free Will

To say that reality is good to men is to say that it is provident. Such a creator god as Augustine himself experienced and as biblical tradition described will certainly not only wish to look out for His creatures; He will also find the means to do so. Augustine's emphasis on providence reflects the sense of uncertainty and insecurity that, as we have already seen, was a part of the new cultural pattern, but it must be said that he carried his sense of God's constant concern to extraordinary lengths. He wrote that even as an infant, "Thy merciful comforts sustained me. Thus it was that the comforts of a woman's milk entertained me; for neither my mother nor my nurses filled their own breasts, but Thou by them didst give me the nourishment of infancy according to Thy ordinance and that bounty of Thine which underlieth all things."[s]

So it was throughout his life. When he left Africa for Italy, he thought he was going in order to secure a more profitable teaching post. Looking back in later years, however, he could see that his so-called "decision" was but a step in the working out of God's plan for his salvation. In other words, the decision to go to Italy was not his; it was God's.

> Thou dealest with me, therefore, that I should be persuaded to go to Rome, and teach there rather what I was then teaching at Carthage. And how I was persuaded to do this, I will not fail to confess unto Thee; for in this also the profoundest workings of Thy wisdom, and Thy ever present mercy [toward us], must be pondered and avowed. . . .
>
> But the cause of my going thence and going thither, Thou, O God knewest, yet revealed it not, either to me or to my mother, who grievously lamented my journey.[t]

There is no doubt that his sense of God's constant providential care gave Augustine the assurance he so greatly desired. Probably one reason for the popular success of Christianity as compared with Stoicism and Neoplatonism was precisely the fact that the notion of a loving father made the workings of providence so vivid and concrete.

But, as we have seen, along with this description of God as a benign father, Augustine made a metaphysical analysis of the Deity in terms of concepts similar to, and in some cases derived from, those of Greek philosophy. Can these two points of view be fused? Consider the problem of evil, for which Augustine had found a Neoplatonic solution. Now, the problem of evil is closely connected with the idea of providence, for if the world is watched over by an infinitely powerful and loving Father, how can evil befall any part of it?

Augustine's philosophical answer to this puzzle was made in terms of the Neoplatonic identification of goodness with reality. Everything, according to this view, is good to just the extent that it is real. God, being supremely real, is supremely good. God's creatures, being in varying degrees less real than God, are in corresponding degrees less good. Their so-called evil is simply the absence of goodness and reality; it is the inevitable consequence of their status as creatures.

If this conception seems paradoxical (and there is much about it that *is* paradoxical), it has some sanction in ordinary English usage. When a watch, for instance, is too slow, we may talk about its "failure" to keep time, and we may attribute this failure either to the incompetence of the workman who made it or to some weakness in the materials of which it is made. In a word, on occasion we attribute evil to something negative (incompetence, deficiency), not to something positive. However, this is not the place to evaluate the Neoplatonic solution to the problem of evil. Rather, we must ask here, "How does this abstract, metaphysical conception comport with the more popular and more appealing notion of a loving father?"

Let us return for a moment to Augustine's journey to Italy and his mother's subsequent distress. Was the journey really a misfortune, as she supposed? Not at all; it only seemed so because she did not know what God intended the journey to produce. It is as if an extremely naïve person watching a surgical operation were to exclaim at the doctor's brutality, not understanding that his use of the knife was calculated to restore the patient to health. The only evil in this case is the ignorance of the person making the judgment. This is precisely the line Augustine took about the nature of evil when he was thinking of God as a wise and loving father.

Thus, for instance, "some heretics" (Augustine meant the Manichees, of course) refuse to acknowledge the omnipotence of God

> . . . because there are, forsooth, many things, such as fire, frost, wild beasts, and so forth, which do not suit but injure this thin-blooded and frail mortality of our flesh. . . . They do not consider how admirable these things are in their own places, how excellent in their own natures, how beautifully adjusted to the rest of creation, and how much grace they contribute to the universe by their own contributions as to a commonwealth; and how serviceable they are even to ourselves, if we use them with a knowledge of their fit adaptations,—so that even poisons, which are destructive when used injudiciously, become wholesome and medicinal when used in conformity with their qualities and design. . . . And thus divine providence admonishes us not foolishly to vituperate things, but to investigate their utility with care; and, where our mental capacity or infirmity is at fault, to believe that there is a utility, though hidden, as we have experienced that there were other things which we all but failed to discover. For this concealment of the use of things is itself either an exercise of our humility or a levelling of our pride; for no nature at all is evil, and this is a name for nothing but the want of good.[u]

It is easy to see that this is very different from the Neoplatonic explanation of evil. From Augustine's point of view, evil is not a metaphysical deficiency (that is, a lack of reality) in the thing itself; it results from a deficiency in *us*, specifically, our lack of knowledge. A plague, a famine, a surgical operation, or a slow watch is not really bad; it only seems so to our shortsighted minds. The loss of life entailed by the plague and the loss of time entailed by the watch are really goods, as we would see if we could but fathom God's great plan. The loss of life in the plague is designed, it may be, to serve as a warning to us to repent before it is too late. The slow watch, perhaps, prevents our catching a train destined to be wrecked and so preserves us for future salvation. The advantage of Augustine's explanation of evil is obvious. Once his initial premise is granted, a little ingenuity can make any conceivable disaster seem good. But, though this makes it attractive to the masses, the explanation is philosophically unsatisfactory, for it rests on an appeal to ignorance: "If we but knew enough, we would see that everything is really all right."

There is yet another point with regard to the nature of evil at which the idea of providence and Neoplatonism fail to fuse. Since, from the Neoplatonic point of view, reality is good and immutable, evil can be defined as mutability. When Augustine was thinking metaphysically he came very close to saying just this; but, of course, from a religious point of view, evil is quite different from mere change, and some change (for example, conversion), far from being evil, is very good.

These two points of view are almost hopelessly mixed up in Augustine's thought, as the following passage shows:

> There is no unchangeable good but the one, true, blessed God; . . . the things which He made are indeed good . . . , yet mutable because made not out of Him, but out of nothing. . . .
> Indeed evil had never been, had not the mutable nature—mutable, though good, and created by the most high God and immutable Good, who created all things good—brought evil upon itself by sin. And this . . . is itself proof that its nature was originally good. . . . For as blindness is a vice of the eye, and this very fact indicates that the eye was created to see the light, and as, consequently, vice itself proves that the eye is more excellent than the other members, because it is capable of light (for on no other supposition would it be a vice of the eye to want light), so the nature which once enjoyed God teaches, even by its very vice, that it was created the best of all, since it is now miserable because it does not enjoy God.[v]

But the "vice" of the eye, which is merely a failure to see, is quite different from the vice of a sinful and perverted human soul, which, as will be seen later, Augustine held to be a positive evil. The latter cannot be adequately described as mere deficiency of some kind.

The problem of reconciling the notion of a loving father with a Neoplatonic conception of ultimate reality is not the only difficulty in which Augustine's conception of providence is entangled. To say that God is provident means that He is a knower and a doer. To add that God is infinite is to say that He knows all and does all. How are His infinite knowledge and activity compatible with man's free will? Ordinarily, for instance, we would credit Augustine with the decision to go to Rome. But if God sent him, how can Augustine be said to have decided? And how can he be given the credit (or the blame, as the case may be) for what occurred?

Augustine, of course, was not unaware of this problem. He sought to distinguish between divine foreknowledge and fate, and he held that only the latter is irreconcilable with human freedom:

In his book on divination, [Cicero] in his own person most openly opposes the doctrine of the prescience of future things. But all this he seems to do in order that he may not grant the doctrine of fate, and by so doing destroy free will. For he thinks that, the knowledge of future things being once conceded, fate follows as so necessary a consequence that it cannot be denied. . . .

What is it . . . that Cicero feared in the prescience of future things? Doubtless it was this,—that if all future things have been foreknown, they will happen in the order in which they have been foreknown; and if they come to pass in this order, there is a certain order of things foreknown by God; and if a certain order of things, then a certain order of causes, for nothing can happen which is not preceded by some efficient cause. But if there is a certain order of causes according to which everything happens which does happen, then by fate, says he, all things happen which do happen. But if this be so, then is there nothing in our own power, and there is no such thing as freedom of will; and if we grant that, says he, the whole economy of human life is subverted. In vain are laws enacted. In vain are reproaches, praises, chidings, exhortations had recourse to; and there is no justice whatever in the appointment of rewards for the good, and punishments for the wicked. And that consequences so disgraceful, and absurd, and pernicious to humanity may not follow, Cicero chooses to reject the foreknowledge of future things. [Holding] either that something is in our own power, or that there is fore-knowledge . . . of those two [he] chose the freedom of the will, to confirm which he denied the foreknowledge of future things; and thus, wishing to make men free, he makes them sacrilegious. But the religious mind chooses both, confesses both, and maintains both by the faith of piety. But how so? says Cicero; for the knowledge of future things being granted, there follows a chain of consequences which ends in this, that there can be nothing depending on our own free wills. . . .

Now, against the sacrilegious and impious darings of reason, we assert both that God knows all things before they come to pass, and that we do by our free will whatsoever we know and feel to be done by us only because we will it. But that all things come to pass by fate, we do not say; nay we affirm that nothing comes to pass by fate; for we demonstrate that the name of fate, as it is wont to be used by those who speak of fate, meaning thereby the position of the stars at the time of each one's conception or birth, is an unmeaning word, for astrology itself is a delusion. . . . It does not follow that, though there is for God a certain order of all causes, there must therefore be nothing depending on the free exercise of our own wills, for our wills themselves are included in that order of causes which is certain to God, and is embraced by His foreknowledge, for human wills are also causes of human actions; and He who foreknew all the causes of things would certainly among those causes not have been ignorant of our wills. . . . Wherefore our wills also have just so much power as God willed and foreknew that they should have; and therefore whatever power they have, they have it within most certain limits; and whatever they are to do, they are most assuredly to do, for He whose foreknowledge is infallible foreknew that they would have the power to do it, and would do it. . . .

It is not the case, therefore, that because God foreknew what would be in the power of our wills, there is for that reason nothing in the power of our wills. For He who foreknew this did not foreknow nothing. Moreover, if He who foreknew what would be in the power of our wills did not foreknow nothing, but something, assuredly, even though He did foreknow, there is something in the power of our wills. Therefore we are by no means compelled, either, retaining the prescience of God, to take away the freedom of the will, or, retaining the freedom of the will, to deny that He is prescient of future things, which is impious. But we embrace both. We faithfully and sincerely confess both. The former, that we may believe well; the latter, that we may live well. . . . Consequently, it is not in vain that laws are enacted, and that reproaches, exhortations, praises, and vituperations are had recourse to; for these also He foreknew, and they are of great avail, even as great as He foreknew that they would be of. Prayers, also, are of avail to procure those things which He foreknew that He would grant to those who offered them; and with justice have rewards been appointed for good deeds, and punishments for sins. For a man does not therefore sin because God foreknew that he would sin. Nay, it cannot be doubted but that it is the man himself who sins when he does sin, because He, whose foreknowledge is infallible, foreknew not that fate, or fortune, or something else would sin, but that the man himself would sin, who, if he wills not, sins not. But if he shall not will to sin, even this did God foreknow.[w]

What can be said of this argument? Clearly, it avoids rather than resolves the issue. There are two different criticisms that can be leveled at Augustine.

(1) *The fact that God knows everything that is going to happen means that man is not free to choose what he does.* To this Augustine replied that God does indeed know everything that is going to happen, but not *before* it happens. To say that He knows it before it happens is to confuse God's nontemporal eternal knowing with our before-and-after temporal knowing. It is true that if I, a finite creature, *know* (not just guess) that on such-and-such a day you will do so-and-so, you cannot be said to be free to do something else. But this is the case only because my knowledge is of a future event before it happens. These distinctions, Augustine held, are irrelevant to the infinite knowledge of a divine creator, who holds all the past and all the future in an eternal present. Whether we accept this defense depends, of course, on whether we regard "eternity" and "eternal knowing" as intelligible concepts.

(2) *The fact that God does everything means that man does nothing.* To this Augustine replied that God chooses to work through human wills. Things are not "fated"; except for miracles (which are direct divine interventions),[12] God's plan unfolds in a regular, orderly way and encompasses human choices, decisions, and acts, which are all a part of the universal order of nature.

Unfortunately for Augustine, this reply does not really resolve the puzzle

---

12 See pp. 132–33, where even this exception is qualified.

about moral responsibility. Responsibility depends on human initiative. Therefore it is not enough for Augustine to reply that God works *through* us, for it is still God who acts. Augustine, however, disguised this from himself by making an irrelevant attack on the notion of fate. It was easy for him to show that fate and responsibility are incompatible and that divine causality and fate are quite different. These two propositions do not, however, give the conclusion triumphantly asserted by Augustine—that divine causality and responsibility are compatible. From the facts that A is incompatible with B and that B is different from C, it does not follow that A and C are necessarily compatible.

The Basic Conflict in Augustine's Account of God

Thus Augustine's difficulties with the idea of divine providence are another example of the basic conflict in his account of God's nature and of his inability to reconcile the conflicting strains that were competing in his mind. On the one hand, Augustine had a metaphysical outlook basically similar to Plato's that, however diluted by mysticism and by his version of Neoplatonism, remained in some major respects rational and Greek. From this point of view it was natural for him to talk of "reality," not of "God," and the properties of this reality were immutability, perfection, goodness, truth. On the other hand, there was a religious strain in Augustine's thought, derived from the canonical writings and, above all, from his great experience in the garden in Milan. From this viewpoint it was natural for him to talk of "God" rather than of "reality," and His important properties were fatherhood, loving-kindness, mercy—in a word, providence.

That these two strains are not completely antithetical is obvious. As has already been said, they overlap at numerous points: in the notion of goodness, in which both the ultimate reality of metaphysics and the God of religion share, and in the belief that God-reality, whatever else it is, is that final end at which all things consciously or unconsciously aim. Such similarities as these, and the fact that a tinge of Neoplatonism had already been introduced into the canonical writings by the author of the Fourth Gospel, probably explain Augustine's failure to see the great difference between the abstractions of metaphysics, reached by a more or less rational analysis, and the Person imaged by religious piety or discovered in religious intuition. For Augustine, God was both ultimate reality and a personality in active contact with humankind.

But what is an infinite personality? For instance, all the persons we know anything about interact socially with other persons, and social interaction entails the idea of some sort of restriction or limitation occasioned for each interacting person by the existence of those with whom he interacts. But an infinite person would act, not *inter*act. Here again we see the difficulty of trying to ascertain what God is like by extrapolating from some finite and limited property of which we have experience to the infinite version of this property. Unfortunately, since the "infinite version" of a finite property would not be a *version* of that property but something utterly different from it, this does not help us understand God's nature. Augustine struggled hard to free himself from naïve anthropomorphism, but to just the extent that he succeeded, his idea of God lost its specifically Christian content. It is necessary to conclude, then, that his attempt to connect the personal God of primitive Christianity with the ultimate reality of Greek metaphysics failed.

Augustine's failure does not necessarily mean that his was a mistaken effort. Indeed, the very possibility of there being a Christian theology depends on the possibility of effecting a solution to this problem, for the essence of traditional Christianity is the notion of an infinite personality. Moreover, the problem is not intractable. Aquinas, for instance, showed far greater skill than Augustine in giving rational interpretation to the basic religious insights he and Augustine shared.

But why bother at all, it may be asked, about theology? Why should religious beliefs need intellectual formulation? Certainly, at the level of piety, many saints and simple Christians have "understood" the notion of an infinite personality and acted in its spirit. And over and over again mystics have held that the whole theological enterprise is unnecessary, because it is possible to know the meaning of the Christian truths in a higher way than by reason.

Perhaps the mystics are right. It is safe, however, to predict that theologians will not give up their attempts to find a rational formulation for their faith just because the mystics hold that theology is a vain and chimerical illusion. And even if there were a fundamental conflict between reason and Christianity, it would not follow, of course, that philosophy must be secular. For, at their furthest bounds—as Bradley pointed out[13]—metaphysics and religion touch. We must remember that Christianity is not the only world religion. And if there are religions less philosophical than Christianity, there are also religions that are more philosophical. Indeed, there is a residuum of mystery, impervious to reason, at the very heart of the Christian gospel. The great problem of the Middle Ages was to establish the limits of this mystery, to define its relation to reason. And the great justification of the Church as an institution, as the medieval theologians saw, was that it canalized, controlled, and, as it were, rendered serviceable for public use the passion and the power—and the privacy—of this mystery.

13 See pp. 84–85.

CHAPTER 4

Augustine: The Created Universe

The Two Cities: Heaven and Hell

From God, the omnipotent creator, we now turn to the world He created. The persistent dualism already encountered in Augustine's conception of God appears dramatically in this philosopher's division of creation into two "cities." On the one hand, there is the city of God, the community of saints; on the other, there is the earthly city, the community of lost souls. This neat division of sheep from goats has existed in God's *intent* from all eternity—of the two communities "the one is predestined to reign eternally with God, and the other to suffer eternal punishment with the devil."[a] But here on earth, until such time as the last judgment come, citizens of the two cities are intermixed and entangled in a life that is neither wholly good nor wholly bad. The saved and the damned live side by side, eating from the same dish. Accordingly, what follows is first a brief description of what Augustine had to say about hell and about heaven and then a discussion in more detail of his view of the intermingled state—that is, the space-time world to which the Greek philosophers and scientists devoted their attention.

As regards hell, the Scripture was, as usual, Augustine's starting point. The Bible says, for instance, that the damned will be eternally attacked by both "worm and fire." Is this to be understood literally or symbolically—and if the latter, in what precise sense? In a long and closely reasoned passage[b] Augustine concluded that it is meant both literally—the bodies of the damned suffer eternally the gnawing of worms and the burning of fire—and symbolically, as an indication of the fact that at the same time their souls are tortured by fruitless[1] repentance. This raises problems: Why is the body not finally devoured by the worms or finally consumed by flames? Can the material fire of hell that burns men's material bodies also burn the immaterial devils?

As regards the first question, Augustine held that since we all know of animals, like the salamander, "which by a miracle of the most omnipotent Creator can live in the fire . . . without being consumed," there is no great puzzle. The second question he regarded as more difficult. We cannot doubt (1) that the fires of hell are material, nor (2) that men and devils suffer together in the same fire.[2] Hence, if the devils have no bodies, as seems likely, they must nevertheless in "some wonderful and inevitable way" experience pain in their souls from the bodily fire. About this, as about all other questions to which no clear and understandable answer seems possible, we must remember that after all we see through a glass darkly. "Until that which is perfect is come," Augustine quoted Paul, we shall know only in part.

At the last judgment, just as the bodies of the damned who have died will be raised, reunited with their souls, and dismissed to hell, so the bodies of the saints will be resurrected, reunited with *their* souls, and lifted up to heaven. There they shall dwell in newly "incorruptible bodies," in "perfect peace each with himself and with the other saints." What power of movement these new bodies will possess Augustine had "not the audacity rashly to define [nor] the ability to conceive." However, he held that we can be certain of one thing: Perfect harmony and obedience will replace the strains and stresses to which our divided bodies and souls at present subject themselves. As regards our minds, they, too, will doubtless experience an enlargement of their powers. Much that now escapes us will then be understood, and as the great design now hidden in mystery is revealed to us, "marvellous discoveries . . . shall . . . kindle rational minds in praise of the great Artificer." Above all, though the details are as yet unrevealed to us, we can be sure that a "full, certain, secure, everlasting felicity" awaits us.[c]

---

1 "Fruitless" because repentance serves no useful purpose for one who is eternally damned.
2 This we know because the Scripture explicitly states the words of Christ: "Begone, you accursed people, to the everlasting fire destined from the devil and his angels"—Matt. 25:41.

In marked contrast to the rather crude anthropomorphism of these passages, with their notion of heaven and hell as future (and physical) states, Augustine, demonstrating a duality closely paralleling that in his conception of God, at times reached a far more mature level of thought.[3] When Augustine was thinking metaphysically, he conceived of God as that perfect reality that completes the partial reality and supplements the deficiencies of all created natures. From this point of view, all creatures, just because they are creatures, are in varying degrees incomplete and unreal. The more real any creature is, the better it will understand God, love Him, and find peace in Him. The less real any creature is, the more deficient its knowledge of God and, accordingly, the more it will mistakenly love other things and be pulled in opposite ways. The behavior of all things, from the motions of the planets in their courses to the complicated movements of animals, is an expression of their various loves. Insofar as their loves are false and mistaken, their movements are erratic, nonconsequential, confused; insofar as they manage to achieve a love of God, their love of this absolutely immutable and supreme reality gives stability and constancy, order and regularity, to their movements.

Man's good, like that of the rest of God's creatures, thus lies in right loving. Augustine meant just this by defining virtue as "the order of love." This is one of the extraordinary aphorisms into which occasionally a whole philosophy of life is condensed. If we understood all that this short definition implies, we would very nearly understand everything of consequence in Augustine's view. Virtue is the order of love: When we love the right objects in the right way we are virtuous, and since the only wholly right object is God, virtue merges with religion. When we love God, an order and harmony is introduced into every aspect, every phase, of our life. This order and harmony is peace. Peace is something that we can attain even in this troubled life if we love God enough. Misfortunes, illnesses, acts of injustice, frustrations of ambitions, all will lose their importance and assume their true scale in the light of our love of God and our complete acceptance of His will and His order. When we come to realize that all such things are false loves, they can no longer affect our peace.

From this point of view, heaven is not a future material state; it is a possible, present spiritual state. It is the peace we achieve through the right ordering of our loves; it is the communion with God that comes through loving Him to the exclusion of everything else. Similarly, hell is not a place of fire and brimstone to be feared after death; it is simply the separation from God that results from our loving other things more than we love Him. Hell is disorder of loves and expresses itself in the violence of our passions, the conflict of our purposes, the frustration of our desires, and confused and hectic living. Hell is taking our petty ambitions and their defeats seriously; hell is trying to keep up with the Joneses; hell is, above all, that conflict within the will that Augustine himself so vividly experienced, that he diagnosed with psychological penetration, and that he traced

3 See pp. 84–85.

to the necessary deficiency of all created things. Heaven is a firm, unified will—an order of our loves; hell is a thwarted, divided will—a disorder of our loves. This great conception, the logical outcome of Augustine's metaphysics, is a long way, certainly, from the literal heaven and hell of pearly gates and eternal fire to which Augustine also clung.

The Earthly Pilgrimage

Augustine used but two terms ("heavenly city" and "earthly city") to designate three states of affairs—blessedness, damnation, and the earthly pilgrimage. Hence, some of the time "earthly city" means the hell to which sinners will be committed after the last judgment; some of the time it means the world in which we presently live (that is, the world before the last judgment)—"a society of mortals spread abroad through the earth." The two cities are at present "intermingled and entangled in this world" and will remain so until they are finally sorted out at the last judgment.

Life in this intermingled and entangled state is a paradoxical drama: The actors live through their parts without having rehearsed them and so do not know how or when the play will end, nor who is the hero and who the villain. Nevertheless, the play is no impromptu performance; the author, who is also, curiously, the players' sole audience, holds the book, and every line is faithfully spoken just as it was written. This analogy can be carried a step further: The author is not only author but also stage designer and, indeed, architect of the theater, and since his play is the only play and this is its only performance, we can be sure that the theater itself was designed with the particular play in mind. Thus, in this intermingled earthly life it is necessary to consider, first, man—the actor, his actions, and the drama of his salvation; second, the physical world—the theater designed for his performance.

Man

Augustine's view of man and of man's place in the universal scheme was determined by two main considerations: first, his conception of God, which was formed of the diverse factors already examined; second, reflection on his own life and experience. What kind of creature must man be if he was created by the Deity of Augustine's conviction? This is a purely analytical inquiry; it involves simply carrying to their logical conclusions the implications of omnipotence, omniscience, and the other qualities attributed to God. Unfortunately, the conclusions Augustine reached in this way did not correspond at every point to the data of introspection. Hence a deep dichotomy appears in his view of man, corresponding to that which has already been examined in his view of God. Moreover, the problems we have encountered in his conception of God carried over into his account of man and served to increase his difficulties.

THE HUMAN PREDICAMENT

In the long centuries of the collapse of classical culture, the idea of there being a "human predicament" gradually emerged. It reflected the sense of insecurity and the pessimism with which man had come to look at his world. Augustine fully shared this mood. He never tired of enumerating the miseries of this life: the dangers by land and by sea, by day and by night; plague, famine, slaughter, bloodshed, social and civil war—"if I attempted to give an adequate description of these manifold disasters, . . . what limit could I set?" Nothing seemed to him more obvious than the misery of the human situation. "Let every one, then, who thinks with pain on all these great evils, so horrible, so ruthless, acknowledge that this is misery. And if any one either endures or thinks of them without mental pain, this is a more miserable plight still, for he thinks himself happy because he has lost human feeling."ᵈ Here at least, in Augustine's sense of the human predicament, the logic of theology and the secret findings of the heart were in perfect accord. From the one side, the logic of divine omnipotence-perfection forced him to debase man, utterly, for if man has any rightful claims, if he possesses any intrinsic value, God's complete preeminence is destroyed. From the other side, when he looked within his own heart, he found that "Thou didst set me face to face with myself, that I might behold how foul I was, and how crooked and sordid, bespotted and ulcerous."ᵉ

It was clear to Augustine that he could do nothing to extricate himself from this terrible situation. His sense of his own helplessness was one of the most vivid facts of his experience. He had struggled for years to lead a good life, but all in vain. When salvation finally occurred, it was none of his doing; it was something that came to him, a gift of God. A voice spoke in the sunlight and his whole world was changed. The corrupt, vitiated, and diseased will that had stubbornly refused to turn—even after Augustine was intellectually convinced that it must—was turned for him by the direct intervention of God. Conversion was something that happened to him, an event to which he contributed nothing. It was simply a part of the role that God had written for him, a particular actor in the cosmic drama.

These facts of personal experience were in complete accord, of course, with Augustine's belief in God's omnipotence and perfection. If Augustine had been able to change himself and had done so, he would have had himself to thank, not God; it would have been his goodness and power, not God's, that was manifest.[4]

---

4 "Where is he who, reflecting upon his own infirmity dares to ascribe his chastity and innocency to his own strength, so that he should love Thee for less, as if he had been in less need of Thy mercy . . . ?"—*Confessions* (Pilkington), II, vii, 15.

Yet despite his sense of incapacity, Augustine felt responsible for his acts. The sinful deeds, the criminal lusts were his even though he was powerless to avoid them. Theological considerations reinforced this feeling of responsibility. For if the acts in question were not his but God's, the pain he suffered for them would be an act of vicious tyranny, not a just punishment; and relief from these pains, when it finally came, would be only long delayed justice, not the act of divine mercy Augustine held it to be.

Here, then, the old puzzles about the reality of sin and the possibility of free will reappear. Augustine had to try to steer a subtle course between the Manichees on the one hand and the Pelagians[5] on the other, both of whom he thought condemned to outer darkness. He had to be true both to the orthodox account of God and to the facts of his own experience. And to make matters more difficult, the facts of his own experience were highly paradoxical: He felt a responsibility for the sinful acts that he felt incapable of avoiding. How could this be?

Augustine decided that he was helpless because his will was diseased and that (following Paul[6]) this was an inheritance from Adam, our first father. But why did Adam sin? Or rather, why did God permit Adam to sin? God, Augustine insisted, had He so chosen, could have created Adam incapable of sin. Foreknowing that Adam would succumb to temptation and that his sin would be inherited by us all, God nevertheless chose to create him with this grave limitation. Why? Augustine concluded that it was a greater demonstration of God's power and glory to create a sinful man and then to use this creature as an instrument of His larger purpose than it would have been to create a sinless man.

This is not easy to understand. To begin with, how could God have created a sinless man? Such a creature would not have been a *man*. This is not just a quibble over the definition of "man." Augustine had already defined sin as a mark of imperfection and deficiency. "I inquired what iniquity was, and ascertained it not to be a substance,[7] but a perversion of the will, bent aside from Thee, O God, the Supreme Substance."[f] A sinless being, therefore, would have to be wholly real, hence not a creature at all. As the shadow of the real (in Platonic terms), as an emanation from reality (in Neoplatonic terms), as God's creature (in religious terms), the world is inevitably less than real. A creature, just because it is a creature, cannot be perfect and must therefore contain *some* evil. Here is another case in which the Neoplatonic metaphysical scheme and the requirements of religion are irreconcilable. A sure sign of this is the fact that Augustine had to fall back on talk about God's "inscrutable" reason for creating sinful man.[8]

---

5 See pp. 65–69.
6 See p. 41.
7 [This he had held when he was a Manichee—AUTHOR.]
8 Occasionally, when he was thinking philosophically, Augustine recognized that God did not have an option—that He could not have created a sinless man. But when he was thinking of God as an omnipotent father, it seemed to him necessary to insist on God's complete freedom of choice.

In any case, whatever God *might* have done, He did create man as a limited being, whose very nature dooms him to sin. Man, that is to say, shares in the character of all created things: Because they have all been made out of nothing, they are all inevitably deficient in some respect. In a clock this deficiency may show up as a tendency to lose time or to wear out quickly; in man it shows up as sin. Sin, in fact, is simply the kind of evil that results from a deficient will.

AUGUSTINE'S ACCOUNT OF SIN

We cannot ask, therefore, how evil entered the world, for evil has always been in the world. As a creature made out of nothing, the world lacks perfection; so, evil being privation, the world is necessarily evil. We can, however, ask how sin, namely, that special form of evil connected with a self-conscious will, came into the world. Naturally, Augustine's answer to this question was based on the account in Genesis. It is written there that Adam was tempted by Satan and ate the forbidden fruit. Who is Satan? He is the chief of those fallen angels whose present function in the cosmic scheme is to plague mankind (under the strict supervision of the Deity, of course). Our search for the causes of our present predicament requires us, therefore, to ask why Satan and the other demons fell. It is important to remember that asking why Satan fell is exactly like asking why Hamlet delayed: According to Augustine, the *ultimate* explanation of the behavior of Satan and of Adam and Eve is that God had assigned them these several roles in the cosmic drama.

> In the beginning [God] created the world full of all visible and intelligible beings, among which He created nothing better than those spirits whom He endowed with intelligence, and made capable of contemplating and enjoying Him. . . . It is He who gave to this intellectual nature free will of such a kind, that if he wished to forsake God his blessedness, misery should forthwith result. It is He who, when He foreknew that certain angels would in their pride desire to suffice for their own blessedness, and would forsake their great good, did not deprive them of this power, deeming it to be more befitting His power and goodness to bring good out of evil than to prevent the evil from coming into existence. . . .
>
> While some [angels] stedfastly continued in that which was the common good of all, namely, in God Himself, and in His eternity, truth, and love; others, being enamoured rather of their own power, as if they could be their own good, lapsed to this private good of their own, from that higher and beatific good which was common to all, and, bartering the lofty dignity of eternity for the inflation of pride, the most assured verity for the slyness of vanity, uniting love for factious partisanship, they became proud, deceived, envious. . . .
>
> If the further question be asked, What was the efficient cause of [the latter's] evil will? there is none. For what is it which makes the will bad,

when it is the will itself which makes the action bad? And consequently the bad will is the cause of the bad action, but nothing is the efficient cause of the bad will. For if anything is the cause, this thing either has or has not a will. If it has, the will is either good or bad. If good, who is so left to himself as to say that a good will makes a will bad? For in this case a good will would be the cause of sin; a most absurd supposition. On the other hand, if this hypothetical thing has a bad will, I wish to know what made it so; and that we may not go on for ever, I ask at once, what made the *first* evil will bad? . . . The only thing that can be suggested in reply is, that something which itself had no will, made the will evil. I ask, then, whether this thing was superior, inferior, or equal to it? If superior, then it is better. How, then, has it no will, and not rather a good will? The same reasoning applies if it was equal; for so long as two things have equally a good will, the one cannot produce in the other an evil will. Then remains the supposition that that which corrupted the will of the angelic nature which first sinned, was itself an inferior thing without a will. But that thing, be it of the lowest and most earthly kind, is certainly itself good, since it is a nature and being, with a form and rank of its own in its own kind and order. How, then, can a good thing be the efficient cause of an evil will? How, I say, can good be the cause of evil? For when the will abandons what is above itself, and turns to what is lower, it becomes evil—not because that is evil to which it turns, but because the turning itself is wicked. Therefore it is not an inferior thing which has made the will evil, but it is itself which has become so by wickedly and inordinately desiring an inferior thing. . . .

Let no one, therefore, look for an efficient cause of the evil will; for it is not efficient, but deficient, as the will itself is not an effecting of something, but a defect. For defection from that which supremely is, to that which has less of being,—this is to begin to have an evil will. Now, to seek to discover the causes of these defections,—causes, as I have said, not efficient, but deficient,—is as if some one sought to see darkness, or hear silence. Yet both of these are known by us, and the former by means only of the eye, the latter only by the ear; but not by their positive actuality, but by their want of it. . . .

The nature of God can never, nowhere, nowise be defective, [but] natures made of nothing can. These latter, however, the more being they have, and the more good they do (for then they do something positive), the more they have efficient causes; but in so far as they are defective in being, and consequently do evil (for then what is their work but vanity?), they have deficient causes. . . .

Man, . . . whose nature was to be a mean between the angelic and bestial, He created in such sort, that if he remained in subjection to His Creator as his rightful Lord, and piously kept His commandments, he should pass into the company of the angels, and obtain, without the intervention of death, a blessed and endless immortality; but if he offended the Lord his God by a proud and disobedient use of his free will, he should become subject to death, and live as the beasts do,—the slave of appetite, and doomed to eternal punishment after death.[g]

In other words, since all evil is privation, neither the evil will of angels nor the evil will of man has an efficient cause. Therefore, were it not for the need of accommodating our account to that given in Genesis, it would be unnecessary to conceive of any special temptation of our first parents by Satan. Augustine emphasized the fact that Adam and Eve would not have yielded to Satan's importunings had their wills not *already* been corrupt (that is, deficient). Thus, though Satan in a sense caused man's fall, in a more fundamental sense our fall, like his, was caused simply by a primary deficiency in the makeup of our will.

> Our first parents fell into open disobedience because already they were secretly corrupted; for the evil act had never been done had not an evil will preceded it. And what is the origin of our evil will but pride? For "pride is the beginning of sin." And what is pride but the craving for undue exaltation? And this is undue exaltation, when the soul abandons Him to whom it ought to cleave as its end, and becomes a kind of end to itself. This happens when it becomes its own satisfaction. And it does so when it falls away from that unchangeable good which ought to satisfy it more than itself. This falling away is spontaneous; for if the will had remained stedfast in the love of that higher and changeless good by which it was illumined to intelligence and kindled into love, it would not have turned away to find satisfaction in itself, and so become frigid and benighted; the woman would not have believed the serpent spoke the truth, nor would the man have preferred the request of his wife to the command of God. . . . The wicked deed, then,—that is to say, the transgression of eating the forbidden fruit,—was committed by persons who were already wicked. That "evil fruit" could be brought forth only by a "corrupt tree." But that the tree was evil was not the result of nature; for certainly it could become so only by the vice of the will, and vice is contrary to nature. Now, nature could not have been depraved by vice had it not been made out of nothing. Consequently, that it is a nature, this is because it is made by God; but that it falls away from Him, this is because it is made out of nothing. But man did not so fall away as to become absolutely nothing; but being turned towards himself, his being became more contracted than it was when he clave to Him who supremely is. Accordingly, to exist in himself, that is, to be his own satisfaction after abandoning God, is not quite to become a nonentity, but to approximate to that. . . .
>
> The devil, then, would not have ensnared man in the open and manifest sin of doing what God had forbidden, had man not already begun to live for himself.[h]

Though the distinction between an efficient and a deficient cause is critical to Augustine's argument, it hardly survives a moment's analysis. We might indeed say that an illness was caused by a man's weakened condition (as a result, perhaps, of malnutrition), and some people might be disposed to think of this weakened condition as a deficient cause. But even in his weakened condition the man would not have come down with the illness if a virus had not been present. And, in any case, "weakened condition" is only the name for a particular set of bodily conditions that themselves have positive causes. Further, we attribute causality to this weakened condition rather than to the virus only because the virus does not normally cause illness, or at least not so serious an illness. Hence, on analysis, we find that we are dealing not with a deficient, in contrast to an efficient, cause, but with a very complex set of circumstances—including both the bodily conditions loosely called a "weakened condition" and a virus. If we want to talk a "causal" language we shall have to call all these circumstances the cause. Our attention is drawn to one circumstance rather than another merely because it is "exceptional," that is, statistically unusual. Obviously, nothing here is of the slightest use to Augustine in his effort to designate the will as a deficient cause that does not itself have a cause.

There are still more difficulties in Augustine's argument. Even supposing the concept of deficient cause to be viable and the human will to be such a cause, most of us will find it impossible to see why man is responsible for what occurs as a result of this corrupt will. Just as we would attribute responsibility for the man's illness to whoever was responsible for the malnutrition that caused it, we would surely assign responsibility for man's evil acts to whoever brought about the grave deficiency in the human will—and this is God, on Augustine's own account. Yet Augustine ignored all such considerations and blamed man wholly for what happens as a result of his deficient will:

> Because the sin was a despising of the authority of God, . . . God in His justice abandoned [man] to himself, not to live in the absolute independence he affected, but instead of the liberty he desired, to live dissatisfied with himself in a hard and miserable bondage to him to whom by sinning he had yielded himself. . . . Whoever thinks such punishment either excessive or unjust shows his inability to measure the great iniquity of sinning where sin might so easily have been avoided. . . .
>
> That the whole human race has been condemned in its first origin, this life itself, if life it is to be called, bears witness by the host of cruel ills with which it is filled. Is not this proved by the profound and dreadful ignorance which produces all the errors that enfold the children of Adam, and from which no man can be delivered without toil, pain, and fear? Is it not proved by his love of so many vain and hurtful things, which produces gnawing cares, disquiet, griefs, fears, wild joys, quarrels, law-suits, wars, treasons, angers, hatreds, deceit, flattery, fraud, theft, robbery, perfidy, pride, ambition, envy, murders, parricides, cruelty, ferocity, wickedness, luxury, insolence, impudence, shamelessness, fornications, adulteries, incests, and the numberless uncleannesses and unnatural acts of both sexes, which it is shameful so much as to mention; sacrileges, heresies, blasphemies, perjuries, oppression of the innocent, calumnies, plots, falsehoods, false witnessings, unrighteous judgments, violent deeds, plunderings, and whatever similar wickedness has found its way into the lives of men, though it cannot find its way into the conception of pure minds? These are indeed the crimes of wicked men, yet they spring from that root of error and misplaced love which is born with every son of Adam. . . .

Why is it that we remember with difficulty, and without difficulty forget? learn with difficulty, and without difficulty remain ignorant? are diligent with difficulty, and without difficulty are indolent? Does not this show what vitiated nature inclines and tends to by its own weight, and what succour it needs if it is to be delivered? Inactivity, sloth, laziness, negligence, are vices which shun labour, since labour, though useful, is itself a punishment. . . .

Who can describe, who can conceive the number and severity of the punishments which afflict the human race,—pains which are not only the accompaniment of the wickedness of godless men, but are a part of the human condition and the common misery,—what fear and what grief are caused by bereavement and mourning, by losses and condemnations, by fraud and falsehood, by false suspicions, and all the crimes and wicked deeds of other men? For at their hands we suffer robbery, captivity, chains, imprisonment, exile, torture, mutilation, loss of sight, the violation of chastity to satisfy the lust of the oppressor, and many other dreadful evils. What numberless casualties threaten our bodies from without,—extremes of heat and cold, storms, floods, inundations, lightning, thunder, hail, earthquakes, houses falling; or from the stumbling, or shying, or vice of horses; from countless poisons in fruits, water, air, animals; from the painful or even deadly bites of wild animals; from the madness which a mad dog communicates, so that even the animal which of all others is most gentle and friendly to its own master, becomes an object of intenser fear than a lion or dragon, and the man whom it has by chance infected with this pestilential contagion becomes so rabid, that his parents, wife, children, dread him more than any wild beast! What disasters are suffered by those who travel by land or sea! What man can go out of his own house without being exposed on all hands to unforeseen accidents? Returning home sound in limb, he slips on his own door-step, breaks his leg, and never recovers. . . . Is innocence a sufficient protection against the various assaults of demons? That no man might think so, even baptized infants, who are certainly unsurpassed in innocence, are sometimes so tormented, that God, who permits it, teaches us hereby to bewail the calamities of this life, and to desire the felicity of the life to come. As to bodily diseases, they are so numerous that they cannot all be contained even in medical books. And in very many, or almost all of them, the cures and remedies are themselves tortures, so that men are delivered from a pain that destroys by a cure that pains. . . .

From this hell upon earth there is no escape, save through the grace of the Saviour Christ, our God and Lord.[i]

Let us postpone considering Augustine's account of the redemption in order to examine in a little more detail "this dying life, this living death" we all suffer unless God intervenes to save us.

Though God in His wisdom has devised many punishments to try us, none is as hard to bear as corruption of the will. Sin having corrupted Adam's will, the disease was communicated by him to all his descendants, precisely as children may inherit an infection from their parents. The symptom of this corrupt will is that sense of frustration, helplessness, and sin that Augustine himself so long experienced. Its first sign, in Adam and in ourselves, is the body's disobedience. Before his fall, Adam never desired anything that was not in his power, and he was therefore completely happy. Now, however, we are powerless to control our bodies, which take off on their own accord, humiliate us, and get us into trouble without our being able to control them.[9] The body's disobedience of the mind and will, which are its lawful superiors, is, Augustine held, exactly parallel to the will's disobedience of God, who is its lawful superior. The punishment God designed for disobedient wills is therefore peculiarly fitting.

> If the soul and reason do not themselves obey God, as God has commanded them to serve Him, they have no proper authority over the body and the vices. For what kind of mistress of the body and the vices can that mind be which is ignorant of the true God, and which, instead of being subject to His authority, is prostituted by the corrupting influences of the most vicious demons?[j]

But not only his will lost control over the disobedient body; will is divided against itself. Our will, like Adam's after his fall, is not wholly bad (for if it were it would be absolutely nothing); part of it yearns for the good it has lost and would turn back to this good if it could. But, precisely because it has been corrupted, it is incapable of so turning and must await God's grace. Meanwhile, we all suffer from the kind of division in ourselves that caused Paul's despair— "What I would that do I not; but what I hate that do I"—and issued in Augustine's intensely human prayer, "Lord, make me chaste, but not just yet."[k]

This division of the will does not, of course, mean that

> . . . there are two kinds of minds in us,—one good, the other evil.[10] . . . I it was who willed, I who was unwilling. It was I, even I myself. I neither willed entirely nor was entirely unwilling. Therefore was I at war with myself, and destroyed by myself. And this destruction overtook me against my will, and yet showed not the presence of another mind, but the punishment of mine own . . . the punishment of a more unconfined sin, in that I was a son of Adam.[l]

It follows that "not nature, . . . but vice . . . is contrary to God." Since God made the body, it is good—not perfectly, of course, for like everything else it was created out of nothing, but nevertheless, "in its own kind and degree the flesh is good." In fact, though the corruption of the body—the disease, pain, death that it suffers—is a punishment we now bear, its corruption is a product

---

9 The most notorious example of this rebellion of the body occurs in sexual passion, Augustine thought. This probably explains in part why he regarded the sexual side of life as so monstrous. See *City of God* (Dods), xiv, 16–19, 24, and 26 for a remarkable analysis of sex in the earthly paradise before Adam's fall.

10 [This was the Manichean position, of course—AUTHOR.]

of the initial sin of the soul. "Though from this corruption of the flesh there arise certain incitements to vice, and indeed vicious desires . . . it was not the corruptible flesh that made the soul sinful, but the sinful soul that made the flesh corruptible."[m]

It is easy to see why Augustine adopted this position. Opposed as he now was to Manicheism—indeed, to anything that would give us an excuse to shift the blame for our evil from ourselves—he would not allow us to shift responsibility from ourselves to our bodies. We must not permit ourselves "in our sins and vices to accuse the nature of the flesh to the injury of the Creator." Moreover, according to Augustine, the fact that Christ took on a human body and became man shows that there can be nothing evil in the body per se. One of the lessons the incarnation was designed to teach is that "it is sin which is evil, not the substance of flesh." It is just this that made the position of the Manichees not only wrong but criminally so: God in His mercy gave us this striking demonstration, but the Manichean heretics deliberately ignored it.[11]

Thus it is apparent that Augustine was far from being an extreme ascetic. In contrast to Jerome, who dwelt in the desert and flagellated his body, Augustine demanded only that Christians confine themselves to a simple life and a sober fare. Consequently, it was necessary for him to interpret the radical interim ethic recommended by Jesus in a symbolic fashion.[12] When, for instance, Jesus forbade his disciples to carry purses or to wear shoes, he did not mean for them (or for us) to take this injunction literally. Augustine reasoned that since Jesus and his disciples were poor men ("Thou didst suffer a theft in Thy company: what hadst Thou that the thief might take from?"), it would have been pointless for him to advise his disciples not to carry bags of money. Therefore, "purse" in Jesus' dictum must have been meant, not literally as a bag of money, but allegorically as "wisdom stored up." Similarly, we must understand "shoes" (because they are "dead skins") as "dead unregenerate works," and so on.[n]

In opposition to the rigorous ascetics Augustine went so far as to argue that, since the body is "a part of man's very nature," we ought to care for it. This, of course, should not be construed as meaning that we ought to pamper it, still less that we ought to allow it and its desires to distract us from our true good.

Let us consider Augustine's discussion of food, which is representative of his treatment of all the bodily needs. Since Adam's fall, men have delighted in eating and drinking. Insofar as they succumb to this pleasure and pursue it to the exclusion of their greater good (insofar, for instance, as they choose to eat a hearty meal instead of attending church), they are in danger of eternal torment. On the other hand, it is obvious that we must eat to live. This, indeed, gives us the rule we should follow. To eat for the sake of enjoyment, because of the pleasures

---

11 Augustine, however, found the Pauline epistles awkward, for Paul certainly seemed to hold that the flesh is bad. Since Scripture obviously cannot contradict itself, some elaborate exegesis was necessary.

12 See p. 28.

of taste, is sinful. We should eat only what is necessary for sustenance. But here, God in His wisdom has created a further hazard for us. We might enjoy even the modest minimum necessary to sustain the body. This, as it were, subsidiary pleasure ought to be extirpated if at all possible. How much happier was the lot of pre-Fall Adam, whose desire for food was exactly commensurate with the daily caloric intake necessary for sustenance and who therefore never lusted after food and drink!

> This much hast Thou taught me, that I should bring myself to take food as medicine. But during the time that I am passing from the uneasiness of want to the calmness of satiety, even in the very passage doth that snare of concupiscence lie in wait for me. For the passage itself is pleasure, nor is there any other way of passing thither, whither necessity compels us to pass. And whereas health is the reason of eating and drinking, there joineth itself as an handmaid a perilous delight, which mostly tries to precede it, in order that I may do for her sake what I say I do, or desire to do, for health's sake. Nor have both the same limit; for what is sufficient for health is too little for pleasure. And oftentimes it is doubtful whether it be the necessary care of the body which still asks nourishment, or whether a sensual snare of desire offers its ministry. In this uncertainty does my unhappy soul rejoice, and therein prepares an excuse as a defence, glad that it doth not appear what may be sufficient for the moderation of health, that so under the pretence of health it may conceal the business of pleasure. . . .
>
> Placed, then, in the midst of these temptations, I strive daily against longing for food and drink. For it is not of such a nature as that I am able to resolve to cut it off once for all, and not touch it afterwards, as I was able to do with concubinage.°

Poor Augustine! And what is true of hunger is true of all the other drives:

> There remain the delights of these eyes of my flesh. . . . The eyes delight in fair and varied forms, and bright and pleasing colours. Suffer not these to take possession of my soul; let God rather possess it, He who made these things "very good" indeed; yet is He my good, not these. . . .
>
> In addition to this there is another form of temptation, more complex in its peril. For besides that concupiscence of the flesh which lieth in the gratification of all senses and pleasures, wherein its slaves who "are far from Thee perish," there pertaineth to the soul, through the same senses of the body, a certain vain and curious longing, cloaked under the name of knowledge and learning. . . .ᴾ

Augustine's Ethics

It is clear, given this analysis of the human predicament, that Augustine's ethics will be negative in tone. For the Greeks, ethics was the science of how to be good, and they conceived the good to be attainable by man's own efforts. For Augustine, on the contrary, the good life was attainable only as a gift of God. Moral science, accordingly, consisted not in prescriptions about what to do to attain our good, but in advice about how to avoid getting ourselves into a still deeper hole. For instance, Augustine summed up our "self-regarding" duties, that is, those we have toward ourselves, in the warning that, though we should not think of the body as positively bad, we must be on our guard against treating it as a real good. He thought it much easier to go wrong than right; the safest rule, he held, is to forego all enjoyments and any real cultivation of talents. Though his asceticism may be "moderate" as compared with the position of some of his contemporaries, it is severe by modern—or by Greek—standards.

Next, what about our duties toward others? Just as he rejected extreme asceticism and mortification of the flesh, Augustine rejected the solitary life of the hermit, recognizing the truth of Plato's idea that the life of the wise man must be social. How could the city of God "either take a beginning or be developed, or attain its proper destiny, if the life of the saints were not a social life?" Nevertheless, Augustine had little to say in detail about our social duties. Indeed, his position can be summed up by saying that since we are all together in our miserable condition, and since, moreover, we are all children of one Father, we ought to help one another as much as we can.

In general, Augustine's view of the social life paralleled his evaluation of the body. Just as the body is not bad in itself but, having been corrupted by the sinful will, now torments us, so social life is not bad in itself but, since the Fall, has become a source of trouble by involving us in the "great grievances" of war and ambition that have already been enumerated.

It follows that in this post-Fall world men need the stern discipline of law and authority. Just as the body that once obeyed the will is now in open rebellion and so requires firm discipline, so men can now live a social life only if there exists a ruler with the power to keep rebels and dissenters in order. Doubtless this ruler should, ideally, aim at the welfare of those under him. But, mankind being as corrupt as it is, rulers are only too often criminally selfish. Even so, they ought to be obeyed, because the alternative of civil war is worse than their rule. "Who . . . has not observed with what profound ignorance, . . . and with what superfluity of foolish desires, . . . man comes into this life, so that, were he left to live as he pleased, and to do whatever he pleased, he would plunge into . . . crimes and iniquities?"[q]

Moreover, since God certainly *could* have given men good rulers instead of bad ones, it must be that some divine purpose is being fulfilled by the vicious tyrants who from time to time have reigned as emperors. This purpose is clear: Just as the body has become, by God's decree, a punishment for our sins, so also wicked rulers are a punishment. To revolt against them is therefore to revolt against God.

> We do not attribute the power of giving kingdoms and empires to any
> save to the true God, who . . . gives kingly power on earth both to the pious
> and the impious, as it may please Him, whose good pleasure is always just.
> For though we have said something about the principles which guide His
> administration, in so far as it has seemed good to Him to explain it, neverthe-
> less it is too much for us, and far surpasses our strength, to . . . determine
> the merits of various kingdoms. . . . He who gave power to Marius gave it
> also to Caius Caesar; He who gave it to Augustus gave it also to Nero; He
> also who gave it to the most benignant emperors, the Vespasians, father and
> son, gave it also to the cruel Domitian; . . . He who gave it to the Christian
> Constantine gave it also to the apostate Julian. . . . Manifestly these things
> are ruled and governed by the one God according as He pleases; and if His
> motives are hid, are they therefore unjust?[r]

What is true of bad rulers is also true of bad institutions. Though slavery,
for instance, is undeniably an evil, we should not agitate for its abolition; it was
instituted by God after Adam's fall as a part of the punishment man must suffer
for his sins.

> God . . . did not intend that His rational creature, who was made in His
> image, should have dominion over anything but the irrational creation,—not
> man over man, but man over the beasts. . . . And this is why we do not find
> the word "slave" in any part of Scripture until righteous Noah branded the
> sin of his son with this name. It is a name, therefore, introduced by sin and
> not by nature. . . . The prime cause, then, of slavery is sin, which brings man
> under the dominion of his fellow,—that which does not happen save by the
> judgment of God, with whom is no unrighteousness, and who knows how
> to award fit punishments to every variety of offense. . . . And beyond question
> it is a happier thing to be the slave of a man than of a lust; for even this
> very lust of ruling, to mention no others, lays waste men's hearts with the
> most ruthless dominion. Moreover, when men are subjected to one another
> in a peaceful order, the lowly position does as much good to the servant
> as the proud position does harm to the master. . . . And therefore the apostle
> admonishes slaves to be subject to their masters, and to serve them heartily
> and with good-will, so that, if they cannot be freed by their masters, they
> may themselves make their slavery in some sort free, by serving not in crafty
> fear, but in faithful love, until all unrighteousness pass away, and all princi-
> pality and every human power be brought to nothing, and God be all in all.[s]

In a word, to try to alter or improve existing arrangements implies discontent
with God's program for us. Moreover, such evils as we think we suffer are either
goods in disguise or well-merited punishments. Finally, we must remember that
if the delights of the flesh are inconsequential, so are its pains. "The good man,
although he is a slave, is free; but the bad man, even if he reigns, is a slave,
and that not of one man, but, what is far more grievous, of as many masters
as he has vices."[t]

By urging men to be content with their unhappy lot and to look for their rewards in the other world rather than in this one, Augustine furnished reactionary conservatives and all upholders of the status quo with useful arguments, as well as with the authority of his name. As regards the historical Church, there is, alas, considerable warrant for Marx's gibe that religion is the opium of the people.

It should be clear from these comments that the central feature of Augustine's ethics was his belief that the locus of ethical value is motive rather than accomplishment. Here, of course, his starting point was Jesus' emphasis on the inner life; but Augustine naturally interpreted this simple view in terms of his own experience of a divided will. Hence he concluded that it does not matter how greatly the flesh lusts, providing only that the will itself remains pure and undivided. Even if our body becomes the instrument of another's lust, we remain chaste as long as our will refuses its consent. Thus the Christian virgins who were threatened by the barbarians during the fall of Rome need not have feared for their chastity. It would have been far better, as a matter of fact, for them to endure physical violation than for them to escape it by committing suicide, as some of these women chose to do. Since suicide is always wrong (for "it is unlawful to take the law into our own hands" and thereby anticipate God's timetable for our departure hence), these foolish virgins committed a real sin in order to escape an imaginary one.

> Let this . . . be laid down as an unassailable position, that the virtue which makes the life good has its throne in the soul, . . . and that while the will remains firm and unshaken, nothing that another person does with the body, or upon the body, is any fault of the person who suffers it, so long as he cannot escape it without sin."

Here Augustine was traversing the same field Aristotle had treated in his account of incontinence, and it may be useful briefly to compare the two positions with a view to making clear the change in point of view that Christianity introduced. The first thing that strikes us is that though both Aristotle and Augustine disapproved of incontinence, and though they defined it in similar terms, the tone of the one is quite different from that of the other. Aristotle's dislike of incontinence was rooted in his sense of the dignity of man and in his sense of shame at the sight of someone demeaning himself and his kind. Augustine, too, felt shame, but his was shame at disobedience to the commands of God, not shame at failure to actualize the ideal of man.

Second, Aristotle recognized a point at which temptation (to use Augustine's term) becomes so great that "nobody could resist any longer." At this point, therefore, according to Aristotle, blame disappears. According to Augustine, however, the will ought never to yield and is blamable for doing so regardless of what it is subjected to. Of course, Aristotle, with his confidence in the rationality of man, expected these crucial cases to occur infrequently, whereas Augustine, with his sense of human helplessness, expected them to occur very frequently.

Finally, Aristotle, who was anything but an ascetic, would have characterized as continent many acts that Augustine damned as incontinent. For Aristotle, the man who enjoys music or food or drink was—a man. He who fails to enjoy these things lacked some essential ingredient in human nature. Only the man who enjoys them to excess and chooses them over what he knows to be greater goods was incontinent. For Aristotle, therefore, a good man was incontinent only infrequently; for Augustine, even the best of men could not escape falling daily into many acts of incontinence—yet, paradoxically enough, even so men were always blamable.

Augustine's concentration on motive had still another consequence. It will already have been observed that Augustine did not provide any list of positive duties, whether self-regarding or social. This is explained, of course, by his belief that all activities are trivial, all values are inconsequential, except the one supreme value: getting into a right relation with God. And this consists less in doing specific things than in feeling a certain way about whatever it is we happen to be doing. That is to say, *everything* except the love of God is a snare and a delusion. Insofar as we love things for their own sake, our love dooms us to perdition. Rather, we should love God through them. Thus, if we love light for its own sake or for the sake of the beautiful objects it illumines, we sin damnably. We must learn instead to praise and love God as the author of this good light.

Accordingly, there is nothing in Augustine's work corresponding to Aristotle's detailed analysis of the virtues. This is not merely because Aristotle conceived of morally good acts as "virtues" (that is, dispositions to be cultivated because they are proper to men) whereas Augustine thought of them as "duties" (that is, commands to be obeyed because God has issued them). It is also because Augustine was basically uninterested in conduct. This was due to his belief that, though living morally will not help us greatly, living immorally (which is only too easy) will damn us. Even social duties and good works may, if we are not careful, become a hindrance to our salvation by distracting us from our devotion to God. And, in any case, morality is nothing without religion.

> The virtues which [the soul] seems to itself to possess . . . are rather vices than virtues so long as there is no reference to God in the matter. . . . Some suppose that virtues which have a reference only to themselves, and are desired only on their own account, are yet true and genuine virtues, [but] the fact is that even then they are inflated with pride, and are therefore to be reckoned vices.[v]

For Augustine, in a word, the good was reunion with God from whom, because of Adam's sin, we have become separated. The way back to God was through faith in Jesus—through religion, that is, not through ethics, which is first and foremost concerned with behavior in this world.

The Drama of Salvation

Perhaps enough has been said about man and his feeble efforts to help himself. But we must not forget that his capacities and, indeed, the whole course of his life have been determined by the divine playwright. Since, as was said at the outset, man's role is merely that of an actor who speaks the lines assigned to him, we must now consider the great drama of which his little life is a part. Though there is much in the play about which the playwright has not seen fit to enlighten the actors, they do know that the play is moving toward a tremendous climax, a predestined end. What the actors do not know, and what, of course, they would be supremely interested in knowing, is through which door—to heaven or to hell—each will exit on the curtain line.

This, Augustine held, is a mystery justly hidden from us. One thing, however, we can say: It is possible to make no deductions from the kind of part we seem to have been assigned. Suffering in this life, for instance, is no sure indication of a future relief from pain, nor do good deeds in this life guarantee exemption from hell. For one thing, as we have seen, good deeds do not matter as much as good motives. For another, sinful desire is appallingly hard to eradicate; pride is terribly subtle, and creeps in most secretly. Even those who succeed in leading pious lives are endangered by a natural tendency to take pride in their humility. They please themselves "in Thy good things as though they were their own . . . or as though of their own merits."[w] Even if they recognize that the power to live righteously comes only through God's grace, they congratulate themselves on having been chosen to receive it and so are damned for false pride.

If a man looks within himself and finds nothing but humility and love of God, can he be sure that he is pure? Alas, no. Augustine recognized fifteen centuries before Freud that many of our motives are unconscious:

> My mind, making inquiry into herself concerning her own powers, ventures not readily to credit herself; because that which is already in it is, for the most part, concealed. . . . And no man ought to feel secure in this life, the whole of which is called a temptation, that he, who could be made better from worse, may not also from better be made worse.[x]

No one, therefore, can be certain of salvation. Even those who, like Augustine, have been saved by a special act of divine intervention are not freed from temptations of the flesh. Since relapse is possible at any time, complacency is an acute danger.

Thus our life is desperately hazardous, full of snares; it is irrational in the sense that our past is no clue to our future. We live in suspense up to the moment the play ends. But this is true only because we are ignorant actors. The author of the play knows from the beginning how many will be saved and who they are. When God foresaw that a certain number of angels would fall through prideful disobedience, he determined that a corresponding number of human souls would be redeemed, in order to make up the fixed number of the citizens of the heavenly city and so, as Augustine declared, to "complete the number of the saints."[13]

THE MECHANICS OF SALVATION

Let us now ask how salvation comes to those who are predestined to become citizens of God's city. What, in other words, are the actual mechanics of salvation? The answer to this question, Augustine held, is to be found in the canonical writings. "From this hell upon earth there is no escape, save through the grace of the Saviour Christ, our God and Lord."[y] According to Scripture, Christ became man and suffered on the cross as a sacrifice for our sins.[14] To whom, according to Augustine, was the sacrifice paid? Certainly not to God the Father, as some have maintained, for this suggests a conflict of wills within the Trinity that is quite impossible to allow. Moreover, as Augustine also saw, it involves us in the intolerable thesis that God is wroth with man and has to be bought off by the suffering of an innocent bystander.

Nor can Christ's death be conceived of as a sacrifice paid to the Devil, for the Devil's role in the human drama is purely instrumental. The Devil may *believe* he is fighting God for men's souls, but he is merely another player with a bit part—merely a tool that God uses to work His own ends. The slaughter of Jesus was doubtless precisely the sort of wickedness the Devil would enjoy, but it is ridiculous to suppose that God must sacrifice to him.

Augustine was quite aware of these difficulties. Though he continued to use the traditional biblical language of sacrifice, he developed a novel conception alongside it. Chapter 24 of Book X of the *City of God* is a representative passage. Here Augustine began, characteristically, by declaring that the incarnation is "a great mystery unintelligible to pride." If we set out to lay bare the ultimate purposes of the Deity in sending His only begotten Son to suffer on earth, we are doomed to eternal damnation for our pains. But though we cannot fathom God's final intent, we can at least understand the intermediate purposes by which it was carried out. The Son, then, became man. Why? To demonstrate to us that flesh as such is not evil. Immortal God died on the cross. Why? To show us that death, which may indeed be a punishment for our sins, is not itself a sin. Again, Jesus' death as a common criminal, his humble acceptance of suffering when he might have revealed his godhead and frustrated his proud enemies, shows us how we ought to live and how we ought to die—in piety, humility, and peace. Finally, the fact that God sent His only begotten Son to die for us demonstrates as nothing else could God's great love for us despite our sin.

---

13 In one place, however, Augustine suggested that God might permit this quota to be exceeded.
14 See pp. 40–44.

THE PLAY-WITHIN-A-PLAY

The incarnation, the Passion, and the resurrection are a part of the cosmic drama. In fact, they constitute a play-within-a-play, cunningly contrived to move the actors of the larger play, who, being unaware that the Passion is a play, experience the emotions (or *ought* to experience the emotions) that it was designed by God to evoke in them.[15] Many, it must be confessed, are left unmoved, despite the fact that in the events of his life and death Jesus "called loudly to us . . . crying out by words, deeds, death, life, descent, ascension, crying aloud to us to return to Him."[z] The fact is, of course, that Augustine himself had for many years missed the point of the play-within-a-play. "I did not grasp my Lord Jesus, [did] not grasp the humble one; nor did I know what lesson that infirmity of His would teach us."

Are we then to assume that the playwright is at fault—that the play-within-a-play was poorly written? God forbid. No drama is more skillful, no lesson more obvious, no example more striking. But stubborn, willful pride blinds us to the obvious; arrogant egoism prevents our being moved to respond lovingly to this wonderful example of God's love for us.

Thus, by the drama of the death and resurrection of Jesus, God intended to move our wills, to turn us toward Him and thus permit the process of repentance and conversion to begin with an act of our own initiative. Had He so chosen, of course, God could have saved us by a divine fiat like that by which He created our first parent. But, having created us self-conscious creatures with wills, He preferred to make these wills the instruments of our salvation. It will be seen that this view complements Augustine's doctrine that evil is voluntary. Just as sin consists in wrong choices, so salvation consists in right choices. Of course, our right choices do not help, nor do our wrong choices harm, our omnipotent Father,[16] but salvation begins in that first right choice by which the will turns from false and fleeting goods toward its one true good.

This conception of the redemption is far more enlightened than the primitive notion of bloody sacrifice. Nevertheless, it is not without difficulties. To just the extent that man takes the initiative in the matter of his salvation (however much this may have been contrived and induced by divine plot), he owes his salvation to his own efforts, not to God's mercy. And this, of course, Augustine could only regard as blasphemy. Moreover, from his own personal experience Augustine was sure of man's utter helplessness to take even that first step by himself. The first tiny turning of Augustine's will had come from God in the voice that spoke from sunlight in the garden in Milan.

The old problem thus reappears. If God is all, how can man be anything? Though Augustine repeatedly asserted that "no man acts rightly save by the

---

15 Compare the way in which, in *Hamlet,* the play scene was designed to move the conscience of the king.

16 "God has no need . . . of man's righteousness, . . . whatever right worship is paid to God profits not Him, but man"—*City of God* (Dods), x, 5.

assistance of divine aid," this formula is quite inadequate. It implies that our salvation is a joint enterprise, to which both we and God contribute. But since God's contribution is infinitely great, ours must be infinitely small. The only way to maximize God's mercy and power is to minimize man's initiative.

There was no way for Augustine to extricate himself from this problem without abandoning at least one thesis that he regarded as indispensable. Against the Manichees he wanted to assert human responsibility; against the Pelagians, the need for grace; against them both, the absolute omnipotence of God. He faced different ways at different times. When arguing against the Pelagians, he unconsciously adopted a position hardly distinguishable from that of the Manichees: Man is helpless in the grip of evil. When arguing against the Manichees, he adopted a position (as the Pelagians were acute enough to point out) almost identical to that of the Pelagians: There is no limitation or restriction on the human will.

Why are some men converted easily? others, like Augustine, only with difficulty and with the direct intervention of the Deity? still others, not at all? The answer is that when God created the universe He decided on the proportion in which reality and nothing would be mixed in each finite creature—in angels, men, animals. Had the mixture God decided on for Adam contained a smaller proportion of nothing, Adam would not have sinned, or would have sinned later rather than sooner, or would have sinned less rather than more grievously. And the same is true for all of us, Adam's descendants, for we are also God's creatures. "For [God] by His providence and omnipotence distributes to every one his own portion. . . . If [man's] will remained upright, . . . he should be rewarded; if it become wicked, . . . he should be punished. But even this trusting in God's help could not itself be accomplished without God's help."[a]

Nothing could be plainer. I decide how much gas will be put into my car (and so, correspondingly, how much "nothing" will be left in its tank). In so doing I determine how far my car will run. It is not the car's fault when it stops. Likewise, it is not man's fault when he sins, since his propensity to sin is a function of the amount of nothing God left in his nature. Nor does man's initiative have any more to do with his conversion than the car's initiative has to do with its being taken into the filling station for refill.

Thus, to revert to the analogy of the stage play, it turns out that the world is really a puppet theater. God not only writes the parts; He also pulls the strings from above. This makes the whole performance even more peculiar. Why should God choose in the first place to put on the show of which He is the only spectator? Why should He invent a complicated play-within-a-play that misleads the actors into thinking it is real life? Why should He go to the trouble of all this elaborate pretense—not only the play-within-a-play, but the whole play—when He knows who is to be saved and who is to be damned and when nothing that occurs in the play changes by one iota the decisions that were taken before the play was written?

This brings us to still another puzzle. Why should some be chosen for salvation? According to Augustine, the whole mass of humanity, having inherited Adam's diseased soul, is damned. But quite arbitrarily God selects some of this lot for salvation.

> Almighty God, the supreme and supremely good Creator of all natures, . . . was not destitute of a plan by which He might people His city with the fixed number of citizens which His wisdom had foreordained even out of the condemned human race, discriminating them not now by merits, since the whole mass was condemned as if in a vitiated root, but by grace, and showing, not only in the case of the redeemed, but also in those who were not delivered, how much grace He has bestowed upon them. For every one acknowledges that he has been rescued from evil, not by deserved, but by gratuitous goodness, when he is singled out from the company of those with whom he might justly have borne a common punishment, and is allowed to go scathless.[b]

This seems unjust—but perhaps Augustine would have found modern notions of justice unrealistic and sentimental. Here again, in the concept of justice, we reach a parting of the ways. To us it seems unfair that we should inherit Adam's sin, that we should be doomed for another's deeds. It seems unfair that Adam, who might just as well have been created with fewer deficiencies, should be blamed for what, given his nature, was bound to happen. It seems unfair, supposing ourselves all equally damned, that some few of us should be arbitrarily pulled out of the common cesspool of iniquity. Our modern equalitarian bias inclines us to feel that we should all either sink or swim together.

From our point of view, Augustine's doctrine of predestination is not only immoral but also impracticable. We would find it quite impossible to live by this doctrine or to act as if we believed it. Indeed, even Augustine himself could not. If he had been quite consistent in carrying out the doctrine of predestination, he would not, for instance, have recommended us to pray, to fast, to do good to our neighbor, to struggle against temptation, and so on, because whether or not we do these things is completely irrelevant to whether or not we are to be saved.[17]

This brings us to another point. If Augustine's salvation was predestined, neither his early life nor his struggle to live morally had any bearing on his conversion. Nor did the Church and its sacraments, for his salvation occurred in the garden in Milan, before his baptism and while he was still outside the fold. The fact is that Augustine, like many another mystic, felt his conversion

---

17 Augustine might fairly have claimed that whether or not men pray is itself predestined. But this would make his recommendation to pray even more absurd. In reply he might have argued that it was predestined that he write the *City of God* recommending us to pray. Similarly, the fact that I read Augustine and follow his recommendations may seem to me acts of my free choice, but in point of fact they, too, were arranged by God with a view to my salvation. All these elaborate sequences of events were designed by an omnipotent puppeteer to bring me into a position that he could just as well have induced by a single flip of his wrist.

to be induced directly by God's personal intervention: At the moment of conversion he stood in an immediate relation to the Deity.

But this interpretation of the saved soul's relation to God is unacceptable from an ecclesiastical point of view, which must hold that the Church is the exclusive agency through which souls are saved, the indispensable mediator between God and man. Augustine's difficulty was that he *also* shared this view. Hence, side by side with his mysticism, and quite contradicting its implications, appears another, and a very different, doctrine—that the sacraments, properly administered, are indispensable conditions of salvation, that the Church is the visible embodiment of the city of God, and that its regularly appointed officers have authority to determine the articles of faith and to make use of the secular arm to put down dissenting opinions.

We can trace Augustine's gradual recognition of the importance of the latter point of view to the very beginnings of his career as an administrator. After all, even Paul, mystic that he was, had a lively sense of the need for order and authority, and the growth of the Church in the centuries between Paul and Augustine had made these requirements even more obvious. No one in the fifth century who, like Augustine, had ecclesiastical responsibilities could possibly avoid facing up to the dangers of private religion.

THE DONATIST HERESY

Augustine was confronted with this whole problem when he went to Hippo in 391 as assistant to the aged Catholic bishop. On his arrival, he found that Donatism[18] had become a vigorous rival to the Church. Donatism was in some respects a strange kind of heresy, for it did not differ from Catholicism on points of doctrine. The Donatists merely held the sacraments to be ineffective if performed by unworthy priests. To modern ears, this may sound like a relatively harmless, indeed, a reasonable, point of view that takes account of the danger of the sacraments' degenerating into acts having automatic, or even magical,

---

18 Donatism (so called because the leader of the movement was a bishop named Donatus) originated early in the fourth century in a quarrel about an election to the bishopric of Carthage. During the persecution by Domitian and his successors, many Christians, lay and clergy, had repudiated their Christian vows. After the persecution ended, those who had withstood the temptation naturally looked upon the backsliders as cowards and timeservers. (The situation in the occupied countries after the defeat of Germany in World War II was parallel; those who had been members of the underground wished to deprive those who had made deals with the Nazis of the right to hold office.) When in 311 it was claimed (with what truth is not known) that the newly elected bishop of Carthage had been ordained by such a renegade, a large party of Carthaginians, who may have had other reasons for disliking their new bishop, declared his election invalid and proceeded to choose another bishop. This dissenting organization perpetuated itself and spread, and thus the Donatists got their start.

Donatism was strictly a North African phenomenon and did not spread into other regions. In later centuries, however, similar movements appeared from time to time. For instance, the Waldenses, a group that had a certain popularity in the twelfth century, held views essentially similar to those of the Donatists on the inefficacy of sacraments performed by unworthy priests, and Protestantism in some respects is also a revival of the Donatists' point of view.

efficacy. However plausible Donatism may seem today, the Catholic party at once saw the danger to institutional stability in the Donatists' contention. The authority of the Church depended upon there being no question about the authority of its officers. Similarly, Catholicism had to hold that the efficacy of the sacraments flows from the fact that they are the Church's. If their efficacy depends in any way on the inner worth of the man who happens to administer them, then any good man might perform the Mass, baptize sinners, and so on.[19] But if all good men are equally priests, what happens to the authority of the Church as an institution? And what happens to its claim to be the only door to salvation?

Obviously, the Donatists had to be firmly dealt with. At first Augustine thought they could be defeated by reasoned argument. The truth, he innocently supposed, would prevail against heresy. As it turned out, however, the numerous tracts Augustine wrote to demonstrate to the Donatists their criminal error, the numerous debates in which he met their principal authorities, failed to move them. Hence, Augustine, somewhat unwillingly (for he held that conversion is necessarily voluntary[20]), came around to the view of those Catholics who were urging stronger methods. The support of the imperial authorities was obtained (the more readily, perhaps, since it appears that the Donatists were not only religiously unorthodox but were also social radicals) and a very severe persecution was initiated. The Donatists were proscribed; many were exiled; many others were killed or committed suicide. Gradually, as a result of these measures, the sect lost its grip, and North Africa was momentarily saved for Catholicism, only to be lost a century later to the Mohammedans.

Though this policy may seem cruel to us, as it doubtless did to those who suffered under it, Augustine argued that it was really most humane. "As to the pagans, they may indeed . . . reproach us for the laws . . . enacted against idolators. [However, they ought to thank us, since many of them] have thereby been, and are now daily, turned from idols to the living and true God."[c] In this way the basis was laid and authority was provided for the institution of the Inquisition—for the cooperation of Church and state in the holy work of extirpating heresy and dissent and of saving souls against their wills.

The Donatist controversy not only forced Augustine to appeal for support to the secular arm; it also obliged him to consider the question of the ultimate authority on Catholic faith. Augustine did not recognize the primacy of the bishop of Rome. No man, he thought, is infallible; this is proven by the New Testament stories of Peter's mistakes. If Peter or Cyprian could fall into error,

---

19 The Donatists themselves appear not to have drawn this, the logical, conclusion of their position. They had their own hierarchy and within it insisted on proper subordination. The point that offended the Catholics was that the Donatists' was a *different* hierarchy.

20 This was, of course, an absolutely central thesis for Augustine, following from both his personal experience and his general metaphysical position. It is a good example of the way in which his philosophy and the exigencies of ecclesiastical administration came into conflict.

may not any other man? Accordingly, Augustine reasoned that the final authority is no single individual but a general council. What the majority at such a council holds is sound doctrine and must be accepted. Until a general council is convoked, and while it is debating a matter of faith, we should use our reason to determine the truth as well as we can, bearing in mind on the one hand that God would not have given us reason had He not intended us to use it, and on the other hand that reason is feeble and that it is the worst kind of pride to suppose ourselves capable of penetrating all mysteries.

But though Augustine held that the declarations of a council are sound doctrine, he was not naïve enough to suppose that any council could promulgate the final truth, once and for all. "Who is ignorant," he asked, "that even plenary councils are often corrected by later ones?"[d] The fact seems to be that Augustine had some notion of a gradual and increasing capacity of the human mind to achieve truth and that he was aware of the successive modifications that any formula must inevitably undergo. He found sanction for his belief in the increasing power of the mind in the hints of the Christian revelation in the prophets and in the half-insights of Plato, as well as in his own experience of struggle toward the truth. Doubtless a later council could not *contradict* an earlier one, for this would imply that the earlier council was completely wrong. But it could "correct" the earlier position, that is, modify and improve it in the light of a fuller grasp of the truth. This is a long way from that dogmatic assertion of final and complete truth to which many Christian thinkers were committed— including Augustine himself when, in the interests of ecclesiastical authority, he attacked heresy and put down schism.

AUGUSTINE'S VIEW OF THE SACRAMENTS

In all these ways, then, institutional needs forced Augustine to affirm the special, indeed, the unique, status of the Church, its hierarchy, and its sacraments. Thus, just as "earthly city" had two meanings for Augustine—hell and the pilgrimage of this life, so "city of God" had a double meaning—heaven and the Church. Assuming that the visible Church is the embodiment of the invisible Church, Augustine interpreted every reference in the Bible to the Kingdom of God as a reference to the historical Church as it existed in his day. He therefore concluded that the Church and its members are the body of Christ; and this body—an organism of many parts standing in various relations of ordination and subordination to one another—owes its life and its allegiance to Jesus. From this point of view, the city of God is a very complex structure, very different from the simple and direct relationship in which, when Augustine was thinking mystically, he conceived each soul to stand to God.

There is no easy way to bring these two conceptions of man's relation to God into accord. On the one hand, the requirements of institutionalism committed Augustine to holding that the only way to salvation is through the sacraments administered by regularly ordained priests of the Church. On the other hand, his mysticism and his predestinarianism implicitly denied this. As regards the latter, if we are predestined for salvation (or for damnation, as the case may be), what we do or leave undone is obviously inconsequential. As regards the former, the central fact of Augustine's experience in Milan was direct communion with God, unmediated by any of the Church's sacraments. From this point of view, where mysticism and predestinarianism come together, salvation is a private and individual affair, and the city of God is a community only in the sense of there being a number of individuals who happen to stand in an identical relationship to God. Here the Church and its sacraments are unimportant—the Church, because all the various lines of authority and all the various relationships it involves are irrelevant to the simple, unambiguous relationship in which each saved soul stands to God; the sacraments, because if the soul has not yet turned, they cannot help, and if it *has* turned, they are unnecessary.

Consequently, there is a striking ambivalence about everything Augustine said on this subject. At times, when he was thinking ecclesiastically, he wrote of baptism as "Thy life-giving sacrament," imputing to it a magical effect not unlike that attributed to similar rites by the earlier mystery cults. And this, of course, is the obvious implication of the position he adopted against the Donatists. It is the rite itself (providing, of course, that it is administered by the Church) that is efficacious; it operates automatically, regardless of who in particular administers it. In this connection it is interesting to note Augustine's belief that heretics and schismatics who dare to partake of the sacraments are hurt thereby.

At other times, when he was thinking mystically and forgot his responsibilities to the Church as an institution, Augustine tended to leave the sacraments out of the picture. Thus he asserted that certain Old Testament figures were saved, though they could have known nothing of the sacraments. Though they lived before the Christian revelation, they had had hints of its meaning; they were saved "by faith in this mystery and by godliness of life." And the same applies to us, except, of course, that whereas those pre-crucifixion saints had only the barest of hints to guide and instruct them, we have the wonderful example, the obvious instruction, of Jesus' life, death, and resurrection.

Sometimes Augustine expressed these divergent points of view side by side. Thus, in one passage, he said that his soul had been changed by "faith and Thy sacrament."[e] Augustine never succeeded in resolving the contradiction that lurks in this "and."

Nature and Natural Science

At the beginning of the discussion of "the earthly pilgrimage," the world, as Augustine saw it, was likened to a play of which God is the author. Enough has been said about the drama of salvation. Now we must consider briefly the stage-set, of which God is the designer and builder. This brings us to the physical world, conceived of by Augustine as the stage on which the drama of man's salvation is unfolded.

AUGUSTINE'S DISINTEREST IN SCIENCE

Augustine was basically uninterested in the physical world. First, he lacked the natural curiosity of the old Greek scientists and their modern counterparts. Indeed, curiosity was replaced in his case by the fear of falling into intellectual pride by prying into secrets that God does not wish us to understand. Second, he did not have the incentive shared by the Greeks and modern men: the conviction that the key to happiness and well-being lies in this world. For Augustine, this world was at best a vale of tears, and happiness lay beyond it, in God's city. The otherworldliness that made him, relatively speaking, indifferent to ethics and politics and the other aspects of man's social environment made him even more indifferent to man's physical environment.

Even if Augustine had interested himself in nature, even if he had thought that a study of it would be helpful instead of dangerous, he could hardly have made any significant contribution to natural science. For his view of nature was dominated by an extremely naïve teleology that, by making all answers easy, made impossible the kind of patient and careful investigation that underlies any real scientific advance. For Augustine, the natural world was designed to supplement and enforce the lesson of the resurrection. Why are there seven planets? To remind us of the seven cardinal virtues, to warn us against the seven deadly sins. Just as the road signs that warn, "Slow," or "Curve," were designed by a benevolent Department of Highways to assist us in getting safely to our destinations, so the various features of the physical world were designed by the benevolent Deity to guide us toward salvation.

The natural world was not only designed to instruct us; like the billboards that crowd upon us on the highway, some natural objects serve merely to tempt and ensnare us—and also to punish us. The mighty frame of the universe was, then, created as a stage on which man's life is acted out, and the various plants and animals, the tornadoes, floods, plagues, and other natural disasters are all stage properties that in one way or another contribute to the effect of the play.

It follows that even though man is utterly debased in comparison with the goodness and worth of God, he is the center of the created universe. Man is the end, the purpose, for which it was produced. The fish of the sea, the fowl of the air, cattle and wild beasts, every creeping thing upon the earth—all exist for man's use, either to sustain his life while the play goes on or to test his merits and steel his resistance.

As a result of these beliefs, Augustine did not merely lack a scientific method, as had most of the ancients; his attitude of mind, unlike theirs, was distinctly antagonistic to such a method. This was not only due to the fact that his thought about the world was teleological. In some fields—in certain aspects of social studies, for instance—a teleological approach is helpful; certainly teleology did not prevent Aristotle from making significant contributions in biology. But Augustine's teleology was so naïvely anthropocentric that it was impossible for him to reach an unbiased conclusion. When all phenomena are explained by exactly the same formula, explanation may indeed satisfy some deep psychological need, but it has no objective meaning. When every action, every event, is referable to a single, self-identical cause, all causal distinctions disappear. It is impossible to develop a science of, say, meteorology when all meteorological events without exception are attributed to the same cause. Why did it rain last night? Because God wanted it to. Why did the rain cease at midnight? Because God wanted it to. Why did it not rain this morning? Because God wanted it not to. And so on. To make matters more difficult, the one cause to which Augustine attributed all events was, of course, a will whose motives are by definition unknown to us.

UNCRITICAL OF THE MARVELOUS

Like everyone else, Augustine was struck by the oddities and irregularities of the physical world, and like most people, he was uncritical in accepting reports of oddities—the salamander lives in fire; the flesh of the peacock is antiseptic; the diamond "is so hard that it can be wrought neither by iron nor fire, nor . . . by anything at all except goat's blood"; there is a stone in Arcadia called asbestos because, once it is lit, it cannot be put out; "the Garamantae have a fountain so cold by day that no one can drink it, so hot by night no one can touch it." In one place, Augustine did indeed say that he related only what he himself had witnessed or "what I was told by one whom I can trust as I trust my own eyes," which shows that he had a certain consciousness of the possibility of being taken in by old wives' tales. And he actually checked up on the report that the peacock's flesh is antiseptic. "Taking a suitable slice of flesh from its breast I ordered it to be kept. . . . When it had been kept as many days as make other flesh stinking, it was produced and set before me, and emitted no offensive smell."[f] Augustine's trouble, of course, was that, given his theological presuppositions, he had a predisposition to believe in the miraculous. Like some modern believers in psychic phenomena, he was inclined to accept proof that might not have satisfied more objective observers.

Now, the starting point of any scientific investigation is, first, the observation of an oddity and, second, curiosity about it, coupled with the conviction that it is not really an oddity at all. Since we are deeply convinced today of the regularity (or "lawfulness") of nature, and since this naturally excludes the possibility of there being any real oddity, we assume that there must be factors present on any seemingly odd occasion that are not present on other, "regular" occasions (or factors absent from this occasion that are ordinarily present), and we assume that these factors, as we say, "cause" the apparent irregularity. We call the irregularity "apparent" because we believe that if we can discover the factors in question, we can show that the alleged oddity is merely a part of a more complicated regularity.

To take a very trivial case, suppose that we formulate, on the basis of numerous observations, the rule, "Matches ignite when rubbed on an abrasive surface." Now suppose that we rub a match on such a surface and it fails to strike. This is an oddity. We investigate the circumstances and discover that the match was wet. Further experimentation with wet matches shows that none of them strikes. Therefore, we formulate a revised version of our first rule: "Dry matches ignite when rubbed on an abrasive surface." Obviously, under this rule, the match that did not strike is no longer an oddity. Perhaps, after we have made a number of such revisions, we will reach the point of realizing that rules must always be tentative and subject to correction as new cases turn up.

Thus, today we never take an oddity at face value. For us, it is not a "marvel," something to goggle at, but a challenge. We automatically seek to discover how it fits into the regular sequence of nature. Augustine, in contrast, did take oddities at face value. He was uninterested in them except for theological purposes, and from a theological point of view, their value lies precisely in the fact that they are oddities. That is, to Augustine these natural "wonders" seemed evidence of the marvelous power of God, and he held that they were designed by God as such. Why should a sceptic doubt the miracle of Jesus' bodily resurrection when he has but to open his eyes to observe the "miracle" of the peacock's antiseptic flesh or the Garamantian spring? Nothing could indicate more clearly the radical difference in orientation between our minds and Augustine's, or the limitations of Augustine's approach to nature.[21]

OTHER REASONS FOR AUGUSTINE'S UNSCIENTIFIC APPROACH

Augustine's thinking was limited by the need of conforming to an authoritative text, and, unfortunately, what this text has to say about nature is, for the most part, a compilation of very early Semitic myths. All Augustine's ingenuity, which was considerable, was directed, not toward modifying his initial presuppositions in the light of the facts, but toward bringing Scripture and his personal point of view into agreement. What Augustine achieved was correspondence between two conceptual systems, not correspondence between a conceptual system and the world that is to be "explained."

Again, Augustine assumed that the answers science attempts to discover are either (1) on the surface, easily ascertained, and available to all, or (2) so deeply buried that no one can discover them. In either case, there is no occasion for serious scientific study of nature. Whatever information God intended us to have about the physical world, He wrote in plain language; whatever is not immediately obvious, God does not intend us to know. It is therefore impious, as well as useless, to try to discover it. The Greeks

---

21 The possible limitations of *our* approach are not spoken of here.

> . . . made efforts to discover the hidden laws of nature. . . . And some of
> them, by God's help, made great discoveries; but when left to themselves
> they were betrayed by human infirmity, and fell into mistakes. . . . With their
> understanding and the capacity which Thou hast bestowed upon them . . .
> they found out, and foretold . . . the eclipses of those luminaries, the sun
> and moon . . . and they exulted and were exalted; and by an impious pride
> [they forgot] whence they have the ability wherewith they seek out these
> things.

So, according to Augustine, the Greeks were damned for their pains.

Why did God permit them to go astray? So that by their example we might
see that only the truly humble are likely to escape damnation. It is much safer
to be ignorant than to be wise and fall into pride. "A just man . . . though he
know not even the circles of the Great Bear, [is] better than he who can measure
the heavens, and number the stars, and weigh the elements, but is forgetful of
Thee." [22]

Though the major points in Augustine's view of nature have been discussed,
it would be unfair to Augustine to stop at this point. In the first place, we must
not slip into the anachronism of supposing that there existed in Augustine's day
a fully developed scientific method that he willfully ignored. From the point
of view of natural science, Augustine's otherworldliness was doubtless a decline
from the naturalism of the Greeks, just as his anthropocentric teleology was more
naïve than Aristotle's and less capable of methodological fruition. But the Greek
mind, too, was for the most part foreign to empirical science in the modern sense.
Greek apriority compares in a way with medieval dogmatism; Greek rationalism
was in some respects as antagonistic to the scientific point of view as medieval
theology.

BELIEF IN REGULARITY OF NATURE

In the second place, and more important, one aspect of Augustine's attitude
toward nature was to prove very fruitful in the long run. Augustine, of course,
believed in miracles, and at times he wrote about them in his usual vein. Thus,
"God . . . does not disdain to work . . . miracles . . . that He may thereby
awaken the soul . . . to worship Himself."[g] But occasionally Augustine rose to
a more interesting view: Since everything is caused by God, it follows that
everything is in the way of being a miracle. In other words, the so-called miracle
is no more miraculous than anything else that happens. It merely *seems* miraculous because it is unusual.

---

22 Augustine's attack on anatomy was characteristic: "With a cruel zeal for science, some medical
men, who are called anatomists, have dissected the bodies of the dead, and sometimes even
of sick persons who died under their knives, and have inhumanly pried into the secrets of the
human body"—*City of God* (Dods), xxii, 24.

[Men] say that all portents are contrary to nature; but they are not so. For how is that contrary to nature which happens by the will of God, since the will of so mighty a Creator is certainly the nature of each created thing? A portent, therefore, happens not contrary to nature, but contrary to what we know as nature. . . .

Even the very things which are most commonly known as natural would not be less wonderful nor less effectual to excite surprise in all who beheld them, if men were not accustomed to admire nothing but what is rare.[h]

Let us recall what has been said here about an oddity's being, from the point of view of modern science, an incentive to make descriptions of natural behavior more precise and more complete. Belief that the oddity is only apparent, faith in the regularity of nature, must exist in the scientist prior to, and as a condition of, any inquiry that vindicates that belief.[23] Without this belief, without this faith, no scientist would even undertake, let alone devote his whole life to, the kind of research that yields results.

Now, a miracle or a portent is *prima facie* an oddity. And Augustine's point in the passage just quoted was that its oddity is in us, not in the event itself. It looks odd just because it is rare; actually, it is not odd at all. Augustine, then, shared the modern scientist's disbelief in the objective reality of oddity. This conviction of Augustine's followed logically from his conception of the omnipotence of the divine nature. With Augustine it did not issue in scientific achievement for the reasons already examined—he was not really interested in the natural world or its doings, and, except for this facet of his belief, his point of view was antagonistic to the scientific attitude. But in this one respect Augustine made a great contribution: He provided a rationale for belief, despite all appearances to the contrary, in the basic orderliness of nature. The perpetuation of this Augustinian belief through the Middle Ages made possible the scientific achievement that came when men's minds finally turned from the other world to this one. Without this deep conviction—this faith that all oddities are only apparent—modern science could never have taken even its first steps.

History

Finally, in this discussion of the earthly pilgrimage, we come to Augustine's conception of human history. His point of view should be clear from what has

23 Of course, faith in the orderliness and regularity of nature is not "vindicated" in any particular experiment or, indeed, in any particular set of experiments. All that can be vindicated is the belief that some particular oddity is not an oddity. The belief that no oddities are really oddities is an act of faith not subject to proof. Here again it is obvious that religion and metaphysics "touch." See pp. 84–85.

been said about his view of natural science. Like the prior acts of a play, man's past throws light on his future. The history of humanity was designed by God to instruct and to test us. All the events of man's history are lessons from which, if we will but look, we can learn what is necessary for salvation. Long before the great revelation in the person of Jesus and the events of his life (which are themselves, of course, a part of human history), God granted mankind "certain signs" by which the "mystery of eternal life was revealed." In particular, the history of the Jews was such a sign. Not only the words spoken by the prophets, but "the rites, priesthood, tabernacle, altars, sacrifices, ceremonies"—all aspects of the inward and outward life of the Jews as revealed in their history—"signify and fore-announce" the drama of salvation.

TELEOLOGICAL BIAS

Of course, most of the details of Augustine's historical narrative are vitiated by the same anthropocentric teleology that we have seen at work in his view of natural science. Why, for instance, do heresies flourish? Because the Devil, seeing the pagan temples deserted by the rush to Christianity, discovers that he must do his work of destruction inside the Christian fold. Why do saints suffer? Because God wants to give them the opportunity to win the crown of martyrdom. Why were evil emperors allowed to persecute the Church? Because God has given the demons "power . . . at certain appointed and well-adjusted seasons [to] give expression to their hostility to the city of God by stirring up against it the men who are under their influence." For what purpose was this power given to the demons? So that God "may not only receive sacrifice from those who willingly offer it, but may also extort it from the unwilling by violent persecution." In other words, so that, willy-nilly, the appointed few become martyrs and so fill the quota of the city of God.[i]

Why did Rome, the center of civilization, fall to the barbarians? Not, as the wicked pagans asserted, because Rome had turned away from the old gods to Christianity,[24] but because "divine providence is wont to reform the depraved manners of men by chastisement." In other words, not because Rome had turned to Christ, but because it had not turned soon enough and it had not turned completely.

---

24 It was to meet this pagan propaganda that Augustine wrote the *City of God*. The fall of Rome to the barbarians profoundly shocked the whole civilized world. Jerome, who certainly cannot be accused of being overconcerned with the things of this life, "was so stupefied and dismayed that day and night I could think of nothing [else]. . . . My voice sticks in my throat and even as I dictate this letter sobs choke my utterance. The city which had taken the whole world was itself taken"—quoted in F. A. Wright, *Fathers of the Church* (Routledge, London, 1928), p. 213.

The pagans found it useful to play on this sense of shock. A few years earlier, in 382, the Christian emperor had removed the Altar of Victory from the Senate, over the protests of that body. This act of sacrilege was held responsible for the disasters that followed. How could one hope to win victories when one deliberately offended the goddess of victory? This argument had such appeal that the pen of Christianity's primary publicist was required to reply to it.

AUGUSTINE AND THE GREEK HISTORIANS

Against such facility, scientific history is helpless. Augustine had a ready-made answer for everything. Nevertheless, one should not overlook certain important contributions he made to the study of history. What these contributions were will be clear if Augustine is compared with Herodotus and Thucydides, the greatest of the Greek historians. Though Herodotus and Thucydides were much more scientific than Augustine, their conception of history was in some respects narrower than his. For one thing, though they gave some account of the past, both were primarily concerned with current events. This was not just an accidental limitation. It was a logical by-product of the dominance in Greek thought of the problem of change. That which is subject to flux and to change cannot, Plato held, be wholly real. The subject matter of history is therefore peculiarly unreal, and historians had best limit themselves to writing about those events that come within their own experience or at least fall within their own lifetimes.

But even within the field of current events there was, in the Greek view, much that was irrational, much for which no historical explanation could be found. Aristotle believed that chance plays a considerable role in the causality of events, and Thucydides shared this opinion. For this historian, as for Homer, much "just happened." Thucydides' account of the Peloponnesian War is dominated by his sense of accident: Over and over again men's best-laid plans go astray because of some chance incident such as the death of Pericles at the start of the war.

For Augustine, on the contrary, with his belief in divine providence, nothing happened by chance. Though his actual explanation of historical causation may be worthless, his sense of divine purpose led him to believe that there is unity and direction in everything. For him, human history was a drama unfolding toward a meaningful end, not "sound and fury signifying nothing."

Since, for Augustine, God was a supremely competent dramatist who wrote no irrelevant details into his script, Augustine concluded that nothing is in principle irrational. It is true that *we* may not be able to understand some particular sequence of events, but this is only because we have not yet fathomed God's purpose in causing them to occur. If, and as soon as, we understand that purpose, we will understand the events themselves because we will see how they are means to God's end.

Since, according to Augustine, human history is but the unfolding of the divine drama, history has direction. Everything in the early stages of a well-constructed drama leads up to a climax; everything that follows as the drama hurries to its conclusion reinforces that climax. For Augustine, of course, the climax of human history was the earthly career of Jesus. Everything that occurred before Jesus' birth was designed by God to lead up to that great event; everything after Jesus' resurrection was designed to supplement its great effect.

This view of Jesus' life as the turning point in human history survives today in our system of dating. Instead of dating by olympiads or, as the Romans did, from the year of the founding of Rome, we date everything "B.C." or "A.D." And though for modern historians the birth of Christ does not have the overwhelming importance that it had for Augustine, the concept of direction and climax is still fundamental to the thinking of many. In this history of philosophy, for instance, the treatment of the subject is organized on this principle and is seen from this point of view. Greek philosophical thinking, as the first volume in the series shows, led up to Plato and Aristotle; in that volume, the meaning of the earlier theories is explained in terms of their significance as steps in a developmental system. This does not mean that modern historians have retained Augustine's notion of a divine providence at work, a Deity consciously shaping events so as to produce the historical sequences. But even though they have abandoned the notion of a conscious, guiding purpose, many modern historians recognize the methodological value of a teleological approach. Whether God foresaw and predestined the theories of the Greek philosophers seems a relatively unimportant question to the modern historian, however important it may still be to theologians. What is important to the historian of philosophy is the interrelations of philosophical theories. Unless and until he can show how these theories fit into a developmental pattern, they have no rhyme or reason; they appear to have "just happened." Once the developmental pattern appears, however, they acquire new meaning from the sequential relationships that are disclosed.

Another difference between Augustine and the Greek historians was his universalism as compared with their relative insularity. The Greek historians wrote Greek history; if other peoples appeared in their narratives, it was only insofar as they had some connection with the Greeks. The sense of universal, instead of provincial, history was a new development. It was the drama of *man*, not the drama of Romans or Greeks or Persians, that interested Augustine. Thus the universalism that was a part of the Christian religious message affected his approach to history, and this point of view, too, we have inherited. No one who writes national history today can afford to lose sight of the fact that what he is writing is a part of a larger whole, an act or an episode in a bigger drama, which gets meaning from and gives meaning to that larger history. This sense of the unity of human history is another inheritance from Augustine.

Conclusion

Augustine was not the sort of thinker whose views evoke a neutral response. Those who are not for him are likely to be dead against him. Thus, many people today regard Augustine's point of view as hopelessly unbalanced—a neurotic exaggeration of guilt and sin and an unhealthy otherworldliness that result in almost total neglect of the really serious social and political problems that it is the business of the philosopher to discuss. Such critics will be inclined to take

Augustine's mystical experience in the garden in Milan less as a profound insight into the nature of reality than as a sign of psychic instability.

Others, however, will argue that if Augustine went too far in one direction, the modern world has gone too far in another. Concentration camps, Hiroshima, and Nagasaki have shocked many of us into a painful recognition of man's inhumanity to man. The post-World War II generation is likely to understand Augustine's horror at the depths of iniquity of which men are capable; and even those who reject his specifically Christian interpretations may feel that he gave a truer picture of human nature than that presented by eighteenth- and nineteenth-century philosophers of progress.

At any rate, quite apart from the value Augustine might have as a corrective to certain tendencies in modern life, he is a figure of great importance in the history of the Western mind. As one of the fathers of the Church, he developed ideas that still form a cornerstone of Catholic Christendom. Moreover, it was to him that the leading Protestant thinkers turned when they rebelled against Rome; his views (somewhat differently interpreted by Protestant thinkers, of course) are therefore the theological core of most modern Protestant sects. It is fair to say, then, that Augustinianism, in at least some of its aspects, is still a living view.

Further, since a great many men for a very long time regarded Augustine's views as true, his opinions are of great importance even to those who regard them as profoundly mistaken. For more than a thousand years Augustine's estimate of the miserable predicament of mankind was a basic attitude. This is too long a time for it not to have left an indelible mark on the Western mind. Even those who react most sharply against the Augustinian outlook are therefore likely to find, if they but look, traces of Augustinianism in their own thinking and feeling. Thus, to mention a trivial example, many people today mistrust an antiseptic that does not sting when applied to a wound. The belief that "it can't be good if it doesn't hurt" is Augustinianism at work. And again, even those who do not feel guilty and sinful sometimes have a sense of guilt at feeling guiltless. In a word, the influence of Augustine, passed to us through Calvin and the New England Puritans, is too pervasive to have been escaped wholly by any American. Hence, if we want to understand ourselves, we must for better or for worse try to understand Augustine.

Finally, and apart from history, there is much that even the most hostile critics will agree we can learn from Augustine. His psychological interpretation of the redemption,[25] when separated from the providential play-within-a-play in which he embedded it, is very suggestive to modern minds accustomed to thinking in naturalistic, rather than in supernaturalistic, terms. And his notion of the gradual unfolding of Christian truth[26] is congenial to our own conceptions. Again,

25 See pp. 122–23.
26 See p. 127.

Augustine's dogged effort to reduce his various beliefs to systematic order is an instructive example for us. The very fact that he failed makes his view in some respects more appealing than the undertaking of the later Scholastics. Just because the latter were more successful, their vast, frozen triumphs of logic and intellection are less human, less relevant to our own philosophic strivings, than is Augustine's abortive scheme.

CHAPTER 5

The Medieval Interval

Plato and Aristotle, the two dominant philosophers of the classical period, were teacher and pupil. They lived in essentially the same world, understood its problems in much the same way, and sought a common solution for them. Between Augustine and Thomas Aquinas, the correspondingly dominant figures of the medieval period, there was a similar continuity of thought and feeling, for they were both Christian thinkers and thus had a common core of doctrine and faith. Yet these two figures were separated by no less than eight centuries. This is a long time by almost any standard—longer than the whole of the classical period. And though the rate of cultural change was much slower in the Middle Ages than it is today, a great many new ideas and attitudes developed, new institutions were fashioned, and new values were experienced during the long period between Augustine's death and Thomas' birth. All these changes were naturally reflected in the Thomistic synthesis of the thirteenth century. Thus, though Thomism shared many of the basic insights of Augustinianism, it faced new problems and dealt with old ones in new ways. The purpose of the present chapter is to survey the major changes, cultural and philosophical, that occurred during this eight-century interval, in order to explain the differences in emphasis and point of view that we will encounter in the Thomistic synthesis.

We shall have to confine ourselves to the main developments. The first factor to note is that the medieval interval falls into two main periods. First, there was a period of outward stagnation, during which the West collected its scattered forces and painfully revived from the terrible destruction that had attended the breakup of the Roman Empire. This destruction was so great and the rate of recovery was so slow that even by the ninth century Europe was still immeasurably behind the classical world in every department of life. But in the following centuries (partly because of increasing access to the remains of classical culture) revival became more rapid and life became more vigorous. By the twelfth century something approximating a real renaissance had occurred and a new culture had been achieved.

The Dark Ages

The shock that even Christians experienced at the fall of Rome[1] has already been mentioned. But the city's capture by the barbarians was only the most dramatic episode in a long-drawn-out collapse.[2] The invasions that began in the closing years of the fourth century and continued during the next century were quite different from the forays and incursions of earlier times, in which some wandering tribe briefly eluded the frontier guards and indulged in an orgy of burning and pillaging until it was rounded up and driven off. Now the frontier was not merely broken; it was destroyed. There were no legions left to round up the barbarians, who simply found themselves in possession of invaded territories.

It must have seemed the end of the world. It was the end of *one* world, and no one, least of all the barbarians, knew what shape the new world would have. In some respects, the barbarian conquerors of the Empire were no more unjust than other conquerors, including the Romans themselves. But the conquest of a civilized people by a relatively uncivilized people causes an additional dimension of suffering. Many, certainly, were the wrongs suffered by the native American Indians at the hands of the white Europeans in the sixteenth and

1 See p. 134, n. 24.
2 The Empire had been divided, for administrative purposes, more than one hundred years earlier, and Constantine had established a second capital for the eastern half in Byzantium, which was renamed in his honor. By the fifth century these two parts of the Empire had become virtually separate states, and though the Eastern Empire managed to survive in an attenuated way for another thousand years, it had little influence on Western thought.

seventeenth centuries; but the sudden conquest of the United States today by those same Indians would entail even greater wrongs. Not merely would we be dispossessed of our lands (as the Indians were dispossessed by our forefathers); there would be all the distress unintentionally created by the conquerors as a result of their inability to understand or to manage the complicated and delicately balanced processes of the more advanced culture.

This comparison is not far-fetched. Compared with the culture of the Empire, that of the barbarians was—barbaric. They were nomads who knew no law except the unwritten tribal customs they brought with them from their primitive communities in the East; with their conquests, therefore, rough justice succeeded Roman juridical system. Yet without the mature jurisprudence that the Romans had gradually developed, the complex economic and social institutions of the Empire could not possibly survive. Urban life, which had already suffered during the disasters of the third century, now largely disappeared, not to revive for centuries. Commerce and industry, which had depended on the stability of a uniform imperial economic system (consider, for instance, such a simple but vital relationship as Italy's dependence on wheat from Africa) and on such facilities as a uniform coinage and the wonderful Roman roads that tied all parts of the Empire together, disintegrated.

After the barbarian invasions the organic society of the Romans was replaced by numerous small-scale, self-sustaining, and marginally existing units, largely agrarian in nature—depending for survival on their own abilities, and isolated not only physically but also culturally. Life holed up for a long winter, and men's energies were focused on the problem of staying alive.

Under circumstances such as these, arts and letters naturally suffered. Because of the indifference and the downright hostility of the Christians, and because of the vicissitudes of war and invasion, almost the whole body of ancient literature and learning was lost. Of Plato's work the Middle Ages knew only the *Timaeus*, which, because of its myth of a creative demiurge, medieval men took to be the work of a fumbling seeker after Christian truth. Of Aristotle's writings only a part of the works on logic survived; of Epicurean Atomism, only a hundred lines of Lucretius' poem. Nor was there any new writing of significance or originality to take the place of the old. Boethius (480–525) wrote the *Consolations of Philosophy*, which had an immense vogue in the Middle Ages, and translated the Aristotelian works on logic referred to above, together with Porphyry's *Introduction to Aristotle's Categories*.[3] More characteristic of the period was Isidore of Seville (560–636), whose *Etymologies*—a hodgepodge, encyclopedic mass of information and misinformation on every conceivable subject—was a primary authority for the whole of the early Middle Ages.

In these catastrophic times men not only lost the art of writing; they also largely lost the art of reading. In the time of Augustine's youth, the second half of the fourth century, even a Christian got a reasonably good classical education.

---

3 This Porphyry was a Neoplatonist, the disciple and biographer of Plotinus. See p. 8.

A few generations later, literacy was a rarity even among the ruling classes. In the eighth century, Charlemagne complained that the clergy themselves did not know enough Latin to interpret Holy Scripture or to conduct the Church's services properly:

> Often in recent years when letters have been written to us from monasteries, . . . we have recognized . . . uncouth expressions; because what pious devotion dictated faithfully to the mind, the tongue, uneducated on account of neglect of study, was not able to express in the letter without error. Whence it happened that we began to fear lest perchance, as the skill in writing was less, so also the wisdom for understanding the Holy Scriptures might be much less than it rightly ought to be. . . . Therefore, we exhort you not only not to neglect the study of letters, but also with most humble mind, pleasing to God, to study earnestly in order that you may be able more easily and more correctly to penetrate the mysteries of the divine Scriptures. . . . We desire you to be, as the soldiers of the Church ought to be, devout in mind, learned in discourse, chaste in conduct, and eloquent in speech.[a]

The Church

This, then, was truly a "dark" age. That anything survived at all was chiefly the result of the Church's existence. Yet it is astounding that the Church itself did not go under along with everything else, for the conquering barbarians were either pagans or, what was worse, Arians. The Church flung itself with passionate zeal into the mission of converting Arians and pagans to orthodoxy. In 496 Clovis, the Frankish king, was baptized and the conversion of his people began. One hundred years later missionaries were dispatched to Britain to convert the barbarian conquerors of that former Roman province. By the end of the Dark Ages Christianity was more widely spread and orthodoxy more firmly entrenched than before the barbarian invasions began.

One reason for this extraordinary success was the missionary fervor of the orthodox Christians; another was the skill and competence of a number of the bishops of Rome; still another was the fact that the barbarian conquerors, even the Arians, found it advantageous (just as Constantine had before them) to deal with an established institution. Then, too, there was the fact that, in the vacuum of power created by the wreck of the Empire, the Church naturally attracted support that might have gone in better times to other groups. Thus, like the one bank that manages to keep its doors open during a period of economic depression, the Church emerged from the ordeal stronger than it had been before the fall of Rome, but, by the same token, profoundly changed from the primitive institution of early times.

THE RISE OF THE PAPACY

In those early days the Church's organization had been episcopal (that is, governed by bishops), not papal. Even as late as the end of the fourth century, when the Empire was in dissolution, the dominant feeling in the Church was opposed to accepting political responsibilities. It was, as we have seen, only after considerable hesitation that Augustine concluded that the Church might call on the secular arm for help, and rare were the political bishops who, like Ambrose, dictated to sovereigns on the grounds of their ecclesiastical prerogatives.

By the next century, however, the beginnings of a double development were discernible. The bishops of Rome not only claimed primacy over all the other bishops; they also asserted a supreme temporal authority. Against the other bishops, for instance, Pope Leo I asserted the "Petrine" doctrine. This rests on Jesus' remark to Peter (Matt. 16:18), "On this rock[4] I will build my church . . . and I will give unto thee the keys of the kingdom of heaven." These verses had occasionally been quoted by bishops of Rome in earlier centuries to demonstrate the importance of their see; they now became the basis for asserting supremacy. As the inheritors and successors of Peter, the bishops of Rome claimed to be the heads of the Church. Characteristic was Leo's conception of the sources of papal authority. "Our Lord Jesus Christ . . . made St. Peter the head of [all the apostles], that from him as from their head his gifts should flow out into all the body. So that if anyone separates himself from St. Peter he should know that he has no share in the divine blessing. . . . It is reasonable and just that . . . the holy Roman church, through St. Peter, the prince of the apostles, is the head of all the churches of the whole world," and so on.[b]

The doctrine of papal primacy over the other bishops was extended to primacy over Christian kings and princes. As long as the Christian Church had faced a pagan Empire, it had been possible to maintain, as Augustine did in essence, the doctrine that the Church and the State were independent powers, each supreme in its own sphere. But once the secular arm became Christian, though the popes often continued to give expression to the two-power doctrine, they felt that the situation had changed: A Christian king, *qua* Christian, was subject to the pope. This was clearly stated as early as the fifth century. Pope Gelasius I did, on occasion, maintain that "[Christ] separated the kingly duties and powers from the priestly, according to the different functions and dignity proper to each. . . . Christian Emperors should stand in need of priests for their eternal life, and priests for their part should employ the aid of the imperial government for the direction of temporal matters."[c] But despite this formal separation of the two powers, it is clear that Gelasius had a sense of the primacy of the spiritual arm:

> There are two chief powers by which this world is governed . . . : the sacred authority of the prelates and the kingly power. Wherein the burden

4 [The Latin word *petra* means "rock"; *Petrus* means "Peter"—AUTHOR.]

laid upon the priests is the heavier, in that they will have to render an account at the divine judgment even for the kings of men. You know, most clement son,[5] that although you are placed in rank above all the race of men, nevertheless you bow your neck in devoted submission to those who are set in charge of matters of religion. You look to them for the means of your own salvation.[d]

After all, in a society in which the soul's salvation is the primary and, indeed, the only real motive for human conduct, it is logical that he who "binds and looses," who owns the keys to heaven and to hell, should be supreme.

These initial claims were powerfully reinforced a few centuries later by several convenient forgeries that seemed to give legal sanction to papal claims. Of these the most famous and the most influential was the so-called Donation of Constantine, an eighth-century document purporting to be an edict of the emperor Constantine. It not only ordained that the bishops of Rome should "have the supremacy . . . over all the churches of God in the whole world," but also relinquished to the popes the imperial power itself—giving over to them "our palace, . . . as also the city of Rome and all the provinces, districts and cities of Italy or of the western regions . . . by our inviolable gift."[e]

The culmination of this whole process came in the second half of the eleventh century during the pontificate of Gregory VII,[6] who was an ardent protagonist of papal supremacy in its most extreme form.[7] This formidable and energetic man not only required all bishops to swear an oath of allegiance but undertook to extract similar submission from all temporal sovereigns. Though petty rulers might have been willing to accept this theory—or might not have been strong enough to resist it—the great princes found it unpalatable. The result was a long, bitter struggle, complicated by all sorts of crosscurrents, in which the popes managed to block the formation of a unified political organization in Europe,[8] only to lose out eventually, at the beginning of the modern period, to the spirit of nationalism and to the national territorial state.

5 [The pope is addressing the emperor—AUTHOR.]

6 Gregory, who was born in humble circumstances, rose rapidly in the Papal Curia and became pope in 1073. He died in 1085.

7 The so-called "Papal Dictate," some excerpts from which follow, was probably not written by Gregory himself, but it expresses his point of view: "(1) That the Roman Church was established by God alone. (2) That the Roman pontiff alone is rightly called universal. . . . (8) That he alone may use the imperial insignia. (9) That all princes shall kiss the foot of the pope alone. . . . (12) That he has the right to depose emperors. . . . (16) That no general synod may be called without his order. (17) That no action of a synod and no book shall be regarded as canonical without his authority. . . . (19) That he can be judged by no one. . . . (22) That the Roman Church has never erred and will never err to all eternity. . . . (23) That the Roman pontiff who has been canonically ordained is made holy by the merits of St. Peter. . . . (24) That by his command or permission subjects may accuse their rulers. . . . (27) That he has the power to absolve subjects from their oath of fidelity to wicked rulers."

For the full list see Thatcher and McNeal, *A Source Book for Medieval History*, pp. 135–38.

8 It is not suggested that papal policy alone was responsible for the Empire's failure. See pp. 153–56.

The nature of this struggle may be illustrated by a brief account of a single dramatic episode in the investiture controversy. In 1075 Gregory suspended certain bishops who held sees in the imperial domain. Since bishops were ecclesiastical officers, it might be supposed that there could be no question of the pope's right to appoint (and so to remove) them. But the bishops were not merely ecclesiastical officers; they were also temporal lords and, as such, subjects of the emperor Henry IV. It was certainly arguable, therefore, that the emperor had the right to assure himself of their loyalty. This was not merely a legal question. Since half the land of Germany was in the hands of the Church, it was essential for Henry to control the policies of those who administered this immense ecclesiastical property. He therefore refused to recognize the Pope's action in removing the bishops. When Gregory complained, the emperor replied by calling a council of the German clergy and persuading them to vote to depose him. Gregory retorted by excommunicating Henry.

> He has refused to obey as a Christian should, he has not returned to God from whom he had wandered, he has . . . done many iniquities, he has despised the warnings which . . . I sent to him for his salvation, he has cut himself off from thy church. . . . Therefore, by thy authority, I place him under the curse. It is in thy name that I curse him, that all people may know that thou art Peter, and upon thy rock the Son of the living God has built his church, and the gates of hell shall not prevail against it.[f]

Challenged by this terrible threat, Henry found that his support evaporated. He was obliged to withdraw his edicts against Gregory and to humiliate himself publicly by kneeling in the snow at Canossa (1077) to pray for the Pope's forgiveness. This was not the total victory for Gregory that it might seem. If canon law gave the Pope the power to "bind and loose," it also required him to forgive the true penitent. Hence Henry's action frustrated Gregory's plans to enter Germany and remove the emperor from his throne. On the whole, therefore, Canossa was a draw, and though Gregory's successors abandoned his extreme position, they continued to pursue his policies in a more cautious way.

Thus, by the eleventh century the Church was no longer the otherworldly society of brothers that it had been at its inception. Partly as a result of the exigencies of the time, partly because of the ambition of its rulers, it had grown into a great secular institution; the popes had become temporal monarchs with great power—and with far greater pretensions to power than any of the secular sovereigns.

MONASTICISM

We may wonder at the fact that, during this long process of secularization, the Church's sense of spiritual mission survived. But survive it did, chiefly because of two movements that will now be discussed.

The first of these was monasticism, which by a curious coincidence had its origins in the fifth and sixth centuries, at precisely the time when, as we have seen, the grounds were being laid for the Church's claims to temporal power and worldly ends. Monasticism, considered in its essence, was nothing but a conscious and determined effort to return to the original otherworldliness of the Church. It can be said without too much exaggeration that, while the popes and the hierarchy were rendering unto Caesar the things that were Caesar's, the monks tried to render unto God the things that were His. The interplay and conflict between these two tendencies of the Church colored the whole epoch.

Withdrawal from the world in order to lead a solitary life was an early form of Christian worship. But the life of the hermit was feasible only in the warm climates around the southern Mediterranean coast. When Christianity spread to the harsher climates of northern Europe, separation from the world became possible only when groups of like-minded individuals banded together. In this way monasteries got their start. They gave sanctuary and provided the privacy judged necessary for concentrated communion with God. Unfortunately, however, many who called themselves monks were inspired not by a love of God but by the relative ease and security that the monastic life assured. Living by no rule, they lived as they liked and brought the monastic ideal into disrepute. As St. Benedict noted early in the sixth century, "In assuming the tonsure they are false to God, because they still serve the world in their lives. . . . Their law is their own desires, since they call that holy which they like, and that unlawful which they do not like. . . . They are governed by their own appetites and senses."

Hence Benedict drew up a rule for the governance of monastic societies that became the model for monastic life throughout the Middle Ages.

> *The qualities necessary for an abbot.* The abbot who is worthy to rule over a monastery ought always to bear in mind by what name he is called and to justify by his life his title of superior. . . . The abbot should know that the shepherd will have to bear the blame if the Master finds anything wrong with the flock. . . . The freeman is not to be preferred to the one who comes into the monastery out of servitude, unless there be some other good reason. . . . For whether slave or free, we are all one in Christ [Gal. 3:28] and bear the same yoke of servitude to the one Lord, for there is no respect of persons with God [Rom. 2:11]. . . . Therefore, the abbot should have the same love toward all and should subject all to the same discipline according to their respective merits. . . .
>
> Above all, the abbot should not be too zealous in the acquisition of earthly, transitory, mortal goods, forgetting and neglecting the care of the souls committed to his charge, but he should always remember that he has undertaken the government of souls of whose welfare he must render account. . . .
>
> *Taking counsel with the brethren.* Whenever important matters come up in the monastery, the abbot should call together the whole congregation [that is, all the monks], and tell them what is under consideration. After hearing

the advice of the brothers, he should reflect upon it and then do what seems best to him. . . .

Humility. Brethren, the holy Scripture saith: "And whosoever shall exalt himself shall be abased; and he that shall humble himself shall be exalted" [Matt. 23 : 12]. . . .

Now the first step of humility is this, to escape destruction by keeping ever before one's eyes the fear of the Lord, to remember always the commands of the Lord. . . .

The second step of humility is this, that a man should not delight in doing his own will and desires, but should imitate the Lord. . . .

The third step of humility is this, that a man be subject to his superior in all obedience for the love of God, imitating the Lord. . . .

The fourth step of humility is this, that a man endure all the hard and unpleasant things and even undeserved injuries that come in the course of his service, without wearying or withdrawing his neck from the yoke. . . .

The sixth step of humility is this, that the monk should be contented with any lowly or hard condition in which he may be placed, and should always look upon himself as an unworthy laborer, not fitted to do what is intrusted to him. . . .

The seventh step of humility is this, that he should not only say, but should really believe in his heart that he is the lowest and most worthless of all men. . . .

The eleventh step of humility is this, that the monk, when he speaks, should do so slowly and without laughter, softly and gravely, using few words and reasonable, and that he should not be loud of voice. . . .

The twelfth step of humility is this, that the monk should always be humble and lowly, not only in his heart, but in his bearing as well. . . .

Now when the monk has ascended all these steps of humility, he will arrive at that perfect love of God which casteth out all fear [I John 4 : 18]. . . .

Divine worship at night [vigils]. During the winter, that is, from the first of November to Easter, the monks should rise at the eighth hour of the night; a reasonable arrangement, since by that time the monks will have rested a little more than half the night and will have digested their food. . . .

How the monks should sleep. The monks shall sleep separately in individual beds, and the abbot shall assign them their beds according to their conduct. If possible all the monks shall sleep in the same dormitory, but if their number is too large to admit of this, they are to be divided into tens or twenties and placed under the control of some of the older monks. . . .

Monks should not have personal property. The sin of owning private property should be entirely eradicated from the monastery. No one shall presume to give or receive anything except by the order of the abbot; no one shall possess anything of his own, books, paper, pens, or anything else. . . .

The weekly service in the kitchen. The brothers shall serve in their turn in the kitchen, no one being excused, except for illness or because occupied in work of greater importance. . . .

The weekly reader. There should always be reading during the common meal, but it shall not be left to chance, so that anyone may take up the book and read. On Sunday one of the brothers shall be appointed to read during the following week. . . .

The amount of food. Two cooked dishes, served either at the sixth or the ninth hour, should be sufficient for the daily sustenance. We allow two because of differences in taste, so that those who do not eat one may satisfy their hunger with the other, but two shall suffice for all the brothers, unless it is possible to obtain fruit or fresh vegetables, which may be served as a third. . . .

The amount of drink. . . . A half-measure of wine a day is enough for anyone, making due allowance, of course, for the needs of the sick. . . .

The daily labor of the monks. Idleness is the great enemy of the soul, therefore the monks should always be occupied, either in manual labor or in holy reading. The hours for these occupations should be arranged according to the seasons. . . .

The ordination of the abbot. The election of the abbot shall be decided by the whole congregation or by that part of it, however small, which is of "the wiser and better counsel." . . . But if the whole congregation should agree to choose one simply because they know that he will wink at their vices, and the character of this abbot is discovered by the bishop of the diocese or by the abbots and Christian men of the neighborhood, they shall refuse their consent to the choice and shall interfere to set a better ruler over the house of God.[g]

These extracts will suggest the particular quality of the monastic ideal. Though it was certainly less rigorously ascetic than the view of, say, Jerome (who, clutching a stone in his hand, prayed alone in the desert), or that of Simeon (who sat for thirty years on the top of a column), it was far from the classical ideal of all-round personal development in a community of like-minded, enlightened gentlemen. The monks, like the Greeks of Plato's ideal community, were an elite—but an elite of self-sacrifice rather than one of birth or talent. Instead of pride, humility was the crown of their virtues. Whereas for the classical philosophers the ideal environment was one in which personality was stimulated and developed, for St. Benedict the ideal environment was a disciplinary background that served to deflate personality and to extirpate, both by example and by punishment, those very qualities that the Greeks had held it important to cultivate.

Of course, monastic society did not by any means live up to the nobility of Benedict's ideal. Despite his injunctions, abbots became men of wealth and property. Like the popes, the monks again and again turned from spiritual to temporal affairs. Simony, corruption, bribery, political maneuvering, and the affairs of Caesar appeared in the monasteries as well as elsewhere in the Church. But as often as this happened, there began a movement of reform that undertook to bring the monastic orders back to the ideals of Benedict, and the larger world of the Church back to its religious duties. Some of these reform movements originated inside the monasteries; some originated in the hierarchy itself, as, for instance, with Gregory VII, who at the same time that he was asserting the Church's claims against the temporal powers was demanding that the Church purge itself of its corruption and luxury. Some of the reformers were intellectuals; others became the leaders of great popular movements that swept up the whole of Christendom into an ecstasy of piety and Christian love.

THE FRIARS: ST. FRANCIS

This brings us to the second of the two movements that, as has been said, saved the Church from collapsing into a purely secular and this-worldly institution. While some reformers, like the Cluniacs and St. Bernard, worked primarily for the reform of the monasteries, others, equally imbued with mystic fervor and endowed with the primitive Church's passion, energy, and self-sacrifice, appealed to society as a whole. One of the most remarkable of the reforming mystics was Francis of Assisi (1182–1226), the founder of the Order of the Friars Minor, which he dedicated to poverty, simplicity, and good works, and which, after more than seven centuries, survives to this day as a potent force in the Church.

Some years after Francis' death, one of the members of his order was commissioned to write his biography. A few excerpts from this *Life of St. Francis* by St. Bonaventura will illustrate one important aspect of the medieval mind.

> There was a man in the city of Assisi, by name Francis, whose memory is blessed, for that God, graciously presenting him with the blessings of goodness, delivered him in His mercy from the perils of this present life, and abundantly filled him with the gifts of heavenly grace. For, albeit in his youth he was reared in vanity amid the vain sons of men, and, after gaining some knowledge of letters, was appointed unto a profitable business of merchandise, nevertheless, by the aid of the divine protection, he went not astray among the wanton youths after the lusts of the flesh, albeit given up unto pleasures; nor among the covetous merchants, albeit intent on his gains, did he put his trust in money and treasure. . . .
>
> But as yet Francis knew not the intent of God concerning him, forasmuch as he was both drawn away unto external things by his father's calling, and weighed down toward earthly things by the corruption inborn in our nature, and had not yet learned to contemplate heavenly things, nor accustomed himself to taste of divine. And, because the infliction of tribulation giveth understanding unto the spirit, the hand of the Lord was upon him . . . , afflicting his body with protracted sickness, that so He might prepare his soul for the anointing of the Holy Spirit. Now when he had regained his bodily strength, . . . he purposed, being as yet ignorant of the divine counsel, to betake himself into Apulia, unto a certain munificent Count, hoping in his service to win glory in arms. [But he had scarcely begun the journey when] he heard the Lord speaking unto him by night as with the voice of a friend, and saying, "Francis, who can do better for thee, the lord or the servant, the rich man or the poor?" And when Francis had made reply that alike the lord and the rich man could do the best, the Voice answered forthwith,

"Why, then, dost thou leave the Lord for the servant, the rich God for a poor mortal?" And Francis said, "Lord, what wilt Thou have me to do?" And the Lord said unto him, "Return unto thy country, for the vision that thou hast seen betokeneth that which shall be spiritually wrought, and is to be fulfilled in thee not by mortal counsel, but by divine." So, when it was morning, he returned in haste toward Assisi, confident and rejoicing, awaiting the will of the Lord.

Thenceforward he withdrew him from the stir of public business, devoutly praying the heavenly mercy that it would deign to show him that which he ought to do. And so by the constant practice of prayer the flame of heavenly yearning was mightily kindled within him, and for the love of his heavenly fatherland he now contemned all earthly things as naught. . . .

Thence that lover of utterest humility betook himself unto the lepers, and abode among them, with all diligence serving them all for the love of God. He would bathe their feet, and bind up their sores, drawing forth the corrupt matter from their wounds, and wiping away the blood; yea, in his marvellous devotion, he would even kiss their ulcerated wounds, he that was soon to be a Gospel physician. Wherefore he obtained from the Lord such power as that he received a marvellous efficacy in marvellously cleansing both soul and body from disease.

· ·

Now Francis, the servant of God, abiding at the church of the Virgin Mother of God, with continuous sighing besought her that had conceived the Word full of grace and truth that she would deign to become his advocate; and, by the merits of the Mother of Mercy, he did himself conceive and give birth unto the spirit of Gospel truth. For while on a day he was devoutly hearing the Mass of the Apostles, that Gospel was read aloud wherein Christ gave unto His disciples that were sent forth to preach the Gospel pattern for their life, to wit, that they should possess neither gold, nor silver, nor money in their purses, nor scrip for their journey, neither two coats, neither shoes, nor yet staves.[9] Hearing this, and understanding it, and committing it unto memory, the lover of Apostolic poverty was at once filled with joy unspeakable. "This," saith he, "is what I desire, yea, this is what I long for with my whole heart." Forthwith he loosed his shoes from off his feet, laid down his staff, cast aside his purse and his money, contented him with one scanty tunic, and, throwing aside his belt, took a rope for girdle, applying all the care of his heart to discover how best he might fulfil that which he had heard, and conform himself in all things unto the rule of Apostolic godliness.

From this time forward, the man of God began, by divine impulse, to become a jealous imitator of Gospel poverty, and to invite others unto penitence. . . .

Many . . . began by his ensample to turn their thoughts unto penitence, and, renouncing all, to join themselves unto him in habit and life. . . .

They . . . began to discuss whether they ought to live among men, or to betake them unto lonely places. But Francis, the servant of Christ, trusting

---

9 [Compare Augustine's symbolic interpretation of this passage. See p. 114—AUTHOR.]

not in his own efforts or those of his Brethren, with importunate prayer enquired the pleasure of the divine will concerning this. Then he was illumined by a divinely revealed oracle, and understood that he had been sent of the Lord unto this end, that he might win for Christ the souls that the devil was striving to carry off. Wherefore he chose to live rather for all men than for his single self, inspired by the ensample of Him Who brooked to die, One Man for all.

. . . .

He restrained his sensual appetites with such strict discipline as that he would barely take what was necessary to support life. For he was wont to say that it was difficult to satisfy the needs of the body without yielding unto the inclinations of the senses.[10] Wherefore he would hardly, and but seldom, allow himself cooked food when in health, and, when he did allow it, he would either sprinkle it with ashes, or by pouring water thereupon would as far as possible destroy its savour and taste. Of his drinking of wine what shall I say, when even of water he would scarce drink what he needed, while parched with burning thirst? . . . The bare ground for the most part served as a couch unto his wearied body, and he would often sleep sitting, with a log or a stone placed under his head, and, clad in one poor tunic, he served the Lord in cold and nakedness.[11]

. . . .

When he was at the hermitage of Sartiano, . . . a grievous temptation of the flesh laid hold on him. When the lover of chastity felt its oncoming, he laid aside his habit, and began to scourge himself severely with a cord, saying, "Ah, brother ass, thus must thou be led, thus must thou submit unto the lash! . . ." Then, impelled by a marvellous fervour of spirit, he threw open the door of his cell, and went out into the garden, where [he] plung[ed] his now naked body into a great snow-heap. . . . Then the tempter departed, routed, and the holy man returned unto his cell victorious, in that, by enduring the external cold in right penitent fashion, he had so extinguished the fire of lust within that thereafter he felt it no whit.

. . . .

When he bethought him of the first beginning of all things, he was filled with a yet more overflowing charity, and would call the dumb animals, howsoever small, by the names of *brother* and *sister,* forasmuch as he recognized in them the same origin as in himself. . . .

When he drew nigh unto Bevagna he came unto a spot wherein a great multitude of birds of divers species were gathered together. . . . They on their part all awaited him and turned toward him, those that were perched on bushes bending their heads as he drew nigh them, and looking on him in unwonted wise, while he came right among them, and diligently exhorted them all to hear the word of God, saying, "My brothers the birds, much ought ye to praise your Creator, Who hath clothed you with feathers and given you wings to fly, and hath made over unto you the pure air, and careth for you without your taking thought for yourselves." . . . He, with wondrous fervour of spirit, passed in and out among them, touching them with his habit,

10 [This, of course, was a problem Augustine had also encountered. See pp. 75–77—AUTHOR.]
11 [Notice how much more ascetic this is than Benedict's rule—AUTHOR.]

nor did one of them move from the spot until he had made the sign of the Cross over them and given them leave; then, with the blessing of the man of God, they all flew away together.

. . . .

When, therefore, by seraphic glow of longing he had been uplifted toward God, and by his sweet compassion had been transformed into the likeness of Him Who of His exceeding love endured to be crucified—on a certain morning about the Feast of the Exaltation of Holy Cross, while he was praying on the side of the mountain, he beheld a Seraph having six wings, flaming and resplendent, coming down from the heights of heaven. When in his flight most swift he had reached the space of air nigh the man of God, there appeared betwixt the wings the Figure of a Man crucified. . . . Accordingly, as the vision disappeared, it left in his heart a wondrous glow, but on his flesh also it imprinted a no less wondrous likeness of its tokens. For forthwith there began to appear in his hands and feet the marks of the nails, even as he had just beheld them in that figure of the Crucified. . . . The right side, moreover, was—as if it had been pierced by a lance—seamed with a ruddy scar, where from ofttimes welled the sacred blood, staining his habit and breeches.[h]

In view of the Church's increasing political commitments and its great wealth and power, it was highly "unrealistic" for Francis to hope for a return to the old ideal of poverty and otherworldliness. Indeed, by the thirteenth century the Church had made itself so indispensable to Western society that any sudden abandonment of its secular role would have been disastrous. It is not surprising, therefore, that Francis failed; what is surprising is the measure of his success. This is testimony alike to the remarkable force of his personality and to the temper of the age. One way of grasping the enormous difference between the Middle Ages and our own time is to ask what would happen to a St. Francis in the twentieth century, with his kissing of lepers' sores, his preaching to birds, and his stigmata. It is much more likely that we would sorrowfully commit him to a mental institution, perhaps for shock therapy with the aim of restoring his sanity, than that we would allow him to inflame our hearts with a love of God and a zeal for poverty.

To understand the mind of the Middle Ages, it is necessary to realize that it was capable of being inflamed. It is not, of course, that the average man of the Middle Ages was an out-and-out otherworldly ascetic. It is rather that even the average man, immersed in the routine of ordinary life, was profoundly touched by an otherworldly appeal. Even when he was most absorbed in this world, he believed that his earthly life derived whatever significance it had from the life beyond. This sense of the transitoriness and the dependency of this life gave an ambivalence to the medieval mind that distinguishes it sharply from the modern mind.

Naturally, this ambivalence also characterized the medieval Church. The history of the Church during the Middle Ages revealed, first, an increasing involvement in this-worldly affairs and, second, a corresponding reaction on the part of those who believed that this involvement was a denial of the original purposes of the Founder and who deplored the vices that power brought in its train. At the practical level, the problem for the Church was to survive institutionally the tensions produced by these conflicts; at the intellectual level, its problem was to formulate a theoretical account of its mission that, while continuing to rest on the Founder's otherworldly beliefs, nevertheless authorized its new activities. As we shall see, one of the greatest achievements of Aquinas was the successful working out of the rationale for this compromise.

Feudalism

So far the gradual development of a great this-worldly institution out of the primitive Church has been examined. Let us now retrace our steps and consider the emergence of those medieval political institutions that were the Church's sole rivals to secular supremacy.

After the confusion of the barbarian invasions, a number of separate kingdoms gradually emerged in the former imperial provinces. A Lombard kingdom was established in Italy; a Gothic kingdom in Spain; a Vandal kingdom (soon to be overrun in its turn by the Mohammedans) in Africa; an Anglo-Saxon kingdom in Britain; a Frankish kingdom in Gaul. In this way, while the Church continued to assert the old imperial universalism, transmuted now into the notion of a universal Catholic Christendom presided over by God's vicar, the old Empire was politically fragmented. A sign of this fragmentation was the gradual development, alongside the original Latin language spoken universally in the Empire, of a number of barbarian tongues—ancestors of the national languages of modern Europe. The seeds of particularism, already sown, were now germinating.

The root of the trouble was the particularistic social structure that the Middle Ages developed. This structure resisted not only the creation of a universal imperial system but even the full development of those lesser units that were the successors of the barbarian kingdoms. The result was that the state in the modern, or even in the ancient, sense could not exist until the collapse of feudalism.

What was feudalism and how did it develop out of the barbarian kingdoms? Fully developed feudalism did not emerge until the chaotic times that followed the collapse of Charlemagne's short-lived empire, but the basis for it was laid even before the final dissolution of the Roman Empire. In those troubled times, as the central government proved incapable of performing its proper functions, more and more responsibilities fell on men of property in the various parts of the Empire. Long before the final collapse, the collection of taxes had been entrusted to landowners, and in the course of time it became the practice to make them—or, perhaps more exactly, to *allow* them to become—responsible for the administration of justice on their own estates. This right, or privilege, was called "immunity," and it prohibited the agents of the central authority from entering such an estate to apprehend criminals or to put down disorder. Another practice, also a sign of the chaos of the times, was called "commendation." In return for a promise of protection, the owner of a small farm might "commend" himself and his property to some greater landowner. After so commending himself, the small farmer would continue to occupy and farm the land as before, but he would no longer be a fully independent owner; he would have exchanged independence for security.

Now, as it happened, the relationship that obtained between a barbarian chieftain and his warrior followers was in some respects not unlike the relationship of commendation. The warriors were free men; so were the small, dependent farmers. The relationship between the warriors and their chief was personal rather than legal, being founded in the main on mutual trust and on the prospect of battles to be fought and won together. Nevertheless, as in the relation of commendation, the warriors felt dependent on the chief, who, in return, recognized that he owed them protection. Hence it was natural for the barbarians, when they settled down in the former imperial provinces, to adopt the similar practices they found there. As a result, in the course of time the relationship of commendation took on some of the color of the chieftain-warrior relationship, while the latter acquired legal status as a result of being defined in terms of commendation.

Again, when a newly settled chief wanted to reward his warrior followers, the most obvious form of pay was land, which had only to be taken away from the native population. The estates so granted were accorded the old Roman "immunities" and so became virtually independent territories, except for the fact that the new owners were bound to their benefactors by those ties of personal loyalty that barbarian warriors owed to their chiefs.

Thus, though the greatest barbarian chiefs now began to call themselves "kings," and though they and their warrior followers settled down into fixed societies that can fairly be called "states," the centralized administration that the Romans had known, the administration that had once tied the whole land into a single system, was not regained. In dividing the land among their followers, the new kings also divided whatever governmental functions had chanced to survive the collapse of the Empire.

Though Charlemagne (about 742–814) organized a central government and was actually crowned emperor, his administration fell apart shortly after his death. In the chaotic times that followed, commendation (interpreted now in terms of the relationships that have been described) was greatly expanded and came to be repeated at every level of society. Eventually, virtually everybody was "commended" to somebody above him and, in turn, had others commended to him. And just as the administration of each kingdom came to be divided among a number of great feudalities, so the administration of each feudality came to be divided among lesser units, the administration of these among still lesser units, and so on. As a result, all administrative and police functions—indeed, authority of every sort—came to be tied to land tenure. To complicate matters, no land was held unconditionally; land was always held from a second party who held it from a third party and so forth. Of course, the condition of tenure was a pledge of service of one kind or another.

The life of the community as a whole thus came to depend on a complex of personal relationships. The Greek (and Roman) notion that every citizen stands in an identical relationship to the state and owes it (or its sovereign) his whole individual loyalty—a notion that many of us share—was replaced in the Middle Ages by the notion of personal loyalty to one's immediate overlord. And, in contrast to our conception of the state's impartial obligation to all citizens, men of the Middle Ages identified governmental responsibility with the overlord's personal responsibility for those who owed him allegiance. Medieval social theory was thus dominated by the concept of status rather than the concept of citizenship.

To understand what feudalism meant to medieval political organization, let us suppose the United States to be organized today on the following basis: The governorship of New York has become an hereditary right of the Dukes of Albany, the governorship of California, an hereditary right of the Earls of Sacramento, and so on—each governorship is hereditary in some great family. It is true that each governor has an overlord, the President of the United States (from whom, long ago, his forefathers received their fief). But as long as each governor, on coming into his inheritance, swears the old oath of personal loyalty, and as long as he annually pays the feudal dues set out in the contract that accompanied the oath (perhaps the gift of a hogshead of wine or a new suit of clothes or the duty of turning up occasionally to "give counsel" or to "kiss hands"), he is sovereign in his own domain.

He is sovereign, that is, as far as his feudal *superior* is concerned. In the governor's domain, the President of the United States (who, in this example, is the apex of the feudal pyramid) may not issue orders or enforce them, collect taxes, or perform any of the functions that we hold to be those of the sovereign. But though the governor is thus sovereign in respect to his relations with *his* feudal superior, his domain consists of fiefs held by lesser lords on the same basis as that on which he holds his from the President: The mayors of San Francisco and Los Angeles, in *their* domains, are independent sovereigns owing only a formal allegiance to the governor of California. So, just as the President's authority breaks on the feudal independence of the governors, the authority of each governor breaks on the feudal independence of the mayors, their authority, in turn, breaks on the independence of the lesser fiefs, and so on down to ward and precinct bosses.

And now, to make matters still more confused, suppose that all sorts of feudal cross-relationships exist. Suppose that the Duke of Albany has inherited a summer home in Santa Barbara; clearly, this makes him the feudal inferior (in California) of the Earl of Sacramento, to whom he owes allegiance. Yet in New York he is an independent agent, owing allegiance only to the President. To add still another element of complexity, suppose that Rotary International is a great landowner. Since all land, on feudal theory, is held in fief from some other person, and since every fief-holder owes personal allegiance to the person from whom he holds his fief, it follows that the president of every local Rotary club is the feudal inferior of somebody or other (he may, of course, be in another connection that same person's feudal superior!), and this relationship cuts directly across the special duties that, as a faithful Rotarian, he owes to the president of Rotary International.

Now let us translate this fantasy back into the terms of the Middle Ages. For "United States" read "Western Christendom"; for President, Holy Roman Emperor; for the governors of the several states, the kings of the various Western countries; for mayors, the great feudal dukes and counts; for ward heelers and dogcatchers, the small barons and knights; for Rotary International, the Holy and Apostolic Catholic Church. This does not much exaggerate the fragmentation of medieval political life. Every small baron had his own court of law, levied his own import and export duties, and warred continually with his neighbors; and the same relationships repeated themselves at each higher stage. At the top was the emperor, to whom, theoretically, the various kings owed feudal allegiance. But the emperor was far too weak to enforce the theory, just as the kings themselves were usually too weak to enforce their feudal rights with regard to their dukes and counts, and so on to the bottom of the line—the great mass of common men, the serfs, who, owning no land, were the superiors of no man.

Chivalry

The Church and feudalism—the two great institutions of the Middle Ages—colored every phase of medieval life. At times they were in conflict, as in the investiture struggle; at times they were in accord, as in the chivalric ideal. This noble conception, emphasizing both private honor and public service, was another characteristic aspect of medieval culture.

ST. LOUIS, KING OF FRANCE

Perhaps the outstanding example of chivalry was Louis IX, king of France. Louis was born in 1214, a few years after the founding of the Franciscan Order. In 1248, leaving his kingdom under a regency, he took the cross and set out to recapture Jerusalem, which had fallen to the Saracens after a brief period of Christian rule. This crusade was a dismal failure, and after six years Louis returned to France to find his barons in revolt. These misfortunes did not deter him from trying once more to recover Jerusalem. In 1270 he organized another crusade, only to die while the expedition was in its second month. He was canonized in 1298.

According to Louis' biographer and friend, the Sire de Joinville,[12] Louis frequently discussed the nature of the chivalric ideal with his knights. "Upright" and "worthy" were the terms that he thought best described it. To be an upright and worthy man was, he held, better far than to be a friar. "Willingly would I bear the title of upright and worthy provided I were such in reality—and all the rest you might have. For uprightness and worth are such great things and such good things that even to name them fills the mouth pleasantly."[i]

What, exactly, did Louis take uprightness and worthiness to mean? In the first place, the upright man is courageous. But more than courage was involved in the ideal.

> For there are many valiant knights in Christian lands, and in the lands of the Saracens, who never believed in God nor in His mother. Whence I tell you . . . that God grants a great gift, and a very special grace, to the Christian knight whom He suffers to be valiant of body, and at the same time keeps in His service, guarding him from mortal sin. And the knight who thus governs himself should be called right worthy because that prowess comes to him by the gift of God. And those [others] may be called valiant because they are valiant of their body, and yet neither fear God nor are afraid of sin.[j]

Besides being courageous, the true Christian knight must be modest, charitable, sober, faithful, and just. Joinville drew on his own conversations with Louis to illustrate how the king exemplified these chivalric virtues.

> For instance, as regards sobriety, Louis. . . put water into his wine by measure, according as he saw that the strength of the wine would suffer it. At Cyprus he asked me why I put no water into my wine; and I said this was by order of the physicians, who told me I had a large head and a cold stomach, so that I could not get drunk. And he answered that they deceived me; for if I did not learn to put water into my wine in my youth, and wished to do so in my old age, gout and diseases of the stomach would take hold upon me, and I should never be in health; and if I drank pure wine in my old age, I should get drunk every night, and that it was too foul a thing for a brave man to get drunk.

And as for humility, Louis

> . . . asked me if I washed the feet of the poor on Holy Thursday. "Sire," said I, "it would make me sick! The feet of these villains will I not wash."

12 Joinville (1224–1317), himself a notable example of the chivalric ideal, was a member of a great feudal house and Seneschal of Champagne. He wrote this biography of his royal friend in 1309, when he was eighty-five years old.

> "In truth," said he, "that was ill said; for you should never disdain what God did for our teaching. So I pray you, for the love of God first, and then for the love of me, that you accustom yourself to wash the feet of the poor."

Louis' horror of sin was such that, like Augustine, he found it natural to describe sin in terms of a loathsome disease:

> "Now I ask you," said he, "which you would the better like, either to be a leper, or to have committed a mortal sin?" And I, who never lied to him, made answer that I would rather have committed thirty mortal sins than be a leper. . . . And he answered, . . . "You should know that there is no leprosy so hideous as the being in mortal sin. . . . When a man dies, he is healed of the leprosy in his body; but when a man who has committed mortal sin dies, he cannot know of a certainty that he has, during his lifetime, repented in such sort that God has forgiven him; wherefore he must stand in great fear lest that leprosy of sin should last as long as God is in paradise."

But Louis' ideals of charity and humility did not apply to Jews. Apparently, he held that it was no sin to mistreat them:

> He told me that there was once a great disputation between clergy and Jews at the monastery of Cluny. And there was at Cluny a poor knight [who] asked that they should bring to him the greatest clerk and most learned master among the Jews; and they did so. Then he asked the Jew a question, which was this: "Master," said the knight, "I ask you if you believe that the Virgin Mary, who bore God in her body and in her arms, was a virgin mother, and is the mother of God?"
> And the Jew replied that of all this he believed nothing. . . . Whereupon [the knight] lifted his crutch and smote the Jew near the ear, and beat him to the earth. Then the Jews turned to flight, and bore away their master, sore wounded. And so ended the disputation.
> The abbot came to the knight and told him he had committed a deed of very great folly. But the knight replied that the abbot had committed a deed of greater folly in gathering people together for such a disputation; for there were a great many good Christians there who, before the disputation came to an end, would have gone away misbelievers through not fully understanding the Jews. "And I tell you," said the king, "that no one, unless he be a very learned clerk, should dispute with them; but a layman, when he hears the Christian law mis-said, should not defend the Christian law, unless it be with his sword, and with that he should pierce the mis-sayer in the midriff, so far as the sword will enter."

Here, of course, the man of action, mistrustful of learning and disputation, is speaking. For Louis, as for St. Francis, simple faith was enough:

> The holy king . . . said that we ought to believe so firmly the articles of faith that neither from fear of death, nor for any mischief that might happen

to the body, should we be willing to go against them in word or deed. And he said that the Enemy is so subtle that, when people are dying, he labours all he can to make them die doubting as to some points of the faith. For he knows that he can in no wise deprive a man of the good works he has done; and he knows also that the man is lost to him if he dies in the faith.[k]

Though Louis may have been close to Francis in faith and piety and in devotion to a life of apostolic charity, he had a strong sense of rank and held that a man ought to dress and act according to his place in society. A knight ought to maintain the dignity of the outward, as well as the virtue of the inward, man. "You ought to clothe yourselves well and suitably, so that your wives may love you the better, and your people hold you in the greater honour."[1]

As king, Louis therefore felt it incumbent on himself to maintain an elaborate court ceremonial. At a "full court" at Saumur in 1241—"the best-ordered court that ever I saw," according to Joinville—

> . . . at the King's table ate, after him, the Count of Poitiers, whom he had newly made knight at the feast of St. John; and after the Count of Poitiers, ate the Count of Dreux, whom he had also newly made knight; and after the Count of Dreux the Count of la Marche; and after the Count of la Marche the good Count Peter of Brittany; and before the king's table, opposite the Count of Dreux, ate my lord the King of Navarre, in tunic and mantle of samite well bedight with a belt and a clasp, and a cap of gold; and I carved before him. . . .
>
> In order to guard the king's table there were there my Lord Imbert of Beaujeu, who was afterwards Constable of France, and my Lord Enguerrand of Coucy, and my Lord Archamband of Bourbon. Behind these three barons stood some thirty of their knights, in tunics of silken cloth, to keep guard over them; and behind these knights there were a great quantity of sergeants. . . .
>
> [The banquet] hall is built after the fashion of the cloisters of the white monks of the Cistercian order. But I think there is none other hall so large, and by a great deal. And I will tell you why I think so—it is because by the wall of the cloister, where the king ate, surrounded by his knights and sergeants who occupied a great space, there was also room for a table where ate twenty bishops and archbishops, and yet again, besides the bishops and archbishops, the Queen Blanche, the king's mother, ate near their table, at the head of the cloister, on the other side from the king. . . .
>
> At the end of the cloister, on the other side, were the kitchens, the cellars, the pantries and the butteries; from this end were served to the king and to the queen meats, and wine, and bread. And in the wings and in the central court ate the knights, in such numbers, that I knew not how to count them.[m]

Louis' sense of feudal status showed, too, in his dealings with the king of England. When his council protested that Louis was treating that monarch too leniently after having defeated him in battle,

. . . the king replied that he knew well that the King of England had no right to the land, but that there was a reason why he should give it him, "for," said he, ". . . a very great honour accrues to me through the peace that I have made with the King of England, seeing that he is now my liegeman,[13] which he was not aforetime."[n]

THE MEDIEVAL POLITICAL IDEAL

Though there was thus a very considerable area of identity between the chivalric and the monastic ideals, there was also considerable difference between them. Whereas the monk retired from this world to avoid contamination, Louis and Joinville lived in this world—Louis because it was his duty as king, Joinville partly because it was his duty in his lesser station and partly because, quite frankly, he enjoyed this world.

St. Francis, too, lived in this world, but he did not live of it. By living in it, he hoped to convert it to the monastic ideal that St. Benedict had thought only an elite could achieve. Louis, for his part, had a noble but less otherworldly ideal. Though it was imbued with Christian idealism, his was nonetheless a political ideal. In the instructions the dying king left for his heir, he put first, it is true, the individual Christian's private duty to his God: "Fair son, the first thing I would teach thee is to set thine heart to love God; for unless he love God none can be saved." But most of Louis' testament was taken up with a Christian prince's political responsibilities.

> Maintain the good customs of thy realm, and abolish the bad. Be not covetous against thy people; and do not burden them with taxes and imposts save when thou art in great need. . . .
>
> Give heed that thy servants and thy subjects live under thee in peace and uprightness. Especially maintain the good cities and commons of thy realm in the same estate and with the same franchises as they enjoyed under thy predecessors. . . . For because of the power and wealth of the great cities, thine own subjects, and specially thy peers and thy barons, and foreigners also, will fear to undertake aught against thee.
>
> Love and honour all persons belonging to holy Church, and see that no one take away, or diminish, the gifts and alms made to them by thy predecessors. . . .
>
> Bestow the benefices of holy Church on persons who are righteous and of a clean life, and do it on the advice of men of worth and uprightness. . . .
>
> Use diligence to have good provosts and bailiffs. . . . Labour to free thy land from all vile iniquity, and especially strike down with all thy power

13 [The same conception of status affected Joinville's relations with Louis. Before the king set out on his crusade, he "summoned all his barons to Paris, and made them take oath that, if anything happened to him while away, they would give faith and loyalty to his children." Though he asked Joinville to do the same, and though Joinville was the king's devoted friend and admirer, Joinville "would not take the oath, because I was not his liegeman" (*Joinville's Chronicle of the Crusade of St. Louis*, in *Memoirs of the Crusades* [Marzials], p. 164)—AUTHOR.]

evil swearing and heresy. See to it that the expense of thy household be reasonable.°

Louis certainly dealt facilely with the difficult problems of the relation of Church and state and the growing conflict between the retrogressive, divisive interests of the great feudalities and the new centralizing aspirations of the monarchy. These were questions that he was content to leave to the jurists and the philosophers. But the fact that such questions are suggested by, or implied in, what he did say, shows that a new day had dawned. Because men had gradually and painfully built a stake for themselves in the present, this-worldly problems once again came to be important.

The nature of this stake in the present is suggested in Louis' testament. "Maintain the good cities and the commons," he urged his son. And, significantly, he emphasized the wealth and power of the burghers as a counterpoise to the feudal barons. The locus of power was beginning to shift to wealthy commoners. Urban culture, which had been virtually destroyed when the Empire collapsed but which was eventually to supplant feudalism, was reviving. Doubtless the "good cities" were as yet but small islands scattered here and there in the great sea of rural poverty, superstition, and ignorance. But they, not the manors and not the baronial castles, were the womb in which new life was stirring.

All these new currents of thought and feeling, all these changing attitudes toward life, would have to be taken into account by the philosophical synthesis that was finally to emerge as the crowning achievement of the Middle Ages.

Art and Letters

ARCHITECTURE

The twelfth and thirteenth centuries were a period of great artistic flowering. Shortly before the middle of the twelfth century, architects discovered how to carry the weight of a heavy stone ceiling on a system of ogival vaulting. This simple and flexible engineering device made possible a much lighter and freer architectural style—the Gothic—which was characterized by the use of pointed arches and extensive fenestration. Among the earliest buildings in which the new engineering principles were employed were the abbey church of St. Denis (begun in 1137) and the cathedrals of Noyon and Senlis. In the cathedrals of Paris (begun in 1163) and Rheims (begun in 1211) the style achieved its definitive form, and in the Sainte Chapelle (begun in 1244 by St. Louis to house a precious relic of Christ's Passion) it may be said to have reached its height. In this building extraordinary lightness and grace were achieved by carrying the stone vaults on a series of slim external buttresses, which left virtually the whole of the wall area free for treatment in a series of colorful stained-glass windows.

Thus, in the course of a single century, a style was achieved that provided an almost perfect medium for expressing the religious aspirations of the men of the age. In this respect, the twelfth century is reminiscent of the fifth century B.C., which saw the development of another architectural style that likewise focused and canalized esthetic impulse without artificially restricting it, and so enabled men to express their esthetic feelings with clarity and precision. And just as the stylistic achievement of the Periclean age coincided with the flood of building and sculpture released by the enthusiasm that came with victory over the Persians, so, in the twelfth and thirteenth centuries, by another happy coincidence, the development of the Gothic style coincided with such an outpouring of religious energy that soon the face of Europe was covered with the noble evidences of Christian piety.

PAINTING AND POETRY

During the same period, the first harbingers of a "sweet new style" in painting appeared. Whereas earlier painters, executing compositions that displayed stiff figures against solid gold backgrounds, had achieved their effects by a kind of somber monumentality, Giotto (1267–1337) dispensed with frozen gesture and hierarchical pose. He painted men and women who lived, breathed, and moved about in a natural world, men and women who experienced the same human emotions—tenderness, joy, sorrow—as the spectators themselves.

This new interest in nature and in man was reflected not only in the plastic and graphic arts but also in poetry—indeed, in every department of life. Sometime during the twelfth century, an unknown author wrote the story of Aucassin and Nicolete:

> 'Tis how two young lovers met,
> Aucassin and Nicolete,
> Of the pains the lover bore
> And the sorrows he outwore,
> For the goodness and the grace,
> Of his love, so fair of face.
> Sweet the song, the story sweet,
> There is no man hearkens it,
> No man living 'neath the sun,
> So outwearied, so foredone,
> Sick and woful, worn and sad,
> But is healéd, but is glad,
>   'Tis so sweet.[P]

The story *is* sweet—romantic, sentimental, this-worldly. Aucassin was all a hero should be: "fair was he, goodly, and great. His hair was yellow, in little curls, his eyes blue and laughing." And Nicolete was all a heroine should be: "Her locks were yellow and curled, her eyes blue and smiling, her face featly fashioned, the nose high and fairly set, the lips more red than cherry or rose in time of summer, her teeth white and small; her breasts so firm that they bore up the folds of her bodice as they had been two apples." But because she lacked the noble birth that Aucassin's proud parents thought indispensable in their son's bride, these were ill-starred lovers. Imprisonment, wars, kidnappings, magic, and Saracens kept them separated until it was discovered that Nicolete, far from being low-born, was the daughter of the king of Carthage. Meanwhile, Aucassin had succeeded to his father's estates, and the two lovers were finally united to live happily ever after.

> Then Aucassin wedded her,
> Made her Lady of Biaucaire.
> Many years abode they there,
> Many years in shade or sun,
> In great gladness and delight.
> Ne'er hath Aucassin regret
> Nor his lady Nicolete.
> Now my story all is done,
>   Said and sung!

Another popular poem was *The Romance of the Rose*,[14] an elaborate allegory of courtly love that appealed to a somewhat more sophisticated, but equally this-worldly and romantic, audience.

> Beside the spring a while I stayed,
> Admiring how the crystals made
> Mirrors for all the lovely things
> That filled the garden. . . .
> From all things mirrored there I chose
> A rose bush, charged with many a rose, . . .
> Thousands of roses! Deeply hued,
> No one in this wide world has viewed
> Such rich profusion; some as yet
> Mere buds, which therefore had not met
> The rude winds' kiss, while others were
> Half opened, and such beauty rare
> Displayed as no man would despise
> Who once upon them cast his eyes;
> For roses which are fully blown
> Will soon begin to let fall down
> Their petals, while the tender new
> Fresh buds, as yet untouched by dew,
> Will keep their beauty while the sun

---

14 This poem's first part, from which excerpts are given, was written by Guillaume de Lorris about 1225, when St. Louis was a lad and when Joinville and Thomas Aquinas were babes in arms.

His course through three full days will run. . . .
The God of Love, whose bow was bent
With deadly aim, where'er I went
Pursued my steps, and took his stand
Beneath a fig-tree, close at hand
To where, with arm aloft, I sought
To pluck the Rose whose beauty brought
Me hither; then he took a shaft
And placing it with bowman's craft,
Drew the string taut against his ear
With mighty arm, for he that gear
Knows how to handle; straightway flew
The shaft from it, which surely knew
Its fatal target; through my heart
Quick pierced the golden-headed dart. . . .
With bounding step the God of Love
Hastened toward me, and stood above
My prostrate form, then gaily cried:
"Vassal! In vain have you denied
Yourself my prisoner; no dread
Or gloom need haunt you, cheer instead.
The readier you do my will,
The quicker I shall be to fill
Your heart with joy. . . ."
I answered: "Sir, to you I give
Myself as long as I shall live:
Before God, I will never fight
Against you, Lord; yours is the right. . . .
Your vassal grants the homage due."

Clearly, a society that sympathized with Aucassin and Nicolete and enjoyed *The Romance of the Rose*, with its appreciation of natural beauty and its characterization of the god of love as a feudal overlord, could not have been utterly absorbed in the life to come. Yet the life to come was always in the minds of the men of this age. Dante[15] could feel for Beatrice a love as secular as that described by Guillaume de Lorris or—for that matter—by Shakespeare in his sonnets. But for Dante, earthly love symbolized celestial love. This was no mere rationalization by means of which he escaped the guilt he might otherwise have felt because of the strong sexual passion he experienced. On the contrary, because Dante and all other medieval men perceived the visible universe in the context of an invisible one, *all* experiences, not merely sexual love, had an added dimension that is largely lacking in modern life. This added dimension, this enriched meaning, is revealed in Dante's sonnet:

15 Dante was born in 1265 in Florence. He lived there, playing a considerable part in the life of the city, until he was exiled by political opponents in 1302. From that year until his death he lived in various cities in Italy under the protection of different princes. He died in 1321.

To every heart which the sweet pain doth move,
   And unto which these words may now be brought
   For true interpretation and kind thought,
Be greeting in our Lord's name which is Love.
Of those long hours within the stars, above,
   Wake and keep watch, the third was almost nought
   When Love was shown me with such terrors fraught
As may not carelessly be spoken of.
He seem'd like one who is full of joy, and had
   My heart within his hand, and on his arm
   My lady, with a mantle round her, slept;
Whom (having waken'd her) anon he made
To eat that heart; she ate, as fearing harm.
   Then he went out; and as he went, he wept.[q]

If we took this sonnet as a purely "literary" production (as it might well have been if it had been written by a nineteenth- or twentieth-century poet), we could read it fairly straightforwardly. But in the context of Dante's life as a whole and in view of what is known about his philosophy, it is clear that the Beatrice of *The New Life* is not only the young Florentine woman, Beatrice Portinari, who married another man and died at an early age; she is also a transcendental principle in the universe. In *The Comedy,* we are told that it was Beatrice who descended into Limbo to summon Virgil to act as Dante's guide through Hell and Purgatory. The symbolism is complex but exact. Virgil, who represents secular knowledge, can conduct Dante only as far as the Earthly Paradise; beyond that point, Beatrice, who represents divine love, becomes his guide. The last hazard that Dante encounters before he meets Beatrice is a wall of flame, the purging fire of Purgatory. Though this so terrifies him that he is incapable of moving, Virgil has but to remind him that he will "see Beatrice when this wall is past" and his "hard paralysis" is at once dissolved.

A lady came in view . . .

My soul—such years had passed since last it saw
   that lady and stood trembling in her presence,
   stupefied by the power of holy awe—

now, by some power that shone from her above
   the reach and witness of my mortal eyes,
   felt the full mystery of enduring love.[r]

Dante's early, sexual love for Beatrice had survived all the vicissitudes of a long and difficult life, but at the same time it had been purged by these vicissitudes and transformed into a nobler passion. Thus, in the poems and also in Dante's thought, "Beatrice" names both the woman Beatrice Portinari and the messenger of the Blessed Virgin.

Accordingly, we should perhaps revise our reading of *The Romance of the Rose*. The "God of Love" of that poem is certainly a pagan Pan, but he is also the Christian Savior. So, too, the pain the lover experiences from Cupid's darts can be interpreted as the anguish felt by the Christian mystic separated from his God.

Such identifications were possible for men of the thirteenth century because they no longer felt a chasm between the this-worldly and the otherworldly, between the secular and the divine. In this respect, as in so many others, the century was a period of transition. As has been seen, the chasm was bridged in Dante's case by the conversion of an earthly love into a religious passion. This can be taken as a sign of the fact that, even when they seemed secular-minded, men of the Middle Ages viewed the natural world sacramentally. Thirteenth-century man was far from abandoning the Christian notion that this life is a sacrament. But he *was* abandoning the old view that this world is in hostile opposition to the other world. Instead, he conceived of this world as a means to the other. If Dante's love of God perfected his love for Beatrice, his love of Beatrice was, in his view, the means by which he mounted to the love of God.

Thus, in a way, Dante returned to the Greek view, recounted in Plato's *Symposium*, that love can be the ladder by which the soul mounts from lower to higher things. But whereas for Plato the highest love was an intellectual love of the abstract Form of the Good, for Dante it was a Christian love of the omnipotent Father. These complex relationships precisely parallel those in which, as we shall see, Thomas held the realm of nature and the realm of grace to stand.[16]

Science

BARTHOLOMEW THE ENGLISHMAN

It was some time before the new appreciation of nature that was reflected in the art and literature of the twelfth and thirteenth centuries issued in any very profound study of nature. In many respects, it must be said, twelfth-century science had advanced little beyond Isidore of Seville.[17] One of the most popular writers on scientific subjects in the Middle Ages was Bartholomew the Englishman. A few passages from his book *On the Properties of Things* (written about 1230) will show the state of scientific knowledge at the beginning of the thirteenth century.

16 See pp. 212–14.
17 See p. 141.

> Matter and form are principles of all bodily things; and privation of matter and form is naught else but destruction of all things. And the more subtle and high matter is in kind, the more able it is to receive form and shape. . . . And matter is principle and beginning of distinction, and of diversity, and of multiplying, and of things that are gendered. For the thing that gendereth and the thing that is gendered are not diverse but touching matter. . . . Of form is diversity, by the which one thing is diverse from another, and some form is essential, and some accidental. . . . And when form is had, then the thing hath its being, and when form is destroyed nothing of the substance of the thing is found. . . . Form maketh matter known. . . . Nothing is more unknown than is matter; for matter is never seen without form, nor form may not be seen in deed, but joined to matter.

Though Bartholomew was indebted to Aristotle for this discussion, he did not *use* the Aristotelian concepts he borrowed; he merely described them in a confused—and confusing—way. Aristotle's influence also appears, at least verbally, in Bartholomew's account of perception:

> The sight is most simple, for it is fiery, and knoweth suddenly things that be full far. The sight is shapen in this manner. In the middle of the eye, that is, the black thereof, is a certain humour most pure and clear. The philosophers call it crystalloid, for it taketh suddenly divers forms and shapes of colours as crystal doth. The sight is a wit of perceiving and knowing of colours, figures, and shapes, and outer properties. Then to make the sight perfect, these things are needful, that is to wit, the cause efficient, the limb of the eye convenient to the thing that shall be seen, the air that bringeth the likeness to the eye, and taking heed, and easy moving. The cause efficient is that virtue that is called animal. The instrument and limb is the humour like crystal in either eye clear and round. It is clear that by the clearness thereof the eye may beshine the spirit, and air; it is round that it be stronger to withstand griefs. The outer thing helping to work, is the air, without which being a means, the sight may not be perfect. It needeth to take heed, for if the soul be occupied about other things than longeth to the sight, the sight is the less perfect.

Representative of Bartholomew's treatment of specific phenomena is his account of magnetism, the rainbow, and the sapphire.

> If an adamant be set by iron, it suffereth not the iron to come to the magnet, but it draweth it by a manner of violence from the magnet, so that though the magnet draweth iron to itself, the adamant draweth it away from the magnet. It is called a precious stone of reconciliation and of love. For if a woman be away from her husband, or trespasseth against him: by virtue of this stone, she is the sooner reconciled to have grace of her husband.

. . . .

The Rainbow is impression gendered in an hollow cloud and dewy, disposed to rain in endless many gutters, as it were shining in a mirror, and is shapen as a bow, and sheweth divers colours, and is gendered by the beams of the sun or of the moon. And is but seldom gendered by beams of the moon, no more but twice in fifty years, as Aristotle saith.

. . . .

The sapphire is a precious stone, and is blue in colour, most like to heaven in fair weather, and clear, and is best among precious stones, and most apt and able to fingers of kings. Its virtue is contrary to venom and quencheth it every deal. And if thou put an addercop [spider] in a box, and hold a very sapphire of Ind at the mouth of the box any while, by virtue thereof the addercop is overcome and dieth, as it were suddenly. And this same I have seen proved oft in many and divers places.

As regards astronomy, Bartholomew had this to say:

All the planets move by double moving; by their own kind moving out of the west into the east, against the moving of the firmament; and by other moving out of the east into the west, and that by ravishing of the firmament. By violence of the firmament they are ravished every day out of the east into the west. And by their kindly moving, by the which they labour to move against the firmament, some of them fulfil their course in shorter time, and some in longer time. And that is for their courses are some more and some less. For Saturn abideth in every sign xxx months, and full endeth its course in xxx years. Jupiter dwelleth in every sign one year, and full endeth its course in xij years. Mars abideth in every sign xlv days, and full endeth its course in two years. The sun abideth in every sign xxx days and ten hours and a half, and full endeth its course in ccclxv days and vj hours.

His account of leprosy—that disease that filled men of the Middle Ages with horror—contains a fairly detailed bit of observation but soon lapses into hearsay and old wives' tales.

Universally this evil hath much tokens and signs. In them the flesh is notably corrupt, the shape is changed, the eyen become round, the eyelids are revelled, the sight sparkleth, the nostrils are straited and revelled and shrunk. The voice is hoarse, swelling groweth in the body, and many small botches and whelks hard and round, in the legs and in the utter parts; feeling is somedeal taken away. The nails are boystous and bunchy, the fingers shrink and crook, the breath is corrupt, and oft whole men are infected with the stench thereof. The flesh and skin is fatty, insomuch that they may throw water thereon, and it is not the more wet, but the water slides off, as it were off a wet hide. Also in the body be diverse specks, now red, now black, now wan, now pale. The tokens of leprosy be most seen in the utter parts, as in the feet, legs, and face; and namely in wasting and minishing of the brawns of the body.

To heal or to hide leprosy, best is a red adder with a white womb, if the venom be away, and the tail and the head smitten off, and the body sod with leeks, if it be oft taken and eaten.[8]

ARISTOTLE AND MEDIEVAL SCIENCE

Some of the chief differences between the work of thirteenth-century writers like Bartholomew and the work of earlier writers like Isidore of Seville resulted from the fact that during the twelfth century many of the major works of Aristotle had become accessible to the West. In earlier times, only a portion of Aristotle's writings on logic were known, and it cannot be doubted that the discovery of his major works, together with the writings of his Arabian commentators, was one of the chief influences operating in the more vigorous intellectual life of the twelfth and thirteenth centuries.[18] From their reading of Aristotle, men not only acquired the wealth of information he had accumulated; they also encountered a method radically different from the authoritarian debates of earlier medieval scholarship. It was sensationally empirical compared with anything the West then knew, and, moreover, it yielded knowledge on all sorts of subjects concerning the natural man and the natural world, about which the West was growing curious.

It took some time, of course, for medieval men to assimilate the Aristotelian method.[19] They found it easier at first simply to take advantage of the new (that is, new to them) information the Aristotelian writings contained. Thus, though Bartholomew cast his brief discussions of such concepts as change, individuality, and genus in vaguely Aristotelian terms, it seems never to have entered his head to use these concepts, as Aristotle himself had, in an empirical study of nature and of natural change.[20] Though he was content to quote his "authorities" quite as uncritically as Isidore had, Bartholomew had the advantage of having in Aristotle an authority of somewhat better standing than Isidore's.

The age's acceptance of a divinely inspired Scripture doubtless influenced it to accept authority in other fields as well. Moreover, it must be remembered

18 When the followers of Mohammed conquered Syria and the other parts of Asia Minor, they found there an essentially Greek culture that had stemmed from the conquests of Alexander the Great. Here the works of the classical philosophers were preserved, though often in Syriac or Hebraic translations. These the Mohammedans translated into Arabic and took with them as they swept across North Africa and into Spain. Finally, in the eleventh century, with Christian expansion into Spain, cities like Toledo became points of contact between the Latin culture of the West and the Arabic culture of the Mohammedans. Soon Christian scholars began translating various Arabic works, and about the middle of the twelfth century a regular corps of translators was set up by the Archbishop of Toledo. Among the works rendered into Latin and so made accessible to the West were Aristotle's *Physics*, *Metaphysics*, and *De Anima*.

19 As a matter of fact, Aristotle met with great hostility in many quarters, for his views seemed to conflict with fundamental Christian theses. For an attempt by Aquinas to show that this conflict was only apparent, see pp. 226–28.

20 There is, for instance, nothing in Bartholomew at all comparable to Aristotle's detailed study of a chicken embryo at various developmental stages.

that ascertaining the facts, which seems so important to us, was of less concern to men of the Middle Ages. It was overwhelmingly more important to them to know what was required for salvation. About things that did not touch one's faith—about the properties of sapphires or the cure for leprosy, for instance—it did not matter a great deal whether or not one went wrong.

VINCENT OF BEAUVAIS

This attitude, radically different from the modern, is expressed very clearly in the Prologue to Vincent of Beauvais' [21] *Speculum Maius:*

> Moreover I am not ignorant that Philosophers have said many contradictory things, especially concerning nature. For example, some have judged the air to be naturally hot, as Aristotle and Avicenna; while others, as Seneca, have pronounced it to be cold. Some also assert that a serpent's venom is frigid, as doth Isidorus; others again will have it to be ardent, of whom is Avicenna. Seeing however that in these and suchlike matters either part of these contradictories may be believed or disbelieved without peril to our Faith, therefore I admonish the reader that he abhor not this book if perchance he find such contradictions in many places, and under the names of divers authors; the more so as I have herein undertaken not the office of a composer but that of a compiler. Wherefore I have taken small pains to reduce the sayings of the Philosophers to concord, striving rather to repeat what each hath said on every matter, and leaving the reader to put faith in one or the other judgment after his own choice. For, seeing that even many physicians seem to dissent one from another in their judgment of the complexion, degree, or quality of simple medicines, we must reflect that the very complexions of men and animals and fruits of the earth differ according to the diversities of regions, so that one of the same kind may be here an antidote, there a poison. For (to cite an example) the black poppy is written in physicians' books for a poison; yet in our parts men take it for food. Likewise Avicenna and Rhasus count the stag's tail as venomous; which, however, is constantly denied by physicians in our country.[t]

Though, from our point of view, Bartholomew and Vincent were fundamentally unscientific, the age was capable, given time for the Aristotelian leaven to take effect, of the first beginnings of what can be called a scientific attitude. This is apparent when one compares Bartholomew's accounts of the rainbow and of perception with those of Roger Bacon, who lived in the second half of the century.[22] Whereas Bartholomew and Vincent merely gave uncritical reports of what other writers had said, Bacon undertook to give a single account—to

---

21 Vincent (about 1190–about 1260) was Louis IX's librarian. His encyclopedic work, which was written some years later than Bartholomew's, was divided into three parts—the Mirror of Nature, the Mirror of Doctrine, and the Mirror of History. It was intended to summarize in a systematic manner the whole body of knowledge available at the time.
22 See pp. 296–97.

combine the views of his various authorities into one consistent view. And whereas they relied entirely on documents, he had some insight into the need for empirical observation.

The influence of Aristotle in the revival of the scientific spirit has been emphasized, but another factor of great importance was the recovery of Euclid's *Elements*. This resulted in the reestablishment of the axiomatic method as the paradigm of scientific explanation. Moreover, the later Scholastics,[23] unlike the Greeks, saw the relevance of mathematics to physics and attempted to formulate the laws governing moving bodies in exact, quantitative terms. At the same time there was a beginning of experimentation, though it was not yet systematic and experiments were more often used to illustrate doctrines already adopted on other grounds than to gain knowledge. It is not important to us, however, to estimate the ratio, at any given time, between innovative and retrogressive forces. What is important is to see that an advance, however slow and halting, was under way.

The Universities

Finally, in this brief account of the cultural renaissance that occurred in the twelfth and thirteenth centuries, the role played by the universities must be mentioned. During the revival of learning attempted by Charlemagne at the end of the eighth century, a number of monastic and cathedral schools had been founded. But these schools were not equipped to teach large numbers of students and were, in any case, concerned primarily with giving prospective clergymen the education necessary to perform their duties. It must also be remembered that in these early centuries the body of knowledge was too scant to form the basis for any very extensive curriculum, even if there had been any desire to expand the scope of education.

But the gradual expansion of men's intellectual horizons that has been described in the preceding pages awakened a great desire for knowledge. The medieval universities, which were the response to this desire, did not, of course, spring up all at once, fully formed. At first there were no buildings, no faculties, not even a corporate institution; there were only groups of young men, eager to be taught, who gathered together and hired someone to instruct them. As the number of students grew, it became necessary to provide for their organization and discipline, and statutes governing the conduct of students and teachers were laid down. These tended to follow the model of the already existing medieval guilds. Originally, indeed, "university" was a term applied to any corporation; only gradually did it come to mean a corporation of teachers and students.

---

23 Representative of these thinkers are John Buridan and Nicholas of Oresme. See p. 323.

Since, like any other guild, this corporation of teachers and students set requirements for the admission of apprentices to the rank of master, examinations and qualifications for degrees came into being. A degree, it will be seen, was thought of primarily as a license to join the other masters in the teaching of students, which, of course, was the business of this guild of scholars. Soon, as various distinct faculties were organized, the degree itself became specialized. Besides the faculty of theology, there were faculties of law (canon and civil), medicine, and the arts. The tremendous desire for education, the founding of numerous universities, the private and royal munificence that assisted in this work, the diversity of subjects taught—all these testify to the way in which, in this age, men's interests were broadening, expanding beyond the field of purely religious matters.

Philosophy During the Medieval Interval

So far in this chapter a description has been given of the ideas, institutions, and attitudes that emerged during the eight-century interval between Augustine and Thomas. We have seen that during the last two centuries of this period there was a remarkable revival of this-worldly interests, reflected in science, arts, manners and customs, and political institutions. The central problem of thirteenth-century philosophy was to find a place for these this-worldly ends in a scheme of life that still had a basically otherworldly orientation, and the great achievement of Thomism was its success in solving this problem.

But before we study this Thomistic solution we must examine philosophical developments during these eight centuries. For these, too, were elements in the whole cultural complex for which a satisfactory rationale had to be found.

This will be an easy task, for, with the exception of Boethius and an occasional compiler like Isidore of Seville, there were virtually no philosophical thinkers between Augustine's time and the middle of the eleventh century. To this generalization there is a solitary exception, John Scotus Erigena. He was remarkable not only in that he philosophized at all, but especially in that he philosophized in the grand manner. Though as an isolated phenomenon he had but slight influence on the history of philosophy, the intrinsic interest of his work requires us to examine his position at least briefly before passing on to the philosophical debates that made up the immediate background of Thomism.

John Scotus Erigena

John Scotus Erigena (about 810–about 877) was born in Ireland (in those days the Irish were called *Scoti*), studied Greek in an Irish monastery at a time when a knowledge of Greek was almost lost to the West, went to France about 847, and taught at Paris in the Palace school that Charlemagne had founded. He soon became involved in disputes over the touchy theological questions of free will and the Eucharist. In an effort to avoid the extreme type of predestinarianism that made prayer, the sacraments, and the Church meaningless, he went too far in the opposite direction and fell into a form of Pelagianism. As a result, his opinions were condemned in 855. His views on the Eucharist (he denied the Real Presence of Christ's body and blood in the bread and wine and held that the sacrament has only a symbolic and commemorative significance) also involved him in difficulties, and it was ordered that his book on this subject be burned. The edict was carried out so successfully that no copy of this work survives. Perhaps as a result of these misadventures, John undertook the safer task of translating into Latin a number of Greek texts that the scholars at Paris had acquired some years earlier but had been unable to read.[24] After a time, however, he turned to philosophy and wrote *On the Division of Nature*, the work on which his fame chiefly rests.

Perhaps the most striking thing about John's philosophizing was his interest in synthesis. Unlike the generation of philosophers that immediately preceded Aquinas, he was less concerned with resolving technical problems than with working out an overall, synoptic world view. It so happened that the Greek texts he had translated at Paris were deeply influenced by Neoplatonism, which, with its emphasis on the fundamental unity of the world, would obviously have a strong appeal for a writer with a synthetic drive. But John was not, of course, simply a philosopher with a synthetic drive; he was also a Catholic Christian. Therefore, his synthesis had to be a Christian synthesis, interpreting philosophically the various Christian insights that had been codified in the Church's dogmas.

NATURE

John's starting point was the nature of reality. All things, he held, are basically divided between "things that are" and "things that are not." Taken together, the "things that are" and the "things that are not" are called "nature." Nature, then, is the sum of reality. How, we may be disposed to ask, can "things that are not" be included in the totality of all that is? Surely, if they are not, they are not a part of reality. This objection is based on the assumption that there is a simple disjunction between being and nothingness. However, according to John, none of the "things that are not" is sheer nothing. There are several modes of nonbeing, including those of (1) sinful man (who, through sin, has lost his integral nature), (2) changing particulars (for what becomes, both is and is not), (3) potential being (for what is merely potential is not yet actual), and (4) anything that, because of its superior reality, is "beyond our intellect." If these, then, are the "things that are not," what are "the things that are"? John's answer was

24 This seemingly harmless undertaking also ended in misfortune. See p. 184.

that "those things only truly are, which are comprehended by the intellect alone."[u]

The Platonic provenance of this distinction is obvious. The universe, according to Plato, is basically divided between (1) entities that are objects of knowledge (that is, the forms) and (2) entities that are not objects of knowledge. Plato himself largely identified this second class with the changing particulars of sense perception (physical objects and their shadows and reflections). But the Neoplatonists, recalling that Plato had also held the Form of the Good to be beyond knowledge and being,[25] reasoned that it must be included in the second class of entities—not because, like sense particulars, it is too inferior to be an object of knowledge, but because it is too superior. John, it will be seen, followed this line of reasoning and simply took the additional step of identifying the Form of the Good with God.

GOD

In John's view, then, God is "beyond being" and so may fairly be said "not to be." But how can this be reconciled with the Christian contention that we know a great deal about God—that He is a creator, that He is provident, just, good, powerful, and so on? Clearly, John had to deal with this apparent contradiction between his Neoplatonic metaphysics and Christian dogma.

John's answer was that there are two ways for finite minds to approach God—an affirmative way and a negative way. The affirmative way consists in asserting, for instance, that He is being, that He is good. Although such assertions are not wholly true, they are not wholly false. God is, for instance, more like goodness than like badness, more like being than like nothingness. Nevertheless, because such positive assertions are not wholly true, they are misleading unless supplemented by corresponding negative assertions. If we say that God is being, we must add that He is not being; if we say that He is good, we must add that He is not good. Of course, if we took the negative assertions by themselves, they would be as misleading as the affirmative statements taken by themselves. For when we say that God is not being, we do not mean that He is nothing. He is not being, not because He is less than being, but because He is more than being. He is not good, not because He is bad, but because He is more than good.

It would seem, then, that all assertions made in the affirmative must be supplemented by assertions made in the negative and, conversely, that all assertions made in the negative must be supplemented by assertions made in the affirmative. However, instead of making pairs of assertions ("God is good, but not good"), John combined the affirmative and the negative in single assertions of the form, "God is supergood."

25 See pp. 8–9 and 13.

> God, then, is called essence, but properly he is not essence, to whom nothing is opposed; therefore he is . . . superessential. Likewise he is called goodness, but properly he is not goodness; for evil is opposed to goodness; therefore [he is] supergood, more than good. . . . We are obliged to understand in the same way concerning . . . truth. For falsity is opposed to truth, and for this reason properly he is not truth; therefore he is . . . more than true, and more than truth. . . . He is not properly called eternity, since temporality is opposed to eternity; therefore he is . . . more than eternal, and more than eternity. . . .
>
> He is called essence, truth, wisdom and other things of this kind not properly but translatively.[v]

Since this is a difficult conception, an analogy may be helpful. Suppose that someone looking at Michelangelo's *Last Judgment* remarks, "That's quite a pretty picture." "Pretty picture, indeed!" we might retort. "That's the shape of things to come." We would be saying, in effect, that words that adequately characterize calendar art ("pretty picture") really shouldn't be used in reference to Michelangelo's art; if Maxfield Parrish painted pictures, we are tempted to say, then Michelangelo didn't. But, of course, Michelangelo *did* paint pictures, and it would be false to deny it. In the same way, according to John Scotus, though it is false to deny that God is good (for He *is* good), it is misleading to say *merely* that He is good, for men are good, animals are good, even spinach is good. And the same arguments apply, of course, to the attribution of any other qualities, or characteristics, to God.

It will be seen that here John was traversing, but in a much more sophisticated way, the considerations that led Augustine to attribute infinite power, infinite goodness, and infinite knowledge to God.[26] But though John's argument did not involve an "extrapolation to infinity," as did Augustine's, it was not without difficulties.

For instance, though "superessential" sounds high-powered, does it mean anything more on analysis than the simple negative, not-essence? In fact, since being and goodness are admittedly finite categories that are meaningful only in terms of human experience, is it possible to attach any meaning whatever to "more than being" and "more than good"? John believed he could answer these questions.

> [Though the] divine essence is not essence, because it is more than essence, . . . nevertheless it is [rightly] called essence, because it is the creator of all essences. . . . It is not quantity because it is more than quantity. . . . It nevertheless is not unfittingly denominated quantity . . . because it is the principle and cause of all quantity. Concerning quality too, we should

26 See pp. 85–94.

understand not otherwise. For God is no quality. . . . But indeed quality is most often predicated to him . . . because he is the author of all quality.ʷ

CREATION

This brings us to the question of creation and the problem of the relation between God and the world. John began his discussion of these matters with a paradox. If God makes the world, He must move. But how can He who is immutable move?

DISCIPLE.²⁷ I cannot grant motion to God, who alone is immutable, nor does he have anything to which he could move himself, since all things are in him, even more since he himself is all things. But I cannot deny making of him, when he is the maker of all things.

MAGISTER. Therefore you will separate motion from making.

DISCIPLE. Not that indeed, inasmuch as I see that they are inseparable from each other.

MAGISTER. Therefore what are you going to do?

DISCIPLE. I do not know; and therefore I strenuously implore you to open some way for me, and free me from this great difficulty.

MAGISTER. Receive therefore this succession of reasoning. . . . Was not God before he made all things?

DISCIPLE. He seems to me to have been.

MAGISTER. Therefore making was an accident in respect of him. For what is not co-eternal and co-essential with him, is either something outside of him or something befalling him.

DISCIPLE. I should not have believed that there is something else beyond him and outside him; [nor] that he is subject to accident. [For if he is subject to accident] he is not simple, but a certain composite of essence and accidents. . . .

MAGISTER. Therefore God was not, before he made all things.

DISCIPLE. He was not, for if he was, he would have been subject to the accident of making all things, and if he were the subject of the accident of making all things, we would understand motion and time in him. . . .

MAGISTER. Therefore his making is co-eternal and co-essential with God.

DISCIPLE. I believe and understand this.

MAGISTER. Are God and his making, that is his action, two distinct things, or one, simple, and individual thing?

DISCIPLE. I [now] see that they are one. For God does not receive number in himself, since he alone is innumerable. . . .

MAGISTER. Therefore in God there is not one thing, which is being and another making, but for him being itself is also making. . . . Therefore when we hear that God made everything, we ought to understand nothing other than that God is in all things, that is, subsists as the essence of all things. For only he himself truly is per se, and only he himself is everything which

27 [John wrote *On the Division of Nature* in the form of a dialogue between a teacher and a student—AUTHOR.]

> is truly said to be in those things which are. For nothing of those things which are, truly is per se. But whatever is truly understood in him receives by a participation of him, the one who alone truly is per se. . . .
>
> Therefore God is rightly called love, because he is the cause of every love, and he is diffused through all things, and collects all things into one, and returns to himself by an ineffable regression, and terminates the amatory motions of the whole creature in himself.[x]

John was attempting to make two main points here. First, the concepts of making and creating, like the concepts of being and goodness, apply to God only in a metaphorical sense; if we try to apply them literally, they involve us in all sorts of paradoxes. Second, and more important, the transcendence of the Creator and the dependence of the creature (two doctrines on which Christianity insisted) are contradictory.

A Platonic assumption underlies this reasoning, namely, that the cognitive status of an object always reflects its metaphysical status. If an object is metaphysically independent (if it exists in its own right, independently of anything else), one can know it completely without taking account of any other object. On the other hand, if an object is dependent on some other objects for existence, it can be fully known only when the objects on which it is metaphysically dependent are known. Now, consider any object, say, some particular horse, Old Dobbin. Is Dobbin a self-sufficient and unconditioned object of knowledge? Clearly he is not; to understand Dobbin it is necessary to compare him with other horses, to study the principles of mammalian zoology, and so on. It follows, in John's language, that Dobbin is not "truly himself per se." So far, of course, John's reasoning was entirely in accordance with Christian doctrine, which held that Dobbin's being is entirely dependent on God, his creator. But John went on to argue that dependence cannot be a one-way relationship. If Dobbin is not a self-sufficient object of knowledge, this is because he does not have a distinct and independent essence. If Dobbin does not have an independent essence, he is an appendage to God. If he is an appendage to God, then we cannot know God completely without knowing Dobbin just as we cannot know Dobbin completely without knowing God.

This can be put in other terms. If God stands in an external relation to the world (which is what the doctrine of transcendence seems to require), then the world stands in an external relation to God. Transcendence implies distinctness; distinctness implies independence. On the other hand, dependence implies inclusiveness and inclusiveness is the denial of transcendence. We cannot have it both ways, according to John. Since his conception of the nature of knowledge committed him to assert dependence, he had to give up transcendence. But this could hardly satisfy the Church, which held transcendence to be every bit as important as dependence. Let us, however, postpone consideration of this dogmatic difficulty[28] to continue the exposition of John's view.

28 See pp. 182–84.

THEOPHANIES

So far we have seen that John argued that God created the world by causing it to progress from His "beyond being" nature. Is it possible to define this particular kind of dependence somewhat more precisely? As a start, it may be said that John held the world to be a "theophany" of God, that is, an "apparition," or appearance, of God. It would be easy to misunderstand this concept, for a term like "appearance" suggests to most people something illusory or, at least, unreal as it stands. (We say, for instance, that the thing lying on the road is "really" a stick, though in the twilight it "appears" to be a snake.) But John did not want to hold that the world is "mere" appearance. The created universe is not a mistake we make about God; it is the way God chooses to reveal Himself to us: "God is not only said to be divine essence, but also that mode, by which he shows himself in a certain manner to the intellectual and rational creature." [y]

The active voice of the verb—"God shows Himself"—reveals John's meaning. The ways we interpret the world—the categories we employ and the "divisions" we make—are not merely subjective attitudes of ours. For the human minds that do the judging and dividing are themselves parts of the theophany that they judge and divide. Hence, even though the created universe is not wholly real (for reality in its innermost nature is "beyond being"), it is not a subjective fantasy. To intellectual and rational creatures (and it was God's choice, of course, that there be such creatures), the superessential unity shows itself as distinct substances standing in various logical and spatiotemporal relations to one another.

Perhaps an example will help clarify this difficult notion. As I drive along a highway, I get a succession of views of a mountain in the distance. Which of these views is "correct"? The answer is, all and none. All, in the sense that each is a view of the mountain; none, in the sense that none is more than a view of the mountain. The very fact that we use the phrase "a view of" indicates our recognition of the limitation of each of these experiences. Perhaps you will say that the totality of possible views of the mountain will be the completely adequate experience of the mountain. Alas, even this totality is inadequate. In the first place, I could never experience all the possible views. In the second, even if I could experience them, they would be only a plurality of views, whereas the mountain itself is a unity.

Well, perhaps you will say that the mountain's experience of itself (supposing it to be conscious) would be a wholly adequate experience. But insofar as it has a mind like ours, a mind that divides and classifies, the difficulty remains. For the difficulty is not so much with *us* as with the nature of experience. Experience is inevitably experience *of*. It is just the nature of intellect to be at a distance, to be "of" things instead of *being* things—to distinguish, to classify, to pluralize.

It would seem, then, that there is indeed a difference of the kind John distinguished. There is a contrast between any experience of the mountain (whether mine or the mountain's own), and the mountain itself, complete, unitary, undivided. That is, to put the analogy aside, there is a contrast between any *experience* of God (whether mine or God's own) and God Himself, complete, unitary, undivided.

Now to return to the analogy and to summarize John's position in its language; there is a twofold relation between the mountain and any experience of it. First, there would be no experience if there were no mountain; second, the truth of the experience depends on what it reports about the mountain. Hence the mountain may fairly be described as the source of the relative being and truth of the various experiences of it, and the various experiences may be described as creatures produced by the mountain, as "apparitions" of it.

The trouble with this is that it is only an analogy. The mountain is not God; it is only a relatively distinct, relatively dependent substance like myself. The mountain, therefore, is not the sole source of the being and the truth of my experiences of it. After all, insofar as I interpret the experiences, I, too, contribute something to their being and truth. My experience of the mountain is a joint product, in which the mountain and I are both involved. The relation between God and His apparitions is, in this respect, less like that of the mountain and my view of it than it is like the relation between an object and its mirror image. Suppose that you have a room hung with many mirrors. These mirrors take in one another's washing, as it were—each reflects the reflections of all the other mirrors and thus gives the impression (or "apparition") of an endless vista of apartments. This, according to John, is precisely what Jesus meant by saying, "In my Father's house are many mansions." Though the house is one and the same, it appears multiple and divided to those who dwell in it.

If you allow that the mirrors exist, you have to accept their reflections as veridical, for it is the nature of mirrors to reflect. Similarly, if you grant the existence of human minds, you have to allow that the superessential unity is divided and classified, for it is the nature of the rational and intelligent creature to divide and classify. But why mirrors, why human intellects? To ask this question, John would have replied, is to fall into presumption and arrogance. It is our business to describe faithfully what God has willed (that is, to describe the principles by which we divide and classify), not to try to discover why He willed what He has willed. This is beyond human understanding. Indeed, even to talk about the divine "intent" is to talk in terms of the way the room looks from the perspective of our particular mirror. It is to divide the "beyond being" unity of God according to human concepts of volition, choice, and decision.

KNOWLEDGE IS ILLUMINATION

Another important conclusion follows from these arguments: Knowledge is illumination. For if everything that exists is an aspect of the divine nature reflected from some perspective or other, then in knowing the things around us we know God—not, of course, God as He is in His superessential nature, but

God insofar as He has externalized Himself. Whatever analysis philosophers and psychologists may make of sense perception and intellection as temporal processes going on in us and dependent on physical changes in our sense organs and in the cortex of our brain, John, as a Christian, held that all knowledge is fundamentally and basically an act of grace by means of which God illumines our minds.

> The theophany is made from the condescension itself of the wisdom of God to human nature through grace, and by the exaltation of the same nature itself through love. . . .
> The divine essence per se is incomprehensible, but joined to an intellectual creature it appears in a marvelous way, so that itself, I mean nothing but divine essence, appears in that creature. [The] ineffable excellence [of the divine nature] surpasses every nature participating of it, so that nothing else besides itself occurs in all intelligences, although per se, as we have said, it appears in no way.[z]

Or, as John put it in an analogy of his own, the sun can be seen only through the medium of the air. Yet we do not see the air; we only see the light that pervades it. It is the combination of air and light that makes vision possible, though, of course, the roles of the sun and of air in this process are quite different. The air is merely the passive medium that the sun utilizes to make itself manifest, insofar as it can be manifest, to minds like ours.

FOURFOLD DIVISION OF NATURE

This brings us, finally, to John's fourfold division of nature, that is, to his analysis of all that is. Even though nature is truly one and "beyond being" and any divisions and distinctions we make are simply those that this superessential one "condescends" to have us make, the basic categories we use to divide nature nevertheless constitute a metaphysical scheme. There is, first, the nature that creates and is uncreated; second, the nature that creates and is created; third, the nature that is created and does not create; fourth, the nature that neither creates nor is created. These are (1) God, (2) the Platonic archetypes, (3) the physical world, (4) God. In other words, God issues into the world and returns from it to Himself. [29]

As for the first division, nature that creates and is not created, we need only remind ourselves that, in Himself, God is not conscious; He does not know Him-

---

29 When "issues," "returns," and "divine progression" are spoken of, one must not, if one wants to understand John's view, think of an evolutionary process in time, for space and time are themselves but products (at the level of the third division of nature) of the divine creativity. Here again, John held that because human concepts are rooted in finite experience, language is inadequate. We can agree; but is it not more than language that fails? If we are not to think of the progression as temporal, how *are* we to think of it? This is a problem that we have met before and will encounter again (see pp. 11–12).

self.[30] The progression of nature begins only when God creates His mind—when, that is, He becomes conscious and thinks the archetypes. The archetypes are not, of course, independent existents; they are merely ideas in the divine mind, or, more precisely, they *are* the divine mind. Hence they differ from Plato's forms, which were independent of the demiurge and which therefore limited the demiurge's creativity.

The archetypes, or "primordial causes," as John called them, form the second division of nature. They are created (by God's thinking them) and creative (because, as primordial causes, they are the sources of the essences of the various particular objects of this world). The primordial causes are goodness, being, life, wisdom, truth, intelligence, reason, virtue, justice, health, greatness, omnipotence, eternity, and peace. Though *we* distinguish them as a plurality, considered in themselves they are one. We think of them as a plurality because our knowledge of them is derived from our experience in the sense world. And in the sense world, the concentrated essence is scattered into a diversity of objects.

Any healthy thing (say, a college sophomore) may also be good and virtuous. To say that this sophomore is good, healthy, and virtuous is to say that he partakes (to a finite degree, of course) in these archetypes, that these characteristics have been produced in him by the action of these primordial causes. Just as the unity of the room gets broken up into the numerous reflections in the mirrors, so the unity of the archetype gets broken up into the particulars of sense perception that participate in the essences in question. It will be seen that the primordial causes are both the ways in which we characterize God and the exemplars of such goodness, justice, and truth as we encounter here on earth. It is because they are ideas of God that we characterize Him truly (though inadequately) when we call Him good, just, and true; it is because they are the causes of sense experiences that we become acquainted with these ideas and so can use them to characterize Him.

The physical world, then, as John conceived of it, has its being through participation in the primordial causes, just as they, in their turn, have their being through God's thinking of them. According to John, this third division of nature, created and not creative, longs to return to the "beyond being" source from which it has issued. And so we come, at last, to the nature that neither creates nor is created. That is, we come to God, conceived of now, not as the creative source from which the progression issues, but as the goal for which it longs and toward which it moves.

Thus it can be said that God "is the beginning, middle and end. The beginning, because all things which participate in essence are from him; but the middle, because they subsist and are moved in him and through him; the end, indeed, because they are moved to him seeking the quiet of their motion and the stability of their perfection."[a]

---

30 Compare what was said above about the difference between the mountain and its consciousness of itself.

IS JOHN'S VIEW CHRISTIAN?

So far the main outlines of John's metaphysics have been sketched in an attempt to suggest that it was designed to serve as a synoptic scheme that would incorporate all creation. From this point of view, the various special sciences— physics, psychology, liberal arts, theology—are simply investigations, at successive levels of division, of one nature. The purely philosophic test of such a philosophical scheme is its capacity to do this without contradiction, distortion, or omission. But a Christian philosophy must meet a special, additional test: It must be in harmony with Christian insights. For a Catholic Christian like John, this means that it must be in harmony with Christian insights as interpreted by the Church. Let us see whether John's metaphysics meets this additional test.

There are certainly some aspects of Christian teaching that lend themselves naturally to interpretation in Neoplatonic terms. This is especially true of the doctrines of the incarnation and the redemption, the original formulations of which had indeed been touched by some of the influences that subsequently gave rise to Neoplatonism.[31] It is therefore possible, without putting excessive strain on Christian dogma, to regard the incarnation of Jesus and his redemption of sinful man as concrete, personalized instances of John's whole metaphysical scheme. In a sense, the progression of the created universe out of God can be described as an incarnation, and its return to God, as a redemption.

John's scheme is, however, less successful in interpreting other important Christian doctrines. Though John's metaphysics is purportedly a rational system, it is constantly on the verge of collapsing into subjectivism and mysticism. A doubt has already been expressed here as to whether concepts like "superessential" and "timeless progression" are meaningful, and it seems that the "beyond being" doctrine is really incompatible with the objective validity of knowledge, which, according to this doctrine, is a private affair between the soul and its God. In a word, John's system dissolves the outer universe: Physics is not even Plato's "likely story"; it is just the way God has chosen to reveal Himself to man.

These particular aspects of John's thought were perhaps congenial to the age in which he lived, but the later Middle Ages became increasingly unsympathetic to his mystical and otherworldly tendencies. Mysticism, as we have seen, is always closely associated with religious individualism, and an age that saw the full development of orthodox, institutional Christianity could hardly accept a view that, if pressed to its logical conclusion, seemed to by-pass the Church. Again, as men's interests turned more and more to this world and its affairs, it seemed less and less satisfactory to describe the world as merely an "apparition" of God. No Christian philosopher would, of course, for a moment *repudiate*

---

31 See pp. 50–54.

mysticism and otherworldliness. But John's Neoplatonism encouraged him to carry these aspects of Christian theory to a point that orthodox Christianity regarded as "dangerous." Hence, later generations of medieval philosophers sought a new basis for their thought, a basis from which they could both affirm the reality of the natural world and rehabilitate the autonomy of natural knowledge.[32]

John's Neoplatonic version of a Christian synthesis is entangled in an even more formidable difficulty. In denying transcendence and in affirming that God created the world out of His own nature, John wiped out the sharp metaphysical and valuational contrast between an infinite sovereign and his puny and helpless subjects, thus destroying the basis for many of the most characteristic Christian insights. The medieval conception of man's duties and man's finitude, the importance of humility, the awfulness of pride, the hope of salvation, the threat of damnation—all these depended on there being an absolute distinction between God and man. Certainly, at the third level of nature, at which God externalizes Himself, Creator and creature are in a sense distinct, though it is very difficult to understand exactly what this distinctness amounts to. However, the fourth level, at which the progression reverses itself and creature returns to Creator, clearly implies that man is absorbed in the divine. In other words, immortality is achieved only at the cost of abandoning personal survival; man seems finally to disappear into, to merge with, God. This, clearly, is blasphemy as well as heresy.

Further, it follows from John's Neoplatonic premises that sin and evil are unreal. For if the universe is an apparition of God—if all that exists is God's own essence—obviously, all that is, is good. The created universe (God externalized) is like a beautiful and harmonious picture executed on so large a scale that we cannot see all of it at once. Though the little section on which our eye happens to light may seem black, it is in fact only a bit of shadow that the divine artist has put in to heighten the overall esthetic effect. If we could see the whole composition, we would see that any particular part that looks ugly is really beautiful, and so on. And, in any case, sin and evil, even hell itself, must disappear with the rest of creation when the universe returns to the Creator.

Naturally, John tried to find a way of reconciling his metaphysics with the orthodox Christian position. One illustration of his procedure will be given. The book of Genesis states explicitly that God created the world out of nothing. How can this be reconciled with John's view that He created it out of Himself? Well, said John, in the first place, the author of Genesis was addressing simple people in a language they could understand; we cannot expect this account to be technically correct or to stand up to philosophical analysis. But, as a matter of fact, it *is* true in a sense to say that God created the world out of nothing,

32 See pp. 212–15, 235–37, and 304–09.

for the divine nature is "beyond being" and so, in the technical language of John's metaphysics, is "nothing."

This kind of defense requires a very loose interpretation of Scripture, but John could also rest his case on a large number of Augustine's dicta. This is not surprising since, as we have seen, Augustine was deeply influenced by Neoplatonism. However, John's main authority, whom he repeatedly cited, was "St. Dionysius the Areopagite," St. Paul's Athenian convert, whose writings were among those John had translated into Latin for the benefit of the Paris scholars who knew no Greek. Since, as is now known, this author was actually not an early Christian but a Neoplatonist who wrote much later, toward the end of the fifth century, it is easy to see how John found in these allegedly canonical writings invaluable proof of his impeccable orthodoxy.

THE NEOPLATONIC PROBLEM

Not only John but all philosophers of the Middle Ages treated the writings of the Pseudo-Dionysius (as the unknown author has been called since the forgery became known) with the greatest reverence. This created a curious philosophical problem, for, as we have seen, Neoplatonic metaphysics and Christian orthodoxy are in many respects deeply antagonistic. Indeed, they are so far apart that it is unlikely, except in view of the mistaken belief that the Pseudo-Dionysius was the divinely inspired convert of St. Paul, that John or anyone else could have supposed they would combine.

The Church saw plainly enough that John's use of Neoplatonism and the Pseudo-Dionysius was heretical, but it did not at first know how to deal with the resulting embarrassment. From the historical perspective we now have, we can see that John's work demonstrated that the attempt to construct a Christian metaphysics on a Platonic basis was a blind alley. But it is easier to see that a new start was necessary than to see how one could have been made. In the first place, medieval thinkers could not throw Neoplatonism overboard altogether. The authority of Augustine, of the Pseudo-Dionysius, and of the other Christian writers tinged in varying degrees with Neoplatonism meant that no Christian philosophy could wholly ignore these elements. Moreover, what was the new basis of thought to be? Philosophizing in the grand, system-making manner died away after John's abortive attempt, not only because his successors were less able than he, but also because the essential element—a new conceptual scheme— was lacking. When, as a result of the rediscovery of Aristotle's writings, such a scheme became available, systematic thinking resumed. The problem was to find a way of doing justice to the Neoplatonic, mystical, otherworldly, and illuminationist tendencies in the Christian tradition without allowing them to run away with the system and plunge it into heresy. This task, as we shall see, was largely accomplished by Thomas and his successors.[33]

33 See pp. 234–35 and 304–09.

The Controversy over Universals

After the brief light afforded by John's genius, the philosophical scene darkened for another two hundred years. When, in the second half of the eleventh century, philosophizing again began, it was in an altogether different manner and on a decidedly lesser scale. The thinkers of the eleventh century were not metaphysicians but logicians. Rather than constructing all-inclusive systems, they devoted themselves for the most part to painstakingly thorough examination of two very technical problems—the status of universals and the relation between the spheres of faith and reason.

These were questions that had to be settled before the great synthesis of the thirteenth century could be undertaken. For, though everyone agreed that Christian truths were above reason in the sense that their truth was guaranteed by the Christian faith in revelation and by the authority of the canonical writings, it was desirable, if only for pragmatic reasons, to prove these truths by rational argument. The crusades as well as an expanding trade, were bringing Western Christians into contact with infidels who found it easy to ridicule the simplicities of unreasoned faith. And, at home, heresy continued to divide the Christian fold.[34]

Against infidels and heretics, reason was an indispensable weapon. But what was its proper domain? Were all Christian truths accessible to reason? If not, where and how was one to draw the line beyond which reason could not go? Moreover, reason was obviously a dangerous instrument; Christian philosophers had not been able to free it from the stigma of its pagan origin. All Christians knew it was presumptuous to suppose that the finite human intellect could probe the depths of the infinite, and they could point to many thinkers besides John Scotus Erigena who had been led into heresy by wicked confidence in their ability to discover a rational truth. It is clear, then, that the determination of a legitimate sphere for the use of reason was critical for the Middle Ages. Until such a sphere was delimited and justified, no philosophical system developed by rational arguments, as all such systems must be, could be secure.

In order to define the relation between faith and reason, it was necessary to determine the nature of reason's proper object. This brings us to the much disputed question of the nature and the status of universals. This, of course, was

---

34 The eleventh-century philosopher, St. Anselm, wrote: "I have been often and most earnestly requested by many [to write down] the proofs of a certain doctrine of our faith. . . . This they ask, not for the sake of attaining to faith by means of reason, but that . . . they may be always ready to convince any one who demands of them a reason of that hope which is in us. [For] this question . . . infidels are accustomed to bring up against us, ridiculing Christian simplicity as absurd"—*Cur Deus Homo*, translated by S. N. Deane (Open Court, 1903), I, i. So, too, St. Thomas: "[Since] some . . . , like the Mohammedans and pagans, do not agree with us as to the authority of any Scripture, [it is impossible to appeal to authority against them]. Wherefore it is necessary to have recourse to natural reason, to which all are compelled to assent"—*Summa Contra Gentiles* (English Dominican Fathers), I, ii.

anything but a new problem; the theory of forms, as worked out by Plato and modified by Aristotle, was the major classical solution to it. Unfortunately, since most of the writings of these philosophers were unknown in the early Middle Ages, medieval thinkers, aided by mere hints of what the classical solution had been, had to find their own answer. It is instructive to contrast the ways in which classical and medieval philosophers tackled this problem and to note how the medieval solution to what was a purely philosophical question was grievously complicated by the fact that this question impinged at certain points on Christian dogma.

Let us examine, then, the way in which the problem of universals was understood in the Middle Ages. There was general agreement among philosophers that, apart from revelation, men have but two modes of cognition—perception and reason. It was also agreed that what perception knows is particulars, that is, the various individual objects of the spatiotemporal world. Reason, on the other hand, knows universal truths—that a straight line is the shortest distance between two points, that the interior angles of a triangle equal two right angles, that all men are mortal, and so on. Certainly, as philosophers of the modern period have discovered, there are grave problems about perception. But philosophers of the Middle Ages were not much interested in perception and its objects, for sense perception obviously cannot yield knowledge of God or any of the great truths of Christian religion. Hence, if men are to know these truths (in distinction from accepting them on the authority of faith and revelation), it must be by means of reason. Accordingly, the attention of philosophers of the Middle Ages was focused on the nature of reason and the status of "universals," as the objects of reason were called.

Men of the Middle Ages tended to approach this question by considering the signification of names. Words like "Socrates" and "Plato" name individual particulars experienced in sense perception. What do words like "man" name? The medieval answer was that they name universals, which are cognized by reason. But what, exactly, *is* a universal? Medieval men thought that the answer to this question must lie among the alternatives set forth by Porphyry[35] in his *Introduction to Aristotle's Categories:*

> At present, . . . I shall refuse to say concerning genera and species whether they subsist or whether they are placed in the naked understandings alone or whether subsisting they are corporeal or incorporeal, and whether they are separated from sensibles or placed in sensibles and in accord with them. Questions of this sort are most exalted business and require very great diligence of inquiry.[b]

---

35 This Porphyry was the Neoplatonic writer whose *Introduction*, as translated by Boethius (see p. 141), was one of the chief sources of information about Greek philosophy available to men of the Middle Ages.

MEDIEVAL REALISM

It was characteristic of the medieval attitude toward knowledge that men of the Middle Ages were content to restrict themselves to choosing among Porphyry's alternative solutions to the problem of universals. Indeed, their discussion of this problem consisted in comment on, and exegesis of, the passage quoted above. The first of Porphyry's alternatives that recommended itself was the notion that universals are real entities, separate from sense particulars and subsisting incorporeally.

John Scotus Erigena's position was typical of this "realistic" (so called because universals were held to be real in their own right) solution. It was inevitable that he would be a "realist." That the individuals Socrates and Plato are less real than the universal "man" follows, of course, from his conception of nature as a progression through eternal exemplars to physical objects: "God has constituted all men simultaneously in that first and one man, whom he made to his image, but did not produce them at once in this visible world, rather at certain times and in certain places bringing the nature, which he had founded simultaneously, into visible being."[c]

In John's view, therefore, every individual particular (say, "the triangular thing which is seen by the bodily sense in some matter") is only an image, or reflection, of its eternal archetype. It is possible for men to move from sense perception of the former to rational knowledge of the latter precisely because the former depends on the latter for whatever being and truth it possesses. "Geometrical bodies, whether they be formed in phantasies of memory or in some sensible matter, subsist in their rational ideas, lacking all phantasy and all matter, above all that which is perceived by bodily sense or fashioned in memory."[d] In other words, John distinguished three kinds of entities named by the word "triangle": (1) the independently real universal, (2) the sense object, and (3) the memory image. Just as the memory image is dependent on the sense object, being "imprinted from the sensible figure through the corporeal sense on the memory," so the sense object (for example, the triangle drawn in chalk on the blackboard) is dependent on "that very triangle which remains uniformly in the discipline itself," the universal "triangle," which is nonspatial, nontemporal, and incorporeal.

Perhaps the eleventh- and twelfth-century thinkers—Odo of Tournai, Anselm, William of Champeaux,[36] for instance—who adopted realism as a solution to the problem of universals should have been warned by the company in which they found themselves. If they did not take John's disaster to heart, it was because

---

36 Odo (d. 1113) taught at the Cathedral school of Tournai and subsequently became Bishop of Cambrai. Anselm (1033–1109) was born in northern Italy, studied in France, and was Abbot of Bec and later (1093) Archbishop of Canterbury, in which office he had a bitter struggle with the king over investitures. William (1070–1120) taught at the Cathedral school of Paris and became Bishop of Châlons-sur-Marne.

they did not think the problem through to the point at which they could see the connection between John's realism and his tendency to pantheism and because, considered superficially, realism seemed wholly concordant with Christian doctrine. The view that particulars are less real than universals and that they derive their truth and being from their participation in these archetypes fit in very neatly with accepted doctrine about the relative unreality of this world as compared with the next. Moreover, some difficult orthodox dogmas were rendered less difficult by the realistic interpretation of universals. Consider the problem of original sin, over which Augustine had so long struggled. If each individual man is a separate reality, it is difficult, if not impossible, to understand how all men could have sinned in Adam's sin. But if the universal "man" is real, then anything that happens to the universal affects all the particulars subsumed by it. Just as Dobbin, by virtue of being a horse, cannot help having a mane, a tail, and hooves, so you and I, by virtue of being men, cannot help having corrupt wills.[37]

However, those who carried realism to its extreme conclusion found themselves in theologically hot water. The notion that universals are more real than particulars suggests that more general universals are more real than less general ones. At the same time, it suggests that as one ascends the scale of reality, one reaches new levels of creativity. This leads to the notion of a hierarchy of successively more general and more creative universals—man, rational animal, animal, living being, being as such. Each higher universal includes the lower ones that emanate from (and depend on) it, and the highest of all, which is God, therefore includes the whole universe. Thus realism seems to lead straight to pantheism. And pantheism, as we have seen, is a doctrine the Church must detest, for it identifies creature with Creator and so provides a philosophical warrant for human pride. If we men are a part of the divine being (however small a part!), we have no reason for humility.

Nor were theological questions of this kind the only difficulties that realism had to face. Though some of the metaphysical problems that had caused Aristotle to abandon Plato's idea of the "separation" of the forms were probably not recognized by medieval thinkers, it was easy, even in the Middle Ages, to make the realists (whose version of realism was, in any case, not as sophisticated metaphysically as Plato's had been) look very silly. One knows where Dobbin is and what sort of existence he has; but what sort of existence can "horse" have apart from Dobbin, Bucephalus, and all the other particular horses? If, for instance, the only truly real aspect of Dobbin is his horseness and the only truly real aspect of Bucephalus is *his* horseness, does it not follow that Dobbin and Bucephalus are identical? The realists did not know how to reply, and their critics (assuming the validity of Porphyry's oversimplified alternatives) therefore concluded that universals must be purely mental products.

37 This was the reasoning of Odo of Tournai.

NOMINALISM

Some of the more extreme of these critics may have gone even farther and concluded that a universal is merely a name—merely the noise "horse" or the wiggles "horse" written on paper. Whether or not anyone actually held this view,[38] it is obviously even less adequate than realism. The universal cannot *be* the wiggles or the noise; the wiggles and the noise are marks that *stand for* something—either for particulars or for universals, if there are universals. Obviously, then, talking about the marks cannot throw any light on the nature and status of the things (whatever they are) to which the marks refer. Consider the difference between the wiggles (or the noises) "Dobbin" and "horse": "Dobbin" has six letters, one of which is a capital, and "horse" has five letters, none of which is a capital. But this is completely irrelevant to the difference between a particular, Dobbin, and a universal, "horse." What the wiggles "Dobbin" means is Dobbin—a particular, four-footed, sway-backed beast. What the wiggles "horse" means is—horse. But what *is* horse? We are back where we started. Either there are only particulars or there is a special sort of entity of which the term (in this case, the wiggles or the noise "horse") is the sign.

Extreme nominalism was therefore no solution to the problem of universals. And it had the further disadvantage of conflicting with Christian doctrine. For instance, as the realists pointed out, nominalism was in open conflict with the dogma of the Trinity.[39] If Plato, Socrates, and Aristotle are one only in the sense that the name "man" can be applied indifferently to all three of them, then Father, Son, and Holy Spirit are one only in the sense that the name "God" can be applied indifferently to all three of them. "How," Anselm, the realist, asked, "can we expect anyone who does not even understand that many men are one man to comprehend how several Persons, each of whom is Himself a God, can yet be also one God?" In a word, if (as the nominalists claimed) only individuals are real, it follows either that God is one or that there are three Gods. In either case, the Trinitarian godhead of orthodoxy, the notion that God is both one *and* three, is denied. Roscelin went so far as to point this out, and, at the Council of Soissons in 1093, he was obliged to repudiate his teaching.

CONCEPTUALISM

Clearly, neither extreme realism, which held universals to be wholly independent objects, nor extreme nominalism, which denied any sort of objective status to universals, was acceptable—either on epistemological or on theological grounds. Some sort of compromise seemed to be in order. And it seemed that an acceptable view would necessarily agree with realism in rejecting nominalism's

---

38 The view being discussed is often attributed to Roscelin (about 1050–1120), but it is by no means certain that he held it in this extreme form.

39 For an account of the formulation of the orthodox position on the Trinity, see pp. 63–64.

contention that universals are merely names but that it would accept nominalism's contention that universals are not wholly independent, Platonic forms.

Now, as a matter of fact, Aristotle's revision of the Platonic theory of forms was essentially the kind of compromise the medieval philosophers were seeking.[40] Forms, Aristotle had held, are neither wholly independent entities nor wholly subjective mental states. They exist apart from the activity of minds in that they are embedded in, and indissolubly bound to, the particulars of sensation. Yet the human mind, by observing a number of similar particulars, has the capacity to separate the universal from them and to consider it in isolation. Accordingly, what the universal word names is a mental product (that is, the form "collected" by the mind); but it is not *merely* a mental product, for it is based upon real similarities in the objects themselves.

The compromise finally worked out by medieval philosophers was strikingly similar to Aristotle's theory, though, because the Middle Ages was largely ignorant of Aristotle's views, it was virtually an independent achievement. The medieval version of the compromise is sometimes called "conceptualism" because it is based on the notion that what the universal word names is not a Platonic form but a concept formed by the mind. If the universal is a concept, it follows that without the activity of human intellects there would be no universals. On this point, the nominalists were correct and the realists mistaken. But, given the "collective" activity of human intellects, a universal is a real entity with an objective reference. On this point, the realists were correct and the nominalists mistaken.

Abelard

The distinction of working out this medieval compromise belonged to Peter Abelard. Before discussing his formula, let us look briefly at his life. His tragic career shows the extent to which dogmatism, piety, and otherworldliness dominated his age. Yet his own complex personality—ambitious, passionate, disputatious, rationalistic—shows how vast an oversimplification it would be to suppose that there were no exceptions to this dominant pattern.

Abelard was born near Nantes, in western France, in 1079. He was destined by his father for a military career, but he soon "forsook Mars for Minerva" and set out as a wandering student to study "the art of disputation wherever it was flourishing." At Paris this art was flourishing under the realist, William of Champeaux, one of the best-known teachers of the day.[41] So thither Abelard went. Finding William's theories unsatisfactory, Abelard (who did not hide his light

40 In the classical debate on the status of universals, Plato's view corresponded to medieval realism and the Sophists' to nominalism.
41 See p. 187, n. 36.

under a bushel) undertook to correct him: "By the most patent arguments I compelled him to change his opinion; indeed, to abandon it." This certainly did not make for a happy relationship, and Abelard offended still further by setting up a rival school and attracting all William's pupils. William was the first, but not the most formidable, enemy Abelard made in this way.

While he was in Paris, Abelard met and fell deeply in love with a young girl, Héloïse, the niece of a canon of Notre Dame. When a child was born to the lovers, Héloïse's uncle sought to legitimatize the relationship by insisting on their marriage. To this Abelard and Héloïse agreed, but Héloïse insisted on keeping their marriage a secret lest it interfere with Abelard's career. This, naturally, was not at all to the canon's liking, and in revenge he caused Abelard to be attacked and emasculated by a band of ruffians. Héloïse took refuge in a convent, and Abelard himself, when he recovered, withdrew from teaching and retired to the monastery of St. Denis.

Meanwhile, he had been accused of heresy and orders had been given to burn his writings. Yet Abelard could not, or would not, hold his tongue, and wherever he went he stirred up trouble for himself. He antagonized the monks of St. Denis by pointing out that their patron could not possibly be the famed Dionysius the Areopagite, as they fondly supposed. Driven from there, he retired to a monastery in Brittany; but he was soon forced to leave. Returning to Paris, he resumed teaching and writing only to give new ammunition to his enemies, who once again accused him of heresy—this time, at the Council of Sens in 1141. He was condemned in 1142 and died, a broken man, the same year. Throughout this period of distress and frustration he maintained a correspondence with Héloïse. Their letters have survived as testimony to their mutual devotion.

Abelard's account of the nature and status of universals is contained in his *Glosses on Porphyry*—in other words, in a commentary on Boethius' commentary on Porphyry's *Introduction* to Aristotle's logic. His approach was rigorous, analytic, unhistorical—the prototype of the "scholastic" method that was to dominate thought during the rest of the Middle Ages and to give its name to the philosophy of that period. Abelard made no attempt, for instance, to consider Boethius' or Porphyry's positions as a whole; he analyzed the text before him sentence by sentence, phrase by phrase. Nor did he realize that the historical context in which Boethius and Porphyry wrote might be relevant to what they said or to how they said it. He assumed their statements to have timeless meanings that could be extracted and explicated for the benefit of less intelligent readers by the logician. The development of such a scholastic method was natural—indeed, inevitable—in an age accustomed to referring all questions to an authoritative text. In fact, Scholasticism was simply the extension of the program of scriptural exegesis to philosophy and the systematic employment of this program in the analysis of metaphysical, epistemological, and other problems.

Of course, Abelard did not expound Boethius' writings merely in order to ascertain Boethius' views; he used this exposition as a stick with which to beat his opponents. What emerged in the course of this process was a new view,

Abelard's own, based on his authorities but different from anything to be found in the work of Boethius or Porphyry themselves.

> There are then three questions, as Boethius says, secret and very useful and tried by not a few philosophers, but solved by few. . . . These questions, however, he passes over in this fashion, saying: *At present I shall refuse to say concerning genera and species this, whether they subsist, etc., or whether subsisting they are corporeal or incorporeal, or whether,* when they are said to be incorporeal, they should be separated *from sensibles, etc., and in accord with them.*[42] This last can be taken in different ways. For it can be taken this way, as if to say: I will refuse to make the three assertions stated above concerning them. . . . We are able so to expound the words, *and in accord with them* that we may add a fourth question, namely, whether genera and species, so long as they are genera and species, must have some thing subject to them by nomination, or whether, if the things named were destroyed, the universal could still consist of the meaning only of the conception, as this noun *rose* when there is not a single rose to which it is common. But we shall investigate these questions more carefully later.
>
> Now, however, let us follow the introduction literally. Note that when Porphyry says: *at present,* that is, in the present treatise, he intimates in a way that the reader may expect these questions to be solved elsewhere. *Most exalted business.* He states the reason for which he abstains here from these questions. . . . *And requiring greater diligence of inquiry,* for although the author is able to solve it, the reader is not able to inquire into it. Greater diligence of inquiry, I say, than yours. *This, however.* Having stated these things concerning which he is silent, he states those which he does treat of. . . .
>
> Let us return now, as we promised, to the above stated questions, and inquire carefully into them, and solve them. And since it is known that genera and species are universals and in them Porphyry touches on the nature of all universals generally, let us inquire here into the common nature of universals . . . , and let us inquire also whether they apply only to *words* or to *things* as well.[e]

Abelard began by attacking and holding up to ridicule various rival views. His criticism of William of Champeaux's extreme realism will serve as an example of his procedure:

> Certain philosophers, indeed, take the universal thing thus: in things different from each other in form they set up a substance essentially the same; this is the material essence of the individuals in which it is, and it is one in itself and diverse only through the forms of its inferiors. If these forms should happen to be taken away, there would be absolutely no difference of things, which are separated from each other only by a diversity of forms, since the matter is in essence absolutely the same. For example, in individual

42 [This is the passage from Porphyry quoted on p. 186—AUTHOR.]

men, different in number, [that is, in the different individuals of the species man] there is the same substance of man, which here is made Plato through these accidents, there Socrates through those. . . .

Although authorities seem to agree very much upon [this opinion], physics is in every manner opposed to it. For if what is the same essentially, although occupied by diverse forms, exists in individual things, it is necessary that one thing which is affected by certain forms be another thing which is occupied by other forms, so that the animal formed by rationality is the animal formed by irrationality, and so the rational animal is the irrational, and thus contraries would be placed in the same thing at the same time. . . .

[It also follows from this] opinion that rationality and irrationality are . . . in Socrates. But since they are in Socrates at the same time, it is proved that they are in Socrates and in an ass at the same time. But Socrates and the ass are Socrates. And Socrates and the ass are indeed Socrates, because Socrates is Socrates and the ass, since obviously Socrates is Socrates and Socrates is the ass. . . .

Moreover, how should we explain the plurality of things under substance if the only diversity were of forms while the subject substance remained at bottom the same? . . .

Whence, consequently, it is manifest that the opinion in which it is held that absolutely the same essence subsists at the same time in diverse things, lacks reason utterly. [f]

Having thus disposed of mistaken conceptions, Abelard was free to develop his own view. It was more profitable, he believed, to begin with a consideration of words than to begin with a consideration of things. For, though he had proved that there are no universal things, it was obvious, he thought, that there are universal words. "A *universal* word . . . is one which is apt by its invention to be predicated singly of many, as this noun *man*. . . . A *particular* word is one which is predicable of only one, as *Socrates* when it is taken as the name of only one." [g] Since there is a Socrates-thing named by the word "Socrates," there is no puzzle about particular words. But there is no distinct man-thing named by the word "man." This creates a very great puzzle about universal names. "The question is raised, then, since . . . according to Boethius every idea has a subject thing, how this applies to the ideas of universals." [h] It was precisely this puzzle, of course, that had forced the nominalists to conclude that universal words are "totally unrelated to signification."

But though it is true that universal words "signify no one thing," and though it is also true that all that exists are individuals, it does not follow that universal words are "empty of meaning." The seeming paradox is resolved when one recognizes that the mind has the power to form abstractions. Thus the mind can form ideas not only of individual particulars (ideas of Socrates and of Plato) but of parts or aspects of these particulars. Since a number of individuals may have similar parts or aspects, these similar parts form the basis for a significant (that is, non-empty) universal idea. So, in addition to the idea of Socrates and the idea of Plato, I can form the idea of man. The former are derived directly from my perception of Socrates and my perception of Plato; the latter is also derived from my perception of Socrates and Plato, but in a more complex way. I can abstract Socrates' rationality and his animality from his concrete individuality (in just the way that I can look at the red color of a ball without thinking about its sphericality), and I can do the same with Plato, Aristotle, and other men. In this way—by considering these aspects of Socrates, Plato, Aristotle in isolation from the rest of their individual natures—I can form the idea of man, namely, the idea of a rational animal. It follows that, though the universal does not have a distinct and separate object as the realists supposed, it is not merely an empty noise as the nominalists maintained. Its object is an abstraction, but it is real *as abstracted*. Rationality is not something that exists apart from Plato and Aristotle and other individual men. But though the concept "rational animal" is a mental product, it is not an illusion, for there *are* rational individuals.

The conceptions of universals are formed by abstraction, and we must indicate how we may speak of them alone, naked and pure but not empty.

And first concerning *abstraction*. In relation to abstraction it must be known that matter and form always subsist mixed together, but the reason of the mind has this power, that it may now consider matter by itself; it may now turn its attention to form alone. . . . For example, the substance of this man is at once body and animal and man and invested in infinite forms; when I turn my attention to this in the material essence of the substance, after having circumscribed all forms, I have a concept by the process of abstraction. Again, when I consider only corporeity in it, . . . that concept likewise . . . is formed also by abstraction with respect to other forms than corporeity, none of which I consider, such as animation, sensuality, rationality, whiteness.

Conceptions of this sort through abstraction seemed perhaps false and vain for this reason, that they perceive the thing otherwise than it subsists. . . . But this is not so. For if one understands otherwise than the thing is constituted, in such manner that one considers it manifestly in such a nature and property as it does not have, certainly that understanding is empty. But that is not what is done in abstraction. For, when I consider this man only in the nature of substance or of body, and not also of animal or of man or of grammarian, obviously I understand nothing except what is in that nature, but I do not consider all that it has. And when I say that I consider only this one among the qualities the nature has, the *only* refers to the attention alone, not to the mode of subsisting, otherwise the understanding would be empty. . . . The understanding considers separately by abstraction, but does not consider as separated. . . .

Now, however, that many things have been shown concerning the nature of abstraction, let us return to the *conception of universals* which must always be formed by abstraction. For when I hear *man* or *whiteness* or *white* I do not recall from the meaning of the noun all the natures or properties which are in the subject things, but from *man* I have only the conception although confused, not discrete, of animal and rational mortal. . . . Wherefore the understanding of universals is rightly spoken of as alone and naked and pure, that is, alone from the senses, because it does not perceive the thing as sensual, and naked in regard to the abstraction of all and of any forms, and pure with respect to discreteness because no thing whether it be matter or form, is designated in it. . . .

With this analysis as a basis, Abelard could return to Porphyry:

> Consequently, *having examined these things, let us proceed to the resolution of the questions concerning genera and species proposed by Porphyry,* which we can do easily now that the nature of all universals has been shown.
>
> The first question, then, was to this effect, whether genera and species . . . signify something truly existent, or are placed in the understanding alone, etc., that is, are located in empty opinion without the thing, like the following words, chimera and goat-stag which do not give rise to a rational understanding.
>
> To this it must be replied that in truth they signify by nomination things truly existent, to wit, the same things as singular nouns, and in no wise are they located in empty opinion; nevertheless, they consist in a certain sense in the understanding alone and naked and pure, as has been determined. . . .
>
> The same can be said in the second question which is as follows: whether subsisting they are corporeal or incorporeal. . . . The universal names themselves are called both corporeal with respect to the nature of things and incorporeal with respect to the manner of signification, because although they name things which are discrete, nevertheless they do not name them discretely and determinately.
>
> The third question, of course, whether they are placed in sensibles, etc., follows from granting that they are incorporeal. . . . Universals are said to subsist in sensibles, that is to signify an intrinsic substance existing in a thing which is sensible by its exterior forms, and although they signify this substance which subsists actually in the sensible thing, yet they demonstrate the same substance naturally separated from the sensible thing. . . . Genera and species are understood, but are not, outside sensible things. . . .
>
> With respect to that which we understand here as the fourth question, as we noted above,[43] the following is the solution, that we in no wise hold that universal nouns are, when, their things having been destroyed, they are not predicable of many things inasmuch as they are not common to any things, as for example the name of the rose when there are no longer roses, but it would still, nevertheless, be significative by the understanding, although it would lack nomination; otherwise there would not be the proposition: there is no rose.[i]

It will be noted that Abelard's treatment of the problem of universals involved shifting the emphasis from metaphysics to logic and psychology. Instead of trying to determine the ontological status of universals, he examined the process by which we arrive at universal concepts. The advantage of this procedure was

43 [See p. 192—AUTHOR.]

that the answer to the psychological question introduced certain distinctions that took Abelard beyond the oversimplified alternatives Porphyry had presented. It was not just a question, Abelard saw, of whether there is or is not a real object corresponding to the universal word. Though it is true that all that exists are individual particulars, various such particulars have similar properties. Consider several distinct individuals—Plato, Socrates, Aristotle. These individuals have an observable "likeness"—all three of them are capable of reasoning. By concentrating our attention on this "likeness" (this we are enabled to do by the mind's power to abstract), we form the universal idea, rationality. It may be said that this common likeness is the "common cause" of the universal concept signified by the universal word. A universal therefore exists in two ways: (1) It exists in the individual particulars as a common likeness, and (2) it exists in the human intellect as a concept formed as a result of the intellect's having focused its attention on the likeness.[44]

The problem of universals was (and still is, as a matter of fact) a serious problem. Before philosophers could philosophize about other matters, it was essential for them to demonstrate that a science of philosophy is possible. This meant demonstrating that universal statements and universal words refer to something, and this, in its turn, meant showing that universals, as the objects signified by the universal words, somehow exist. Until their foundations could be thus secured, metaphysics, theology, and all the other sciences were suspect.

Half the task of resolving any problem consists in discovering the right questions to ask. It is clear that in asking, "How do universal concepts arise in the mind?" Abelard adopted a fruitful line of approach. Although his psychology was certainly sketchy, and although his account left many questions unresolved, his view became the basis for discussion of this problem by subsequent medieval thinkers. In laying down the main lines for a solution to the controversy over universals and in showing how the possibility of there being scientific knowledge might be vindicated, Abelard helped make possible the great synthesis of the thirteenth century.

The Faith-Reason Controversy

Though the medieval attempts to solve the problem of universals were complicated by religious considerations, the problem itself is one that every philos-

---

44 Theological considerations, as a matter of fact, required Abelard to hold that universals exist in a third way: as the ideal prototypes used by God as models when He created the world. For, not content (as a modern writer might be) with the *fact* that similarities exist among the individual particulars of experience, Abelard proceeded to ask in typical medieval fashion, "Why do these similarities exist?" He arrived at the answer, "Because God created them similar." "But how did God come to do this?" "Because He was working from eternal archetypes." So, in the end, he too turned to Platonism and to the Middle Age's understanding of the *Timaeus*.

ophy must face and try to solve. The faith-reason controversy, on the other hand, is peculiar to Christian philosophy and arises only because the Christian philosopher accepts the authority of revelation. The classical mind, for its part, rested on no special revelation; what it knew it had discovered through its own efforts. This was possible because the things the Greeks were primarily interested in—man, the state, nature—were all possible objects of cognition.

However, as soon as men began to long for a supernatural and infinite object, it was clear that there had to be some sort of extranatural access to the desired object. And, since it was also clear that this extranatural access was not accorded to all men, it was argued that we should have faith in the authority of those who had received a special revelation. This simple scheme, as we have seen, soon proved insufficient. What if those to whom God revealed Himself contradicted one another? What if the language in which they reported their revelation was so ambiguous as to make the revelation itself unclear? And, since revelation operated at best only in one department of life (though this was doubtless the most important), were we to depend on reason elsewhere? If so, where was the frontier between the domain of reason and the domain of faith? And was reason or was faith to adjudicate disputes about the location of this frontier? [45]

At first it was easy for philosophers to assume that faith and reason do not conflict—that they yield identical conclusions. Since they held that God is the perfection of reality and truth, it seemed evident to them that He must operate in a perfectly rational manner. Moreover, they could not believe that the God who endowed men with rational minds did not intend them to use these minds to establish communication with the rational order He had decreed. Examples of this point of view, which seems rather naïvely optimistic in the light of subsequent developments, can be found in John Scotus Erigena's writings. He maintained that

> There is no doubt [that reason and authority] both flow from one fountain, namely divine wisdom. . . . Consequently no authority should frighten you away from these things, which the rational persuasion of right contemplation firmly teaches. For true authority does not oppose right reason, nor right reason true authority. . . . True authority seems to me to be nothing other than truth discovered by virtue of reason and committed by the holy Fathers to words for the use of posterity.[j]

But, unfortunately, John did not *prove* that faith and reason do not conflict; he merely *asserted* that they do not. And his opponents showed fairly conclusively that, as a matter of fact, the Church's faith and John's reason did conflict. If

45 A somewhat similar situation has developed in the United Nations. The Charter provides that in the Security Council the five great powers shall have a veto on all save "procedural matters," which shall be decided by a majority vote. But there are borderline cases in which it is difficult to say whether a given issue is a procedural matter. To put the matter more generally, when a watchman is required, who watches the watchman?

John himself had seen the necessity of choosing between faith and reason, it seems likely that he would have chosen reason: "We should follow reason which investigates the truth of things, and is overpowered by no authority, and is impeded in no way." The basis for this choice was his conviction that "reason is prior in nature, but authority in time. For although the nature has been created simultaneously with time, nevertheless the authority did not begin to be from the beginning of time and of nature. But reason has arisen with nature and time from the beginning of things."[k] In other words, God created the universe according to a rational plan before He revealed Himself in it. It follows that "every authority, which is not approved by true reason, is seen to be weak."

It is doubtful that John understood all the implications of his position, but it is plain that, pressed to its logical conclusion, this position is diametrically opposed to the fundamental presuppositions of the medieval mind—that the Holy Scripture is the revealed word of God and that the Church's interpretation of Scripture is definitive and binding. Since it was evident to some churchmen, if not to John himself, that John's premises led to this disastrous conclusion, they thought it the better part of wisdom to abandon the premises. These churchmen were also gravely dissatisfied with the "art of disputation" that fascinated Abelard and many of his contemporaries. Not understanding the epistemological problem with which the disputants were concerned, these churchmen concluded that the dispute over universals was both trivial and wicked—trivial because the disputants were wasting their time, and wicked because, by expending their energy on such trivial matters to the neglect of their religious duties, they were putting themselves in imminent danger of damnation.

ST. BERNARD

St. Bernard of Clairvaux (1091–1153) was representative of this fairly widespread antirationalism. Bernard, the son of a French knight who was killed on a crusade, joined the Cistercian Order (a great reforming order whose aim was to purge monasticism of its worldliness) in 1122. So deep was his devotion that "he lived for a year in the cell of the novices, and yet did not know that it had a vaulted roof."[46] In 1125 he was appointed abbot of a newly established Cistercian monastery at Clairvaux. Although Bernard was a mystic who would have preferred to live in retirement from the world, his reforming zeal plunged him into active life. He hated the secularism and the political involvements of the papacy as much as he hated the rationalistic pretensions of philosophers —and these hatreds were based on much the same grounds. He became a maker and breaker of popes, a vigorous opponent of ecclesiastical corruption, the driving force behind the Crusades, and a major political power in the Europe of his day. He also wrote several works of mystical devotion and a number of hymns.

46 See Jacobus de Varagine's *Life of St. Bernard* (written about 1250).

Like the earliest Christians, Bernard held that the earth and our life on it are at once a test of our Christian faith and a punishment for sin. Men are "strangers and pilgrims" painfully working their way back from the darkness into which Adam's prideful sin has cast them. On this pilgrimage men are not free agents but are desperately in need of God's grace.

For the rest, Bernard's theology was simple: "My philosophy is to know Jesus and Jesus crucified." This might have led a more logical mind to conclude that ecclesiastical apparatus is unimportant to salvation,[47] but Bernard insisted vigorously on all the traditional orthodox dogmas.

Though Bernard thought he needed dogma, he was sure that he did not need philosophy, with its rational justification of faith. He had been fortunate enough to have a mystical experience of God.

> I confess, I say in my folly, that the Word has visited me and that many times. And though he has often entered into me I have never known when he came. I have felt his presence, I remember that he has been present, and sometimes I have been able to foretell his entrance, but never to perceive his coming or his going. . . . He did not enter by the eyes, for he is without color, nor by the ears, for he is without sound, nor by the nostrils. . . . How then did he enter? Or can it be that he did not enter because he did not come from without, not being of those things that are without? But neither did he come from within, for he is good and I know that in me there is no good thing. . . . How then you ask, when his ways are thus altogether unsearchable, could I know that he was present? Only by the movement of my heart have I been aware of him. In the flight of vices and the restraint of carnal affections I have perceived the power of his virtue. In the examination and reproof of my secret faults I have admired the profundity of his wisdom. In the amendment, however small, of my ways I have experienced his goodness and gentleness. In the renovation and reformation of my mind and spirit, that is of my inner man, I have seen the fashion of his beauty. And as I have reflected on all these things I have been overwhelmed by his greatness.[1]

Like Tertullian,[48] Bernard reveled in the incomprehensibility of this experience: "I believe though I do not comprehend, and I hold by faith what I cannot grasp with the mind." He believed that humility and love, not learning and scholarship, prepare the mind for the secret and mysterious entrance of the Word. Philosophy, he felt, is not only useless; it is a pitfall for the unwary—as Abelard's unfortunate career only too plainly showed. Abelard, in his pride of intellect, was not content to dispute about the status of universals, itself a sufficiently dangerous matter. He also undertook to dispute about theology and wrote a

47 See the discussion of the relation between mysticism and institutional Christianity, pp. 54–57.
48 See pp. 64–65.

book in which he showed that the Church fathers contradicted themselves and one another on numerous matters.[49]

Today, most of us might be disposed to accept at face value Abelard's protests that he meant no harm and that he wished merely to provide young scholars with useful training in logic and debate. But what modern men understand by "Christian kindness" was no part of St. Bernard's makeup. Bernard judged that, at best, Abelard was guilty of criminal folly; he ought to have known that young minds are weak and pliable and that the display of all the contradictions into which certain eminent theologians had fallen could easily upset the faith of youthful readers. Therefore, Abelard should be punished, and his writings should be suppressed.[50]

But, of course, for Bernard the real criminal was not so much the individual Abelard as it was reason, with its lust for proof and evidence. Since, once we enter the rational road, there seems no end save the blind alley of heresy and damnation, we ought, Bernard held, to refuse to enter it at all. Suppose, for instance, the question occurs to us, "How can man achieve union with God without becoming submerged in the divine nature?" We must not try to *understand* this union; we must try to *experience* it:

> As a tiny drop of water falling in a quantity of wine seems to disappear and take on the taste and color of the wine; as iron reddens and grows incandescent in the fire and loses its original form; as air inundated by sunlight seems to become transformed into light itself—so that it is no longer illuminated but is itself a source of illumination, so the saints lose their human passions and are wholly absorbed in God. How can God be everything, if there survives in man something human? Without doubt the substance survives, but under another form, another power, another glory.

These metaphors, interestingly enough, stem from the Neoplatonic writings that John Scotus Erigena had drawn on. Bernard was quite right, therefore, in

49 This work, called by Abelard *Sic et Non* ("Yes and No"), enumerates 158 different propositions, for example, baptism is necessary to salvation; Christ became flesh and dwelt among us; God is triune. Abelard listed first the assertions of the fathers who affirmed, and next those of the fathers who denied, each of these propositions. Abelard did not question the authority of the Bible (he was not the eighteenth-century rationalist that some have attempted to make of him). He did, however, hold that the Church fathers are not infallible and that therefore we should not simply accept them as authority. To show that we must go beyond the fathers to the Bible itself was his purpose in *Sic et Non*. Abelard did not want to make sceptics of his readers; he wanted to show them that the truth has to be searched for: "By doubting we come to inquiry, by inquiring we discover the truth."

50 "Peter Abelard is a persecutor of the Catholic faith and an enemy of the cross of Christ. Outwardly he is a monk but inwardly he is a heretic. . . . His inexperienced auditors who . . . are scarcely able to bear the first elements of the faith, he introduces to the mystery of the Trinity, to the holy of holies, to the chamber of the King. . . . With Arius [he] distinguishes grades and steps in the Trinity; with Pelagius he prefers free will to grace; with Nestorius he divides Christ. . . . Thus traversing almost all sacred subjects he boldly attacks them from end to end and disposes of each in a damnable manner"—Letter 331, quoted in McGiffert, *A History of Christian Thought*, Vol. II, p. 224.

refusing to press for a rational understanding of the felt relationship. Any attempt to "explain" it would undoubtedly have led him into the same pantheism that had ensnared John. But it is difficult for a mystic to be content with the felt certainty. of his mystical experience, and Bernard himself did not succeed at this endeavor. Because he wanted to communicate it and to convince others of its truth and importance, and because he wanted to demolish Abelard, Bernard resorted to the use of discussion and argument.

The difficulty of avoiding all rational discussion is, indeed, so obvious that most medieval thinkers recognized that some sort of compromise had to be reached. Many formulas were proposed. Representative was Anselm's[51] reformulation of Augustine's famous "I do not know in order to believe; I believe in order to know."[52] Anselm held that "no Christian ought in any way to dispute the truth of what the Catholic Church [teaches]. But always holding the same faith unquestioningly, loving it and living by it, he ought himself so far as he is able to seek the reasons for it. If he can understand it let him thank God. If he cannot let him not raise his head in opposition but bow in reverence."[m] Like the diplomatic phrasemaking that sometimes resolves an international stalemate, this formula serves a useful purpose only so long as no one asks what it means. We ought to accept what the Church teaches. But what exactly *does* the Church teach? Abelard's *Sic et Non* showed that this is anything but clear. Again, we ought to seek the reasons for our faith "so far as we are able." But how able *are* we? What seems to one man an adequate proof of some article of faith may seem to others inadequate.

ANSELM'S PROOF OF GOD'S EXISTENCE

Anselm's own proof of the existence of God is a case in point, for there have been endless disputes about its adequacy. Let us examine this proof.

> Be it mine to look up to thy light, even from afar, even from the depths. Teach me to seek thee, and reveal thyself to me, when I seek thee, for I cannot seek thee, except thou teach me, nor find thee, except thou reveal thyself. Let me seek thee in longing, let me long for thee in seeking; let me find thee in love, and love thee in finding. Lord, I acknowledge and I thank thee that thou hast created me in this thine image, in order that I may be mindful of thee, may conceive of thee, and love thee; but that image has been so consumed and wasted away by vices, and obscured by the smoke of wrong-doing, that it cannot achieve that for which it was made, except thou renew it, and create it anew. I do not endeavor, O Lord, to penetrate thy sublimity, for in no wise do I compare my understanding with that; but I long to understand in some degree thy truth, which my heart believes and loves. For I do not seek to understand that I may believe, but

---

51 See p. 187, n. 36.
52 This may be contrasted with Bernard's statement on the same subject, quoted on p. 199.

I believe in order to understand. For this also I believe,—that unless I believed, I should not understand.

And so, Lord, do thou, who dost give understanding to faith, give me, so far as thou knowest it to be profitable, to understand that thou art as we believe; and that thou art that which we believe. And, indeed, we believe that thou art a being than which nothing greater can be conceived. Or is there no such nature, since the fool hath said in his heart, there is no God? (Psalms 14 : 1). But, at any rate, this very fool, when he hears of this being of which I speak—a being than which nothing greater can be conceived— understands what he hears, and what he understands is in his understanding; although he does not understand it to exist.

For, it is one thing for an object to be in the understanding, and another to understand that the object exists. When a painter first conceives of what he will afterwards perform, he has it in his understanding, but he does not yet understand it to be, because he has not yet performed it. But after he has made the painting, he both has it in his understanding, and he understands that it exists, because he has made it.

Hence, even the fool is convinced that something exists in the understanding, at least, than which nothing greater can be conceived. For, when he hears of this, he understands it. And whatever is understood, exists in the understanding. And assuredly that, than which nothing greater can be conceived, cannot exist in the understanding alone. For, suppose it exists in the understanding alone: then it can be conceived to exist in reality; which is greater.

Therefore, if that, than which nothing greater can be conceived, exists in the understanding alone, the very being, than which nothing greater can be conceived, is one, than which a greater can be conceived. But obviously this is impossible. Hence, there is no doubt that there exists a being, than which nothing greater can be conceived, and it exists both in the understanding and in reality.

And it assuredly exists so truly, that it cannot be conceived not to exist. For, it is possible to conceive of a being which cannot be conceived not to exist; and this is greater than one which can be conceived not to exist. Hence, if that, than which nothing greater can be conceived, can be conceived not to exist, it is not that, than which nothing greater can be conceived. But this is an irreconcilable contradiction. There is, then, so truly a being than which nothing greater can be conceived to exist, that it cannot even be conceived not to exist; and this being thou art, O Lord, our God. . . .

I thank thee, gracious Lord, I thank thee; because what I formerly believed by thy bounty, I now so understand by thine illumination, that if I were unwilling to believe that thou dost exist, I should not be able not to understand this to be true.[n]

COMMENT ON ANSELM'S PROOF

This argument, which is the celebrated "ontological" proof of the existence of God, is characteristic of much medieval philosophizing—a blend of awkwardly expressed reasoning and touching piety. It starts from the assumption that we have an idea of an absolutely perfect being, defined as a being than which nothing greater exists. The question is: Does the being so defined exist in reality as well as in idea? Anselm held that this being must exist in reality as well as in idea, for to say that the most perfect being exists only in idea involves a contradiction. It would not be most perfect if it existed only in idea. Suppose that this most perfect being does exist only in idea. We can certainly *think* of a being exactly like this being in all respects except one: The second being has the added perfection of existing. This second being would therefore be more perfect than the first one, and so we contradict ourselves in calling the first one most perfect. It is clear, then, that a being that does not exist cannot be most perfect and, conversely, that the most perfect being must exist. In other words, the than-which-nothing-could-be-greater being would not be than-which-nothing-could-be-greater if it did not exist.

It is evident that Anselm's proof is open to attack at two main points: (1) Do we in fact have an idea of an absolutely perfect being? (2) Is existence indeed an "added perfection"? That is, is a being that exists necessarily greater (more perfect) than one that does not exist? Both these assumptions were challenged almost immediately by a monk named Gaunilo, and they have been points of discussion for philosophers and theologians from that day to this.

Let us take up point (1) first. Gaunilo noted that the sceptic who is not convinced of God's existence would not grant Anselm's assumption that men have an idea of a most perfect being. To this Anselm could have replied that he was not trying to convince sceptics that God exists, but to provide Christians with a rational understanding of Christian truth. ("I believe in order to understand," not "I understand in order to believe.") In any case, he would have maintained that he could *prove* that men have an idea of a perfect being. This proof runs along Platonic lines and fits in with Anselm's tendency toward Platonic realism, which has already been noted. According to Plato, even though none of us has even seen an absolutely equal pair of sticks, we have an idea of absolute equality (that is, we cognize the form "equality" in and through sense experience of sticks that are only roughly equal). If we did not know the form, we would not be able to recognize that the sticks are nearly equal. Similarly, according to Anselm, we have various experiences of "degrees of perfection"—for instance, we experience some things as better or more beautiful than others. We can make this kind of relative judgment only because we have a standard of comparison: the idea of absolute perfection.[53]

It will be seen that the argument here turns on a question that has already been considered, namely, how can a finite mind transcend its finite experience

---

53 Anselm's argument here is similar to one of Thomas' proofs of the existence of God (see pp. 216–18), but Thomas did not agree with Anselm that men necessarily have a clear idea of God as the most perfect being. See *Summa Theologica*, Pt. I, Ques. 2, Reply Objs. 1, 2, and 3.

and reach an understanding of an infinite object? [54] What a finite mind feels to be an intellectual grasp of an infinite object may be only an emotive response. It is necessary, indeed, to distinguish between the rich emotive and conative meaning of words like "perfection" and the kind of meaning needed for philosophical communication. Consider the word "communist," which arouses strong emotions in many Americans but which most people do not bother to define precisely. Consequently, when A calls B a communist, he tells us more about himself than about B. He tells us that he dislikes B, that he believes B is a menace to the "American way of life," and so on; but he does not tell us what characteristics of B's form the basis of his dislike. Perhaps B actually is a member of the Communist Party, but perhaps B has only advocated withdrawal from Vietnam, whereas A is in favor of a nuclear attack there.

Similarly, no one would deny that "most perfect being" has a very strong emotive meaning. The question is whether Anselm could formulate this meaning firmly enough for it to serve as the basis of a rational proof of the existence of God.

Let us pass on to point (2). Allowing that men have an idea of a most perfect being, does it follow that a being corresponding to this idea must exist? Gaunilo invited Anselm to think of the most perfect conceivable island. This ideal island would have a wonderful beach, just the right kind of surf, coconut palms, and whatever other features seem appropriate. Certainly, one would also *think of it* as existing, for a nonexistent island, however attractive its other features, would not be especially desirable. But the fact that one cannot help thinking of this most perfect island as existing does not prove that it exists. As Gaunilo said, "If a man should try to prove to me by such reasoning that this island truly exists, . . . either I should believe that he was jesting, or I know not which I ought to regard as the greater fool: myself, supposing I should allow this proof; or him, if he should suppose that he had established with any certainty the existence of this island."°

To this Anselm could and did reply that the criticism rests on an equivocation. "Most perfect" has one meaning when applied to "island," another when applied to "being." Thus, to have the idea of the most perfect island is not to have the idea of the most perfect being. The fact that the island does not necessarily exist is therefore irrelevant to the question of whether God necessarily exists. This reply, it must be allowed, seems effective against Gaunilo's criticism in the form in which he stated it. But it raises a difficult question for Anselm: Is not any "most perfect" of which men can think on the order of Gaunilo's island rather than on the order of Anselm's God?

Moreover, Gaunilo's argument can be restated in more effective form; one can ask whether existence is indeed an "added perfection." Anselm's whole case depends on the assumption that it is. If existence is not an added perfection,

54 See pp. 174–76.

no contradiction is involved in admitting that the most perfect being exists only in idea. And Gaunilo's real point is that existence is *not* an added perfection. An island that really exists is more useful than one that is merely thought about, but the island itself is the same whether it exists or does not exist. It may be said that the existence or nonexistence of the island affects *us* and our attitude toward the island, but it does not affect the inner essence of the island.

If one wants to call existence a "property" of existing things (in the sense that color is a property of colored things), it is important to see that it is a special kind of property. Doubtless, one adds something to the nature of an uncolored thing by coloring it, but one does not add anything to the *nature* of a nonexistent thing by bringing it into existence.

Put this way, it may seem obvious that Gaunilo was correct and that Anselm was mistaken. But the matter is not quite this simple. The fundamental question is: How do we get from thought to things? There certainly seems to be a distinction between thoughts and the things thought about, for not all thoughts are true. But if this distinction is valid, what, generally, makes thoughts true? Specifically, can the perfection and consistency of the thinking that goes into thoughts make these thoughts true? Consider, for example, one of the most perfectly consistent thought processes that can be found—the thinking that goes into the proof of a theorem in Euclidean geometry. Are the theorems in which this thinking results true? Many people would draw a distinction. They would say that the theorems are valid, not true,—or, perhaps, that the propositions are only "hypothetical." For instance, we do not say, categorically, that triangles have interior angles equal to 180°; we say, hypothetically, that *if* anything is a plane figure enclosed by three straight lines, then that thing has interior angles equal to 180°. Thus, from this point of view, the perfection and consistency of geometrical thinking does not prove that such-and-such entities, for example, triangles, exist outside thoughts. The perfection and consistency apply only to the relation of one thought to some other thought. And this relation is doubtless a necessary relation—*if* one thinks of a Euclidean triangle, one must think of it as having interior angles equaling 180°. Similarly, from this point of view, the most one can maintain with respect to God is that, *if* one thinks of a most perfect being, one must *think* of it as existing. But it does not follow, of course, that the being necessarily thought of as existing necessarily exists.

This line of reasoning will certainly not satisfy everyone. Some people will ask, "If, when we think about triangles, we are not thinking about real entities, what in heaven's name *are* we thinking about?" "Are you going to say," they will continue, "that mathematical thinking is merely private and subjective—like daydreaming, only more organized?" We are obviously back to the central Platonic question about the forms: The triangle of perception cannot be the object of mathematical thinking; therefore, if mathematical thinking is not a subjective fancy, it must have some nonmaterial, nonperceptual object, the form "triangle."

Since the ontological argument for God's existence is tied to this extremely difficult question, it is easy to see why there has been such a long debate about its validity. In general, the ontological argument will seem plausible to those who incline toward Platonic realism, for the realist conceives the object known (the universal) to be present in the knowing mind, illuminating it, as it were. If this is true of even the most ordinary universal, it will obviously be even more true of God, if He is conceived of, not as a particular being, but as the most universal of universals. By the same token, the ontological argument will seem implausible to those who incline toward nominalism, and since realism is rather out of fashion today, the ontological argument also tends to be out of fashion.

Of course, one does not have to be a medieval realist to accept the ontological argument. Hegel, for instance, held that the distinction between thought and its objects is a distinction within thought, for he did not see how, otherwise, mind could ever know anything other than its own states. Believing this, he also held that consistent thoughts are not only valid but true. In other words, the totality of thoughts is the totality of reality, and the ontological argument (on these premises) is entirely correct.

Perhaps enough has been said to suggest that there is more to the ontological argument than appears at first sight—more than appears in the debate between Anselm and Gaunilo. This argument is, indeed, another major parting of the ways in philosophy. What seemed to Anselm so easy—to prove the existence of the God of whose existence he was already assured by faith—turned out to be anything but simple. As long as philosophers were not sufficiently acute to see the complex questions that the attempt to prove God's existence opens up, the faith-reason controversy seemed no great problem. But in the coming years the "art of disputation" that Abelard and his colleagues practiced began to reveal some of the complications. And when proofs become suspect, the relation between faith and reason is inevitably left in suspense. If, even in an age of faith, men cannot get on without using reason, they need to know where it is appropriately used and where it should be set aside. They need a logical canon that shows what a valid proof is, and if this canon discloses that certain articles of Christian faith cannot be proved, they need a theological canon that shows how reason and faith are related at the point at which reason leaves off and faith takes over. Here again, the work of the philosophers of the eleventh and twelfth centuries helped clear the ground for the systematic thinkers of the thirteenth century.

Summary

In this chapter we have considered the long interval between the fifth and the thirteenth centuries, between Augustine and Thomas. The extent to which philosophy suffered from the collapse of the Empire and the loss of classical culture is evident from the fact that it virtually disappeared for many centuries. Except for the brief and almost accidental career of John Scotus Erigena, there was no philosophical thought—let alone any thinking of the first rank—until the second half of the eleventh century.

When philosophy finally emerged again, it became absorbed in two very technical, and, in a sense, very limited, problems—the status of universals and the relation of reason to faith. Yet the possibility of the great systems of the thirteenth century depended on the attempts made in the eleventh and twelfth centuries to state these technical issues clearly and to at least make a start toward solving them satisfactorily. For, though a Christian philosophy by definition acknowledges the ultimate authority of Christian revelation, it must, as far as it claims to be *philosophy,* also aim at making an objective and rational formulation of its articles of faith. Before Christian philosophers could even begin to work on such a formulation, they had to justify the use of reason and show that rational analysis of belief was possible. And, since reason was obviously concerned with universals, with making general assertions rather than particular ones, it was clear that in order to justify reason they had to establish the existence, in some sense, of universals. Finally, the disputations of the eleventh and twelfth centuries prepared the way for the philosophical work of the thirteenth century not only by resolving certain preliminary problems but by sharpening men's minds and helping them to forge an instrument of logical analysis capable of dealing adequately with a central problem of medieval philosophy.

What was this problem? It was, of course, one of the central problems any intellectual age has to face: the problem of finding a philosophical rationale for the beliefs, values, and attitudes of ordinary men. In the thirteenth century, this naturally meant giving philosophical form to Christian truth. It was the old problem Augustine had unsuccessfully sought to solve. And after Augustine, during the Dark Ages, it had lain in abeyance, for piety had seemed enough and men had been too intent on surviving and assuring themselves of salvation to worry about philosophical precision.

If the passing centuries had gradually fashioned a keener logical instrument than Augustine had possessed, they had also added a new dimension to the philosophical task. The philosophical problem that confronted the thirteenth century was not simply to do better than Augustine what he had tried to do. It was not merely to work out a philosophical statement of Christian belief, but to incorporate in that statement the new insights and attitudes, the new this-worldly concerns that had gradually emerged in the twelfth century. The problem, of course, was still to create a Christian philosophy; but in the interval the conception of Christian philosophy had expanded to include political, social, ethical, and esthetic considerations that the earliest Christians had written off as paganism. Let us now turn to an examination of this immense undertaking.

CHAPTER 6

Thomas:
Metaphysics

Thomas was the son of a count of Aquino and was born in 1225 (or late in 1224) at his father's castle, Rocca Secca, near the great Benedictine Abbey of Monte Cassino, in southern Italy. There, at Monte Cassino, he received his early education. At the age of ten he was sent for six years to the University of Naples, where he came under the influence of the newly formed and energetic Dominican Order. In spite of his family's opposition, he joined this Order and continued his education, at Paris and at Cologne, under its auspices. In 1257 he took his degree, Doctor of Theology, and settled down to a life of lecturing and writing, interrupted by frequent journeys in the service of his order and the Church. He died on March 7, 1274, when he was not yet fifty years of age, while on the way to Lyons to attend a Church council.

Our discussion of Thomism will be divided into two main parts—an account of Thomas' metaphysics and an account of his conception of man. In connection with the former, which occupies the present chapter, his proofs of the existence of God and his conception of God's infinite and perfect nature will be discussed. This chapter will also give brief accounts of Thomas' views of the physical world and of angels. The next chapter will deal with Thomas' psychology, ethics, and politics and will conclude with an account of some of the theological problems that were created for him by his conception of man.

The Central Problem

Thomas' intellect was of the same rank as Plato's and Aristotle's; with him we reach another philosophical mountain peak. Indeed, he stands functionally to the Middle Ages as Plato and Aristotle do to the classical world. Like them, he gave a definitive answer to the major intellectual problems of his times. What were the problems that Thomas set himself to solve? And why did they seem important? They were, in part, purely dogmatic; that is, they were problems related to the old task of working out a consistent theology, of systematizing the hodgepodge of seemingly contradictory dicta in the work of the Church fathers.

This undertaking has little more than academic interest for most people today. But Thomas was more than a theologian, and the problems of his time were more than purely theological problems. For, during the preceding century, the world had so changed and broadened that any exclusively theological or radically otherworldly scheme would have been unsatisfactory in Thomas' time. Some of the most important of these changes—the novel art forms, the Crusades and their manifold results, the new interest in natural science, the rise of the universities—have already been discussed. Thomas' major problem, and that of all thinking men of his day, was to find a way of incorporating the new interests and the new knowledge to which they gave rise into the religious orientation that, of course, still dominated the Western mind. Or, since virtually all of men's knowledge about extrareligious matters was derived from such writings of the ancients as were then accessible, it may just as well be said that Thomas' major problem was to reconcile the Christian notion of God and what it implied about man and nature with the old classical world view.

CLASSICAL AND CHRISTIAN VIEWS CONTRASTED

For the classical mind the essential human problem was how to get in a right relationship with oneself and with one's fellow men. Though classical philosophers often differed about exactly where and how to strike the balance, they all held that the human problem could be solved with human resources and that it was soluble *here*, on this earth. The problem, as they saw it, was how to be happy. And they agreed that the solution of this problem required knowledge of one's natural and social environment. Whether one was an activist like Aristotle or a passivist like Epicurus was, from the point of view of these classical philosophers, less important than the fact that both the activists and the passivists held the ethical problem to be a this-worldly one.

In contrast, the Christian's outlook on life and its problems was determined by his belief in an omnipotent God who was at the same time a loving father. The supreme—indeed, virtually the only—concern of the early Christian was to get into a right relation with his God-father. And he held this right relation to be defined by God, not by man. That is, God (as omnipotent ruler) decrees certain rules that man (as subject) must obey with utter punctiliousness. But at the same time God (as loving father) wishes not merely strict obedience, but free and loving service. Though God's commands are duties, the good man performs them in the same spirit as that in which a loving and trustful son obeys his wise and loving human father. The good man, the man who conforms to his divine father's wishes, will doubtless be happy. For happiness, the Christians held, is a by-product of man's goodness, and goodness lies in establishing a proper filial relation to God. Correspondingly, they defined badness as separation from God, as the wrong kind of relationship, which results when men fail to do God's commands or when they do them in a niggardly and unfilial manner. For the early Christian, who expected the end of the world momentarily, nothing mattered except his relation with God.

But as time went on and the world did not end, and as the Church grew in power and responsibility, men could no longer disregard the old ethical, social, and political questions with which the classical mind had been concerned. Thus the issue involved in the faith-reason controversy reappeared. Just as it was discovered that reason could not be wholly dispensed with, though no one was able to define its exact relation to faith, so it was discovered that this world and its problems did indeed require attention, though—once again—no one quite knew how the this-worldly questions were related to the transcendentally important other world and *its* problems.

What was true in the fields of epistemology and ethics and politics was also true in physics and psychology. The early Christian view that man commits the sin of intellectual pride if he inquires too much or too carefully about the workings of nature had gradually weakened. If the physical universe was still held to be a vale of tears, it was proving to be a very deep vale, and men could hardly avoid giving some attention to their sojourn there. Interest in medicine, for instance, appeared, and with it a recognition that the pagans had something of value to say on this subject. It was not that men's sense of the primacy of religious concerns and of the supreme importance of the Christian revelation had diminished. It was rather that, as men slowly emerged from the darkness of the early Middle Ages and as they began to rebuild culture and civilization, they inevitably felt renewed interest in this-worldly things. Consequently, it became necessary to find a place in their scheme of things for the natural man and his natural pursuits.

Thus, as has been said, the central problem for Thomas and the Middle Ages was to reconcile the Christian and the classical views of man and his world. It was easy for the earliest Christians to reject the classical conceptions of the world as wicked paganism, but by the thirteenth century men recognized that, despite all its deficiencies, the classical world view contained values that could be ignored only at the cost of corresponding deficiencies in their own points of view.

THE INFLUENCE OF ARISTOTLE

This recognition required considerable intellectual and moral maturity. Indeed, it is doubtful that a philosophical synthesis of classical and Christian insights could have been achieved but for the series of lucky accidents by which, as we have seen, the major works of Aristotle became available to Western scholars at precisely the time when the Western world could best appreciate his thought.

Unhappily, this new light was disturbing to settled ways of thought. Not only was the empirical-naturalistic point of view of Aristotle antagonistic to the Neoplatonic mysticism that had so long dominated Christian thinking, but some of the conclusions Aristotle himself had drawn from his basic principles contradicted cherished Christian dogmas. Aristotle had held, for instance, that the world is eternal and uncreated; it seemed (to some at least) that he had denied personal immortality. It is not surprising, therefore, that the teaching of Aristotle's theories met with great hostility. As early as 1210, fifteen years before Thomas' birth, the authorities at Paris forbade the teaching of Aristotle's natural science. A few years later the *Metaphysics* was also banned, and these interdicts were renewed several times during the century. In 1277, just after Thomas' death, the various attempts to reconcile Aristotelianism and Christianity (Thomism, of course, was one of the chief) were condemned both at Oxford and at Paris.[1]

It thus took courage as well as acumen to maintain, as Thomas did in effect, that the Christian insights were one-sided and that they required supplementation—that man is certainly a child of God, but that he is also a natural animal. It is fashionable today to speak contemptuously of the conservatism of Thomism, but in its own day it was progressive and forward-looking. Today, with the enormous advances made in the natural sciences, we would not go to Aristotle for information about man, but in Thomas' day where was one to turn but to the Greeks? And among the Greeks, who was wiser than Aristotle?

---

1 Soon, however, and largely as a result of Thomas' work, the tide turned. The Dominicans were the first to rally solidly behind their brother; in 1278 this order officially accepted Thomism. Thomas was canonized a half-century later, in 1323. In the sixteenth century it was decreed that he ranked equally with the four great Latin fathers—Ambrose, Augustine, Jerome, and Gregory. And in 1879 Pope Leo XIII pronounced that Thomism should be the basic theory of the Roman Catholic Church.

THE MAGNITUDE OF THOMAS' TASK

We should not underestimate the difficulty of the task to which Thomas set himself. It was one thing to recognize, as Thomas did, that the classical mind had made significant discoveries in the fields of physics, epistemology, logic, ethics, and politics, and to see that in these fields, at any rate, the Christian view required supplementation. It was quite another thing actually to work out the needed synthesis, for with their notion of a divine and infinite father, the Christians had done much more than merely introduce a new dimension; they had radically altered the conception of every part of the classical scheme. Consider nature: Instead of the closed system of naturally caused events that the Greek physicists had conceived it to be, it became for the Christians a stage setting on which the drama of salvation unfolded. Instead of a system of events horizontally related by spatiotemporal relations, it became a set of symbols vertically related to God's inscrutable purpose. Or consider man: For the Greeks he had been the summit of spatiotemporal existence, containing in himself, at his best, the necessary ingredients for as good and as successful a life as could be conceived of. For the Christian, man was, in Augustine's words, "crooked, sordid, bespotted and ulcerous"—at once helpless and depraved. How could any sort of synthesis be effected between two such radically different views?

Part of Thomas' achievement was finding a formula for reconciling the pagan and Christian world views. But he did not stop there. He actually applied this formula to various specific problems in physics, epistemology, ethics, and so on, and thus tied the various special sciences together in a single, all-inclusive science. In this respect Thomas went far beyond any earlier thinker, Christian or pagan.

Basic Concepts

REASON AND REVELATION

The first tasks of the Christian philosopher, Thomas thought, must be to define and delimit the domain of philosophy and to justify the use of a rational method of inquiry. This was necessary because, as he well knew, many important churchmen (St. Bernard, for instance) maintained that philosophy should not concern itself in any way with the articles of faith. In opposition to this anti-intellectualism, Thomas held that it is possible to demonstrate many religious truths by the natural light of reason. He did not mean, of course, that reason is wholly independent of Christian revelation. On the contrary, for Thomas the philosophical undertaking rested on prior acceptance of the great principles of Christian faith. This was true in two respects:

(1) The truths known in revelation form the first principles from which we go on to prove other truths by rational argument. The fact that these first

principles cannot be proved is not a valid objection to their use as a starting
point, for no science proves its own first principles. Here, of course, Thomas
was following Aristotle's contention that each science is simply the logical
demonstration of the conclusions that follow from principles that *that* science
accepts as its starting point. As Thomas himself put it,

> As the other sciences do not argue in proof of their principles, but argue
> from their principles to demonstrate other truths in these sciences, so this
> doctrine does not argue in proof of its principles, which are the articles
> of faith, but from them it goes on to prove something else. . . . However,
> it is to be borne in mind, in regard to the philosophical sciences, that the
> inferior sciences neither prove their principles nor dispute with those who
> deny them, but leave this to a higher science; whereas the highest of them,
> viz., metaphysics, can dispute with one who denies its principles, if only
> the opponent will make some concession; but if he concedes nothing, it can
> have no dispute with him, though it can answer his arguments. Hence Sacred
> Scripture, since it has no science above itself, disputes argumentatively with
> one who denies its principles only if the opponent admits some at least of
> the truths obtained through divine revelation. Thus, we can argue with
> heretics from texts in Holy Scripture, and against those who deny one article
> of faith we can argue from another. If our opponent believes nothing of
> divine revelation, there is no longer any means of proving the articles of
> faith by argument, but only of answering his objections—if he has any—
> against faith.[a]

(2) In addition to serving the axioms from which the theorems of a Christian
philosophy are deduced, the truths of revelation serve as guides in the actual
process of developing such a philosophy. Just as it is easier for us to solve
mathematical problems if we can look up the answers in the back of the book
and then work backwards from them, so the fact that we have prior knowledge
(in revelation) of the Christian truths we want to prove makes it possible for
us to demonstrate many truths that we would otherwise find it impossible to
prove.

Aristotle, Thomas held, is a case in point. Aristotle could and did demonstrate
some truths about God by unaided reason—but not enough, unfortunately, for
his salvation. Christians, guided by truths that they know first in revelation (and
that Aristotle, of course, did not know at all), find it possible to prove much
more about God than Aristotle did. Even so, however, there are important truths
that remain forever outside the sphere of reason. These must be accepted on
faith.

To summarize Thomas' position on this point, it may be said that he made
a double distinction. First, he distinguished between philosophy and theology:
Philosophy is what can be proved by the natural light of reason; theology is
whatever rests on faith. Second, he distinguished between revealed and natural
theology: The latter is the part of the former that is susceptible of proof. Thus,

philosophy and theology overlap. Some of the truths that rest on faith (and so belong in the field of theology) are demonstrable (and so belong in the field of philosophy). Natural theology is the name Thomas gave to the set of propositions that constitute the field of knowledge in which faith and reason overlap.

If all this is true, it is clear that philosophy (that is, of course, physics, ethics, and politics as well as natural theology) and revealed theology cannot possibly conflict. However, Thomas wanted to maintain more than this. He wanted to hold not merely that revelation does not contradict reason, but that revelation supplements reason. "Sacred doctrine also makes use of human reason, not, indeed, to prove faith (for thereby the merit of faith would come to an end), but to make clear other things that are set forth in this doctrine. Since therefore grace does not destroy nature, but perfects it, natural reason should minister to faith as the natural inclination of the will ministers to charity."[b]

This, of course, was Thomas' way of resolving the faith-reason controversy. Is his formula satisfactory? Does grace really "perfect" nature? Thomas would have replied that the whole body of his *Summa* is a demonstration of this thesis, for the *Summa* is a rational inquiry, and its conclusions (he would have maintained) are not only in harmony with, but are illumined by, the truths of faith.

THE UNIVERSE AS A HIERARCHY OF SUBSTANCES

With the assurance, then, that reason is a reliable, if limited, instrument, one may ask what, specifically, reason declares the world to be. Since Thomas took Aristotle as his guide, the basic outlines of his metaphysics are Aristotelian. With Aristotle, he held the universe to be a collection of individual substances that can be defined in terms of matter and form.

By adopting this position, Thomas found it possible to avoid the dualism that infected Augustine's view. As we have seen, this Christian dualism always tends to collapse into monism, usually by way of an otherworldliness and mysticism that regard the realm of nature as basically unreal. In Thomas' work there is hardly a trace of this Neoplatonic strain. According to Thomas, the universe is not irrevocably sundered into two spheres, the realm of grace and the realm of nature. There are not two kinds of existents, but one kind—subject, of course, to continuous gradation as form becomes more and more actual. The created world is not an unreal shadow somehow vaguely imitating the one true reality, God. Creatures and Creator form one universe, a single, continuous hierarchy. Here, it may be noted, the basis for Thomas' assertion that grace perfects nature instead of destroying it has been stated in metaphysical terms. In Christian dualism, the reality of nature is destroyed by the superior reality of the realm of grace; in Thomas' view, nature is perfected by grace. Nature, that is, is matter illumined and made actual by its form.

This formulation not only gave Thomas' world view a unified structure; it supplied Thomas with a large mass of material that could be incorporated into this world view. For, since he equated nature with what Aristotelian science revealed, he had in Aristotle's writings the whole "matter" of his own philosophy. This needed only to be actualized by form (conceived of by Thomas as the truths of Christian revelation) in order to become a completely adequate philosophy.

In general, then, Thomas' position was that, in order to understand anything, we need to know, first, what Aristotle said about it and, second, what light Christian revelation throws on Aristotle's view. Thus, with regard to the nature of man, Thomas maintained (1) that what Aristotle said about human psychology in the *De Anima* is true and important. Man *is* a natural being with natural functions. And as a natural being, he has natural ends, which Aristotle adequately described in the *Ethics* and the *Politics*. But (2) man is more than the natural being Aristotle supposed him to be. Christian insight discloses that he is also a child of God. As such, he has another and a higher end—loyalty and obedience to God, his father and his creator.

Similarly, as regards Aristotle's conception of God, Thomas held that it is true as far as it goes, but that it does not go very far. God is indeed, as Aristotle held, the summit of the hierarchy of substances. He is pure actuality, pure activity, pure intelligence, a being whose perfection inspires the universe's movement. Yet there are deeper truths about the divine nature that were inaccessible to Aristotle—truths that God makes known only to His chosen people. As the Christian knows, God is more than the metaphysical perfection Aristotle conceived Him to be; He is a creative providence, a loving father, an exacting ruler. Once again, these higher insights do not contradict what unaided reason discloses. Hence the demands of reason are not denied; they are satisfied even while they are transcended. The metaphysical unity of the world is preserved even though two distinct cognitive powers are required for its adequate comprehension.

METHOD OF ARGUMENT

So much for the Thomistic world scheme in outline. Before a detailed examination of it is undertaken, a few words must be said about the method of argument by which Thomas developed these views. This method was similar to that employed by Abelard in *Sic et Non*[2] inasmuch as it consisted in setting out arguments, derived from various authoritative sources, for and against certain important theses. But Thomas went far beyond Abelard both in the way in which he organized the successive theses into a systematic whole and in the exhaustive manner in which he examined and either refuted or affirmed the various alternatives under each thesis. Although it certainly cannot be maintained that Thomas' arguments for his own position and against rival views are always valid, it must be allowed that, *given his presuppositions,* he is on the whole convincing.

His standard procedure was to raise a question and then to list, one after

2 See p. 200, n. 49.

another, a number of answers to it that he held to be mistaken but for which some authority or other could be cited. He then stated, in summary form, the argument in support of each of these answers. The next stage of the discussion was introduced by the phrase, "On the contrary," after which a counterauthority was cited in support of the answer that Thomas himself proposed to defend. The citation of a counterauthority was followed by an argument for Thomas' own answer, and this, in turn, was followed by separate replies to each of the rejected answers. In this final stage of the discussion Thomas attempted to show either that the mistaken answer was based on confusion about what was being proved or that the authority quoted in its defense was misunderstood. In other words, he aimed at showing that the conflict among authorities was only apparent and that, when rightly understood, they all supported the position he had reached by rational argument.

The difference between this exhaustive method and the partial method of Abelard's *Sic et Non* is an index of the advances made in logic and argumentation in the century between Abelard and Thomas. It was easy for the early Scholastics to affirm that faith and reason could not conflict, but this assertion was bound to remain unconvincing as long as various canonical authorities could be cited for and against the same thesis. Thomas, however, developed a method that actually resolved these contradictions; accordingly, the claim that faith and reason did not conflict was no longer a bare assertion.

Another feature of the Thomistic method—but one that it is impossible to appreciate without reading through the whole of the *Summa*—is the systematic way in which the successive theses are unfolded. So far only Thomas' systematic treatment of each particular thesis has been noted, but the *Summa* is not just a vast hodgepodge of separate assertions. It is, in fact, a huge, logically organized structure of propositions, in which the place of every proposition is determined by its logical relations to all the others—to those on which it depends and to those that depend on it. The *Summa* can, indeed, be taken as a reflection—at the level of thought—of that structured, ordered hierarchy of matter and form that Thomas held the whole universe to be.

Now, having examined at least the main outlines of the Thomistic enterprise and having gained some understanding of Thomas' method, let us see how Thomas employed this method to establish what can be known about God, man, and the world.

Proofs of God's Existence

That God exists is, of course, an article of faith; but it is also, Thomas held, a proposition capable of proof by natural reason. Thomas offered, in all, five proofs of God's existence. In each, he started with some particular occurrence (for example, some fact of experience, like motion) and argued that, but for such-and-such an attribute of the divine nature, it would never have occurred. Thus Thomas' proofs have a causal form: The changes that we observe occurring can only have God for their cause.

The existence of God can be proved in five ways.

The first and more manifest way is the argument from motion. It is certain, and evident to our senses, that in the world some things are in motion. Now whatever is moved is moved by another, for nothing can be moved except it is in potentiality to that towards which it is moved; whereas a thing moves inasmuch as it is in act. For motion is nothing else than the reduction of something from potentiality to actuality. But nothing can be reduced from potentiality to actuality, except by something in a state of actuality. Thus that which is actually hot, as fire, makes wood, which is potentially hot, to be actually hot, and thereby moves and changes it. Now it is not possible that the same thing should be at once in actuality and potentiality in the same respect, but only in different respects. For what is actually hot cannot simultaneously be potentially hot; but it is simultaneously potentially cold. It is therefore impossible that in the same respect and in the same way a thing should be both mover and moved, i.e., that it should move itself. Therefore, whatever is moved must be moved by another. If that by which it is moved be itself moved, then this also must needs be moved by another, and that by another again. But this cannot go on to infinity, because then there would be no first mover, and, consequently, no other mover, seeing that subsequent movers move only inasmuch as they are moved by the first mover; as the staff moves only because it is moved by the hand. Therefore it is necessary to arrive at a first mover, moved by no other; and this everyone understands to be God.

The second way is from the nature of efficient cause. In the world of sensible things we find there is an order of efficient causes. There is no case known (neither is it, indeed, possible) in which a thing is found to be the efficient cause of itself; for so it would be prior to itself, which is impossible. Now in efficient causes it is not possible to go on to infinity, because in all efficient causes following in order, the first is the cause of the intermediate cause, and the intermediate is the cause of the ultimate cause, whether the intermediate cause be several, or one only. Now to take away the cause is to take away the effect. Therefore, if there be no first cause among efficient causes, there will be no ultimate, nor any intermediate, cause. But if in efficient causes it is possible to go on to infinity, there will be no first efficient cause, neither will there be an ultimate effect, nor any intermediate efficient causes; all of which is plainly false. Therefore it is necessary to admit a first efficient cause, to which everyone gives the name of God.

The third way is taken from possibility and necessity, and runs thus. We find in nature things that are possible to be and not to be, since they are found to be generated, and to be corrupted, and consequently, it is possible for them to be and not to be. But it is impossible for these always to exist, for that which can not-be at some time is not. Therefore, if everything can not-be, then at one time there was nothing in existence. Now if this were true, even now there would be nothing in existence, because that which does not exist begins to exist only through something already existing. Therefore, if at one time nothing was in existence, it would have been impossible for anything to have begun to exist; and thus even now nothing would be in existence—which is absurd. Therefore, not all beings are merely possible, but there must exist something the existence of which is necessary. But every necessary thing either has its necessity caused by another, or not. Now it is impossible to go on to infinity in necessary things which have their necessity caused by another, as has been already proved in regard to efficient causes. Therefore we cannot but admit the existence of some being having of itself its own necessity, and not receiving it from another, but rather causing in others their necessity. This all men speak of as God.

The fourth way is taken from the gradation to be found in things. Among beings there are some more and some less good, true, noble, and the like. But *more* and *less* are predicated of different things according as they resemble in their different ways something which is the maximum, as a thing is said to be hotter according as it more nearly resembles that which is hottest; so that there is something which is truest, something best, something noblest, and, consequently, something which is most being, for those things that are greatest in truth are greatest in being, as it is written in *Metaph.* ii. Now the maximum in any genus is the cause of all in that genus, as fire, which is the maximum of heat, is the cause of all hot things, as is said in the same book. Therefore there must also be something which is to all beings the cause of their being, goodness, and every other perfection; and this we call God.

The fifth way is taken from the governance of the world. We see that things which lack knowledge, such as natural bodies, act for an end, and this is evident from their acting always, or nearly always, in the same way, so as to obtain the best result. Hence it is plain that they achieve their end, not fortuitously, but designedly. Now whatever lacks knowledge cannot move towards an end, unless it be directed by some being endowed with knowledge and intelligence; as the arrow is directed by the archer. Therefore some intelligent being exists by whom all natural things are directed to their end; and this being we call God.[c]

These arguments may be taken as representative of Thomas' reasoning. It is instructive to compare them with Anselm's proof of the existence of God.[3] To begin with, Thomas denied that we have a clear and distinct idea of God. "To know that God exists in a general and confused way is implanted in us by nature. . . . This, however, is not to know absolutely that God exists; just as to know that someone is approaching is not the same as to know that Peter is approaching, even though it is Peter who is approaching."[d]

Moreover, Thomas held that even if Anselm was correct in believing that we have a clear and distinct idea of God, he was mistaken in believing that

3 See pp. 201–06.

by analysis of this idea we can prove the existence of the object that the idea represents. "Granted that everyone understands that by this name *God* is signified something than which nothing greater can be thought, nevertheless, it does not therefore follow that he understands that what the name signifies exists actually, but only that it exists mentally."[e] In other words, Anselm's argument proves only that if we think of God at all, we must *think* of Him as existing; it does not prove that He actually exists.

In contrast, each of Thomas' proofs begins, not with an alleged idea, but with an empirical fact. No one doubts that motion occurs, that events have causes, that there is order in the world, that there are degrees of temperature, and so on. Thomas' position was simply that the only way to account for such facts is on the hypothesis that God exists and that these are His effects. No exception can be taken to this method of argument; it is, indeed, the only kind of argument that can be used to prove the existence of objects not immediately accessible to perception. But unless one can show that it is absolutely impossible to account for the effect in any other way, the conclusion of this kind of argument is only probable. And to rule out other possibilities is usually very difficult. Suppose, for instance, that M's body is discovered lying in a pool of blood in a locked room. The more keys to this room there are, the less reasonable it is to argue that N, who has a key, is the murderer. Even if one can prove that N has the only key to the room, this does not warrant concluding that N murdered M, for N might have lent his key to O, or P might have stolen it and then replaced it in N's pocket. Corresponding considerations apply to Thomas' arguments. If the facts that he adduced can be accounted for in any other way, however unlikely, his arguments do not *conclusively* establish the existence of God; at best, they only show that it is likely that He exists.

So, to be specific, one must ask: Can motion be accounted for without the assumption of a first, unmoved mover? Many people, undoubtedly, will agree with Thomas (and with Aristotle) that the whole world process must have been inaugurated by an initial movement. What, then, can be said in reply to the Atomists, who not only expressly denied the need for a first cause but asserted that the notion of such a cause is meaningless? No matter how far back in time one goes, they said, one can always find a cause for any specific movement—this cause is, of course, some other movement of the same kind (fall of atoms, according to Atomism). As long as there is an infinite series of motions, *any particular* motion can be explained by other motions. Hence the need for a first cause to explain the occurrence of motion does not arise.

The question, however, is whether such an infinite series of motions (or causes) is conceivable. Thomas, of course, denied that it is. In reply, the series of positive integers—1, 2, 3, 4, 5, and so on—could be cited. It is clear that this series does not have a last term, since after any number n, however large, there is another number $n + 1$. Similarly, it could be said that before any time t, however remote in the past, there was an earlier time $t - 1$, in which motion was occurring. If there is no greatest positive integer, why need there be any first motion?

Why, as a matter of fact, if the notion of a greatest positive integer is really a contradiction in terms, is not the same thing true of the notion of a first, unmoved mover? Thomas began by arguing that every event must have a cause, and, since he denied that an infinite series is possible, he concluded that there must be a first cause. But since a first cause is uncaused, his conclusion contradicts his original contention that every event has a cause.

THE FIRST THREE PROOFS

It might appear from this that Thomas' argument is easily disposed of. But the matter is not really this simple. It actually depends on what one means by "account for" in the sentence, "Is there any way to account for motion other than by the hypothesis of an unmoved mover?" If what we are interested in is an account of some particular motion (say, the combustion of a piece of wood), we can give such an account inside the system of motions of which this motion is a part. We can, as the Atomists would have said, trace this motion back to other motions, and these to still other motions, and so on "as far as we like," that is, as far as any useful purpose will be served thereby. Or, to put the matter in more modern terms, we can find a description of this event that can be made as general as we wish it to be. But all such descriptions, however general, will be descriptions *inside* the system of motions. In general, then, if we want to give an account of some event A, we do so in terms of some other event B. (It does not matter if, in another connection, we give an account of B in terms of A. In the same way, we define a word in terms of other words inside the system of words that we call a dictionary. Sooner or later every word is defined by words that it helps to define.)

Suppose, however, that what interests us is not some particular motion or event but the system of events or motions as a whole. It follows from what has just been said about the nature of explanation that we can give an account of the system as a whole only if we can find something outside the system to relate to it, just as we can account for events *inside* the system only by relating them to other individual events. But, of course, if we *do* find some outside event, the "system as a whole" is not a whole but merely a part of a larger system. Consequently, no account (at least, no "account" as it has been defined here) can be given of the universe, that is, of the totality of things that are.

This, it will be seen, was precisely the conclusion Thomas himself reached. He did not oppose the contention of the Atomists (whom we may continue to take as representing the scientific point of view) that it is impossible to give the same kind of account of the totality as we give of its parts. He differed from the Atomists in insisting that some *other* kind of account of the totality can be given. Now, the Atomists were chiefly concerned with trying to give an account of particular events. They were quite uninterested in the totality; indeed, they would have argued that there is no totality of the universe (in the sense of a complete system, with bounds), just as there is no totality of positive integers.[4] Accordingly, they held that the man who expects to find answers to questions about the totality is doomed to disappointment. Thus it is clear that the conclusions the Atomists drew—that the universe (that is, everything that is) is not going anywhere, that it is not coming from anywhere, that it has no meaning or significance—were entirely correct in terms of the Atomists' definition of meaning. Thomas, on the other hand, had the kind of mind that is chiefly interested in the totality. He saw that if any account of it is possible, this account must be in terms other than those in which we explain parts. His name for these other terms was "God."

This basic difference in outlook is a part of what is involved in the so-called conflict between science and religion. The advantages of the kind of account (within systems) that science gives are obvious. This kind of account is public (in the sense of being readily communicable) and verifiable; it gives man control over the natural processes it describes, thus making possible the immense technological achievements on which modern civilization rests. This kind of account is, indeed, so successful and so useful that most scientists refuse to have anything to do with less precise, less verifiable accounts. And, being by nature primarily interested in the description of natural processes, these scientists are not troubled by the limitations of range to which this choice commits them.

On the other hand, the religious man is so interested in questions about the totality—where it is coming from, where it is going—that he is willing, if necessary, to resort to accounts of quite a different kind—to "faith," for instance. Here, then, we come to a fundamental parting of the ways. This often happens in philosophical inquiry, since the function of philosophical analysis is not so much to find "the" answer as it is to make clear what the alternative answers are.

These comments apply to Thomas' first and second proofs, and to his third proof also, insofar as any clear meaning can be attached to the distinction he drew between the possible and the necessary. The fourth and fifth proofs require some additional comments.

THE FOURTH PROOF

The fourth proof also appeals to an empirical fact—the fact that differences of degree exist. Thomas argued that such differences can be accounted for only on the hypothesis of an objective standard. It is meaningless, Thomas held, to talk about "more" and "less" except in terms of a norm from which these are deviations, and this norm, this absolute criterion, is God. But though we cannot talk about "more" or "less" without *some sort* of standard, it does not follow that this standard must be absolutely objective. The argument only proves the existence of an absolutely objective criterion if we assume an absolutely objective "more" and an absolutely objective "less," and this is precisely the point at issue.

This comment can also be stated in terms of the distinction that has been

4 Thus we come back, in another connection, to the dispute about infinite series.

drawn between "accounts inside the system" and "accounts of the system as a whole." Comparisons inside the system are meaningful, but conclusions drawn from them are always relative to the area of the system included in the account. If we want to arrive at a more definitive comparison, we can take a larger part of the system into account. Since the system is indefinitely large, it is always possible for us to get a more definitive comparison than the one we have at the moment, however definitive this comparison may be. That is, we can always find another criterion for checking our present criterion of "more" and "less"; and all these criteria are within the system as a whole. Thus, for ordinary purposes of checking our conclusions up to any degree of precision we choose, we do not need an absolute criterion at all. On the other hand, if we want an absolutely objective criterion of "more" and "less," we must go outside the system to a consideration of the totality, and so to a different *kind* of account.

THE FIFTH PROOF

Much the same considerations apply to the fifth proof, "from the governance of the world." Arguments that are valid about governance inside the system are not relevant to the governance of the system as a whole. But here a prior point must be dealt with. Does the argument about governance really hold even with respect to events *inside* the system? The ends toward which inanimate things appear to be aiming may be in fact only projections of our human hopes and fears. If so, it is unnecessary to assume "the existence of an intelligence which directs them to their end," that is, God. Consider, for instance, the temperature range of this planet. Temperatures very much colder or very much hotter than those that occur on earth would make life as we know it impossible. Thomas could have argued that, since we cannot suppose that the temperature itself has willed to adjust itself to our needs, we must conclude that it was directed to this good end by a divine intelligence. But this conclusion does not follow. First, this temperature range is "best" from our point of view merely because we have an interest in the continuation of the human race—a matter in which we are, after all, somewhat prejudiced witnesses. And, second, we know that all sorts of temperature ranges exist on other planets. This planet happens to be one that permits life like ours, and so—there is life like ours. What seems to be design may in fact be coincidence. If we were dealt a straight suit of spades on the first and only occasion anybody anywhere played bridge, we might regard this "good thing" as evidence of purpose on somebody's part. But when we know that millions upon millions of hands of bridge are being played, it should not surprise us that this combination is sometimes dealt. That it happens to be dealt to us is "best," but we do not attribute it to a kindly providence looking out for our interests in preference to those of the other players.

To summarize this long discussion, it can be said that if Thomas' proofs are valid, he has so far established the existence of (1) an unmoved mover who is

(2) the first cause of all that is, (3) an absolutely necessary being, (4) the final criterion of value, and (5) the governor and designer of the universe. But *are* the proofs valid? This depends on whether the empirical facts to which they appeal can be accounted for in some way other than by tracing their causes back to God's activity. And to this question, as we have seen, it is impossible to give a simple answer. Whether or not we think the empirical facts can be accounted for in some other way will depend on how we define "account" and on whether we are satisfied with the kind of account that can be given of parts inside systems. Since this is a "parting of the ways," let us pass without further discussion, to other characteristics of the divine nature that Thomas believed could be demonstrated.

God's Nature

GOD IS NOT BODILY, NOT MATERIAL, NOT COMPOUND

Providing that one accepts the theorems already discussed, it is easy to prove these three new ones. God is not bodily, for He is an unmoved mover, and bodies do not move unless they are moved.[f] He is not material, for what is composed of matter and form is bodily.[g] He is not compound, for compounds are posterior to their parts, and God has already been shown to be the first being.[h]

GOD IS HIS OWN ESSENCE

This is an extremely important theorem,[i] but, unfortunately, it is a very difficult one for modern minds to understand. Let us begin by recalling that for Thomas, as for Aristotle, "essence" was the that-about-a-thing-that-makes-it-what-it-is. Now, it is clear that neither Socrates nor any other finite thing is identical with its own essence. This is true in two senses. First, a part of the essence of Socrates is his humanity, and, because there are other men, humanity transcends Socrates. Second, in Socrates, besides his essence, there are various "accidents." For instance, Socrates may be sitting or standing or sleeping, and these states are not a part of that which makes him what he is. So, in one sense Socrates (and all other created, finite things) is more than his essence, and in another, he is less than his essence. But with God the situation is different. There are no accidents in God (as can easily be shown),[5] and He is the only instance

---

5 An accident is by definition something extraneous, something "superadded," not necessary to the nature of the thing that has it. (Standing, for instance, is an accident of Socrates, for Socrates is Socrates whether he sits or stands.) Hence the accident must have some cause other than the thing that has it. (Socrates' nature is not the cause of his standing; something else—the presence of a body in the room—is the cause of his standing.) But nothing about God can be caused by anything outside His nature, for He is the first cause and the cause of everything else. Hence there can be no accident in God. See *Summa Theologica*, Pt. I, Ques. 3, Art. 6; *Summa Contra Gentiles*, I, xxiii.

of Himself, as has already been proved. Hence God is neither more nor less than His essence; He is identical with it.

This can be stated in another way. In order to understand most things (everything except God, Thomas would have maintained), we have to pass *beyond the thing itself*. Consider what is required to understand Socrates—knowledge of Periclean Athens (which is certainly not a part of Socrates' essence), knowledge of the Sophistic movement, and so on. It is fair to say that this condition, or limitation, results from the fact that no finite thing such as Socrates is its own essence. Essence, we must remember, is the that-about-a-thing-that-makes-it-what-it-is; it is that which, when known, gives real knowledge of the thing in question. Clearly, we do not know Socrates fully unless we know, among other things, whether the "Socrates" of Plato's *Republic* is a true portrait of the man Socrates. Hence, Socrates is obviously not his own essence.

Granting this, is it not entirely possible that nothing is its own essence? that everything is known by and through its relations to other things? Thomas' answer to this question, though never stated explicitly, must have been that, just as the possibility of any comparative judgment implies that there is an absolute standard of comparison, so the possibility of any truth at all implies that there is an absolute truth. This truth must be its own essence, for every relative truth necessarily depends on essences beyond itself.

This is basically the old argument that there must be an absolute truth because even the attempt to deny it reaffirms it. Is it true that all truth is relative? If so, there is at least one nonrelative truth, and the assertion that all truth is relative is false. The reasoning here is similar to that by which Plato sought to prove the existence of the Form of the Good. The only difference is that, though Plato and Thomas argued in much the same way for the existence of an absolute truth, each naturally defined this truth in accordance with his own conception of knowledge and being. But the difference is less than might be expected, for when Thomas was considering God, the infinite substance, he abandoned the Aristotelian doctrine of the immanence of form on which he insisted as long as he was discussing finite substance. Thomas' God, like the Platonic Form of the Good, was transcendent and creative, the source of such knowledge and being as the rest of the world has.

When we move from the finite to the infinite—from that which holds *inside* a system to that which holds of a system *as a whole*—we find that *all* conditions are removed, including the condition that knowledge of an object depends on our passing outside that object to the system of which the object is a part. This follows from the fact that, since God is His own essence, there is nothing beyond Him to pass *to*. And this, in turn, means that the human intellect cannot compass God, for it is the nature of the human intellect to pass from part to part. The rules governing what happens inside the system do not apply to what happens outside the system. The most that can be said, Thomas concluded, is that there must be an infinite, creative power outside the system that produced it and sustains it. We can know *that* God is and *that* He is His own essence, but we cannot know *what* that essence is.

GOD IS PERFECT

It follows from the fact that God is His own essence that He is completely actual. Since there is nothing outside God on which His existence depends, His nature is completely realized, that is, completely actual. This can be seen if God is contrasted with a material substance. In the latter, form is only relatively actual; its degree of actuality depends on the intransigency of the particular matter in which it happens to be operating. The form "oak," for instance, never achieves all that it has in it to be. But God, being a nonmaterial substance and being identical with His own essence, cannot be other than absolutely actual. Now, to say that God is wholly actual is simply another way of saying that He encompasses all perfections. "Just as matter, as such, is merely potential, so an agent, as such, is in a state of actuality. Hence, the first active principle must needs be most actual, and therefore most perfect; for a thing is said to be perfect in proportion to its actuality."[j]

GOD IS GOOD

That God is good follows by definition from what has already been proved. Since being is good it is clear that the more being anything has, the better it is. God, who is supremely actual, is therefore supremely good.

> Goodness and being are really the same, and differ only in idea; which is clear from the following argument. The essence of goodness consists in this, that it is in some way desirable. Hence the Philosopher says: *Goodness is what all desire.* Now it is clear that a thing is desirable only in so far as it is perfect, for all desire their own perfection. But everything is perfect so far as it is actual. Therefore it is clear that a thing is perfect so far as it is being; for being is the actuality of every thing, as is clear from the foregoing. Hence it is clear that goodness and being are the same really. But goodness expresses the aspect of desirableness, which being does not express.[k]

GOD IS INTELLIGENT

The nature of God's intellect is discussed in great detail in both the *Summa Theologica* and the *Summa Contra Gentiles*. The following is one of the arguments used to prove that God has knowledge.

> Now a self-mover moves itself by appetite and apprehension: for suchlike things alone are found to move themselves, since it is in them to be moved

and not to be moved. Wherefore the moving part in the first self-mover must needs be appetitive and apprehensive. Now in that movement which is by appetite and apprehension, the appetent and apprehender is a moved mover, while appetible and apprehended is a mover not moved. Since then that which is the first mover of all, which we call God, is a mover altogether unmoved, it follows that it is compared to the motor which is a part of the self-mover as the appetible to the appetent. Not, however, as the appetible to the sensitive appetite, because the sensitive appetite is not of the good simply, but of this particular good, since also sensitive apprehension is only of the particular; and that which is good and appetible simply, is prior to that which is good and appetible here and now. Therefore the first mover must be the appetible as an object of the understanding: and consequently the mover that desires itself must be an intelligent being. Much more therefore is the very first appetible an intelligent being; because that which desires it becomes actually understanding through being united to it as an intelligible object. Therefore it follows that God is intelligent, if it be supposed that the first mover moves itself, as the early philosophers maintained.[l]

Not only is God intelligent; He possesses the most perfect knowledge.

To prove this, we must note that . . . the immateriality of a thing is the reason why it is cognitive, and that according to the mode of immateriality is the mode of cognition. Hence, it is said in *De Anima* ii. that plants do not know, because of their materiality. But sense is cognitive because it can receive species free from matter; and the intellect is still further cognitive, because it is more *separated from matter and unmixed*, as is said in *De Anima* iii. Since therefore God is in the highest degree of immateriality, as was stated above, it follows that He occupies the highest place in knowledge.[m]

So far, so good. But does not the very perfection of God's knowledge exclude the possibility of His having knowledge of such insignificant matters as men and their affairs? Aristotle thought so. He held that God's knowledge is exclusively self-contemplative.[6] It was of great importance to Thomas to deny that this conclusion follows, for the notion that God is providential (that is, that He has a knowledge of "things other than Himself," especially, a knowledge of men) was an absolutely crucial point of Christian doctrine. Let us see how Thomas proceeded.

His first step was to attempt to show that God knows things other than Himself:

For the knowledge of an effect is sufficiently obtained from knowledge of the cause: wherefore *we are said to know a thing when we know its cause.*

6 The faulty texts available to Thomas misled him as to the extent of his deviation from Aristotle on this point.

Now God by His essence is the cause of being in other things. Since therefore He knows His own essence most fully, we must conclude that He knows other things also. . . .

Moreover. Whoever knows a thing perfectly, knows whatever can be said truly of that thing, and whatever is becoming thereto by its nature. Now it is becoming to God by His nature to be the cause of other things. Since then He knows Himself perfectly, He knows that He is a cause: and this is impossible unless He knows His effect somewhat. Now this is something other than Himself, for nothing is cause of itself. Therefore God knows things other than Himself.

Accordingly taking these two conclusions together, it is evident that God knows Himself as the first and *per se* object of His knowledge, and other things as seen in His essence.[n]

However, to satisfy the requirements of the dogma of providence, it was necessary to show not merely that God knows things other than Himself, but that He knows individual things. Otherwise, of course, He could not care for men. Thomas recognized that the arguments against divine knowledge of particulars are extremely difficult to meet. Three such arguments will be cited. (1) Particular things are constantly coming into being and passing away. Since God's knowledge is unchangeable, He cannot know a changing flux. (2) Some particular things are contingent. Since God's knowledge is certain, what merely "may be" is unknowable by God. Taken together, these two arguments connect with the Platonic thesis that physics is only a "likely story." If Plato was correct, the physical world is not sufficiently stable to be an object of divine contemplation. (3) Everyone agrees that real knowledge, even in man, is knowledge of forms, not of particulars. How much more must this be true of an infinite mind than of a finite one like man's.

To these arguments Thomas replied as follows:

We shall prove . . . that God cannot be lacking in the knowledge of singulars.

For it has been shown that God knows other things in as much as He is their cause. Now God's effects are singular things: because God causes things in the same way as He makes them to be actual; and universals are not subsistent, but have their being only in singulars, as is proved in 7 *Metaph.* Therefore God knows things other than Himself not only in the universal but also in the singular. . . .

Again. . . . From the fact that [God] is His own being it follows that in Him are all the perfections of being as in the first source of being, as we have shown above. Therefore it follows that every perfection of knowledge is found in His knowledge, as in the first fount of knowledge. But this would not be if He were lacking in the knowledge of singulars: since the perfection of some knowers consists in this. Therefore it is impossible for Him not to have knowledge of singulars. . . .

Again. The first movable is moved by a motor that moves by intellect and appetite, as was shown above. Now a motor by intellect cannot cause movement unless it knows the movable as naturally inclined to local movement, and that is as existing here and now, and consequently as a singular. Wherefore the intellect that is the motor of the first movable knows the first movable as a singular. But this motor is either supposed to be God, and thus our point is proved, or else it is something beneath God. And if the intellect of this motor is able by its own power to know a singular which our intellect is unable to know, much more will the divine intellect be able to do so. . . .

Further. If God knows not singulars which even men know, this would involve the absurdity which the Philosopher urges against Empedocles, namely that *God is most foolish.*°

It will be noted that the major assumptions underlying all Thomas' replies are (1) reality consists not of forms alone but of *individual substances,* which are a union of form and matter; (2) we know any object *x* when we know its cause; (3) cause and effect are somehow "alike." Proposition 1 is specifically Aristotelian and anti-Platonic; proposition 2 has been affirmed by rationalists of every age, including both Plato and Aristotle; proposition 3 is one of the great "partings of the way" as between the classical and medieval minds, on the one hand, and the modern mind, on the other.

GOD IS VOLITIONAL

The doctrine of providence required, of course, not only that God *know* singulars (especially, that He know men), but that He *care* for them. This means that there must be will in God. But Aristotle had argued that, because god is perfect, he lacks nothing, and that, lacking nothing, he has no reason to will. The object of will is something that would bring the willer's present potentiality to actuality. How, then, can will be attributed to God, who is wholly actual and needs nothing to complete Him?

Thomas attempted to avoid this embarrassing conclusion by arguing that (1) God wills Himself, and (2) in willing Himself, He wills the existence of His creatures. As regards the first point:

Now everything has this disposition towards its natural form, that when it does not have it, it tends towards it; and when it has it, it is at rest therein. It is the same with every natural perfection, which is a natural good. This disposition to good in things without knowledge is called *natural appetite.* Whence also intellectual natures have a like disposition to good as apprehended through an intelligible form, so as to rest therein when possessed, and when not possessed to seek to possess it; both of which pertain to the will. Hence in every intellectual being there is will, just as in every sensible being there is animal appetite. And so there must be will in God, since there is intellect in Him. And as His knowing is His own being, so is His willing.[p]

As regards the second point:

> Every thing desires the perfection of that which it wills and loves for its own sake: because whatever we love for its own sake, we wish to be best, and ever to be bettered and multiplied as much as possible. Now God wills and loves His essence for its own sake: and it cannot be increased or multiplied in itself, as appears from what has been said: and can only be multiplied in respect of its likeness which is shared by many. Therefore God wishes things to be multiplied, because He wills and loves His essence and perfection.
>
> Moreover. Whosoever loves a thing in itself and for its own sake, loves in consequence all the things wherein it is found: thus he who loves sweetness for its own sake, must needs love all sweet things. Now God wills and loves His own being, in itself and for its own sake, as we have proved above. And all other being is a participation, by likeness, of His being, as was made sufficiently clear by what we have said above. Therefore, from the very fact that God wills and loves Himself, it follows that He wills and loves other things.[q]

GOD IS CREATOR

We now come to the question of creation. Aristotle (and the pagans in general) had held that there is no creation out of nothing and that the world is eternal. Thomas, of course, had to hold the contrary, for it was a cardinal article of faith that God created the world and that He did so, not as an artist fashions an object out of a preexistent material, but by divine fiat, out of nothing. But all production men know anything about is of the former kind. Is it possible for us to attach any meaning to the notion of an activity so different from anything in our experience?

Thomas' reply was, in effect, that this difficulty results from a failure to distinguish between thinking about parts of a system and thinking about the system as a whole. Insofar as one thinks in terms of the emergence of particular things inside a system, the notion of creation out of nothing is indeed meaningless, as the Atomists claimed. All human experience is of movement and change inside systems, and these do imply the prior existence of something that is moved and changed. But the limitations that apply to events inside a system do not apply to the emergence of the system as a whole. Philosophers fall into the mistake of supposing that creation out of nothing is impossible because they use inappropriate concepts: They carry over from their thought about events inside the system the notions of change and movement (which are valid there) to their thought about the system as a whole. Then they triumphantly discover that these notions do not apply to the totality. But this only proves that such a transfer is illegitimate and should not have been made in the first place.[7]

This argument shows only that creation is not change. We may agree; but we must still ask what creation is if it is not a change in the state of affairs. The following considerations may help. We know (supposing, of course, that the previous Thomistic arguments are correct) that there is a completely good and completely real being who owes His goodness and reality to nothing beyond His own nature and who is completely self-explanatory. We also know that there are other beings who owe whatever goodness, reality, and intelligibility they possess—indeed, who owe their very existence—to something beyond themselves. Ultimately, since we have to reject the possibility of an infinite series, we must conclude that the latter owe what they possess of these qualities to that being who possesses these qualities supremely. To say that God created the world out of nothing is simply to say that there is nothing that does not owe its being, goodness, intelligibility, and reality to God. Stated in this way, the doctrine of creation is self-evident, for any being anywhere (and any goodness or truth) either is or is not self-dependent and self-explanatory. If it is, it is God; if it is not, it depends on (and so flows from as an effect of) some other being. The same considerations apply to this second being, and so on until, ultimately, we come to a being that *is* self-dependent. This being is God.

But, one might object, why call this "creation"? If this is what Thomas meant, "creation" is surely a very misleading term. The answer is, of course, that for better or worse, Thomas was forced to use this term. The best he could do was to try to make sense of it, even if the sense he made was a very long way from the crude, anthropomorphic meaning of the term as it was originally used. This is typical of the kind of problem that frequently confronts any thinker who professes to base his views on an authoritative text. How true to that text is he if he changes everything but its terminology? Thomas would have argued, of course, that Genesis was written for "ignorant people"; that its author, being divinely inspired, knew very well what he was about; and that he himself, as a commentator, did not change that meaning but only expressed it in clear and technical language.[r]

Whether this is a satisfactory reply, one must judge for oneself. For our purposes it is more important to understand the three major theses that underlie this view of creation: (1) the doctrine of degrees of truth, goodness, and reality; (2) the doctrine that the existence in any degree of a quality, or character, implies its existence somewhere in supreme degree; (3) the doctrine that the quality

---

7 "The ancient philosophers . . . considered only the emanation of particular effects from particular causes, which necessarily presuppose something in their action; whence came their common opinion that *nothing is made from nothing*. But this dictum has no place in the first emanation from the universal principle of things"—*Summa Theologica*, Pt. I, Ques. 45, Art. 2, Reply Obj. I.

in its supreme degree is the "cause" of all its lesser manifestations and that they are its "effects."

The next question is: Why should God want to create a world? Why should He, who knows the world in idea as a part of His own essence, wish it to exist outside Himself? Or, put into the less theological language that has just been used, why should there be the various lesser degrees of truth, goodness, and reality in addition to these qualities in their supreme degree? Thomas said that this is a question we cannot answer, for it surpasses our understanding. It is only possible to say that there is everywhere an observable tendency of the good to diffuse itself. The good man, for instance, shares his good with others and makes their lives better. Taken at its lowest level, this tendency can be seen in our desire to have others read a book we have enjoyed or to share an experience we find satisfying. In God, who is the supreme good, this tendency expresses itself in the creation of the world.[8]

Granting, then, that God desires to create a world, we can see why He should create one in which many *different* degrees of truth, goodness, and reality exist. That is, we can see why there should be many different levels of reality, or species of creatures—inanimate objects, plants, animals, men, angels—rather than a single level, or species. Only in a variety of levels of reality could the richness of the divine nature be reproduced. Of course, the divine nature cannot be reproduced *perfectly*. If it could be, creature would be God, and this is a contradiction in terms. Nevertheless, God wished to make the universe as perfect as a created thing can be. Since a single creature could be given only some one aspect of the infinite variety of the divine nature, God chose to create a plurality of creatures, which represents His nature more adequately.

It can be said that, in the same way, though no single photograph, or series of photographs, can "do justice to" a statue that a sculptor has produced, many different photographs, taken from different angles, are a more adequate representation of it than is a single "reproduction." Of course, to speak of a photograph as a "reproduction" is a misnomer. No two-dimensional object is really even very much *like* a three-dimensional object, let alone a reproduction of it. A photograph is at best a poor, inadequate creature. Since the creation of a facsimile is excluded on the grounds that this would not be a creature at all, but another God, it follows that the only way to reproduce the richness of three-dimensionality is to make a large number of two-dimensional creatures. The diversity and the multiplicity of the creatures are thus the echo of the infinity of the original.

GOD IS PROVIDENTIAL

To say, finally, that God is providential is only to spell out what is implied in the last two theses. Since God, by His intellect and His will, is the cause of all things, it follows that "the exemplar of every effect should pre-exist in

Him." And to say this is to say that God acts providentially, for "the exemplar of things ordered towards an end is, properly speaking, providence."[t]

God's providence operates not merely with respect to the general outlines of events (in the way in which a client might set certain general conditions for an architect—the size of the house and its site—and leave the rest to the latter to work out), but even with respect to the individual being of every substance. God's providence, for instance, does not merely determine that there will be such-and-such species, but that there will be such-and-such individuals in these species.

Several conclusions follow:

First, since every event, being a part of God's providential plan, has a cause, what we call chance is merely a sequence of events that lies outside some particular causal series, not outside causal series altogether. The meeting of two servants at the market place may appear to them fortuitous, for each arrived there in the course of pursuing his own duties. But it is not chance that brought them together, for "their master . . . purposely sent them to meet at the one place, in such a way that the one has no knowledge of the other."[u]

Second, it is a part of God's providence that there be a science of nature, for He has chosen that His will should operate through secondary causes. Democritus and the Epicureans were not mistaken in supposing that every event has its cause in a regular and systematic way; they were wrong in holding that this excludes providence. Effects proceed from definite causes precisely because God in His goodness has willed the preservation of order in the universe.[v]

Nevertheless, miracles are possible, for God can will at any time to produce an effect directly, without the mediation of secondary causes. Such an event is outside, but not contrary to, the order of nature.[w]

Third, despite the fact that divine providence both foresees all that will happen and causes it to happen as it has been foreseen, Thomas maintained that some events are truly contingent.

> Divine providence imposes necessity upon some things; not upon all, as some believed. For to providence it belongs to order things towards an end. Now after the divine goodness, which is an extrinsic end to all things, the principal good in things themselves is the perfection of the universe; which would not be, were not all grades of being found in things. Whence it pertains to divine providence to produce every grade of being. And thus for some things it has prepared necessary causes, so that they happen of necessity; for others contingent causes, that they may happen by contingency, according to the disposition of their proximate causes.[x]

It is easy to see why Thomas found it necessary to make this assertion. Unless there is contingency, human freedom is illusory, and with freedom goes moral responsibility. But it must be allowed that at least a *prima-facie* contradiction is involved in holding both that events inevitably occur (because God "prepares their causes") and that they do not necessarily occur. Let us postpone for the present a consideration of whether Thomas managed to avoid this contradiction.[8]

The Physical World

We now turn from Creator to creature, from God to the universe of things. For Plato and Aristotle, exposition of God's nature was merely the capstone to physics; for Thomas, physics was an appendage to theology. For Thomas, indeed, the chief task of the physicist was to provide an adequate interpretation of the account of creation given in Genesis (thereby removing any occasion for scepticism) and to reconcile Aristotle's physics with this biblical account. For instance, it is said in Genesis that "God divided the waters that were above the firmament" and that He "called the firmament heaven." However, we know on the authority of Aristotle (as well as by sense perception) that water is "by nature heavy, and heavy things tend naturally downwards. . . . Further, water is fluid by nature, and fluids cannot rest on a sphere, as experience shows. Therefore since the firmament is a sphere, there cannot be water above it."[y] How can we reconcile these apparently contradictory theses?

To begin with, we must be clear about what has to be reconciled with what. The first rule always is "to hold the truth of Scripture without wavering." Since *"these words of Scripture have more authority than the most exalted human intellect . . . we cannot for a moment doubt"* that the waters are where Genesis says they are.[z] What we have to do, therefore, is to show how—experience and Aristotle to the contrary—water can be above the heavens. The waters above the firmament may not be in a fluid state at all, but in a solid state; the firmament, which is certainly seen as concave from below, is not necessarily convex when seen from above; and so on. Into the detailed and often ingenious arguments with which this and similar difficulties are disposed of, we need not follow Thomas.

In addition to the work of biblical exegesis to which, in Thomas' view, the physicist was committed, it was (Thomas thought) both possible and desirable to formulate the basic principles of a philosophy of nature—possible because the created universe is essentially rational; desirable for many reasons, but especially because a knowledge of this rational order must move us to love and praise its divine author.

In general, Thomas followed Aristotle faithfully in formulating the principles of physics, but since he interpreted Aristotle's principles from a theological point of view foreign to Aristotle's own thinking, he had to face problems that Aristotle

8 See pp. 282–85.

himself had not encountered. According to Thomas, all the many movements that can be observed in the universe—the behavior patterns of animate and inanimate things everywhere—are nothing but the ways in which all these things, each in its own way, seek God. Aristotle, of course, had said much the same thing, but without the religious overtones: Everything, he had maintained, seeks its good and its fulfillment. But Aristotle had also attempted, by means of careful observation and experiment, to make generalizations about the various motions by which different kinds of things actually fulfill themselves. Thomas almost wholly lacked this interest. He was content simply to make the general point that God is the good—the end and the fulfillment—of every created thing. His attention was concentrated elsewhere, on certain philosophical and theological problems created by this formulation.

DUAL CAUSALITY

How, for instance, can sin and error be explained if everything seeks God? The answer is that not everything seeks God directly. Most things, including man, know God so inadequately that they take certain subordinate goods as their immediate ends: The center of the earth, which the falling stone seeks, is that stone's good; the jam jar on the closet shelf is the child's good; and so on. Yet, according to Thomas, in seeking out these various, personal, and limited goods, they are *also* seeking out God, the supreme good common to them all.

It may seem that this reply only substitutes one puzzle for another. How can a thing seek such different ends at the same time? Must it not choose between aiming at "its own perfection" and aiming at "a divine likeness"? How, for instance, can the jam on the closet shelf or the fall of a stone through space *be* "a divine likeness"? Yet this is precisely what Thomas had to maintain.

It will be easier both to understand this difficulty and to see why it was so important for Thomas to resolve it if the difficulty is rephrased in causal terms. This is permissible since (as it is not difficult to show) whether one talks of "goods" or "ends" or "causes" is entirely a matter of convenience.

The Aristotelian universe that Thomas accepted is a hierarchy of individual substances in which the place of each substance is determined by its degree of actuality. At the bottom of the hierarchy, being and reality fade into nothingness—into the mere possibility of being something. At the top of the hierarchy is God, who, as we have seen, is pure actuality, complete being, perfect fulfillment. No other substance is wholly actual, but every substance is actual to the extent that it *is* at all. Insofar as it is already something, it has form; insofar as there is something about it that might be but is not yet, it is matter. Everything has in it a drive to become, insofar as it may, fully and actually all that it might be. Thus, all movement and change is a coming-to-be, a fulfillment of something's nature.

Consider some substance A, which is completed by B. B is A's *good*. Since B is what A, insofar as A is able, aims at, it can also be said that B is A's *end*.

Again, since A's recognition of B's goodness is what moves A to act, it can be said that B is the *cause* of A's action. Thus the problem of a duality of goods can be restated in causal terms: How can there be two causes for A's behavior—B *and* God?

When the problem is stated in this way, the importance of the dual-causality doctrine becomes apparent. If we are forced to say that *either* B *or* God is the cause of A's behavior, and if we adopt the first alternative, we end in a completely secular philosophy: B is A's cause; C is B's; D is C's; and so on. We have a godless universe in which, because God is inefficacious, knowledge of reality does not depend in any way on the divine nature. If, on the other hand, we adopt the second alternative, we have to conclude that changes on earth are the direct products of divine activity. We have to say, for instance, not that fire causes heat, as it certainly seems to, but that "God causes heat in the presence of fire." Things, that is to say, are not real, nor is their apparent causal efficacy real. They are merely the symbols of a reality separate from them and above them.

From Thomas' point of view, there were two main objections to the latter alternative. First, his empirical bent was too strong for him to feel any sympathy with a view that denied the reality of the sense world. Naturally, this objection would not have troubled Neoplatonizing Christians with an otherworldly bias. But the second objection must, Thomas thought, give even them pause. If the natural world is not real, God's creative act and Christ's incarnation are both illusions, and God is not a transcendent being since there is nothing for His nature to transcend.

Thus it was essential, from Thomas' point of view, to show that there is double causality. In the following proofs, it will be noted that Thomas directed his argument chiefly against those who accepted the second alternative presented above. Since there was general agreement in his day that God is efficacious, he could afford to ignore the secular alternative. It was only necessary for him to show that God's causality does not exclude real causality in the things themselves.

> He who gives a principle, gives whatever results from the principle: thus the cause that gives gravity to an element, gives it downward movement. Now to make a thing actual results from being actual, as we see to be the case in God: for He is pure act, and is also the first cause of being in all things, as we proved above. If therefore He bestowed His likeness on others in respect of being, in so far as He brought things into being, it follows that He also bestowed on them His likeness in the point of acting, so that creatures too should have their proper actions. . . .
>
> Again. To take order away from creatures is to deny them the best thing they have: because each one is good in itself, while altogether they are very good on account of the order of the universe: for the whole is always better than the parts, and is their end. Now if we subtract action from things, the order among things is withdrawn: because, things differing in nature are not

bound together in the unity of order, except through the fact that some are active and some passive. Therefore it is unreasonable to say that things have not their proper actions. . . .

It is, also, clear that the same effect is ascribed to a natural cause and to God, not as though part were effected by God and part by the natural agent: but the whole effect proceeds from each, yet in different ways: just as the whole of the one same effect is ascribed to the instrument, and again the whole is ascribed to the principal agent. . . .

Further. It belongs to the dignity of a ruler to have many ministers and various executors of his rule: because the greater the number of his subordinates of various degrees, the more complete and extensive is his dominion shown to be. But no government can compare with the divine in point of dignity. Therefore it is fitting that the execution of divine providence be committed to agents of various degrees.[a]

These arguments are unequal in value. One of them rests entirely on an uncertain analogy—that God is like a king who rules through ministers of state. Another rests on a purely verbal distinction; whether one says that the instrument or the agent produces the effect—whether one says that the nail is driven in by the hammer or by the carpenter—is merely a matter of terminology. The argument from "order" is suggestive, but it does not seem to establish what is desired. It might be argued, (indeed, Berkeley and the Occasionalists later did argue) that the regularities that can be observed in nature are directly caused by God and that all causality is vertical (from God to thing) rather than horizontal (from thing to thing). Other arguments—for instance, that real being implies real activity—are, however, valid if Thomas' basic premises are allowed.

For example, suppose that some individual A is completed by another individual B. What completes B? Some other individual C. Obviously, therefore, B, taken by itself, is only the relative fulfillment of A. In the long run, A is completed by the C that completes B. What completes C? Some other individual D. Hence, in the longer run, D is the fulfillment of A—and so on for E, F, G, and so forth. It is clear that a finite individual adequate to complete A does not exist, for every finite individual is deficient in some way and thus requires completion. On the other hand, Thomas' basic contention was that there is a final state of completion, that is, God, in which this whole series of relative completions is fulfilled.[9] Hence it can be said that though, relatively speaking, A is completed by B, it (and every other individual particular), absolutely speaking, is completed by God. And since, as we have seen, it matters not whether one talks of "goods" or of "causes," it can just as well be said that both B and God are the causes of A. It is A's knowledge (either obscure and unconscious or distinct and rational) of B and of the fact that B will complete A's present deficiency that induces A to take B as its end. But A must also see (either obscurely or clearly) that C is B's end, that D is C's, and so on. Hence, there is involved in A's knowledge

9 See pp. 217–18.

of B's goodness (the knowledge that moves A to act) a knowledge, however faint and obscure, of the goodness of the whole series C, D, E, F, and so on to, eventually, God. Thus it can truly be said that B and God are jointly the cause of A's act.

This may be easier to comprehend if one thinks in terms, not of causes (comings-to-be), but of explanations (comings-to-understand). Any individual A is relatively intelligible through some individual B, but it is ultimately intelligible by the totality of things that are. To say that the sinking of the nail in the wood is caused by both the hammer and the carpenter may be to concoct a mere verbalism, but to say that such-and-such a theorem is proved by such-and-such another theorem *and* by the whole body of theorems that constitute Euclidean geometry is to make an important observation about the nature of knowledge.[10]

THEOLOGY AND THE SCIENCES

The conception of dual causality, described above, determined Thomas' conception of the relation that obtains between theology and the other sciences. In a purposively structured universe, all scientific knowledge is teleological in character. Since all things aim at ends, the movements they make are efforts to realize these ends. Hence, if we want to understand some particular object's behavior, we must ask why (to what end) it is moving. Suppose we see a child trying to climb onto a kitchen stool. "What is he about?" we ask. "Why is he struggling to get onto the stool?" His behavior becomes clear, acquires a pattern, as soon as someone tells us that there is a jam jar on the closet shelf. Now, from Thomas' point of view, the study of jam jars (and other human goods) is the domain of psychology. But though the child is striving for the jam jar, he is also seeking (however little his childish mind may understand this) the divine likeness. It follows that his behavior also falls into the domain of theology. Every science is per se the knowledge of ends. The special sciences are devoted to the various limited ends (the personal perfections) that individuals seek. But since theology is the science of God, and since God is the supreme end that all things seek, all the special sciences eventually pass over into—or, rather, are "perfected" by—theology. Physics, psychology, botany, and the other special sciences give us true knowledge, but only about relative ends. Therefore, they all require supplementation by theology, which gives us knowledge about the perfect and complete end. Theology is in fact the "queen" science, to which all the other

---

10 Another example of dual causality is what goes on in a play. When Macbeth cries, "Out, out, brief candle!" he is responding to the news of his wife's death. Word of this death, brought by the doctor, might therefore be said to be the "cause" of the exclamation. (It also "explains" it. If we are asked, "Why did Macbeth cry out?" we answer, "Because he had just heard that Lady Macbeth had died.") But in a larger sense, the cause of Macbeth's exclamation is his ambition and Duncan's assassination and the knocking at the gate and the murder of Banquo and the flight of Macduff—indeed, the whole play. (So it is the play as a whole that illumines and explains any particular part of it—for instance, this exclamation.)

sciences are subordinate in the way in which the various relative ends of individual substances are subordinate to the absolute end that is the final completion of them all.

LIMITATIONS OF THOMAS' METHOD

Thomas' conception of the method of physics was naturally determined by his conception of the physical world as a hierarchy of individual substances seeking God. In order to understand the behavior of any particular substance, Thomas thought it necessary to ascertain the means by which that substance fulfills both its long-range end (that is, God) and its private, short-range end.

This brings us to a difficulty that turns on the now familiar distinction between events within a system and the system as a whole. Even if we allow Thomas this distinction (which, as we have seen, is the basis of a major parting of the ways in philosophy), it does not follow, as Thomas himself assumed, that the teleological method of approach is valid in both domains. Doubtless this method is appropriate for studying the system as a whole, that is, for investigating an object's long-range fulfillment, since this is nothing but that thing's role in the divine plan for the universe. But is the method equally appropriate for investigating short-range fulfillments? In particular, if the object being investigated is not human, is it possible to ascertain what its private end is?[11]

Thomas' answer was that the purpose of any thing is what it does "most of the time"—or, rather, what it does when nothing is interfering with it. This follows logically from the basic assumptions that form is everywhere striving to become actual and that movement is the process by which form accomplishes this end. Everything experiences a deficiency and looks around for what will complete it. It is "natural," therefore, for everything to busy itself with the process of fulfillment.

This means that Thomas thought it possible to discover the ends that an object seeks by simply observing that object's behavior. Since, as anyone can see, a stone *always* falls to earth unless something holds it up, Thomas confidently concluded that falling to earth is what fulfills stones. Unfortunately, his reasoning here was circular. What things do is what fulfills them, and what fulfills them is what is "natural" to them. But what is natural to them is in point of fact what they do. Consider the falling stone. If Thomas had been asked, "Why does the stone fall?" he would have replied, "Because it is fulfilling itself and realizing the purpose of the intelligent substance that (ultimately) directs it." If he had been asked, "But how do you know that this is the stone's end?" he would have answered, "Because experience shows that this is what stones do when left to their own devices." Thomas ascertained the purpose by examining the behavior

---

11 As a matter of fact, of course, even with human beings there are serious difficulties. How many people know the "real" reasons for what they do? And how many will divulge these reasons when they do know them?

and then explained the behavior in terms of the purpose. This amounts to explaining the behavior by itself and says no more than that stones fall because they fall.

To make matters worse, Thomas based his conception of the purposes of particular objects on overhasty observation of the objects' behavior, for what really interests a teleologist like Thomas is not behavior itself but the purpose behind it. Hence his specific formulations of "purpose" (which is nothing but a projection of observed behavior) were inadequate. The behavior of stones is not adequately described by saying that they fall, or the behavior of fire, by saying that it rises. But the teleologist never discovers the inadequacy of his formulations, for the purposes he finds inevitably "explain" the behavior in question satisfactorily. After all, the alleged purpose is nothing but another way of talking about the observed behavior.

This is a criticism, it should be noted, not of Thomas' basic assumptions that everything strives toward ends and that the universe is a vast teleological structure, but of the procedure by which, having made these assumptions, Thomas proposed to find out what the ends are. This methodological criticism is logically independent of the question of whether the universe is in fact such a system, and, historically speaking, the fallacies in the teleological method were pointed out long before any serious attack was made on the belief that the universe in all its parts was created by a beneficent God. These fallacies, which may seem obvious to men of the twentieth century, did not occur to Thomas and his contemporaries because they were basically uninterested in facts; their minds leapt ahead to God and His plans. One must not presume that they were stupid whereas modern men are clever, for their science served very well for what interested *them*. It was not until men began to be interested in facts for their own sake, instead of for God's sake, that the Thomistic method began to present difficulties. When that time came, not only the teleological method in physics but the whole Thomistic world view collapsed.

Angels

Material substances occupy the lower levels of the hierarchy of substances; angels occupy the upper levels, immediately under God. Thomas devoted a large part of the *Summa Theologica*—much more, in fact, than he assigned to physics—to an account of their nature and attributes.

This part of Thomas' philosophy is perhaps the most foreign to modern readers, who may be puzzled, to begin with, to know why he took the existence of angels for granted. In the first place, of course, the Bible mentions angels, and (as we have already seen) he thought it necessary to "hold the truth of Scripture without wavering." Second, and quite apart from the Bible, the existence of angels had been assumed by so many writers—pagan, Mohammedan, and Christian—for so many centuries that it would have been unthinkable for any medieval writer not to take angels seriously.[12] Third, the metaphysical scheme Thomas had evolved, with its continuous hierarchy of individual substances, required that there be a whole series of beings between God and man. Moreover, given the basic assumption of "no gaps," it was possible to deduce what must be the properties of such creatures—the general nature of their intelligence and their will, for instance. And, finally, the properties thus deduced turned out to agree point for point with those assigned to angels by the religious tradition. Here, then, is another example of the remarkable way in which the Thomistic metaphysical scheme provided a rational underpinning for the articles of Christian faith and incorporated all the heterogeneous beliefs of the time into a single world view. Physics, physiology, theology, and now angelology—all the different sciences of that age were unified through interpretation in terms of the concepts of form and matter.

The principal problem Thomas had to face in his angelology was this: If angels are incorporeal (and so lack matter), it seems to follow that they are fully actualized and hence indistinguishable from God. This difficulty caused St. Bonaventura and other thinkers to argue that angels, like men, are composed of form and matter. Thomas' principle of continuity, however, required that beings higher than man have higher intelligences. Since it is the business of intellect to know form, a higher intellect must know form more directly and more adequately than a lower one. Now, the human intellect (precisely because form is embedded in matter in man) knows form only insofar as it can collect it from the particulars known in perception. A being higher than man, who therefore knows form more adequately, must be independent of sense experience for its knowledge of form. Hence such a being cannot have a body with bodily organs that know by means of sense organs.

At the same time, Thomas was fully aware of the necessity of distinguishing between angels and God. This he did by drawing an ingenious distinction between the kind of potentiality involved in matter and the kind of potentiality involved in a finite intellect. Angels, it is true, are not potential in the first sense. But they are potential in the second sense, and this fact preserves the supremacy of God and distinguishes the angels from Him.

The most important conclusion that follows from the notion of the incorporeality of angels is that there is only one of each species. There can be more than one cow or horse because these forms (or species) are of the kind that can be embedded in matter, and matter differentiates individuals of the same species. But angels have no matter and so can differ only formally, that is, they differ as a horse and a cow differ, not as two horses differ.

12 In Greek philosophy of the classical period there were no angels, though Aristotle held that superhuman intelligences move the planetary spheres. Neoplatonism, however, introduced various grades of being between the Absolute and the human soul, and monotheistic religions like Christianity and Mohammedanism found it convenient to supplement their one God with various ministers, messengers, and other lesser spirits.

Thomas gave an exhaustive classification of the angelic species, of which he held there are many.[13] It appears that they fall into three main groups, each of which is divided into three subordinate groups. These are Seraphim, Cherubim, Thrones, Dominions, Virtues, Powers, Principalities, Archangels, and, finally, at the bottom of the angelic hierarchy, mere angels. They are distinguished from one another by the different degrees of adequacy of their knowledge of God. It is not necessary for us to go into the details of these arrangements. Instead, let us turn back to fill in the gap left at this point in our study between the sphere of material things and the sphere of angels.

---

13 The angelic species "exist in exceeding great number, far beyond all material multitude. . . . The reason for this is that, since it is the perfection of the universe that God chiefly intends in the creation of things, the more perfect some things are, the greater the abundance in which they are created by God"—*Summa Theologica*, Pt. I, Ques. 50, Art. 3, Ans.

CHAPTER 7

Thomas: Psychology, Ethics, Politics

The Psalmist was literally correct when he declared that man is a little lower than the angels. As the lowest of the intellectual substances, man is immediately below the lowest angel; as the highest of the corporeal substances, he is just above the highest animal. He is thus unique: No other corporeal substance has an intelligence, and no other intelligent substance has a body. It is man's place in the hierarchy of substances that both causes the human predicament and creates the possibility of man's extricating himself from it.

Like the angels in that he knows universal truths and has a will that is free to choose what is good, like the animals and lower creatures in that he is bound to sense experience and to sensuous appetites, man is presented with problems that are peculiar to him. The bodiless angels do not experience, and therefore do not have to withstand, the lusts of the flesh.[1] Knowing God more adequately

---

1 Angels are capable, however, of pride and envy. Some of them have sinned in this way and have fallen.

than man can know Him—at least in this life—they love Him more deeply and truly than man can. Animals and lower creatures never experience the conflict of will that plagues mankind—but for exactly the opposite reason. Stones "naturally" fall and, in so doing, achieve their small perfection; even animals, who are capable of more varied movements and more complex perfections, see but one good at a time—the satisfaction of a present appetite. Only with intellect, which can contemplate alternatives, does the possibility of choice (and so of choosing the worse rather than the better alternative) arise. Yet, because mankind is capable of a beatitude that no animal can attain, no man would choose to be animal for the sake of escaping the pangs of conscience and the conflict of desires.

Psychology

Psychology, in Thomas' view, differs in no essential way from the other sciences. Every science, as we have seen, studies the way in which individual substances strive to complete themselves at some particular level of the hierarchy. We call our study of this striving as it occurs at the human level "psychology." The basic question for psychology is: What are the modes in which form becomes actual in the individual amalgams of formed matter that we call men? In accordance with the general principle that every lower is matter to every higher and every higher is form to every lower, it is clear that the human soul contains the lower souls that are the forms of animal and plant bodies even while it completes and transcends them. Thus it would be a mistake to suppose that the human person contains three distinct souls. On the contrary, though the powers of the nutritive soul (as it appears in plants) and of the appetitive soul (as it appears in animals) are contained in the human soul, they are transformed there by the relation in which they stand to intelligence and by the higher ends that they serve. Let us now take up in turn Thomas' discussion of the three faculties of the soul.

THE NUTRITIVE FACULTY

The nutritive faculty consists of a group of three powers—nutrition, growth, and reproduction. Even the most elementary of these activities transcends the simple movements of which inanimate objects are capable. Contrast the fall of a stone through space, for instance, with the transformation of one substance (food) into another (flesh and blood) that nutrition and growth entail.

Further, there is an order of progressive complexity among these three powers. Growth is a more complex affair than nutrition, and reproduction is still more complex. Nutrition and growth both take place in the individual's own body; reproduction involves a relation between this individual and another.

Reproduction is thus the link between this group and the next higher group of activities, all of which involve an "extrinsic" relation, that is, not merely a relation with another individual (as in reproduction) but *awareness* of that other.

THE FACULTY OF SENSATION

This brings us to the second faculty of the soul, that of sensation. First, Thomas distinguished among the five special senses, each of which is tied to a special organ of sensation and makes us aware of a special type of quality. Lowest of all are those that involve the sense organ's actually acquiring the quality that is sensed. In touch, the hand that senses the cold of the water and the back that senses the heat of the sun actually become cold and hot. On the other hand, in sight, the eye that senses green does not *become* green. Thomas' way of stating this relatively simple point involved, as usual, a complicated terminology that makes it difficult for modern minds, accustomed to a totally different vocabulary, to understand him. He distinguished between two kinds of "immutation"—natural and spiritual. Touch involves a purely natural immutation; sight involves a purely spiritual immutation. Between these lie the other senses, which (in various ways) involve both types of immutation.[a] What this means is quite simple: In sensing heat, the organ becomes hot. Heat, in its natural being, is received into the thing heated. This is "natural immutation" because the whole nature of the thing or quality in question is transmitted. In the case of vision (say, seeing green), the whole nature is not transmitted; green, the natural quality, is not received into the eye. What, then, is transmitted? What is received? To Thomas the answer seemed obvious. It is Aristotle's sensible form. The eye comes to be filled with the form "green," just as wax takes the form of a signet but not its matter. This process Thomas called "spiritual immutation."

Nobody, once the terminological fog has been penetrated, would deny that there is a difference between touch and vision. But today we are likely to feel that the distinction between natural and spiritual immutation throws little light on this difference. In order to understand why Thomas regarded it as so significant, it is necessary to bear in mind that he was almost exclusively interested in system. What concerned him was to demonstrate that the created universe is, throughout, an ordered structure in which every feature has a place rationally related to that of every other. The distinction between natural and spiritual immutation, which may seem trivial to us, provided Thomas with a rational basis for ordering the special senses in respect to one another, from touch (at the bottom), through taste, smell, and hearing, to vision (at the top).

So far we have been considering sensation as the experience of some object or quality that is actually present to the sense organ. But in addition to being able to touch hot things or to see green ones, we can remember or imagine having done so. This brings us to a set of powers that are more complex but that still belong to the faculty of sensation.

Now we must observe that for the life of a perfect[2] animal, the animal should apprehend a thing not only at the actual time of sensation, but also when it is absent. Otherwise, since animal motion and action follow apprehension, an animal would not be moved to seek something absent. . . .

Again, we must observe that . . . the animal needs to seek or to avoid certain things, not only because they are pleasing or otherwise to the senses, but also because of other advantages and uses, or disadvantages; just as the sheep runs away when it sees a wolf, not because of its color or shape, but as a natural enemy. So, too, a bird gathers together straws, not because they are pleasant to the sense, but because they are useful for building its nest. Animals, therefore, need to perceive such intentions, which the exterior sense does not perceive. Now some distinct principle is necessary for this, since the perception of sensible forms comes by an immutation caused by the sensible, which is not the case with the perception of the above intentions. . . .

For the retention and preservation of these forms, the *phantasy* or *imagination* is appointed, being as it were a storehouse of forms received through the senses. Furthermore, for the apprehension of intentions which are not received through the senses, the *estimative* power is appointed: and for their preservation, the *memorative* power, which is a storehouse of such intentions. . . .

Now, we must observe that as to sensible forms there is no difference between man and other animals; for they are similarly immuted by external sensibles. But there is a difference as to the above intentions: for other animals perceive these intentions only by some sort of natural instinct, while man perceives them also by means of a certain comparison.[b]

There are several points worth noting in this account. In the first place, it illustrates the principle that every lower power is transformed and perfected by its presence in a higher-level soul. At the human level, intelligence mediates the "estimative power" that men and animals share; the animal's capacity to react to advantageous and disadvantageous circumstances (something that, as Thomas rightly saw, is itself more complex than the simple capacity to react to the immediately pleasurable or painful) becomes still more complex in man. Man does not simply react to the advantageous by seeking it and to the disadvantageous by avoiding it. He can compare one advantageous situation with another, or an advantageous with a disadvantageous situation (unlike an animal, he does not "automatically" run when confronted with an enemy). Thus intelligence gives estimation another dimension by presenting it with alternatives that sense alone cannot envisage.

But why did Thomas assume that sensation, estimation, memory, and imagination are separate powers? Today this would be regarded as an open question,

---

2 [For "perfect" read "natural," and see previous comments (pp. 238–39) on Thomas' assumptions about nature and the natural—AUTHOR.]

to be settled by empirical investigation. Thomas, however, simply took for granted that every distinct type of behavior must be attributable to a distinct power of the soul.

> As nature does not fail in necessary things, there must needs be as many actions of the sensitive soul as may suffice for the life of a perfect animal. If any of these actions cannot be reduced to one and the same principle, they must be assigned to diverse powers; since a power of the soul is nothing else than the proximate principle of the soul's operation.[c]

Because he found it intellectually unsatisfactory to end with a large number of completely separate powers, Thomas had to cast about for some way to bring these powers into unity. He accomplished this, as we have seen, by applying the principles of hierarchy, continuity, and system. Though the powers are distinct, they fulfill, and are fulfilled by, one another; thus, after all, order and unity are established in diversity.

THE RATIONAL FACULTY

Finally, we come to the rational faculty—those powers that transcend plant and animal natures and so mark man off as belonging, with the angels, to the realm of intellectual substances. Here, as at the level of the sensitive soul, we are dealing with two kinds of powers—those that know objects and those that behave toward them. Just as sensation becomes self-conscious knowledge at the level of the rational soul, so appetite becomes volition.

These two powers—knowledge and will—are distinct but mutually dependent. On the one hand, what we will determines what we know. For instance, our desire for such-and-such an end leads us to ascertain (often by complicated thought processes and scientific knowledge) the means thereto. On the other hand, what we know determines what we will, not only because the limitations of our knowledge determine what particular objects or states of affairs we will to attain, but also because the *level* of our knowledge is reflected in the level of our willing. Knowledge that is merely sensation never rises above "estimation" and appetite— movements of approach and avoidance. Knowledge that is rational and scientific is reflected in deliberation and choice.

Let us examine these two powers of the rational faculty, turning first to cognition. According to Thomas, this power is divided into two subpowers, one active, the other passive. Thomas reasoned that the intellect must have a passive power because (unlike God) we men do not know everything all at once. Until we learn to do quadratic equations, our intellects have merely a potentiality for this kind of knowledge, in the way that the acorn, until it grows to be an oak, has (or is) merely the potentiality of being an oak. Since we know things potentially before we know them actually (and, of course, know many things potentially that we never come to know actually), the human intellect has a "passive power."

The difference between the merely sensitive soul and the rational soul can now be reformulated in terms of this concept of the passive intellect. A plant, for example, an acorn, has the potentiality to be but one form—in this case, an oak. A man's intellect has the potentiality of acquiring knowledge about, and so of becoming, an infinite number of forms; indeed, the intellect may become, in this sense, the whole universe. Of course, the intellect does not become another thing in the same way that the acorn becomes the oak. In knowing "horse," the intellect does not become a horse; Socrates does not change into Dobbin. Rather, the intellect acquires the intelligible species "horse" that is embedded in Dobbin.

This is clearly an even higher type of "immutation" than the spiritual immutation involved in sight, just as sight is a higher type of immutation than the natural immutation involved in touch. For, in thought, it is the intelligible, not the sensible, species that is transferred. It is not the particular aspects of the situation (this-green-here-and-now, Dobbin) but its universal aspects ("color," "horse") that are transferred to, and acquired by, the intellect when it thinks. True, the intellect is stamped (to this extent it is passive) with the form of the thing "out there," as wax is stamped with the design of the seal; but it is, as it were, not the design of *this* seal (still less, the material of the seal), but design in general that is transferred.

There is another important difference between intellect and sensation that Thomas, characteristically, felt he had to attribute to a distinct power in the soul. Objects write, as it were, upon passive sense organs; we experience visual sensations as long as our eyes are open. If Dobbin is there and if we look in his direction, we cannot help but see him. But we would never experience the *form* "horse" unless our intellects operated actively to extract the form from the individual substance out there in which it is embedded.

As Thomas pointed out, if Plato had been correct about forms' having an independent existence, there would be no need to presuppose the existence of an active intellectual power. Forms would then impress themselves on the passive intellect in the way in which sense objects impress themselves on the sense organs.[3]

> But since Aristotle did not allow that the forms of natural things exist apart from matter, and since forms existing in matter are not actually intelligible, it follows that the natures or forms of the sensible things which we understand are not actually intelligible. Now nothing is reduced from potentiality to act except by something in act. . . . We must therefore assign on the part of the intellect some power to make things actually intelligible, by the abstraction of the species from material conditions. And such is the necessity for positing an agent intellect [that is, an active power in the intellect].[d]

3 This is true, of course, only according to the *Aristotelian* view of the relation between form and matter, in which form, because it is necessarily embedded in matter, is not fully actual. According to *Plato's* view (expressed in Aristotelian, not Platonic, terminology), all forms are fully actual because they are wholly independent. Hence forms do not require to be *made* actual.

This conception of the active power of the intellect was necessary, or so Thomas believed, to complete his theory of knowledge; but it also had the immense advantage of enabling him to prove that the soul, despite its union with the obviously mortal body, is immortal. For "all corruption consists in separation of form from matter. . . .[4] Where there is not composition of form and matter, there can be no separation of the same: wherefore . . . there can be [no] corruption."

Granting the basic Aristotelian and Thomistic assumptions about form and matter, it does indeed seem that the part of man that is independent of the body and active in its own right will survive that corruption of the body called death. But, unfortunately for Thomas, if matter corrupts, it also individualizes. Hence, as Aristotle seems to have concluded, what is immortal is not the personal soul of each individual man but some sort of general, supra-individual soul.[5] Since personal immortality was of the first importance both to Christian piety and to Christian theology,[e] it was necessary for Thomas to labor mightily to extricate himself from this heresy. We need not go into the long and ingenious arguments with which he attempted to prove his case.[f] Nevertheless, it is instructive to note the way in which theological considerations continuously affect the Christian philosopher's position—even on such a seemingly nontheological matter as the question of the psychology of cognition.

Since Thomas' study of the rational faculty passes at this point from psychology to theology, let us turn our attention to the soul's second intellectual power, volition. We have already seen that, just as rational knowledge has its roots in sensation, so volition has its roots in animal appetite and in even more elementary drives. Articulate human will is, in fact, simply a manifestation, at a relatively advanced stage, of the basic urge of every creature to fulfill itself, to make what is potential about itself actual, to complete itself.[6]

What, then, are the features that distinguish will from other levels and types of fulfillment? Since all these features result from the fact that the fulfillment called will is self-conscious, let us begin by contrasting it with lower-level fulfillments that are not self-conscious.

According to Thomas, the end of every inanimate object, for example, a stone, is to be located in a particular part of space, namely, the center of the created universe. Its nature is therefore completed and fulfilled by a single kind of movement—a simple fall through space. Because animals, on the other hand, have a variety of ends—sleeping, eating, and sexual activity, for instance—they

---

4 [Change, in which matter loses one form and acquires another, is a case in point—AUTHOR.]

5 It is not certain that Aristotle himself held the active intellect to be identical in all men [for a discussion of this point, see W. D. Ross, *Aristotle* (Methuen, London, 1930), pp. 148–53]. But most of his Arabian commentators, whose writings were widely read in the West, had adopted this position, and therefore, in the minds of most churchmen, Aristotelianism was associated with a denial of personal immortality.

6 Everything that is a fusion of matter and form not only *is* but *acts*, precisely because it is the nature of form to become actual and to fulfill itself insofar as may be.

perform a great variety of movements. Animals have a variety of ends because anything felt by them as advantageous is *ipso facto* an end for them. Yet these various ends do not conflict because, by and large, the animal sees only one of them at a time. If an animal is thirsty and there is something drinkable about, it drinks; it cannot read the sign beside the waterhole, "Poisoned," and so does not know that the water is dangerous. For an animal, in other words, everything is wholly black or wholly white, either good or bad; choice is no problem. An animal does not, in fact, *choose*—it responds by a "natural instinct," as Thomas called it, to the sensed advantages or disadvantages of its situation.[7]

Man, on the other hand, can read; that is, his intellect, with its extended memory, sees ends as temporally and contextually relative rather than as absolute. The water is good now—one naturally inclines to drink; the water's aftereffects, in a few minutes or hours, are bad—one naturally inclines not to drink. One is pulled in two directions at once, the magnitude of the "pulls" depending on (1) how thirsty one is and (2) how dangerous one thinks the poison in the water is. By taking thought, man can resolve this conflict (and, of course, many similar dilemmas of policy). Knowing that he will be traveling in a desert, he asks the chemists in a laboratory to find a substance that will purify water. Clearly, human (that is, willed) behavior, though even more diversified than animal behavior, is far more orderly. But the orderliness of will is not the order of a simple pattern, like that of inanimate behavior; its unity is achieved through man's being able to make a plan and act on it.

It is obvious that this capacity for forward planning depends on man's ability to compare particular desirables (to compare, for example, the value of preserving life with the value of reducing taxes by spending less on chemical research). This consideration led Thomas to distinguish a second feature of will, as compared with unconscious fulfillments. For, according to Thomas, it is possible for man to compare desirables only because he has a criterion for choice. But different criteria yield different choices. (If human life is "precious," we say, "Hang the cost of chemical research." But if life is "cheap," we may decide that the money can be better spent elsewhere.) Hence, according to Thomas, all criteria must themselves be evaluated by other criteria, and these, ultimately, by some absolute criterion. That is to say, since infinite series are impossible, there must be a terminus to every means-end series; since ultimately all (relative) ends must be means to other (higher) ends, there is a single, final, supreme end to which all other ends lead as means in a single, hierarchical structure. Man has the power, moreover, to grasp in its general outlines (though not to know in detail) the nature of this supreme end. Hence he is capable of tracing for himself the position of every good in relation to every other good in this single means-end hierarchy and so of resolving the various specific conflicts between rival goods that occur in his daily life.

This can be put differently: Animal appetites have sense particulars for their

7 This is, of course, the "estimative power." See p. 245.

objects; human appetites have universals of some sort for theirs. Just as an animal knows only particulars (for example, "master-feeder-punisher"), so an animal experiences only particular desires ("food now," "sleep now"). Precisely as we, being men, can pass from the particularity of sense knowledge to a knowledge of the universal "man" embedded in this particular "master-feeder-punisher," so we can rise to a knowledge of "good"—the universal embedded in the particular desirables experienced by animals. It may be said, then, that when what moves us is not merely some particular desirable, but a knowledge of value, the moving force is "will." Everywhere in the universe, Thomas held, things are seeking what completes and fulfills them. This is why rocks fall, flames rise, and the planets turn. This is why animals eat, sleep, and hunt. Will is simply the character that this generic thrust toward completion assumes in a rational creature who *knows the good* that completes him.

A third distinction that Thomas drew between will and other types of fulfillment must be mentioned: Will involves deliberation. A rock naturally falls if nothing hinders it; appetite (whether in animals or men) operates automatically. An animal, he held, "naturally" inclines toward anything experienced as desirable; when it is hungry and food is available it eats. This is also true of man *if* nothing appears in consciousness to complicate the situation. Unless a conflict of goods presents itself to us, we naturally will that which seems to us good, just as the animal naturally seeks its particular desirable and just as the stone naturally falls. For to see that anything is good is simply to see that it corrects some present deficiency (that is, that it is form relative to this present matter). Hence, unless a conflict of goods appears, will is as automatic and as necessary as appetite.

However, because men have extended memories and because they are capable of abstract knowledge, such conflicts almost always occur. Hence, will is a vastly more complicated business than appetite. Animal appetite, for the most part, fixes on only one desirable at a time (food now, sleep now). The human intellect gives us the power of looking before and after. Memory, foresight, the power to generalize and compare—these faculties all result, as a rule, in several goods' being present in consciousness at once. The result is that, instead of inclining automatically toward the single desirable particular present now in sensation, we usually have to choose among several goods.

How, then, do we choose between two goods a and b present in consciousness now? We need, as Thomas pointed out, some principle of choice. This can only be some higher, longer-range good c. Now, if a is seen to be a means to c, whereas b is not, we would certainly choose a. But the situation is seldom so simple, for if a is a means to long-range good c, b is likely to be a means to some other long-range good d. Hence another "principle" is required to help us choose between c and d, for until we make *this* choice, we obviously cannot choose between a and b. This second principle must be some still greater, still longer-range good in terms of which c and d can be appraised. We proceed in this way, Thomas thought, until we reach some good n, which is the last end, at least for present purposes.

In *this* calculation, whatever we take as our end (for example, national security) is not itself a matter of choice. Of course, in another situation national security might be an intermediate end to some still higher end; in this case, it would enter into the choice-calculation, and something else would be our end— say, the establishment of a world government (for which, under certain conditions, we might sacrifice national security). But, regardless of whether national security is a means in some other situation, it is the intended end in *this* situation. Accordingly, in Thomas' view, we work our way down to a choice between *a* and *b* on the basis of which is the best (that is, the most efficient and direct) means to national security. If *a* happens to be the policy of negotiating with the Chinese Communists and *b* the policy of launching a preventive war against them, deliberation is likely to be long and difficult.

Of course, this means-end calculation (which Thomas called "counsel") may begin at the other end—that is, we may begin by setting ourselves some long-range end, say, health, and then carefully and deliberately plan a program for achieving it. It is indicative of Thomas' intellectualistic bias that he usually thought of counsel in the latter way.

THE FREE WILL

Apart from his interest in demonstrating that the various powers of the soul constitute a systematic hierarchy, Thomas' chief goal in the study of psychology was probably to lay a basis for a solution of the problem of free will. For, though psychological in origin, this question has immense theological and ethical implications.

Although Thomas recognized that the term "free" is ambiguous and is "employed in many ways," he failed to distinguish these ways with sufficient precision and so, as we shall see, fell into confusion. One type of freedom that he *did* distinguish is "freedom from coercion." The will, he maintained, can never be coerced, or forced. He did not mean, of course, to deny that terror or pain sometimes causes us to do things that defeat our real ends instead of fulfilling them. But on such occasions, according to Thomas, we cannot be said, strictly speaking, to have *willed* the things that defeat us.[g] To will is by definition to aim at what we want because we see, or believe, that it fulfills us. Hence cases of coercion are not cases of will. Hence, again, the will is never coerced.

The will, then, is always free in the sense of being voluntary. But this type of freedom is irrelevant in the present context, for necessity in the sense of coercion is not what is usually attributed to the will by those who deny its freedom.

A second, more important kind of freedom may be called "freedom of contingency." We have already seen that, according to Thomas, animal appetite naturally seeks whatever it experiences as desirable, and that this characteristic of appetite is inherited by will. This is the necessary thrust toward completion that all things without exception share. Now, there is one object and one alone that is wholly good. This, of course, is God. Therefore, when man thinks about God, he cannot help desiring Him. Here, then, man has no freedom; his will is as inevitably determined to love God as the appetite of an animal is determined to seek its "desirable."

But all other things, because they are only partially actual, are only partially good. A picture that is esthetically satisfying may be economically bad—it costs too much for one's pocketbook. A dish that is tasty and therefore gastronomically good may be rich in calories and so dietetically bad. Every choice is a decision to take "this" instead of "that." The "this" one takes is doubtless good in its own right, but insofar as it excludes the "that" (which is also good in *its* own right), the "this" is bad.

Thus, except as we attain to a full knowledge of God, all the objects of our thought are, for the purposes of volition, "contingent singulars."[h] They have some good aspects, some bad ones. They are not, therefore, necessary objects of will. Thomas' conclusion was that though we will *some* things necessarily (the supreme good and, indeed, any good experienced without conflict or complication), we do not will *most* things necessarily. "The will does not necessarily will *whatever* it desires."

Unfortunately, the adverb "necessarily" in this sentence is ambiguous. Suppose that I buy the picture that is esthetically good but economically bad. Buying the picture is certainly not "necessary" in one sense of the word, for there are circumstances in which I might not buy it—for instance, if I have just lost a large amount of money gambling and I am seriously in debt. But, as a matter of fact, I have just been left a large amount of money unexpectedly. In a word, circumstances vary, and as they vary, my volition naturally changes. In this sense, buying the picture is not an absolutely necessary object of my will. But, given the whole set of circumstances that actually do exist, is my decision to buy it necessary? Many people would say that a psychologist who knew enough about me and the pattern of my previous choices, and also about the particular circumstances that now exist, could have predicted that I would buy it. (And, presumably, in the different circumstances of worry about gambling debts, he could have correctly predicted that I would not buy it.) If this is correct, it follows that, though my volition to buy the picture is not necessary in one (rather technical) sense of the term, it is necessary in the only sense relevant to the free-will controversy.

But Thomas would presumably have denied that a psychologist could make this kind of prediction, for he maintained that there are no circumstances that make the will's choice inevitable. He allowed, of course, that circumstances (for example, winning last night) may make "this" seem better than "that," but he argued that, even so, we can always resist "this" and choose "that." In other words, we have an absolute freedom to will or to abstain from willing.

In fact, Thomas held that even in willing God we have this freedom of control. It is true that *if* we think of God, we cannot fail to will Him, but we can choose not to think of Him.[i] And, obviously, what is true of the supreme good is true of all lesser goods. No matter how powerful the seduction of sense, no matter how much pressure the passions put upon us, no matter how bad the habits we have acquired or how long we have let ourselves remain subjected to them, we can always "resist"; the will, *if it so chooses*, reamins in control of the situation.

> These [natural] inclinations are subject to the judgment of reason, which the lower appetite obeys. . . . Therefore this is in no way prejudicial to free choice.
>
> The adventitious qualities are habits and passions. . . . Yet even these inclinations are subject to the judgment of reason. . . . It is in our power either to acquire them, whether by causing them or disposing ourselves to them, or to reject them. And so there is nothing in this that is repugnant to free choice.[j]

But here the empirical facts are against Thomas. Indeed, it is so clear that unlimited freedom of control does not exist that, as he proceeded, Thomas was forced to admit as much. Thus he allowed that the will has no control over the various acts of the vegetative soul—nutrition and growth, for instance, nor over the action of the heart. And further, as Augustine said, *"the movement of the genital members is sometimes inopportune and not desired; sometimes when sought it fails, and whereas the heart is warm with desire, the body remains cold."*[8,k]

And again, though, generally speaking, the will controls the sensitive powers, "it sometimes happens that the movement of the sensitive appetite is aroused suddenly in consequence of an apprehension of the imagination or sense. And then such a movement occurs without the command of reason, although reason could have prevented it, had it foreseen it."[l]

The fact is that the passions (which are, of course, connected with the sensitive appetite) not only resist the will but on occasion actually master it. "The sensitive appetite has something of its own, by virtue of which it can resist the commands of reason." And again, "it is evident that . . . according as a man is affected by a passion, something seems to him fitting, which does not seem so when he is not so affected; and thus that seems good to a man when angered, which does not seem good when he is calm. It is in this way that the sensitive appetite moves the will."[m]

All these obvious and undeniable facts about human nature show that there are extensive areas of our behavior over which the will, even if it so chooses, does not have control. There seems no way to reconcile these admissions with Thomas' official position that we have complete freedom of control.

Leaving the question of what *areas* of conduct the will can control, we must

---

8 In explaining this phenomenon Thomas followed Augustine: "It is in punishment of sin that the movement of these members does not obey reason. That is to say, the soul is punished for its rebellion against God by the insubmission of that member whereby original sin is transmitted to posterity"—*Summa Theologica*, Pt. I–II, Ques. 17, Art. 9, Reply Obj. 3.

next ask what, precisely, it means to say that the will has control. Thomas' reply was that to say that the will is in control is to say that the will is an unmoved mover. His argument can be set out in the following way. He started from the assumption that some of the time, in some areas, the will can control passion "if it chooses." What causes it to choose or not to choose? One may be tempted to answer that it is the will that chooses to choose to control the passions. But what causes it to choose to choose to control them? Obviously, it is the will that chooses to choose to choose to control them, and so on. It is clear that when we try to trace causes back, we never get beyond the will. It is also clear that the will is not a sequence of causes. Causal series of the kind that occur in nature (or in man, when the passions move him) do not occur in cases of human volition. To say that we will to will to will to will and so on is redundant. It is equivalent to saying simply that we will. Thus, the will is an unmoved mover. Of course, in Thomas' view, every causal series ends, sooner or later, in an unmoved mover. Series in the sublunar world terminate, for instance, in the intelligence that moves the sun. But in human volition there is no *series:* The unmoved mover in us issues directly in what we call the act of will.

With this concept we have reached what was for Thomas the most important sense of freedom. To say that the will is free does not mean that it is *un*caused; it means that the will is *self*-caused, that it is an unmoved mover.

This assertion of human freedom requires qualification in one respect. The doctrine of dual causality teaches that God is *also* the cause of everything that occurs. Accordingly, the human will is not an absolutely unmoved mover; only God is that. In the end, we have to attribute my free choice both to myself and to God.

> Free choice is the cause of its own movement, because by his free choice man moves himself to act. But it does not of necessity belong to liberty that what is free should be the first cause of itself, as neither for one thing to be cause of another need it be the first cause. God, therefore, is the first cause, Who moves causes both natural and voluntary. And just as by moving natural causes He does not prevent their actions from being natural, so by moving voluntary causes He does not deprive their actions of being voluntary; but rather is He the cause of this very thing in them, for He operates in each thing according to its own nature.[n]

THOMAS' APPROACH CONTRASTED
WITH THAT OF MODERN PSYCHOLOGISTS

For the moment, let us postpone asking whether this account of freedom provides a satisfactory basis for the moral life as Thomas understood it and whether it is compatible with the theological dogmas to which he was committed.[9] Instead, let us consider the contrast between Thomas' approach to the

9 See pp. 278–85.

study of psychology and that of modern psychologists. An understanding of some of the differences between the two approaches should help us to a better understanding of them both.

Perhaps the first difference to note is that of method. Thomas started with definitions and deduced their implications (the way he derived the concept of freedom from coercion from the definition of the voluntary is a case in point); modern psychologists prefer to generalize from empirical data accumulated under controlled conditions (What happens to rate of heart beat, blood pressure, and so on when a man "resists" telling a lie?). The result of this methodological difference is that Thomas has a neat and tidy schematic structure that is almost totally irrelevant to actual behavior patterns, whereas modern psychologists have an immense accumulation of empirical data that they cannot seem to fit into any systematic conceptual framework.

Today we not only mistrust a procedure that begins with rigid definitions, but we find Thomas' actual definitions unmanageable. We are, for instance, less concerned with what will *is* than with how it *operates*. We would, indeed, be inclined to say that the only practical definition of will is in terms of how it operates. And to describe how will operates means, for us, to give an account of the various physical, psychical, and symbolic processes that occur when what the ordinary man calls an "act of will" takes place.

When we make such an investigation, we find a very complex situation—not at all like Thomas' self-caused, spiritual act, imposed by the soul on an organic situation and manipulating that situation from outside. Since we hold that a causal relation is always between two events *within* a spatiotemporal system, we cannot deal with anything standing outside such a causal network. And, of course, many people today would deny that anything like Thomas' spiritual act, occurring outside the empirical causal system, does occur. We would interpret the will's apparent lack of relation to its background simply as our own failure to see the connections that *are* there. There is, from the point of view of modern psychology, nothing more extranatural about volition than about, say, the activity of mice in a maze—not that all psychologists would "reduce" voluntary behavior to this level, but that most psychologists, while admitting the presence of all sorts of complicating factors, would claim that whatever happens is part of a causal situation that is (theoretically, at least) capable of analysis.

Moreover, Thomas' view of will seems overly rationalistic. According to Thomas, reason proceeds by surveying certain possible values, deciding which is most desirable, and then dispassionately planning a program for achieving the value settled upon. Finally, when the program has been worked out down to the last detail, it is launched and action begins. That behavior of this general type does occur seems clear; that it occurs very often or that it ever occurs in so straightforward and simple a fashion seems most unlikely. Indeed, instead of holding with Thomas that men aim at things because they see them to be good, a modern psychologist is likely to maintain exactly the opposite: Men judge things to be good because they aim at them. The radical differences in value theory that this shift in orientation signifies cannot be gone into here. It is enough to point out that the modern view tends to minimize the role of what Thomas called "reason" and to treat it as being more often ex post facto than actually operative in behavior; it provides us, *after* we act, with a socially acceptable justification for having behaved as we did.

In addition to holding that much human behavior is, in Thomas' sense of these terms, "natural" rather than "voluntary," most of us would challenge Thomas' contention that there is a sharp dichotomy between "reason" and "passion," between the "deliberate" and the "natural." Reason, we feel, is not simply thoroughly rational, utterly distinct from something else called "passion." A typical modern account, by Gardner Murphy, runs as follows:

> Inner signals of all kinds tend to initiate both inner and outer responses of a high degree of complexity. Sometimes a period of thought ends in a simple verbal summary from which a course of action follows. This overlaps a good deal with what we call the *will*. A man is said to be "making up his mind," and when a certain symbolic summary is achieved, he is said to have "resolved upon" a course of action, which then follows. . . . A . . . generally satisfactory use of this word [will] relates to a *symbolic process* in which a definable period of hesitation is known to precede an overt act.
>
> The hypothesis [is] that verbal cues intervene at the decisive point and lead to the initiation of one response pattern rather than another. [It at least appears to be the case that] inner verbal cues, as conditioned stimuli, can set the muscular mechanism going.[o]

It will be noticed that Professor Murphy thinks of the whole process as will, whereas Thomas thought of will as the final stage in the process. Further, what Thomas called "counsel," Professor Murphy calls "hesitation" (a suggestive difference in terminology!). Quite apart from such obvious terminological differences, their points of view are radically different. We may allow that terms like "impulse" and "drive" beg more questions than they answer—indeed, that they say little more (and, in one sense, less) than Thomas said when he held that it is the nature of form everywhere to fulfill itself by becoming actual. We may allow, too, that the only way of determining "the decisive point" is by the fact that a "verbal cue" happens to intervene there; that we distinguish a verbal cue from a verbalism that is not a cue merely by the fact that in one case a response occurs and in the other it does not; and that saying "response patterns are initiated" is merely a way of saying that changes can be observed to occur. However, all this amounts merely to saying that there is a great deal about human behavior that we do not yet understand and that most of our formulas are in fact questions requiring further investigation.

The real point is that modern psychology's descriptions invite further investigation and suggest lines along which it might profitably be undertaken. Thomas' rationalistic method, on the other hand, not only creates an impression that no problems exist (except logical problems involved in making various conceptual spheres mutually consistent); it forestalls the possibility of progress, even if problems were to occur to us, by throwing us into a realm of timeless acts, spiritual substances, and uncaused activity. It is perhaps well to emphasize that this particular weakness is a result of Thomas' rationalism rather than of his theologism. Many generations of thinkers who were not at all bound by Thomas' dogmatic presuppositions were just as firmly wedded to rationalistic psychology. Psychology, indeed, was one of the last of the sciences to break away from this sort of methodological bias, and it was not until the middle of the nineteenth century—long after dogmatic considerations had ceased to limit thought—that psychology even began to be empirical.

There is, however, one great strength in Thomas' psychology that must be mentioned. A basic fact of human life, as Professor Murphy points out, is "the tension or drive of the living individual. . . . Indeed the personality is apparently definable as a system of tensions or impulses, or acts of will."[p] But what is the relation between the behavior of "living individuals" and the behavior of inanimate particles that is a basic fact about the physical universe and that is the subject matter of physics and the other natural sciences? Until this relation is understood, we live, even at the scientific level, in two worlds—the world of the physicist and the world of the psychologist. This is surely an unsatisfactory state of affairs. But Thomas' account of human behavior—form fulfilling itself—is identical with his account of physical motion, indeed, of motion everywhere. And since his definition of value is also in terms of form realizing itself, his is truly a unified world view. In terms of the facts he knew, he gave a far more systematic account of the universe than modern science has yet been able to give. Of course, our problem is more difficult than his, not merely because we know more facts but because the concepts of matter and form he used as the unifying scheme of his world view seem incapable of being accommodated to the descriptive purposes of modern science. Yet we should not allow the great advances we have made in some departments of knowledge to obscure the extent of Thomas' achievement, taken as a whole and seen in relation to the age in which he lived.

Ethics

In Thomas' view, the science of ethics is concerned with two main questions: What is the good? What should we do to attain it? Let us consider these in turn.

THE GOOD

That all the many different goods at which men aim are to be evaluated in terms of one supreme good seemed to Thomas evident. Otherwise men would be confronted in decision situations by alternatives between which they could not choose since both would be good and there would be no way of telling which was better. Since this would be irrational, there must be one final good to which all others are means.

Clearly, it is essential, if we want to live well and make right choices, to know what this final end is. Now, as Thomas pointed out, Aristotle discussed this question in his *Ethics*. Is it possible to accept his conclusions here, as well as in physics and the other sciences? Thomas replied affirmatively: What Aristotle said about man's end is true to the natural man. Thomas held it important to bear in mind what some Christians had overlooked—that there *is* a natural man. Man is not, as some Neoplatonizing Christians had held, merely soul; his body and its appetites are a real part of his nature, not a punishment inflicted on the soul for some sin committed in a previous, nonbodily existence. Man as an individual substance—a real fusion of matter and form, of body and soul—has a natural good, and that good, "happiness," is just about what Aristotle held it to be.

But, Thomas continued, it must never be forgotten that man is more than Aristotle thought him to be. The pagan philosopher was debarred from knowledge of man's higher, supernatural destination—the knowledge with which Christians are endowed by faith. There is, in fact, a whole range of life and experience from which, as a pagan, Aristotle was completely cut off, and about the end of this part of human life he can tell us nothing. On the other hand, it would be a mistake to suppose that these two parts—the one known to Aristotle by natural reason and the one known to Christians by faith and revelation—are completely distinct. The higher life and its end do not contradict the lower life and its end; rather, the higher end supplements the lower. Thus the highest happiness of the natural man is knowledge, just as Aristotle conceived it to be. And the supernal happiness (a state whose possibility Aristotle did not dream of) is also knowledge—namely, knowledge of God, about whom Aristotle, pagan that he was, had only vague and inadequate information.

That knowledge of God is man's final end follows, according to Thomas, from the general consideration that everything, in its own way, seeks both "its own perfection" and "the Divine likeness."[10] To ascertain man's final end and supreme good is therefore equivalent to ascertaining the perfection of an intellectual substance. But the perfection of any substance is its form, and we already know that the peculiar and special property of an intellectual substance is—naturally!—intellect. Just as a stone fulfills itself by seeking the center of the universe, so an intellectual substance realizes *its* form and so achieves its good by knowing. What is more, in this fulfillment an intellectual substance becomes like God, and more like Him than any lesser creature can ever be.

---

10 Ethics is thus simply a subdivision of physics; it is the study of the mode in which individual substances of a certain level (that is, men) achieve this common fulfillment.

For the knowing mind becomes, in a sense, the known object.[11] It follows that the end of an intellectual substance is knowledge—in particular, knowledge of God, the most perfect and complete truth.

> Now, seeing that all creatures, even those that are devoid of reason, are directed to God as their last end: and that all reach this end in so far as they have some share of a likeness to him: the intellectual creature attains to him in a special way, namely through its proper operation, by understanding him. Consequently this must be the end of the intelligent creature, namely to understand God. . . .
>
> Again. The operation proper to a thing is the end thereof: for it is its second perfection; so that when a thing is well conditioned for its proper operation it is said to be efficient and good. Now understanding is the proper operation of the intellectual substance: and consequently it is its end. Therefore whatever is most perfect in this operation, is its last end; especially in those operations which are not directed to some product, such as understanding and sensation. And since operations of this kind take their species from their objects, by which also they are known, it follows that the more perfect the object of any such operation, the more perfect is the operation. Consequently to understand the most perfect intelligible, namely God, is the most perfect in the genus of this operation which is to understand. Therefore to know God by an act of intelligence in the last end of every intellectual substance.[q]

Though these considerations show that the supreme human happiness is knowledge of God, the *kind* of knowledge of God that is best and most adequate remains to be seen. There is, for instance, a crude, rudimentary knowledge of God implanted in all men, but it is easy to prove that

> . . . this knowledge of God cannot possibly suffice for happiness.
>
> For the operation of the happy must be without any defect: and this knowledge is subject to an admixture of many errors. Some believed that there is no other ordainer of mundane things than the heavenly bodies; wherefore they said that the heavenly bodies are gods. . . . Some, deeming human acts not to be subject to any but a human ordinance, declared that men who cause order in other men are gods.—Accordingly this knowledge of God is not sufficient for happiness.[r]

Nor, according to Thomas, does man's happiness consist in rational knowledge of God like that set forth and demonstrated in Thomas' own *Summa*. For demonstrative knowledge of God is also "subject to the admixture of many errors," and, in any case, it does not attain to God's essence. Furthermore, as Thomas pointed out in a characteristic argument, demonstrative knowledge is perforce limited to

---

11 The form embedded in the object known becomes actualized in the mind of the knower. In Aristotle's metaphor, the wax acquires the form of the seal that is impressed on it.

the educated few; but happiness, being the end of the human species, must be attainable by all men. Hence demonstrative knowledge "does not suffice for man's ultimate happiness."

Nor does happiness consist in the knowledge of God attained through faith. For, though in some respects knowledge by faith is superior to intellectual knowledge, it is not superior *qua* knowledge: "The intellect in believing does not grasp the object of its assent." (In other words, though we know by faith, we do not understand by faith.) Hence, in such knowledge the intellect is imperfect and man cannot possibly be supremely happy.

It is clear, in fact, that the knowledge of God that is supreme happiness is not attained in natural life at all, unless it be in some sort of mystic and enraptured trance.

> The more our mind is raised to the contemplation of spiritual things, the more is it withdrawn from sensible things. Now the divine substance is the highest term to which contemplation can reach: hence the mind that sees the divine substance must be wholly freed from the senses, either by death or by rapture. Wherefore it is said in God's person (Exod. xxxiii, 20): *Man shall not see me, and live. . . .*
>
> Again. Man's last end is the term of his natural appetite, so that when he has obtained it, he desires nothing more: because if he still has a movement towards something, he has not yet reached an end wherein to be at rest. Now, this cannot happen in this life: since the more man understands, the more is the desire to understand increased in him,—this being natural to man,—unless perhaps someone there be who understands all things: and in this life this never did nor can happen to anyone that was a mere man.[s]

Further, complete knowledge is a gift from God. Even after the death of the body, the soul, though freed from the limitations of sense knowledge, does not attain to a knowledge of God by its own, unaided powers. For by its natural powers an intellect knows only as much or as little of an object as it is capable of taking in.[12] It follows that the separated soul, which knows God only by means of its own finite substance, longs for an unmediated, direct knowledge of Him. Hence it falls short of complete happiness (because it lacks complete knowledge) unless God raises it from the level of natural knowledge to the level of a higher knowledge.

One would do well, indeed, to call this higher level "vision" instead of "knowledge." Of course, the vision *is* knowledge, and knowledge in the supreme degree, for in it we are confronted with the absolute truth. But the term "knowledge" suggests the limited, discursive kind of knowing to which men are limited in this life, whereas the "vision of Truth" indicated by the term "vision" is immediate, direct, and nondiscursive. When, "by some kind of

---

12 The example of the wax and the seal is a case in point. The wax takes in (knows) the shape of the seal, but not its color. The eye takes in (knows) the color as well as the shape. See p. 247.

outpouring of the divine goodness," this vision comes to us, it comes all at once. The mind illumined by the divine light sees the "Truth" as a whole, not as a series of distinct parts grasped one after another.

It follows from this that he who sees the vision truly partakes of eternal life.

> For eternity differs from time in that the latter has its being in a kind of succession, whereas the former is all simultaneously. Now it has already been proved that there is no succession in the vision in question, and that whatsoever is seen in it, is seen at once and at a glance. Therefore this vision takes place in a kind of participation of eternity. . . .
>
> It follows from what has been said that those who obtain ultimate happiness from the divine vision, never fall away from it. Because *whatever at one time is, and at another time is not, is measured by time,* as stated in 4 *Phys.* xii. Now the vision in question that makes intellectual creatures happy, is not in time but in eternity. Therefore no one can lose it having once become a partaker thereof.[t]

Perhaps all that needs to be said about these arguments is that they will probably convince only those already convinced. That is, they provide a rationale for beliefs adopted on other, and deeper, grounds. We may suspect that Thomas' proof that the supreme good for all men is knowledge, as well as Plato's and Aristotle's earlier proofs of the same thesis, is but a reflection of personal preference. At least, many medieval Christians continued to hold, despite all Thomas' arguments, that it is not knowledge of God but surrender to Him that is man's supreme good.

THE MORALLY GOOD ACT

So far we have considered Thomas' account of the nature of the supremely good end. Now that the nature of this end has been demonstrated, it is logical to inquire how it can be achieved. According to Thomas, the answer, in general terms, is obvious. Any behavior by which anything anywhere in the universe changes from potentiality to actuality is good, for such a change is a means to that thing's final end, namely, such likeness to God as it is capable of. Thus the stone's fall through space is good because it brings the stone nearer its final end—location at the center of the universe.

But, of course, Thomas was not concerned here with good acts in general; it is specifically human conduct that is the subject matter of the science of ethics. And not even all human behavior falls within the domain of ethics—the various acts of nutrition and growth by which the vegetative soul is realized, though good, are not *morally* good. Moral goodness or badness, Thomas held, is attributable only to voluntary acts. Hence, though the general definition of goodness as fulfillment of form holds for man as well as for all other creatures, moral goodness involves more than is involved in the simple goodness of the behavior by which stones and flames fulfill themselves. Man does not merely behave. Being an intelligent creature, he knows what he does; he deliberates about alternatives and chooses one in preference to another. These psychological facts about the way in which the human soul fulfills itself add complicating dimensions to the study of ethics.

Thomas began this study as he began every other: by distinguishing the several components in the object under analysis—in this case, a human act. As an example, let us take the act of giving alms. In the first place, the act has an external object—the transference of money to another person. An act's external object gives the act its species and so corresponds to the form of a natural object, which determines the name we assign it. We call a particular animal a "horse" because it has a form of such-and-such a kind; we call a particular act "almsgiving" because its external object is of such-and-such a kind. The "primary goodness," as Thomas called it, of an act is derived from its external object. If this object is "suitable" ("suitability" remains to be defined), the act is good; if the object is unsuitable, the act is bad.

In the second place, every voluntary act has an internal object, or end. This is what the agent hopes to bring about by the act. Thus, for instance, I might give alms because I truly wish to help the poor, or because I vaingloriously wish to win a reputation for munificence. Here again, there is a parallel between being and goodness. The goodness, like the being, of every created thing depends in part on other things. Thus human acts "have a measure of goodness" from their end, in addition to the primary goodness they have as acts of a certain kind.[u] In a word, the suitability or unsuitability of the internal (that is, intended) object affects the goodness or badness of the act taken as a whole.

Finally, there are the circumstances of the act. Almsgiving is almsgiving whatever the size of my purse and the extent of the recipient's need, just as Socrates is a man whether sitting or standing, white or black. But though these circumstances, or accidents, do not affect the character of the act taken in itself as an act of this kind, they do bear on its morality. The right (that is, the moral) amount of money to give in alms depends on my present wealth, my other obligations, the circumstances of the recipient, the use he will make of my gift, and so on.

The extent to which end and circumstances affect the morality of our conduct will be apparent if we think of such acts as picking up a straw or stroking one's beard. These acts, considered in themselves (that is, from the point of view of their external objects), are morally indifferent. Done absent-mindedly, they have no end beyond themselves and are thus neither suitable (like almsgiving) nor unsuitable (like adultery). But suppose one of these acts is done deliberately and for some end beyond itself. Suppose, for instance, I stoop to pick up a straw in order to avoid a beggar seeking alms. In this case, picking up a straw gets its character from my end and is judged accordingly.

Thus the analysis of the modes by which men fulfill themselves is more complex than the analysis of the modes by which animals and inanimate objects seek their good. Because men—unlike stones—can foresee the consequences of their behavior, and because, on occasion, they take these consequences into account (that is, when they deliberate before choosing), it is necessary to take consequences into account when evaluating men's acts. But how many consequences should be considered? How long a future ought men take into account? And to what extent are they blamable if, acting with laudable motives, they act in a way that turns out to have evil effects?

> The consequences of an act are either foreseen or not. If they are foreseen, it is evident that they increase the goodness or malice. . . .
> But if the consequences are not foreseen, we must make a distinction. For if they follow from the nature of the action, and in the majority of cases, in this respect the consequences increase the goodness or malice of that action. . . . On the other hand, if the consequences follow by accident and seldom, then they do not increase the goodness or malice of the act; for we do not judge of a thing according to that which belongs to it by accident, but only according to that which belongs to it essentially.[v]

So far we have seen merely that, according to Thomas, object, motive, and circumstances have to be considered in assessing the moral goodness or badness of an action. But whether object, motive, and circumstances are good or bad depends, as we have also seen, on whether they are suitable. The argument remains incomplete, therefore, until "suitability" has been defined. Now, it might seem to follow from Thomas' definition of "good" as that which fulfills desire that every object, every end, is suitable: Unless it fulfills some desire one would not aim at it, and what satisfies desire is good.

Thomas would have admitted that in a certain sense this is true. All being *qua* being is good; every end does satisfy some deficiency and so brings form to actuality. But though all finite being is good in some respects, it is evil in others, namely, those in which it is deficient. Hence every finite end, just because it is a finite end, makes good some deficit but leaves others unsatisfied. We must not forget that good is what fulfills form, and form is not something private, or something variable from individual to individual. What is good in any given case does not, therefore, depend on the momentary whim of the agent; he may, under the influence of some passion, desire something that is not in accordance with his real, long-range good and that therefore, though it fulfills *some* desire and is to that extent "good," does not bring his form nearer actuality. Hence what determines whether an act is good is not simply whether it fulfills some desire (for obviously all acts set out to do *that*), but whether the act is in accord with the objectively characterized form "man," which, being a property common to all men, is a good common to them all. Thus Thomas constantly distinguished between "the good" and "the apparent good"[w] and, like Aristotle, avoided subjectivism by insisting that form provides an objective standard for evaluating conduct. The degree to which conduct fulfills form is the degree to which that conduct is good.

It is now possible to define "suitable." The suitable act is one that, considered in its various aspects, conforms to the universal order of reason, that is, is in accord with the rational structure of the universe envisaged and decreed by God when He made it. This can be put in theological terms: The good will, the suitable will, is one that is in agreement with the divine will as reflected in the ordering of the universe; the bad will, in contrast, is one that goes off on its own, that is out of harmony with the divine will.

Accordingly, in order to understand Thomas' account of suitability we must understand his view of the rational order that—insofar as men succeed in willing in agreement with it—makes men's acts morally good. This order is, of course, nothing but the objectively existing, cosmic means-end structure that has already been considered under the aspect of being. Considered, however, as a rule that ought to govern men's conduct, it is called "law."

LAW

As usual, Thomas began his discussion of law by drawing distinctions. Of the several kinds of law he distinguished, two are relevant to the present discussion— eternal law and natural law. The former is God's decree for the governance of the whole universe.

> Just as in every artificer there pre-exists an exemplar of the things that are made by his art, so too in every governor there must pre-exist the exemplar of the order of those things that are to be done by those who are subject to his government. And just as the exemplar of the things yet to be made by an art is called the art or model of the products of that art, so, too, the exemplar in him who governs the acts of his subjects bears the character of a law. . . . Therefore, just as the exemplar of the divine wisdom, inasmuch as all things are created by it, has the character of an art, a model or an idea, so the exemplar of divine wisdom, as moving all things to their due end, bears the character of law. Accordingly, the eternal law is nothing else than the exemplar of divine wisdom, as directing all actions and move-ments.[x]

All things obey the eternal law, for the pattern of their behavior (the rising of flames, the falling of stones) is nothing but a reflection of this law. Man, however, is as usual more complex than other creatures. Whereas all other things, being bereft of reason, obey the eternal law unknowingly, man has in him a power by which he knows what he is doing. He recognizes the dictates of eternal law and experiences its compulsions as articulate commands. Eternal law as experienced by rational creatures is called "natural law."[y]

The most fundamental precept of natural law, according to Thomas, is to promote good and to avoid evil. To most people today this seems a high-sounding but empty generality. However, for Thomas it was but another application of the basic metaphysical proposition that all being is good and that, accordingly, every substance seeks what fulfills itself and preserves its being. To say that the first precept of natural law is self-preservation should not be understood, of course, as implying that one has a right to build up oneself at the expense of others. Here, as elsewhere with Thomas, egoism, which from a metaphysical point of view may be taken as a primary motif of this philosophy, is limited by the generic notion of form. What one has a right to fulfill is not the particularity of the self, but its generic, formal properties; what natural law looks to is not the individual, but the common, good. Hence a king, for instance, should not take this precept as a justification for self-aggrandizement at the expense of his subjects; rather, he should see it as a command to promote the good of all.

Other, more specific precepts of natural law follow from a consideration of human nature. In man, the general precept to preserve one's life acquires content in rules—rules about sexual intercourse, about the education of offspring, about communal living generally. For instance, if we take account both of what we know about the nature of human nature, that is, the form "man," and of the basic precept to fulfill this form, we can deduce (according to Thomas) a rule to the effect that we ought to avoid offending those among whom we live.

DUTY

This conception brought Thomas to the notion of obligation. As has frequently been pointed out, one of the chief distinctions between the classical and the medieval minds was the absence in the former and the primacy for the latter of the concept of duty. In the classical view, since virtue is knowledge, any failure to achieve goodness is essentially a deficiency in understanding. But Christianity, in introducing the idea of an omnipotent sovereign, inevitably shifted the emphasis from a problem about knowledge to a problem about will. For the Christian, the good consists not so much in realizing a state of affairs as in obeying God's commands. Of course, before men can do His will, they must know it. But about this, Thomas held, there is no great difficulty: The precepts of natural law are "imprinted" on men's minds.[13] Unfortunately, the fact that we know what God commands does not necessarily mean that we do it. Thus, for the Christian, the central problem of ethics is the weakness of our free, human wills. Flames rise—naturally; stones fall—naturally. Inanimate and irrational substances, in a word, obey the dictates of eternal law automatically, without knowing that they do so, and are therefore neither moral nor immoral. Men, in return for the gift of knowledge, have the burden of responsibility. Hence the primacy in Christian ethics of duty.

One important qualification must be made at this point. It is true that the

---

13 Thomas did not, of course, hold that men know the whole of the eternal law (to claim that they do would be to make the fantastic assertion that men understand the working of the universe in all its detail), but he did maintain that they know more or less clearly the part of it that applies to them.

primary problem in ethics is a failure of human will, but Thomas recognized that there is also a cognitive aspect to men's moral failures. Though conscience informs us of what we ought to do (that is, reveals the precepts of natural law and even indicates how they apply in concrete situations), human reason is fallible, conscience occasionally errs. What is to be said of a man who, by following the dictates of his conscience, does something that is actually at variance with divine law? We must not, Thomas held, demand more than that a man do what he honestly thinks is right. If we do something thinking it to be against reason, we sin—whether or not our act is really in accordance with the dictates of reason. Conversely, if we do something thinking it to be right (that is, suitable), we do not sin—even if our act is not suitable. Thomas' way of putting this was to say that "erring reason binds. . . . Every will at variance with reason, whether right or erring, is always evil."[14] This was his formulation, in philosophical terms, of Jesus' preference for the spirit over the letter.

VIRTUE AND DISPOSITION

Men have a duty, then, to obey natural law; or, more precisely, they have a duty to obey the dictates of their own consciences as interpretations of natural law. But this is not yet the sum of morality. It is not enough to do what we should and to do it because we see that we should. We must do the right act from a certain disposition. This requirement merely extends the notion of motive by treating it as an outgrowth of character.

Surely Thomas is correct here. A man might possibly be moved by a sudden impulse—let us say a particularly pathetic appeal—to perform an act of alms-giving. Since internal and external objects and circumstances are all suitable, some people might call the act morally good. But any assessment that considers the act as an atomic, isolated fact is extremely artificial. We need to inquire, before we praise his act, whether this man has a disposition to give alms or whether he has a disposition to look the other way and gave alms on this occasion only because of the especially pathetic appeal. In a word, the man who gives alms at this moment has a past that must be taken into account in assessing the moral value of each of his acts. The way the past operates is through his disposition, or, as we might say, his character. A character is not something born with a man, ready-made; it develops in and through conduct, and as it develops it alters the conduct that develops it. A man develops a charitable character through giving alms, and this character in turn affects what he does and how he does it. Such a man does not have to wait for a particularly pathetic appeal; for him, the charitable motive, produced as it were by successive acts of giving, lies ready to hand and operates on each new occasion.

14 As an illustration of this thesis Thomas chose the most dramatic case possible. Actually, of course, belief in Christ is necessary to salvation; nevertheless, if someone happened honestly to believe otherwise, he would do wrong in becoming a Christian. (See *Summa Theologica*, Pt. I–II, Ques. 19, Art. 5, Ans.)

For this reason, Thomas rightly maintained, it is not enough to act from a certain motive; we must act from a certain disposition as well. A morally good (or virtuous) disposition is one that disposes us to conduct that conforms to right reason; a morally bad (or vicious) disposition is one that disposes us to conduct that conflicts with right reason. This is why a charitable disposition, for instance, is virtuous—it disposes us to give alms, that is, to act in conformity with right reason.[15] On the other hand, a disposition to drink excessively is vicious, because it tends to produce conduct that conflicts with right reason—the wine-bibber is likely to purchase liquor for himself instead of giving alms to the poor.[16]

INTELLECTUAL AND MORAL VIRTUES

The virtues, then, are simply dispositions to act in accordance with the precepts of natural law. In conformity with his Aristotelian model, Thomas classified the virtues as intellectual and moral. The former "perfect the speculative intellect for the consideration of truth"; the latter "perfect the appetitive part of the soul by directing it to the good of reason."[z] To each passion of the appetitive part of the soul there corresponds a virtue—temperance is the virtue of such passions as hunger and sexual desire; fortitude is the virtue of such passions as fear and daring; magnanimity, of hope and despair; meekness, of anger; and so on.

Still following Aristotle, Thomas held that virtue is always a mean between "too much" and "too little." But whereas Aristotle, with his more empirical bent, had reached this conclusion by generalizing from particular moral judgments, Thomas characteristically sought to deduce it from the concept of suitability. Consider, for instance, the virtue of fortitude, which is a disposition about when it is suitable to be fearful and when it is suitable to be daring. Now, the concept of suitability takes us back to the notion of law—of reason as a rule and measure. And a rule is something to which our conduct can fail to conform because of either an excess or a deficiency in measure. Virtue as a disposition to conform to the rule is thus a mean between going beyond or falling short of what is commanded, that is, of what is suitable.

ASCETIC VIRTUES

But what is to be said of the typically Christian virtues of poverty and chastity? Can they be held to conform to the Aristotelian pattern of the mean?

---

15 Of course, a disposition does nothing more than *dispose* us to act in a certain way, that is, give us an initial orientation toward the kind of act in question—in this case, almsgiving. Since in certain circumstances almsgiving will not be in accordance with right reason, we require, besides the disposition, conscience—that is, the application of the precepts of natural law to this particular case of almsgiving with its particular circumstances.

16 "The evil of drunkenness and excessive drink consists in a falling away from the order of reason"—*Summa Theologica*, Pt. I-II, Ques. 55, Art. 3, Reply Obj. 2.

Thomas knew that St. Francis and many other pious Christians who took Jesus' precepts literally insisted that the Christian ideal was an extreme—complete chastity, utter poverty. Nothing more strikingly indicates the way in which Thomas effected a real synthesis of classical and Christian views than the vigor with which, in opposition to such ascetic otherworldliness, he asserted the ideal of balance and moderation—even with respect to the specifically Christian virtues. Poverty, he maintained, is no more a good in itself than is wealth. Each of these states has its snares and pitfalls; each, its opportunities for virtue and achievement.

> In order to elucidate the truth about what we have been saying, we must form our judgement of poverty, by considering riches. External riches are necessary for the good of virtue: since by them we support the body, and help others. Now, things directed to an end must take their goodness from that end. Consequently external riches must be a good of man; not his chief, but, as it were, his secondary, good: because the end is a good principally; and other things, according as they are directed to the end. [But if] they hinder the practice of virtue, they are no longer to be reckoned as a good but as an evil. Hence it happens that the possession of riches is good for some who use them for virtue: while to others it is an evil, because they are withdrawn thereby from virtue, through being either too anxious about them, or too much attached to them, or self-conceited about them. . . .
>
> Man is formed of a nature both spiritual and corporal. Wherefore, according to the divine ordinance, it is necessary that man both perform actions of the body, and attend to the things of the soul: and he is the more perfect, the more he attends to spiritual things: yet man's perfection does not depend on his performing no actions of the body; because, since the actions of the body are directed to what is needful for the maintenance of life, if a man omit them, he neglects his life, which everyone is bound to maintain. Now a man is a fool and tempts God, if he does nothing himself and looks to God to provide him with those things to which he can help himself by his own action. . . . Therefore man must not expect that God will provide for him, without his doing any action whereby he is able to provide for himself: for this is contrary to the divine ordinance and goodness.[a]

Thomas was too good a churchman, of course, to deny that those in holy orders should follow a much more rigorous rule than that appropriate for the laity. But he insisted, first, that even those taking special vows should be careful to avoid excessive otherworldliness and, second, that it does not follow from the fact that it is good for some to take vows and live ascetically that those who do not do so are morally inferior. On the contrary, the principle of division of labor suggests not only that some should specialize in building houses and others in tending flocks, but that some should be busy about temporal things while others are busy about spiritual things. The good of the whole community depends, indeed, on a distribution of effort between spiritual and temporal affairs—on there being "some who attend to the act of procreation, and others who abstain therefrom and give themselves to contemplation."[b]

THEOLOGICAL VIRTUES

So far we have considered Thomas' discussion of the natural virtues, which are the perfection of the natural man—fortitude, justice, friendship, science, and so on. Men are social animals and delight in the society of their fellows; friendship, insofar as it makes this kind of relation possible, is therefore a human good. Men are rational creatures and delight in knowledge; science, insofar as it is an attitude or disposition that aims at, and results in, knowledge, is a human good. But man is more than a natural being, and it is clear that the virtuous dispositions just enumerated will not perfect our highest nature nor produce the beatitude that is our final end. For the realization of our supernatural end, other dispositions are required. These Thomas called the "theological virtues."

> Man is perfected by virtue for those actions by which he is directed to happiness, as was explained above. Now man's happiness or felicity is twofold, as was also stated above. One is proportioned to human nature, a happiness, namely, which man can obtain by means of the principles of his nature. The other is a happiness surpassing man's nature, and which man can obtain by the power of God alone, by a kind of participation of the Godhead; and thus it is written (2 *Pet.* i. 4) that by Christ we are made *partakers of the divine nature.* And because such happiness surpasses the power of human nature, man's natural principles, which enable him to act well according to his power, do not suffice to direct man to this same happiness. Hence it is necessary for man to receive from God some additional principles, by which he may be directed to supernatural happiness, even as he is directed to his connatural end by means of his natural principles, albeit not without the divine assistance. Such principles are called *theological virtues.* They are so called, first, because their object is God, inasmuch as they direct us rightly to God; secondly, because they are infused in us by God alone; thirdly, because these virtues are not made known to us, save by divine revelation, contained in Holy Scripture. . . .
>
> [Since] these two [intellect and will] fall short of the order of supernatural happiness, . . . man needed to receive in addition something supernatural to direct him to a supernatural end. First, as regards the intellect, man receives certain supernatural principles, which are held by means of a divine light; and these are the things which are to be believed, about which is *faith.*—Secondly, the will is directed to this end, both as to the movement of intention which tends to that end as something attainable,—this pertains to *hope*—and as to a certain spiritual union, whereby the will is, in a way, transformed into that end—and this belongs to *charity.* For the appetite of a thing is naturally moved and tends towards its connatural end and this movement is due to a certain conformity of the thing with its end.[c]

That the theological virtues are faith, hope, and love[17] Thomas knew on the authority of St. Paul,[d] and from Thomas' point of view, any account of the moral life that failed to give primacy to these three virtues could not possibly be correct. But it was far from easy to incorporate this transcendental and mystical insight of Paul's into the framework of Thomas' Aristotelian metaphysics.

In the first place, none of the theological virtues involves a mean. Thus there is a radical difference between the love that is a natural virtue and the love that is a theological virtue. Each of the natural virtues is the right management of an appetite, which, after all, is nothing but a love for some sort of sense object. Hence all the natural virtues are concerned with love, and it was possible for Thomas to hold that his position conformed to Augustine's generic definition of virtue (that is, natural virtue) as "the order of love." Temperance, for instance, is concerned with the right ordering of our love for food and drink, and so on.

But the love St. Paul wrote about in his letter to the Corinthians is utterly different. Since it is love of God,

> . . . there is no sinning by excess. . . . Never can we love God as much as He ought to be loved, nor believe and hope in Him as much as we should. Much less, therefore, can there be excess in such things. Accordingly the good of such virtues does not consist in a mean, but increases the more we approach to the summit.[e]

In the second place, though the natural virtues, at least in some degree, can be acquired by our own efforts, the theological virtues are supernaturally induced and depend entirely on God's grace. Consider, first, the natural virtues. In calling them "natural," Thomas did not, of course, mean to imply that we are born temperate, courageous, and just. But he did hold that we are born with a potentiality for these virtues. This potentiality may or may not become actualized. Given a good education, given practice and discipline, the disposition to be temperate about eating and drinking will gradually develop and will become an operative force in our daily life. This much can and does happen without any special divine intervention. But even the man who has cultivated a generally temperate disposition cannot hope to avoid an occasional—and sometimes serious—lapse. Hence the perfect operation of even the natural virtues requires God's assistance.

Still more is God's grace required for the theological virtues, which are concerned, not with human powers, but with the divine nature. Love, for instance, depends on and is limited by knowledge; we cannot love what we do not know. There is no problem, of course, about coming to know that food and drink are goods; the only problem at this level is to order rightly our loves of food and drink. But since our natural knowledge of God is woefully deficient,

17 See pp. 46–47.

our natural love of Him is imperfect. Hence the theological virtue of love, insofar as we attain it at all, is supernaturally induced in us by God's grace.

Even though the theological virtues are thus radically different from the natural virtues, Thomas held that the former supplement (that is, "perfect") the latter rather than substituting for them. The natural virtues are at best only partial and inadequate fulfillments of our natures. It is true that they order our various earthly loves, but our natures cry out, not merely for the kind of satisfaction that comes from the right ordering of temporary and changing affections, but for an absolutely complete and absorbing love. And these qualifications can be met only by the love of God, the absolutely perfect object. Hence love of God is the perfection, the terminus, of all our earthly loves. The same conclusion can be reached by a different line of argument. Intellectual virtue lies in natural knowledge, but since natural knowledge is always incomplete, intellectual virtue is always partial. Accordingly, just as love of God perfects our earthly loves by presenting us with the perfect object of love, faith in God perfects our earthly knowledge by presenting us with the absolute and eternal truth that transcends the truths of reason.

Examination of the good under the aspect of act thus brought Thomas to the point he reached in his discussion of the good under the aspect of end. Though he defined morally good acts as those that promote man's moral end (that is, those that are the means to happiness), it is more exact to say that, in his view, the right ordering of our natural powers *is* natural happiness. His analysis of the moral act, in other words, was merely a description in more detail and in somewhat different language of what he had already set out in his description of the moral end.

The same cannot be said of the relation between the theological virtues and man's supernatural end. Since our supernatural end is not attainable in this life, it is not identical with the theological virtues, for they are attainable in this life providing that God induces them in us. Though the theological virtues are the gift of God's grace, they are, after all, dispositions of the natural man.[18] They are simply the psychological setting in which certain exalted acts of piety and love occur. What, then, is the relation between these divinely induced dispositions and our supernatural end? The dispositions are intimations we receive during this life of the happiness that awaits us after death if we are among the elect. These intimations consist in, first, a certain disposition, or attitude, toward those supernatural principles on which our natural knowledge rests—that is, faith; second, a disposition or attitude of confidence toward the eventual achievement of our supreme end—that is, hope; and, finally, some present measure of that final union with God—that is, love.

Thus, just as Thomas' physics passed over into theology at the point at which he considered the ultimate truth about the workings of the universe, so, in his

18 They are called "virtues" precisely because they are dispositions of the natural man. They are specifically "theological" because they are divinely induced, not naturally cultivated.

ethics, whether he was considering the matter under the aspect of end or of the aspect of act, he again reached theology.

Politics

For Thomas, as for Aristotle, politics completed ethics, for man was a social animal who could attain his natural good only in communities. But, according to Thomas, the state is not only the environment in which man's natural end can be brought to fulfillment; it is also an instrument by which man can be prepared for his supernatural end. It follows that political power is subordinate to theological power and that the state has a dual role.

DUAL ROLE OF THE STATE

First, the state has the negative, disciplinary function of exacting obedience to natural law on the part of those who do not heed the voice of conscience within them. Second, and more important, it has the positive, educative function of producing citizens whose conduct does not merely conform externally to the injunctions of natural law but flows from virtuous dispositions.

> As we have stated above, man has a natural aptitude for virtue; but the perfection of virtue must be acquired by man by means of some kind of training. . . . A man needs to receive this training from another, whereby to arrive at the perfection of virtue. And as to those young people who are inclined to acts of virtue by their good natural disposition, or by custom, or rather by the gift of God, paternal training suffices, which is by admonitions. But since some are found to be dissolute and prone to vice, and not easily amenable to words, it was necessary for such to be restrained from evil by force and fear, in order that, at least, they might desist from evil-doing, and leave others in peace, and that they themselves, by being habituated in this way, might be brought to do willingly what hitherto they did from fear, and thus become virtuous. Now this kind of training, which compels through fear of punishment, is the discipline of laws. Therefore, in order that man might have peace and virtue, it was necessary for laws to be framed; for, as the Philosopher [Aristotle] says, *as man is the most noble of animals if he be perfect in virtue, so he is the lowest of all, if he be severed from law and justice.* For man can use his reason to devise means of satisfying his lusts and evil passions, which other animals are unable to do. [f]

HUMAN, DIVINE, AND NATURAL LAW

The instrument by which the state performs both these functions is law. Because the law that governs states is decreed or legislated by men, Thomas called it "human law"; thus he distinguished it from divine law and natural law.[19] It is important to understand the relation in which human law stands to these more basic promulgations. Now, law in its most general sense is "nothing else but an ordinance of reason for the common good, promulgated by him who has the care of the community."[g] The whole universe is a community, and God, its creator, is also its sovereign. Just as, on a small scale, a king legislates for the good of all his people, so, on a universal scale, God legislates for the good of that cosmic community, the universe. The "laws" He promulgates are simply the ways in which this universe of individual substances behaves. It is divine law, for instance, that flames should rise, that stones should fall, and that the planets should turn about the earth. Conceived of as the body of divine decrees for the governance of this great community, law is simply the way in which the universe fulfills itself. And this same definition, without modification, applies equally well to those lesser communities called states. Here again, Thomas managed to unify a world that is today divided. Today, politics and physics are radically different sciences; for Thomas, a single definition served to formulate both.

Since Thomas defined natural law as divine law applied specifically to the human situation, it might seem that human law and natural law are identical. But here Thomas drew still another distinction. Natural law, as the basic mode of fulfillment of the form "man," is necessarily general. Because men live in communities varying widely in cultural maturity, climate, and geographical location, different codes of justice are needed to fulfill the general requirements of natural law. The function of the human ruler is to obtain the requisite local information, to formulate this as the minor premise of a practical syllogism, and to promulgate the conclusion of this syllogism in the form of a decree, or law, for the guidance of those living under these conditions. Thus, whereas natural law consists in generalities sufficiently broad to hold for the whole community of men, human law consists of relatively detailed decrees applying to those specific communities called states.

Human law, then, is distinguished from divine (and natural) law in two ways: (1) it applies to a lesser community, and (2) it is the articulate decree of a human agent, not simply a metaphysical mode in which the universe operates. But human regulations are *law* only when they are, as it were, the verbal expression of divine law. What makes such regulations law is not the fact that they issue from someone who claims (and is acknowledged) to be a ruler, but the fact that they implement divine law.

THE STATE ESSENTIALLY GOOD

These definitions led to a number of important conclusions. To begin with, they enabled Thomas to deny the old thesis, dating back to the days when

---

19 See pp. 264–65.

Christianity was a minority and a persecuted sect, that God instituted the state as a punishment for men's sins. It is true that the apparatus of laws, regulations, and sanctions that are necessary for the communal life are often irksome. It is also true that bad rulers cause suffering. But these defects should not blind us, Thomas held, to the essential goodness of the state. For the natural man can be satisfactorily fulfilled only by cooperation with others. There is ample evidence, he pointed out, that man's dependence on his fellows does not postdate Adam's fall and that his sociability is, as Aristotle maintained, a part of his nature. For instance, many animals are born with an intuitive knowledge of what is harmful to them and what is necessary to life. Since human beings largely lack instincts, they must learn what is harmful and what is useful. But no child can possibly acquire all this necessary knowledge on his own; he needs teachers and so must live in a group.

> This point is, further, most plainly evidenced by the fact that the use of speech is a prerogative proper to man. . . . Other animals, it is true, express their feelings to one another in a general way, as a dog may express anger by barking . . . . So man communicates with his kind more completely than any other animal known to be gregarious, such as the crane, the ant and the bee.[h]

Again, these considerations made it possible for Thomas to draw a firm distinction between slavery and political subordination, which Neoplatonizing theologians like Augustine had tended to lump together as punishments for sin. The former kind of subjection Thomas held to be wrong; the latter he held to be reasonable and proper, for it is the means by which that social animal, man, fulfills himself. If men are to live in communities, they cannot get on without authority to order their lives. But their ruler should aim at *their* good (principle of political dominion), not at his own (principle of slaveholding).

That communities require a directive principle follows from the general metaphysical thesis stated in the fifth proof of the existence of God.[20] Applied to the state, it runs as follows:

> If it is natural for man to live in the society of many, it is necessary that there exist among men some means by which the group may be governed. For where there are many men together, and each one is looking after his own interest, the group would be broken up and scattered unless there were also someone to take care of what appertains to the common weal.[i]

Thus Thomas returned to the notion, central to his conception of the state, of a ruler who promulgates laws, that is, ordinances of reason for the common good. As Aristotle pointed out, this ruler may be one, few, or many. To ask

20 See p. 218.

which is best is equivalent to asking whether it is more likely that one man or a few men or many men will promulgate rules that are truly laws. Though Thomas allowed that the rule of one, when perverted, is worst, he held that on the whole monarchy is best: "Now it is manifest that what is itself one can more efficaciously bring about unity than several: just as the most efficacious cause of heat is that which is by its nature hot. Therefore the rule of one man is more useful than the rule of many."[j]

IDEAL OF A LIMITED MONARCHY

That the king should be an absolute monarch does not follow, however, from the notion that the rule of one is best. Political absolutism was a notion quite foreign to Thomas—indeed, to men of the whole Middle Ages. One of the signs of modern times was the emergence of the concept of an unlimited sovereign power in society, in contrast to Thomas' ideal of a limited monarchy.

There are, in Thomas' view, a number of different limitations on royal power. First, it is directly concerned only with the natural man and his natural end. The establishment of conditions of peace and security in which the virtuous life can be pursued and the natural talents cultivated is the function of royal power. And just as man's natural end is subordinate to his supernatural end, so kings are subordinate to priests, who provide men with the guidance they must have in order to reach this higher end.

> It is not the ultimate end of an assembled multitude to live virtuously, but through virtuous living to attain to the possession of God. . . . Because a man does not attain [this] end . . . by human power, but by Divine power, . . . the task of leading him to that end does not pertain to human government but to divine. . . . Consequently, . . . kings must be subject to priests.[k]

A king is further limited, even in the area of secular power, by the fact that he is only the agent of the community. The question of whether the rule of one, few, or many is best is not a question about the ultimate source of political power, but simply a question about relative efficiency of administration. The advantage of monarchy lies in the fact that it is more efficient to vest "coercive power" in one than in many. Thus, in the *Summa Theologica*, Thomas said explicitly that political power resides either directly in "the whole people" or in "someone who is the vicegerent of the whole people."[l]

Though Thomas did not write in contractual terms about the relation between a king and his subjects, it is clear that he supposed at least a tacit contract limiting the king's authority to exist between them. The people raise up one man to do for them what they cannot do for themselves—to create peace and security; if he fails to do this, he has violated the contract and may be deposed. These conclusions follow directly from the nature of law as Thomas defined it. Since "law is an ordinance of reason for the common good," an unjust law does not bind, or, more precisely, an unjust decree is not law at all. The central idea here—that might does not make right—is a reflection at the level of politics of Thomas' basic metaphysical concepts. In his metaphysical theory, potentiality is the possibility of actuality; movement toward actuality is always guided by (one might as well say, "is under the authority of") form and therefore partakes in its very essence of the nature of law. But "potentiality" (in the language of metaphysics) is "power" (in the language of politics). Hence Thomas was saying that what sanctions the use of force to compel obedience is not merely the sovereign's possession of power (potentiality) but the end (form) that he has in view in using this power. Thus, whether it is a question of simple substances like stones or of complex organisms like the state, it is impossible to dissociate development from the concept of law and order: Form is everywhere the law and the order of change.

This also explains why, in Thomas' view, there is no need for an explicit contract between kings and subjects. The most fundamental relation in the universe, the relation between matter and form, is in essence a contract. And the conditions of life that obtain (or ought to obtain) in the state are nothing but a reflection, at this level of the hierarchy, of the basic pattern established by God for the whole universe of things. The notion of a formal contract became prominent in political theory only after the Thomistic world view was replaced by a metaphysics that repudiated this idea and substituted for it the concept of fact.

Still another conclusion that follows from Thomas' conception of law is that subjects have a right to rebel. Yet, though a ruler who violates natural law is a king (in law) no longer and so may be deposed, rebellion is at best a hazardous undertaking. Hence, according to Thomas, subjects will be well advised to pray to God for help rather than rely on their own arms. "But to deserve to secure this benefit from God, the people must desist from sin; because by divine permission wicked men receive power to rule as a punishment for sin. . . . Sin must therefore be done away with that the scourge of tyrants may cease."[m]

DEFICIENCIES IN THOMAS' POLITICAL THEORY

Finally, before leaving Thomas' political theory, we should consider a few deficiencies. Most of these result from the same excess of rationalism that caused difficulties in his psychology. In the first place, though Thomas defined the ruler as the source of law and though this is quite compatible with extensive and varied legislative activity on the part of the sovereign, Thomas did not think that legislation would occupy much of the ruler's time. Of course, in the slowly changing world of feudalism, there was not the obvious need that exists today to adjust old laws to new social and economic conditions. Nevertheless, medieval society was by no means static; quite enough change took place in the thirteenth century to make Thomas' theory unrealistic and inflexible even in his own day.

The truth is that his rationalistic bias led him to suppose that the ruler's role is simply to deduce the detailed application of the eternal principles of natural law to his particular society. Once a particular human law is so deduced—say, a statute forbidding murder is promulgated on the ground that this follows as a conclusion from the principle that one should do harm to no man—only the discovery of a logical fallacy somewhere in the syllogistic reasoning or some radical change in the conditions of life would warrant modification.

Further, Thomas' rationalism caused him to overemphasize the part played in holding human societies together, by the formal and explicit decrees of the sovereign, as compared with the part played by custom and tradition. Thus, in the *De Regimine Principum,* he contrasted the "natural instincts" that operate to combine animals into societies with the deliberate and self-conscious motivation that, so he believed, carries men into equivalent groupings. In part, this is simply a reflection of his exaggeration of the role of deliberation; in part, it is a consequence of the juridical bias that any political theory founded on the concept of natural law is likely to have.

Occasionally, however, there is in Thomas' writings a suggestion of a view that would be regarded today as more plausible.

> Now just as the human reason and will, in practical matters, may be made manifest by speech, so they may be made known by deeds; for evidently a man chooses as good that which he carries into execution. But it is evident that, by human speech, law can be both changed and set forth, in so far as it manifests the interior movement and thought of human reason. Therefore by actions also, especially if they be repeated, so as to make a custom, law can be changed and set forth; and furthermore something can be established which obtains the force of law, in so far as, by repeated external actions, the inward movement of the will and the conceptions of the reason are most revealingly declared. For when a thing is done again and again, it seems to proceed from a deliberate judgment of reason. Accordingly, custom has the force of a law, abolishes law, and is the interpreter of law.[n]

Usually Thomas regarded the king, once he is chosen by the people, as the sole source of human law in his state; it is he who decides on the legislation that makes natural law applicable to such-and-such particular circumstances. But any recognition that men are creatures of habit and that custom plays an important role in the regulation of group living leads to quite a different conception of the source of human law. From this point of view, the traditions of the people have an even higher authority than the king's decrees.[21] Worked

---

21 This is exemplified most clearly when a foreign dynasty takes over a going concern whose customs, though different from those of the new rulers, the new king must respect. It is significant in this connection that in the *De Regimine Principum* Thomas for the most part ignored this kind of case (which is certainly the most usual) and devoted his attention to the procedure to be followed in founding new states. This type of situation was easier for him since, in a new state, there are no prior traditions to restrict the king's right to interpret natural law.

out to its logical conclusion, this view would involve a kind of restriction on kingly power that natural law theories do not allow. It cannot be said, however, that Thomas developed these conclusions in any detail or that he made any serious attempt to reconcile the two concepts.

Grace, Predestination, and the Moral Life

The picture of man that has emerged in our study of Thomas' ethics and politics shows him as a twofold creature. On the one hand, he is a rational animal capable of choosing his ends and acting on his choices. The good life at this level consists in developing certain moral and intellectual virtues—habitual dispositions by which the potentialities of the natural man are brought to actuality. On the other hand, as an immortal soul made in God's image, man has a higher end, beatitude. This end, which depends not on ourselves but on God, is not to be achieved in this life. We can approach it, however, by way of the three theological virtues, which may be infused in us by God's grace. These two ends, the natural and the supernatural, are not in any sense rivals. Attainment of the former, which is in our power, is the basis for attainment of the latter, which is simply the former carried to a higher degree.

Though not everyone today will agree with it, this theory has a wonderful logical cohesion resulting from the systematic application of basic metaphysical concepts to the interpretation of moral experience. For a Christian philosopher, however, morality passes over into religion. And, since for a Catholic philosopher religious truth is determined by dogma, it was essential for Thomas that his ethical theory comport not only with moral experience but also with theology. Though this is an extremely delicate question about which there will be many opinions, it would appear that Thomas' ethical theory runs afoul of certain fundamental dogmas. The contradictions in this theory cluster around Thomas' account of free will.

FREE WILL

It is easy to understand why Thomas considered freedom of the will to be essential to morality. As he said,

> If the will were deprived of freedom, . . . no praise would be given to human virtue; since virtue would be of no account if man acted not freely: there would be no justice in rewarding or punishing, if man were not free in acting well or ill: and there would be no prudence in taking advice, which would be of no use if things occurred of necessity. . . .
>
> Man has free choice, or otherwise counsels, exhortations, commands, prohibitions, rewards and punishments would be in vain.[o]

It was precisely because Thomas realized that without human freedom God's punishment of man would be unjust that he defined the will as an unmoved mover, timeless and self-caused. Unless the act of will is such a free, timeless act, his ethical theory falls to the ground.[22] Unfortunately for Thomas, it appears that this concept of freedom is incompatible with the dogmas of predestination and grace.

PREDESTINATION

Predestination is the name for the particular aspect of God's providence that is concerned with man's supreme end. There are in God's mind, as we have seen, exemplars of everything that will happen to everything in the universe. The exemplar of man's direction to the eternal life is called providence. Thus, predestination is a part of providence. Correspondingly, "reprobation" is that exemplar by which God abandons some men to sin and assigns eternal punishment as their lot. As regards reprobation, Thomas was careful to insist that God's providence is not the *cause* of the sin of these men in the way in which it is the cause of other men's virtue. God merely "abandons them," that is, leaves them in the corruption into which they have fallen as a result of Adam's original disobedience. God does not specifically damn them; they are already damned by their own sins. He merely does not intervene to save them.[p]

But this technical distinction hardly extricates Thomas from the difficulty felt by the Pelagians and the Manichees. Failure to intervene when intervention could prevent a calamity is as morally reprehensible as bringing on a calamity by positive action. A man who sits idly by while someone drowns cannot excuse himself on the grounds that it was not he who caused the catastrophe, but the drowning man, by having failed to learn to swim.[23]

Even if we pass over this old problem, we are faced with the puzzle of why God condemns some to damnation and predestines others to salvation. As it stands, this question is ambiguous. If we mean to ask, "Why is it that all cannot be saved?" we already know Thomas' answer.

> The reason for the predestination of some, and reprobation of others, must be sought in the goodness of God. . . . Now it is necessary that God's goodness, which in itself is one and simple, should be manifested in many ways

22 It does not follow, of course, that an ethical theory based on some kind of freedom other than that of a timeless act would necessarily be untrue.

23 This excuse for not giving aid is especially unsatisfactory since, according to Christian doctrine, the drowning man has inherited his natatorial deficiency from his great-great- . . . grandfather Adam (who could once swim but subsequently lost the art). Because of this inherited deficiency, the drowning man *could* not have learned to swim. Indeed, to make matters worse, it turns out, as we shall see, that the same inherited deficiency made it impossible for the drowning man even to begin to want to try to learn to swim. But God, had He chosen to do so, could have induced the man in the water to learn to swim despite all these disabilities—God is, as it were, the man sitting on the bank who disclaims all responsibility, for rescue now as well as for educative measures earlier.

> in His creation; because creatures in themselves cannot attain to the simplicity of God. Thus it is that for the completion of the universe there are required diverse grades of being, of which some hold a high and some a low place in the universe. That this multiformity of grades may be preserved in things, God allows some evils, lest many good things should be hindered, as was said above. Let us then consider the whole of the human race as we consider the whole universe. God has willed to manifest His goodness in men: in respect to those whom He predestines, by means of His mercy, in sparing them; and in respect to others, whom he reprobates, by means of His justice, in punishing them. This is the reason why God elects some and rejects others.q

That some must be damned thus follows from the general metaphysical consideration that the universe must contain all possible grades of being. Accordingly, whether Thomas' way of dealing with the apparent immorality of predestination will satisfy a modern reader depends on whether this reader accepts the basic premises of Thomistic metaphysics.

However, when we ask why some are reprobated to damnation, it may be that we are raising a different point. We may mean to ask, "Why were just these particular men selected for salvation, these others for damnation?" To this question, Thomas could make no satisfactory answer. He could only reply that, since God does nothing arbitrarily, He had His reasons for selecting as He did. Further, we must believe that His decisions were completely His own—that salvation is not a debt God owes men or a reward He gives them for merit.

> Predestination is not anything in the predestined, but only in the person who predestines. [It] depends upon the simple will of God; just as from the simple will of the artificer it depends that this stone is in this part of the wall, and that in another; although the plan requires that some stone should be in this place, and some other in that place.r

GRACE

This brings us to grace, which is even more difficult to reconcile with free will than is predestination. Grace is merely the operation of providence. It is the device by which, as it were, God executes the exemplar of predestination. (Simply by withholding it, He executes the exemplar of reprobation.) With scholastic thoroughness Thomas analyzed grace into sanctifying grace and gratuitous grace, operating and cooperating, prevenient and subsequent, and so on. Into all these subtleties it is not necessary to follow him, but some of his basic distinctions must be noted in order to understand the difficulties he faced.

To begin with, dogma required Thomas to distinguish between man's condition before and after the Fall. Before his fall, Adam had a power of acting virtuously—which Thomas interpreted as a power of cultivating the moral virtues by acting in accordance with God's commandments. That is to say, a power of choice, of following or abstaining from following God's law, was as natural to pre-Fall man as hearing and seeing are natural to post-Fall man. Adam must have had this power because the Fall is comprehensible only as a punishment for sin; Adam must, therefore, have freely chosen the course he followed.

The punishment for Adam's sin was not only mortality, but also the corruption of that integral nature into which he had been born and the corresponding loss of his natural power of free choice. As inheritors of Adam's corruption, we are all sick men; and just as a man weakened by bodily illness cannot do many things that a well man can do, a man with a corrupted moral nature cannot do many things that a man with an integral nature can do. Of course, men are not *totally* corrupted by sin; there are still some "particular goods" that they can perform by their natural endowments and without external assistance, "such as to build dwellings, plant vineyards and the like." But there are many more activities natural to man, activities that pre-Fall Adam could and did do, of which men are no longer capable. In particular, men are now incapable of the cultivation of the virtues that was a part of the nature of integral man. Unlike Adam, who could have avoided sin *had he so chosen*,[24] we cannot avoid sin.[25]

> In the state of integral nature man referred the love of himself and of all other things to the love of God as to its end; and thus he loved God more than himself and above all things. But in the state of corrupted nature man falls short of this in the appetite of his rational will, which, unless it be cured by God's grace, follows its private good, because of the corruption of nature.[s]

To sum up the situation of post-Fall man, it can be said that, left to our own devices, we would all be doomed because of our sin and corruption to the punishment of eternal damnation. God, however, has chosen to elect a certain number to salvation. On these, accordingly, he bestows His gratuitous gift of grace; the others He simply abandons to their fate. How, then, does grace operate in those who are elected to salvation? Grace, it turns out, operates in five distinct stages in the corrupted soul of post-Fall man. "Of these, the first is, to heal the soul; the second, to desire good; the third, to carry into effect the good proposed; the fourth, to persevere in good; the fifth, to reach glory."[t] In other words, post-Fall man needs grace not only to acquire the virtuous dispositions Thomas described in his treatise on morals, but also to put these dispositions, once acquired, into action in specific situations. Indeed, even the first turning of the

---

24 Even the pre-Fall Adam required God's help to "sustain him in the good" (*Summa Theologica*, Pt. I–II, Ques. 109, Art. 8). This raises the question of whether God withdrew His sustaining help. If He did not, how did Adam come to sin? If He did, how can Adam be blamed for his lapse?

25 "Nor in the state of corrupted nature can man fulfill all the commandments of the Law without grace" (*Summa Theologica*, Pt. I–II, Ques. 109, Art. 4, Ans.). "Man by himself can in no way rise from sin without the help of grace" (*Ibid.*, Art. 7, Ans.). So, too, "grace is prior to virtue" (*Ibid.*, Ques. 110, Art. 4).

corrupted soul as it longs for change, even the striving to strive for virtue, is a product of grace and has therefore to wait on God's will.

> Now to prepare oneself for grace is, as it were, to be turned to God; just as whoever has his eyes turned away from the light of the sun prepares himself to receive the sun's light, by turning his eyes towards the sun.[26] Hence it is clear that man cannot prepare himself to receive the light of grace except by the gratuitious help of God moving him inwardly. . . .
> Every prepartion in man must be by the help of God moving the soul to good. And thus even the good movement of free choice, whereby anyone is prepared for receiving the gift of grace, is an act of free choice moved by God.[u]

This drastic conclusion about man's utter helplessness without grace follows inevitably from the doctrine of predestination: "Predestination is not anything in the predestined, by only in the person who predestines." Accordingly, there can be nothing in the soul that merits grace. Even the first, tiniest act of virtue that seems to merit grace is but the product of a prior act of grace.

CONFLICT WITH THOMAS' ETHICS

Dogmatic considerations, it seems, thus invalidate the basic presuppositions of Thomas' treatises on morals and politics. When Thomas was discussing these subjects, he assumed that man (and, of course, he was thinking of post-Fall man) has in him a capacity to become virtuous—a potentiality that can be developed by his own acts and by the education given him by his family and his community. Thomas' whole intent in these sections of the *Summa* was practical—to teach men how to be good. And this implies that goodness (that is, the goodness of the natural man) is in the natural man's power. But the exigencies of dogma clearly required Thomas to hold that the life of virtue was in man's power only before the Fall. Since the Fall, and as a result of Adam's sin, it has not been in man's power. Since the Fall, and unless grace intervenes, man inevitably pursues "false images of good."

But if sin is inevitable without God's grace—if, without grace men cannot even begin to want to strive to rise above their present condition—it is difficult to see how men can be responsible for their wrongdoing. Moreover, if this theological doctrine is accepted, how can it be held that everything naturally seeks its good and that this good is likeness to God? Post-Fall man, it would seem, is an exception to Thomas' most fundamental metaphysical concept.

And, finally, not only does the dogma of grace lead to the conclusion that the life of earthly virtue is no longer in man's power, but it makes meaningless

---

26 [In Plato's myth of the cave, which the language here suggests that Thomas was echoing, the turning is accomplished by the help of a fellow man. For the Greeks, one may say, education (a social process) played the role that grace plays for the Christians—AUTHOR.]

the notion that this life is the basis for man's supernatural end. In his treatises on ethics and politics, Thomas assumed that man's earthly end and his supernatural end are connected by a rationale; he intended his account of the sciences of ethics and politics to be a detailed exposition of this rationale. Ethics tells us how to construct our individual lives here on earth in such a way that their outcome will be beatitude; politics tells us how to organize the state in such a way that its citizens will develop the moral virtues that lead to salvation. But it follows from the dogma of grace that if we are elected, our salvation is inevitable, whereas if we are not elected, we cannot escape damnation. Hence the noble, practical purpose of the *Summa* is thwarted.

Thomas naturally sought to avoid these conclusions and to bridge the gap between his treatises on morals and politics and the requirements of dogma. In spite of the fact that the will is moved by God's grace and, being so moved, is carried infallibly toward salvation, he insisted that it is free. It is true, he said, that

> . . . the predestined must necessarily be saved, yet by a conditional necessity, which does not do away with the liberty of choice. . . .
>
> Man's turning to God is by free choice; and thus man is bidden to turn himself to God. But free choice can be turned to God only when God turns it. . . . It is the part of man to prepare his soul, since he does this by his free choice. And yet he does not do this without the help of God moving him. . . . Even the good movement of free choice, whereby anyone is prepared for receiving the gift of grace, is an act of free choice moved by God. . . . Man's preparation for grace is from God, as mover, and from free choice, as moved.[v]

Clearly, all these formulas appeal to dual causality, but even if that concept were generally acceptable, it would be of no help to Thomas here. Man and God, Thomas said, both cause something to happen, in the way in which, in *Macbeth*, the doctor's news and the larger state of affairs we call the play both cause Macbeth's outburst.[27] But this notion provides no answer to the problem of human freedom. For here it is not a question of *who* causes something, but a question of *how* it is caused. Even if we allow that the doctor, along with Shakespeare, in some sense causes the outburst, it remains to be asked whether he freely causes it—that is, whether the doctor could have chosen otherwise. Granting that dual efficacy occurs, we have yet to inquire whether one of the two causes is free. As soon as the question is put in this form, it is plain that the double-efficacy doctrine, instead of helping Thomas out of this difficulty, plunges him deeper into it. For this doctrine teaches that what every individual does is, after all, part of a whole and conditioned by that whole, in the way in which what the doctor (or Macbeth) does is determined by the play as a

27 See p. 237, n. 10.

whole. The doctrine of double efficacy, if it means anything at all, means that a part of a whole is *never* free to be otherwise.

Fortunately for Thomas' peace of mind, an ambiguity in his concept of freedom (already discussed in connection with his psychology) shielded him from seeing this fatal weakness. Some of the time he used "to be free" to mean "to be an unmoved mover," but some of the time he used it to mean "to be free from coercion." Now "freedom from coercion" is compatible with predestination but is insufficient to account for the reality of the moral life, whereas "freedom of an unmoved mover" is required to account for the reality of the moral life but is incompatible with predestination. The fact that Thomas failed to distinguish clearly between these two senses of freedom lent his theory a specious plausibility. When he was dealing with the difficulties of predestination he could talk about freedom from coercion, and when he was thinking of the moral struggle he could talk about the freedom of an unmoved mover.

That freedom from coercion is compatible with predestination is easily shown, for this kind of freedom means merely that such-and-such a causal sequence passes through a means-end structure, it being a matter of indifference how such a structure itself is caused. But morality and responsibility require, Thomas held, not merely *that* a volition occur, but that the self have control over the body's behavior, and this control, he thought, is that of an unmoved mover. Freedom in this sense is clearly incompatible with the double-efficacy doctrine, which Thomas supposed to be the key to the puzzle of free will. For double efficacy is meaningful only when the finite cause is a part of a larger system (for example, when the doctor's news is a part of the whole system that we call the play). But to call man's will an unmoved mover is to take man outside the system. Then it is no longer a matter of "both-and," but a matter of "either-or." We cannot say, for instance, that both Shakespeare and Bacon wrote *Macbeth*, as we can say that both the doctor and the play as a whole caused Macbeth's outburst. Since Shakespeare and Bacon are mutually independent agents, we must say either that Shakespeare wrote the play or that Bacon wrote it. Similarly, freedom in the sense of the will's being an unmoved mover would make man independent of God. Since this cannot be tolerated for dogmatic reasons, it is necessary to abandon the freedom of an unmoved mover and, with it, the possibility of man's being a free and responsible agent.

It is easy to see why Thomas struggled against the implications of the doctrine of predestination. Today we readily sympathize with his desire to give man a share in the working out of his destiny, with his emphasis on the possibility of self-improvement and accomplishment, and with his generally optimistic and melioristic attitude toward man and his affairs.[28] But it must be allowed that,

28 It is a paradox of cultural history that in the age of the Renaissance, when mankind was visibly standing on the threshold of an era of enormous accomplishment, religion should have chosen to turn its back on this affirmation of human initiative and return to the primitive Church's view of man as helpless and hopeless.

however appealing such an optimistic attitude may be, it was not justified logically as long as Thomas insisted at the same time on the dogmas of predestination and grace.

Conclusion

Though, unlike most earlier philosophical systems, Thomism survives today as a living philosophy, not many people outside the Roman Church are likely to feel much sympathy with Thomas' views. Nevertheless, even his most bitter opponents should not overlook the important cultural role his theory played. Perhaps the most important aspects of this cultural role were, first, the ideal of an all-embracing "summa" of human knowledge and, second, Thomas' success (relative, of course, to the knowledge at his disposal) in actually carrying out this vast project. For, although there are certain conflicts between reason and dogma in Thomas' theory, as we have seen, it must be allowed that, to a great extent, the *Summa Theologica* is a logically cohesive body of propositions encompassing the whole range of medieval knowledge.

No earlier thinker came close to, and few even attempted, such an achievement. Plato, for instance, wrote a number of dialogues in which, with the prodigality of genius, he flung off numerous brilliant—but not always consistent —ideas. When these ideas conflict, it is not easy to say which represent Plato the philosopher and which Plato the dramatic artist. Nor does the difficulty arise merely from the dialogue form in which he wrote. As far as modern commentators can tell, Plato never reached, or at least never wrote down, a view that completely satisfied him. Believing as he did that it is impossible to communicate about matters of real philosophical importance in writing, he ruled out the possibility of making a formal philosophical synthesis at the very start.

Aristotle, for his part, composed a number of separate treatises on a variety of subjects. In these, the reader can trace the way he used his master concepts— matter and form, potentiality and actuality, for instance—as the basis for his treatments of the various special sciences. But though there is in Aristotle the basis for a synoptic world view, he himself did not work out such a view.

What was implicit in Aristotle became explicit in Thomas. Doubtless Thomas' belief in a universal-creative God disposed him to believe in the possibility of a single, universal science. But earlier Christian thinkers had believed in a universal-creative God. Why was Thomas the first to work out a universal, synoptic science? It is not merely that he was abler than the rest. Had he lived even a century earlier, it is inconceivable that he would have written the *Summa.* The West had first to have access to Aristotle; it had also to experience the intellectual renaissance described in Chapter 5. And, perhaps most important, it had to conceive the idea of a university. For a medieval university was simply the concrete embodiment of the Thomistic *Summa,* or, put the other way around, the *Summa* was simply the intellectualized and abstract reflection of the university. The various faculties of the medieval university were no more the independent, sovereign fields of learning that the special sciences are today than were the European nations of the Middle Ages the national territorial states of modern times. In the Middle Ages, just as national identities were not yet frozen, just as Europe was not yet merely a collection of separate nations but was still dominated by a sense of its own unity as Christendom, so in the field of education the separate faculties were not concerned with wholly separate bodies of knowledge but rather with the whole body of knowledge that constituted the heritage of Western man.

Since Thomas' day the notion of an all-embracing world view has remained before philosophy as an ideal. But though many such systems have been proposed, especially in the nineteenth century, none has come close to winning the acceptance that the Thomastic scheme once attained. If the enormous expansion of knowledge has made the construction of a synoptic world view increasingly difficult, many people would say that the fragmentation of experience accompanying this expansion has made achievement of some sort of synthesis all the more desirable.

The fragmentation of modern culture is symbolized in the modern university, which is merely an artificial grouping of special schools. Such unity as exists is a matter of buildings and physical "plant," or, perhaps, of "school spirit," rather than, as in the medieval university, a matter of intellectual kinship and shared love of God. The problem of the modern university is no different from the problem of modern society—how to replace cultural pluralism with some sort of cultural unity.

Any such synthesis would have to differ radically, both in detail and in spirit, from that achieved in the Middle Ages. For a modern synthesis would have to include vast ranges of experience completely foreign to Thomas' basic assumptions. Hence it is vain to hope (as some still fondly do) for a return to Thomism. Nevertheless, from the point of view of the history (and, perhaps, the future) of culture, the study of Thomism ought to have considerable interest. The Middle Ages achieved a level of cultural integration that has since eluded the West, and insofar as it is meaningful to attribute any such achievement to a single individual, it can be said that the Middle Ages owed its cultural unity to Thomas.

CHAPTER 8

The End of
the Middle Ages

Inhibitions of Orthodoxy

Though, as has been said, Thomas' relation, functionally, to medieval thought was roughly equivalent to that of Plato and Aristotle with respect to classical thought, the post-Thomas phase of medieval thought differed in many respects from the post-Aristotle phase of classical thought. For one thing, there was (as we shall shortly see) far more cultural change in the two centuries immediately following Thomas' death than in, say, the two centuries preceding his birth—and still more than in the two centuries following the death of Aristotle. Between 1300 and 1500, social, economic, and political developments drastically altered almost every phase of European life, and soon afterward scientific developments and the application of technology to production further increased the tempo of change. These changes required a more rapid and flexible adjustment than the medieval mind was capable of making. The result was the rapid overthrow of the medieval scheme.

One great reason for the age's failure to respond to the need for flexibility was the existence of the Church with its ideal of orthodoxy. This brings us to another difference between the closing periods of classical and medieval thought. Late classical thought was free to develop within the framework of the dominant conceptual scheme, unrestrained by anything except its sense of the intellectual fitness of that scheme. It was possible, therefore, for it to adjust itself to the great shift from the city-state to the imperial pattern, and to the other cultural changes that occurred. But as soon as the Middle Ages achieved its philosophical climax, the new conceptual scheme became frozen in a rigid orthodoxy. Since any major change inside the dominant system thus became impossible, development in philosophical thought had to take place outside the medieval world view.

This does not mean, of course, that there was not prolonged and vigorous debate regarding many aspects of the Thomistic synthesis. Many Christian thinkers felt, for instance, that Thomas had failed to do justice to the Augustinian point of view, and efforts were made, as we shall see, to soften Thomas' Aristotelianism. But though adjustment was possible on relatively minor points, any really novel thought was forced into open rebellion. The result was unfortunate, both for the dominant view and for the new thought that was emerging. The rebel, unable to assert himself against a dominant opinion that refused to make reasonable concessions, introduced a note of stridency into his arguments. He adopted an attitude of intolerance similar to that which had infected Christianity in its early days, when it too was a rebellious novelty. But now Christianity had become the dominant opinion and was far more unyielding than pagan thought had ever been. As a consequence, a serious split developed in the Western mind. To the new thought Thomism seemed increasingly reactionary; to Thomism the new ideas seemed heretical.

Thus, there was no afterglow in medieval thought corresponding to the long and, on the whole, fruitful process by which the classical mind explored latent possibilities in the basic framework of the Platonic-Aristotelian world view and developed modifications of this view that were satisfactory for centuries. Instead of this gradual change and fruitful development, the medieval synthesis met a dual fate. On the one hand, because Thomism became the official philosophy of the Church, it has survived to our own day virtually unchanged. On the other hand, from the point of view of what may be called "free" thought, Thomism came under attack almost at once, and before three centuries had elapsed, it had been largely overthrown and abandoned. It is symptomatic of the divisiveness of modern times that a philosophy can at one and the same time be everything to some and nothing to others.

Let us now examine the views of some representative thinkers of this final period of medieval philosophy.

Roger Bacon

LIFE

Though Bacon was a contemporary of St. Thomas, he lived in a different intellectual world. His career is therefore a useful reminder that the thought of the Middle Ages was not a block universe. In some respects, as we shall see, Bacon anticipated many of the currents of thought that constituted the wave of the future.

He was born in England, probably about 1214.[1] After studying at Oxford and Paris, he taught at the university of Paris. Later, looking back on this period, he said that, "careless of the crowd's opinion," he had labored from his youth in the sciences and languages; that he had sought the friendship of all the wise men in the West; that he had spent "more than two thousand pounds [a great sum] on occult books and various experiments, and languages and instruments, and tables and other things."

Here a new note is sounded, and even if we knew nothing more of Bacon, we would be able to say that he was a man not wholly typical of his time. This is borne out by both his writings and the treatment accorded him by his contemporaries.

At a time when Greek was virtually unknown in the Western world, Bacon was an ardent advocate of its study. He also held it important to know Hebrew, Arabic, and Chaldean because (as he saw) it was impossible to understand the Bible without them.

> Numberless portions of the wisdom of God are wanting to us. Many books of the Sacred Text remain untranslated, as two books of the Maccabees which I know to exist in Greek. . . . Josephus, too, . . . is altogether falsely rendered . . . : and without him nothing can be known of the history of the Sacred Text. Unless he be corrected, in a new translation, . . . the Biblical history is lost. Numberless books, again, of Hebrew and Greek expositors are wanting. . . . The Church, therefore, is slumbering. . . . It is an amazing thing, this negligence of the Church.[a]

Here Bacon anticipated by almost two hundred years the textual and historical point of view of the Renaissance. He also belonged to that age in his curiosity about the natural world, in his deep contempt for the barrenness of the Scholastic method, in his emphasis on the importance of mathematics and physics, in his insistence on the practical utility of the study of science, and in his sense

---

1 Stewart C. Easton, in *Roger Bacon and His Search for a Universal Science* (Columbia University Press, 1952), presents a study of the few available facts regarding Bacon's life. Bacon probably died about 1292.

of the superiority of direct experience over hearsay and authority.[2] It is not surprising that some modern commentators have concluded that Bacon was, in spirit, wholly a man of our time. This is an exaggeration. Bacon conceived of physics in a way that would have been familiar to Pythagoras and Plato, and his "experimental science," which has often been taken as an anticipation of scientific method in the modern sense, turns out on close examination to be both less original and less earthshaking than some have thought. Indeed, in many respects, and despite his attack on Scholasticism, Bacon remained a Scholastic. He had no doubt that Holy Scripture was the revealed word of God; his philological studies were intended to disclose what God had revealed in the sacred texts; he explicitly accepted the full dogmatic position of the Church and, like Thomas, held theology to be the queen of sciences. He cited authorities—even while attacking other writers' dependence on authority. And he discussed at length and in detail the very questions, such as those related to the status of universals and the nature of the principle of individuation, that were exercising the most orthodox Scholastics.

Rather late in life, Bacon joined the Franciscan Order, but he soon antagonized his fellow friars and was put under close supervision and forbidden to write. This caused difficulties for him when, in 1266, he was instructed by the pope to prepare a treatise setting out the "universal science" on which Bacon had long been working. Although in eighteen months Bacon managed to turn out three long treatises, his eagerness made the time seem long, and he apologized for delay. "The first cause of delay came through those who are over me. Since you have written nothing to them in my excuse, and I could not reveal to them your secret, they insisted with unspeakable violence that I should obey their will. . . . And another obstacle, enough to defeat the whole business, was the lack of funds."[b]

Unfortunately for Bacon, this friendly pontiff soon died, perhaps without even having seen the treatises, and his successor showed no interest in Bacon or his work. For a few years after this disappointment Bacon proceeded with his work without interference, but it appears that he was later accused of "certain suspected novelties" and imprisoned.

He was probably less guilty of "novelties" than of annoying his contemporaries with his sharp tongue. Indeed, he coupled the frankest confessions of his own genius with open expressions of contempt for all the scholars of the age.

2 For instance, in a discussion of geography, Bacon wrote, "Sometimes many things are found written which authors have gathered from reports more than from experience. Pliny was not accurate . . . ; Ptolemy was plainly in error . . . and other authors likewise. Wherefore I shall have recourse to those who have in great measure travelled over the places of this world. Especially in the northern regions I shall follow [Friar William Rubruquis], whom the lord king of France, Louis, sent to the Tartars in the year of our Lord 1253, who traversed the regions of the East and of the North, and wrote these facts to the aforesaid illustrious king. I have examined this book with care, and I have conferred with its author, and likewise with many others who have explored the places of the East and South"—*Opus Majus* (Burke), Pt. IV, Chap. XVI.

Like all the Scholastics, he admired Aristotle, but he was disgusted with the inadequate Latin translations on which, for want of knowledge of Greek, his fellow scholars depended. If he had had his way, he would have burned all these faulty translations; in his eyes, those who made and used them were but "boys who became teachers before they had learned." Nor were the morals of the clergy any better than their scholarship. Anticipating the appraisal of a later generation of reformers, Bacon declared that "the whole clergy is given up to pride, luxury, and avarice. . . . Their quarrels, their contentions, and their vices are a scandal to laymen."[c]

CENTRAL THEME OF BACON'S WORK

Since Bacon's learning was encyclopedic and since Bacon himself was not a completely isolated phenomenon, his work will serve to indicate the state of knowledge among the most advanced intellects of his time. The *Opus Majus*, his chief surviving work and the principal document he prepared for the pope, is a fascinating hodgepodge of information on comparative philology, optics, alchemy, astrology, and many other subjects. Through it all, however, runs a connecting thread. The central theme of the *Opus Majus* is suggested by the alternative title that appears in many manuscripts: *On the Utility of Knowledge*. The book is full of proposals to put knowledge to practical use: to construct great magnifying glasses with which to set Saracen fleets on fire at sea; to use mirrors, "which can be so made and so placed that a single object can be multiplied at will," in order to make one's own army appear to be several and so mislead the opposing forces as to one's strength; to fashion periscopes by means of which a besieging army can peer over the walls of a beleaguered city; and so on.[d] But to emphasize Bacon's attention to technological applications of scientific knowledge is to distort his position. He was clear that the *ultimate* utility of science is in the service of the Church and the perfection of man's knowledge of God.

> By the light of knowledge the Church of God is governed, the common-wealth of the faithful is regulated, the conversion of unbelievers is secured, and those who persist in their malice can be held in check by the excellence of knowledge, so that they may be driven off from the borders of the Church in a better way than by the shedding of Christian blood. . . .
>
> There is one wisdom that is perfect and this is contained in the Scriptures. From the root of this wisdom all truth has sprung. I say, therefore, that one science is the mistress of the others, namely, theology, . . . whose nod and authority the rest of the sciences obey. Or better, there is only one perfect wisdom, which is contained wholly in the Scriptures, and is to be unfolded by canon law and philosophy. [Theology] gathers within its own grasp all wisdom; since all wisdom has been given by one God, to one world, for one purpose. . . . The way of salvation is single, although there are many steps; but wisdom is the way to salvation.[e]

NATURE AND UTILITY OF THE SCIENCES

Having laid down this general principle, Bacon discussed in exhaustive detail, and with a curious blend of naïveté and insight, the ways in which mathematics, "the study of tongues," the various other sciences, and philosophy could be used in interpreting Scripture and illuminating the human mind.

Some extracts from Bacon's account of optics can serve to show that the science of his day, though still weighed down by the symbolism, obscurity, and traditionalism of earlier science, was beginning to be invigorated by a new and relatively empirical point of view.

Having explained the fundamental principles of wisdom, both sacred and human, which are found in the tongues from which the sciences of the Latins have been translated, and likewise in mathematics, I now wish to discuss some principles which belong to optics. . . . It is possible that some other science may be more useful, but no other science has so much sweetness and beauty of utility. Therefore it is the flower of the whole of philosophy and through it, and not without it, can the other sciences be known. We must note, moreover, that Aristotle first treated this science. . . . This book has been translated into Latin. After him Alhazen treats the subject more fully in a book which is extant. Alkindi also has arranged some data more fully, likewise authors of books on vision and mirrors. . . .

Clearly, therefore, in order that there may be no scruple of doubt in what follows, the structure of the eye must be studied, because without this nothing can be known concerning the method of vision. But some writers say less, some more, and in certain things they are at variance. . . . But that I may not draw upon sources of individual opinions to too great an extent, I shall confine my description of the structure of the eye mainly to three authorities —Alhazen in his first book on Perspective, Constantinus in his book on the Eye, and Avicenna in his books; for these writers are sufficient and they treat more definitely the matters in which we are interested. I cannot, however, give the exact words of each, because they are sometimes at variance owing to faulty translation, but from them all I shall form a single statement of the truth. . . . According to Avicenna, and the author on Perspective, and Constantinus, these visual nerves of which we are speaking come out at the bottom of the ventricles of the anterior part. This is the explanation of Constantinus who teaches us to examine the heads of large animals, when they are killed not in the summer or in the heat, and we shall find a small opening in the skull through which the nerve passes, and then we should examine the membrane of the pia mater cautiously lest it be broken. . . . But the two nerves, as we have stated, from the two directions right and left, meet, according to all authorities, and after meeting again are divided. It was, moreover, better that they should meet in the opening than before it or after it. For in either of these cases they would make two openings in the bone of the head, but it is better that the nerve should pass through one opening than through two. The bone is firmer the less it is perforated. Therefore, since nature acts in the better way possible, the junction will be in the opening of the skull, at which place they are again divided. The nerve that comes from the right goes to the left eye and the one from the left to the right eye, so that there is a direct extension of the nerves from their origin to the eyes. For if the nerve coming from the right part of the anterior cell of the brain passed to the right eye, there would be an angle in the common nerve where they meet and the nerve would be bent and would not extend directly to the eye. But this would hinder vision, because vision always selects straight lines as far as possible. . . .

It turns out, however, that Bacon did not conceive the chief value of the science of optics to be its use in improving our eyesight (as modern readers might be inclined to think), nor even in designing mirrors to baffle the Saracens. Its real value, Bacon thought, lies in the fact that it enables us to explicate some of the deep meanings hidden in Holy Scripture.

We have now spoken of the principles of perspective as far as they are necessary for scientific knowledge and for the understanding of their practical applications. I wish now in conclusion to intimate how this science possesses an ineffable usefulness in regard to divine truth. . . . When the truth of the matters set forth in Scripture is known it is very easy for every theologian to draw from them profitably their spiritual meaning. For when it is said, "Guard us, Lord, as the pupil of thine eye," it is impossible to know God's meaning in this prayer unless one first considers how the guarding of the eye is effected, so that God deems it right to guard us according to this similitude. . . .

But we shall not understand the guarding of the pupil except through the science of perspective. For the pupil is the anterior glacialis, which is supported by two humors in front of it and behind it; and is contained in one web and three coats, and receives moreover a constant and unrestricted influx of spirits and forces from the plenteous source of supply in the optic commissure; and thus it requires seven things for its protection. This, then, is the literal exposition, to which the Psalmist wishes the spiritual to be likened when he prays for the guarding of the spiritual pupil, that is, of the soul; for the perfect guardianship of which seven things are necessary, namely, virtue, gift, beatitude, spiritual sense, fruits, and revelation according to the states of rapture, and in addition the continual influx of the gifts of grace from the plenitude of the Crucified. But the principal virtues are seven, namely, three theological, charity, faith, and hope, and four cardinal, justice, fortitude, temperance, and wisdom; by means of which our spiritual pupil must be guarded. Moreover, the gifts of the Holy Spirit are seven, and the petitions of the Lord's prayer are confined to seven. But the beatitudes are eight, as is evident from the fifth chapter of Matthew, and therefore we shall add to the seven guardians of the bodily pupil as an eighth that of the eyelashes, so that as many bodily defenders may correspond to the eight spiritual ones. Now the spiritual senses are five, and those things that are directly allotted to the protection of the pupil are five. . . .

Just as we see nothing corporeally without corporeal light, so it is impossible for us to see anything spiritually without the spiritual light of the divine grace. And just as a moderate distance is required for vision, so that a body is not visible if it is too far off or too near, the same condition is required for spiritual vision. For remoteness from God through unbelief and a multitude of sins takes away spiritual sight, and so also do an excessive presumption of intimacy with God and scrutiny of his majesty.[f]

BACON'S "EXPERIMENTAL SCIENCE"

This brings us to Bacon's account of what he called "experimental science," the part of his work that has excited a number of exaggerated estimates of his modernity. Several preliminary remarks are in order. First, Bacon never managed to say exactly what he meant by this wonderful new science. In particular, he was not clear as to whether it was another special science whose subject matter was somehow different from all the others or a new *method* appropriate for reforming the established sciences. The latter is, of course, what, logically, he should have been expounding, but the former is the point of view he usually adopted. The fact that Bacon did not even see this fundamental distinction shows how far he was from anything like a modern point of view.

Second, Bacon did not distinguish between his new science as merely an educational device (a technique for presenting vividly and dramatically truths already arrived at by more conventional methods) and as a technique for establishing truths previously unknown.

Third, he did not distinguish between observation and experiment, both of which he referred to with a single term. Though he occasionally and faintly saw the value of experiment, what interested him for the most part was simply direct experience as opposed to hearsay and secondhand reporting.

Fourth, he did not distinguish between the role of his new science as a technique for the discovery of truth and what we would call the science's technological utility. It appears, indeed, that what impressed him most about this new science was the advantage he foresaw for it in the field of invention.[3]

All these ambiguities will be evident in the following extracts:

Having laid down fundamental principles of the wisdom of the Latins so far as they are found in language, mathematics, and optics, I now wish to unfold the principles of experimental science, since without experience

---

3 "Machines for navigating are possible without rowers, so that great ships suited to river or ocean, guided by one man, may be borne with greater speed than if they were full of men. Likewise cars may be made so that without a draught animal they may be moved [at incalculable speeds]. And flying machines are possible, so that a man may sit in the middle turning some device by which artificial wings may beat the air in the manner of a flying bird" [*De Secretis Operibus*, quoted in Taylor, *The Mediaeval Mind*, Vol. II, p. 538]. But all this is fantasy; even if his predictions happened later to come true, Bacon himself had not the slightest basis in fact or in theory for making them.

nothing can be sufficiently known. For there are two modes of acquiring knowledge, namely, by reasoning and experience. Reasoning draws a conclusion and makes us grant the conclusion, but does not make the conclusion certain, nor does it remove doubt so that the mind may rest on the intuition of truth, unless the mind discovers it by the path of experience; since many have the arguments relating to what can be known, but because they lack experience they neglect the arguments, and neither avoid what is harmful nor follow what is good. For if a man who has never seen fire should prove by adequate reasoning that fire burns and injures things and destroys them, his mind would not be satisfied thereby, nor would he avoid fire, until he placed his hand or some combustible substance in the fire, so that he might prove by experience that which reasoning taught. But when he has had actual experience of combustion his mind is made certain and rests in the full light of truth. Therefore reasoning does not suffice, but experience does.

This is also evident in mathematics, where proof is most convincing. But the mind of one who has the most convincing proof in regard to the equilateral triangle will never cleave to the conclusion without experience, nor will he heed it, but will disregard it until experience is offered him by the intersection of two circles, from either intersection of which two lines may be drawn to the extremities of the given line; but then the man accepts the conclusion without any question. . . .

He therefore who wishes to rejoice without doubt in regard to the truths underlying phenomena must know how to devote himself to experiment. For authors write many statements, and people believe them through reasoning which they formulate without experience. Their reasoning is wholly false. For it is generally believed that the diamond cannot be broken except by goat's blood, and philosophers and theologians misuse this idea. But fracture by means of blood of this kind has never been verified, although the effort has been made; and without that blood it can be broken easily. For I have seen this with my own eyes, and this is necessary, because gems cannot be carved except by fragments of this stone. . . .

But experience is of two kinds; one is gained through our external senses, and in this way we gain our experience of those things that are in the heavens by instruments made for this purpose, and of those things here below by means attested by our vision. Things that do not belong in our part of the world we know through other scientists who have had experience of them. As, for example, Aristotle on the authority of Alexander sent two thousand men through different parts of the world to gain experimental knowledge of all things that are on the surface of the earth. . . . But this experience does not suffice . . . , because it does not give full attestation in regard to things corporeal owing to its difficulty, and does not touch at all on things spiritual. It is necessary, therefore, that the intellect of man should be otherwise aided, and for this reason the holy patriarchs and prophets, who first gave sciences to the world, received illumination within and were not dependent on sense alone. . . .

Moreover, there are seven stages of this internal knowledge, the first of which is reached through illuminations relating purely to the sciences. The second consists in the virtues. . . .

The third stage consists in the seven gifts of the Holy Spirit, which Isaiah enumerates. The fourth consists in the beatitudes, which the Lord defines in the Gospels. The fifth consists in the spiritual senses. The sixth consists in fruits, of which is the peace of God which passes all understanding. The seventh consists in raptures and their states according to the different ways in which people are caught up to see many things of which it is not lawful for a man to speak. And he who has had diligent training in these experiences or in several of them is able to assure himself and others not only in regard to things spiritual, but also in regard to all human sciences. . . .

Since this Experimental Science is wholly unknown to the rank and file of students, I am therefore unable to convince people of its utility unless at the same time I disclose its excellent and its proper signification. This science alone, therefore, knows how to test perfectly what can be done by nature, what by the effort of art, what by trickery, what the incantations, conjurations, invocations, deprecations, sacrifices, that belong to magic, mean and dream of, and what is in them, so that all falsity may be removed and the truth alone of art and nature may be retained. . . .

For the other sciences know how to discover their principles by experiments, but their conclusions are reached by reasoning drawn from the principles discovered. But if they should have a particular and complete experience of their own conclusions, they must have it with the aid of this noble science. . . .

Yet every now and again Bacon's writing takes on very different tone; pious allegorizing drops out and is replaced by the projection of empirical hypotheses and the invention of ingenious ways to test them. In such passages a very different world view is faintly adumbrated and a wholly new interest is revealed—an interest in discovering the facts just to satisfy one's curiosity as to what the facts are, not an interest in the facts as somehow symbolic of a supersensible realm. Bacon's discussion of the rainbow is a case in point:

Let the experimenter first, then, examine visible objects, in order that he may find colors arranged as in the phenomena mentioned above and also the same figure. For let him take hexagonal stones from Ireland or from India, which are called rainbows in Solinus on the Wonders of the World, and let him hold these in a solar ray falling through the window, so that he may find all the colors of the rainbow, arranged as in it, in the shadow near the ray. . . . And since many employing these stones think that the phenomenon is due to the special virtue of those stones and to their hexagonal shape, therefore let the experimenter proceed further, and he will find this same peculiarity in crystalline stones correctly shaped, and in other transparent stones. Moreover, he will find this not only in white stones like the Irish crystals, but also in black ones. . . . For a difference in the corrugations causes a difference in the colors. And further let him observe rowers, and in the drops falling from the raised oars he finds the same colors when the solar rays penetrate drops of this kind. The same phenomenon is seen in water falling from the wheels of a mill. . . . Likewise when it is raining, if he stands in a dark place and the rays beyond it pass through the falling rain, the colors will appear in the shadow near by; and frequently at night colors appear around a candle. Moreover, if a man in summer, when he rises from sleep and has his eyes only partly open, suddenly looks at a hole through which a ray of the sun enters, he will see colors. . . . Thus in an infinite number of ways colors of this kind appear, which the diligent experimenter knows how to discover. . . .

Since, moreover, we find colors and various figures similar to the phenomena in the air, . . . we are encouraged and greatly stimulated to grasp the truth in those phenomena that occur in the heavens. Further, let the experimenter take the required instrument and look through the openings of the instrument and find the altitude of the sun above the horizon, . . . and let him note the altitude of the rainbow above the horizon; and he will find that the higher the sun's altitude is, the lower is that of the bow, and conversely. By this means he knows that the rainbow is always opposite the sun, and that one line passes through the center of the sun, and through the center of the observer's eye. . . .

After, therefore, the experimenter discovers this, he must then by his experiments learn the size and shape of the rainbow, and for this purpose he conceives a cone of which the apex is at the eye and the base is the circle of the bow, the portion of which appears colored. The axis of the cone is the line mentioned above, which passes through the center of the eye and the center of the sun and the center of the bow to the nadir of the sun. The base of this cone is elevated and depressed according to the elevation and depression of the sun, as we have stated in regard to that line, and as it is depressed it sinks sometimes to the earth, cutting it and cut by it. . . .

The experimenter further tries to find out whether the bow is caused by incident rays or by reflection or by refraction, and whether it is an image of the sun, . . . and whether there are real colors in the cloud itself. . . .

We learn by experiment that there are as many bows as there are observers. For if two observers at the same time stand and look at the bow in the north, and one of them goes westward, the bow will move in a direction parallel to him, and if the other goes to the east, the bow will move in a direction parallel to him, or if he stands still in the original position, the bow will be stationary. . . . For this reason it is impossible for two observers to see one and the same bow, although an ignorant person does not grasp this fact.[g]

Bacon not only proposed a new method for ascertaining the truths of nature. He supplemented his proposal with a short, but interesting, account of the causes of error:

Now there are four chief obstacles in grasping truth, which hinder every man, however learned, and scarcely allow any one to win a clear title to learning, namely, submission to faulty and unworthy authority, influence of custom, popular prejudice, and concealment of our own ignorance accompanied by an ostentatious display of our knowledge. Every man is entangled in these difficulties, every rank is beset. For people without distinction draw the same conclusion from three arguments, than which none could be worse, namely, for this the authority of our predecessors is adduced, this is the custom, this is the common belief; hence correct. . . . Should, however, these three errors be refuted by the convincing force of reason, the fourth is always ready and on every one's lips for the excuse of his own ignorance, and although he has no knowledge worthy of the name, he may yet shamelessly magnify it, so that at least to the wretched satisfaction of his own folly he suppresses and evades the truth. Moreover, from these deadly banes come all the evils of the human race. . . . Therefore nothing is more necessary of consideration than the positive condemnation of those four errors. . . . But although authority be one of those, I am in no way speaking of that solid and sure authority, which either by God's judgment has been bestowed upon his Church, or which springs from the merit and dignity of an individual among the Saints. . . .

All that which our intellect is able to understand and know is small in comparison with those things which in the beginning in its weakness it is bound to believe, such as the divine verities and many secrets of nature and of art completing nature, concerning which no human reason can be given in the beginning; but one must get understanding from God through the experience of the inner light, I mean in the sacred verities of grace and glory, and stirred through the experience of his senses in the secrets of nature and art he must discover their reason.[h]

A comparison of Bacon's and Thomas' views of science will show how complex a matter cultural change is, and how misleading apparently simple questions can be. Was Bacon more modern than Thomas? Yes, and no. Yes, in that, despite all ambiguities and confusions, Bacon did have an idea of the possibility of a truly experimental science, which Thomas wholly lacked. No, in the sense that Bacon was at one with Thomas in the conviction that scientific knowledge must be "perfected" by revelation. Indeed, in one respect Bacon was actually *more* medieval than Thomas. With his Franciscan background, Bacon was far more under the influence of Augustine and the Neoplatonists and so emphasized much more than Thomas the need for divine illumination.

BACON'S CONCEPTION OF PHILOSOPHY

It is particularly in Bacon's conception of philosophy that the Neoplatonic ideal appears. "Philosophy," he held, "exists through the influence of divine illumination." Since there is but one universal truth, which is God's, and since this truth exists in men's minds only as a result of divine illumination, "it is evident" that the labor of even the pagan philosophers "is not opposed to the divine wisdom."[i] The whole history of philosophy is, in fact, nothing but the unfolding—interrupted by periods of relapse and ignorance—of this divine wisdom. The early and perfect philosophers, who were the sons of Seth and

Noah, were followed by evil men. "God darkened the foolish heart of the multitude: and gradually the knowledge of philosophy disappeared until Solomon . . . recalled and perfected it in its entirety." This revival was followed by another period of decline that lasted "until Thales of Miletus took it up again, and his successors broadened it, until Aristotle completed it, as far as was possible for that time."[j] Bacon believed his time to be another period of decline, and it is clear that he conceived of his mission as nothing less than that of launching a new revival of eternal truth.

Since "there is one wisdom in its entirety for mankind," the patriarchs and prophets and other divinely inspired authors of Holy Scripture knew all things —"not only the law of God but all the parts of philosophy." All this knowledge was, as it were, poured into the sacred writings; we therefore cannot completely understand these writings without having mastered it. It was this conception, incidentally, that underlay Bacon's insistence on textual criticism and the study of comparative philology. He believed, however, that not only philology but all the sciences ultimately obtain their value from the fact that they throw light on the meaning of God's word[4] and thereby assist us in finding the way to salvation.

Duns Scotus

With Duns Scotus, who was born about the year of Thomas' death, we encounter a mind much more typical than Bacon's of the Middle Ages and of the Scholastic tradition. Yet in certain important respects, as we shall shortly see, his views were signs that changes were encroaching.

LIFE

About Duns's life almost nothing is known. He was born, presumably, in Scotland, about 1265. In his youth, he became a member of the Franciscan Order. He studied and subsequently taught at Oxford, wrote voluminously, taught in Paris, acquired a tremendous reputation for the subtlety of his reasoning, and in 1307 was sent by his order to Cologne, where he very shortly died.[5]

There is also great uncertainty about the authenticity of certain works long attributed to him,[6] and this, coupled with the extremely technical character of his vocabulary, has made it difficult for modern commentators to agree about either the nature of his views or their historical significance. To some he has

---

4 An example has been quoted from Bacon's discussion of optics.
5 *The Dictionary of National Biography*, however, casts doubt on even these scanty data.
6 For a recent (and inconclusive) discussion of this much debated question, see F. Copleston, *A History of Philosophy* (Newman Press, Westminster, Md., 1950), Vol. II, pp. 477–81.

seemed a typical example of the barren triviality of Scholastic metaphysics and logic. Indeed, the term "dunce," used in reference to a stupid fellow or an ignoramus, was derived from his name. More recently, however, with the recognition of the importance of rigorous conceptual analysis, the precision of Duns's mind has come to be more generally appreciated, though today few outside the Roman Church find much significance in his metaphysical scheme.

As to the nature of this metaphysical scheme, it is not clear whether Duns was primarily an Aristotelian with a dash of Augustinianism or an Augustinian with a dash of Aristotelianism. An attempt to settle this question will not be made here. This account will be confined chiefly to a discussion of the principal points of disagreement between Duns and Thomas. This section will deal with Duns's views with regard to (1) theory of knowledge, (2) the nature of individuality, (3) the relative primacy of intellect and will, and (4) the limits of natural theology. In connection with Duns's differences from Thomas on these issues, it will be shown that, though Duns regarded himself as defending orthodoxy against dangerous Thomistic innovations, he was actually preparing the way for its overthrow.

(1) DUNS'S THEORY OF KNOWLEDGE

In general, Duns accepted the Aristotelian-Thomistic theory of knowledge: Human knowledge begins with the sensing of particulars; by a process of abstraction, men "collect" from several experiences of similar particulars the universal embedded in all those particulars. But Duns introduced some major modifications into this theory in an effort to correct what he regarded as the deficiencies in Thomas' position.

In the first place, whereas Thomas held that man's mind is limited to knowledge based on and derived from sense experience and is thus fundamentally different from and inferior to the divine mind, Duns denied that man's mind is *naturally* limited in this way. According to him, the human mind is naturally capable of direct knowledge of form, knowledge unmediated by sense experience. Why, then, does it lack this capacity in its present post-Fall state? Though Duns suggested several possible explanations for this limitation, the most probable appeared to him to be (and here he followed Augustine) that it is a punishment imposed on mankind for Adam's sin.

To most twentieth-century men the question of whether such-and-such a characteristic of the human mind is pre- or post-Fall will seem, at best, trivial. We might be inclined to say that a limitation that has been shared by all men since Adam's day is, in effect, a part of human nature. But this only shows the radical gap between our time and the Middle Ages. From a metaphysical and theological point of view, the distinction Duns was concerned with is of fundamental importance. As Duns pointed out, if the human mind were naturally limited to knowledge derived from sense experience, the science of metaphysics would be impossible. For metaphysics, medieval philosophers universally agreed, is concerned with being in its widest determination, not merely with being at the level of the forms of material things. Nor, so it would seem, would rational knowledge of God be possible, if the human mind were so limited (for He is certainly a nonmaterial being). Hence, Duns reasoned, the whole program of Thomas' *Summa Theologica* was actually undermined by Thomas' own theory of knowledge; if this theory were correct, men would have to depend entirely on faith and revelation for their knowledge of God.[7]

UNIVOCITY AND EQUIVOCITY

This criticism of Thomas can be put another way. First, however, it is necessary to introduce one of the most characteristic of Duns's ideas—that of the contrast between univocity and equivocity. Consider, for instance, the term "dog" as applied to the canine animal, to the star *Sirius*, and to the fish *squalus acanthias*. When we call *Sirius* the Dog Star, we are using "dog" in a different sense from that in which we use it when we call a St. Bernard a dog. The term "dog," that is to say, is predicated equivocally of stars, fishes, and St. Bernards. But when we call St. Bernards and Dalmatians dogs, we are using the term "dog" in a single sense, that is, univocally. The equivocal use of a term causes no trouble if we know it is equivocal. But suppose a foreigner who does not know English well happens to come across a reference to the Dog Star or the dogfish. Knowing that the canine animal is called "dog" in English, he may infer that the star and the fish also bark.

The attempts of Christian thinkers to make inferences about God's nature may go wrong in a similar way. They argue that He is good, that He exists, that He is truth, and so on, using terms that describe states of affairs in human experience. For instance, chocolate ice cream is good and men exist. Of course, they hasten to add that, unlike ice cream, God is *all*-good; that though men have being, He is an *infinite* being; and so on. The difficulty in this procedure has already been pointed out in connection with Augustine's views. By insisting on the infinity of the divine attributes, do theologians not take them altogether out of human experience? Do we really have any idea of what *absolute* goodness and *absolute* being are?[8]

This question can now be restated in terms of Duns's distinction between univocity and equivocity. If being, as predicated of God and ourselves, is equivocal, how can we make inferences from what we know to be true of ourselves to what is true of God? Since we cannot, we must (Duns held) maintain that being is univocal. In order to maintain this plausibility, we must further maintain

7 Duns could find high canonical authority to support his contention that natural knowledge of God is possible. See pp. 304–05.
8 See pp. 100–01 and 174–75.

that a knowledge of being as such, not merely of material *being*, is natural to the human mind.

But though this theory saved Duns from having to admit that we have no rational knowledge of God, it involved him in another difficulty. If being is univocal in man and God, is not man divine? Is Duns not impaled on the horns of the old dilemma? To the extent that infinite being and finite being are alike, a natural knowledge of the former is possible; but, to just that extent, God and man are the same sort of thing. On the other hand, to just the extent that God and man are different sorts of things, natural knowledge of God is impossible. Clearly, it is of interest at this point to know in exactly what respects Duns held them to be alike and in what respects he held them to be different.

It would seem, to begin with, that, *qua* being, they are both something as opposed to nothing—both infinite being and finite being *are*. This we can surely accept. But if infinite being and finite being differ save in this one respect, we are thrown back on the problem of how we can know God's nature. If we know only that God's being, like ours, is not nothing, we certainly do not know much about Him.

Duns sought to avoid this meager conclusion by arguing that infinite being and finite being are alike in a second, very important respect: In both, essence and existence are indissolubly joined. But in thus extending our knowledge of the divine nature, it would seem that Duns reverted to a position that is pantheistic in its failure to distinguish sharply between Creator and creature, between the divine and the human. It was precisely in order to avoid this conclusion that Thomas denied that essence and existence are necessarily connected in finite beings.

However, Duns believed that he had found a way of escaping the trap of pantheism. This consisted in analyzing the concepts of "alike" and "different" and drawing a distinction between them that had not occurred to Thomas. In order to explain Duns's position on this point, it is necessary to introduce another of his characteristic ideas—that of the "formal distinction in respect to the thing." Duns pointed out that there is an obvious distinction between an objectively real difference (for example, the difference between Socrates and Plato) and a merely subjective or mental difference (for example, the difference between Aristotle's and Plato's conceptions of Socrates). That there is such a distinction everyone would of course agree. But Duns wanted to hold that between the objective kind of difference (which he called a "real distinction") and the subjective kind of difference (which he called a "rational distinction"), there is a third kind of difference (which he called a "formal distinction"). This is, as it were, a mean between two extremes. It is less objective than a "real" difference but more objective than a purely subjective, mental one. It is a formal distinction, but it is objectively *there* in the things distinguished, not merely made by the mind. Duns defined the formal distinction as that which exists between two entities each of which can be thought of by itself, though they are so closely united that even God Himself could not separate them.

This notion of the formal distinction may be a little difficult to grasp when described in Duns's Scholastic terminology. But there is no doubt that in singling out the formal distinction he put his finger on an important characteristic of some objects of our experience. For instance, there is a difference between asserting that seven is the largest prime number less than ten and asserting that seven is the number one greater than six, and this difference is neither completely subjective nor completely objective. Though neither of these truths could exist without the other (for they entail each other), they are nevertheless distinct truths. The distinction between them is one made by thought but nevertheless objective, that is, it is a formal distinction in respect to the thing.

Duns's next step was to show that the formal distinction is relevant to the particular problem in hand, namely, the threat of pantheism. He proceeded in the following way. There is, after all, a difference between infinite and finite being in respect to the relation between essence and existence. Though it is true that, in both, essence and existence are indissolubly joined, they can be thought of separately in the case of finite being. That is, there is a formal distinction between the essence and the existence of finite beings but not between God's essence and His existence. Or, to put the matter somewhat differently, Duns denied that it is necessary to choose between saying that God's being and man's being are identical and saying that they are wholly different. They are, he maintained, alike *and* different, and their particular kind of alikeness and difference is that described in the formal distinction. This makes them alike enough for there to be a natural knowledge of God and different enough for Duns to escape pantheism.

THE STATUS OF UNIVERSALS

A second major difference between Duns's and Thomas' theories of knowledge concerns the status of universals. This, too, grew out of Duns's insistence that the human mind is capable of real objective knowledge of things. It has been said that Duns (and Thomas, of course) accepted the basic Aristotelian scheme. But this scheme contained a grave ambiguity. It is not clear whether Aristotle believed that the mind makes or discovers the distinctions (for example, those between form and matter, particular and genus) that he employed in his philosophy. Duns believed that this ambiguity had infected Thomism. He was determined to validate these distinctions as objective and to do so without lapsing into the extreme position of the medieval realists whom Abelard had attacked. That is to say, he held that genus must be a real object of knowledge, not merely a way human minds look at things; yet he also held that genus is not a separate existent—not, that is, a Platonic form. How can this be?

Duns thought the answer lay in his formal distinction. We do not, he held, have to choose between asserting that genus is wholly objective (that there is a "real" distinction between particular and genus) and admitting that it is only subjective (that there is merely a "rational" distinction between particular and genus). There is a third possibility, namely, that the distinction between particular and genus is "formal," that there is a real difference between them but that they are not separate entities.

DIVINE ILLUMINATION AND HUMAN KNOWLEDGE

Duns also differed from Thomas regarding the role that divine illumination plays in human knowledge. No Christian thinker, of course, would for a moment deny that complete knowledge of the ultimate reality is beyond human capacity unless God by an act of grace illumines our minds. But what about our knowledge of natural objects? Is it adequate in itself, or does its truth too depend on divine illumination? Can we obtain an adequate knowledge of falling stones, for instance, by studying physics, or must this knowledge be "adequated" by God?

It is easy to see how Platonism and Aristotelianism became the bases for rival answers to this question. In insisting that, ultimately, all truth depends on the Form of the Good, conceived to be a transcendent and separate entity, Plato provided the basis for the position Augustine and his followers adopted. By identifying the Form of the Good with God, they arrived at the desired conclusion: Divine illumination is necessary for true knowledge of natural objects. Aristotelianism lent itself just as naturally to the opposite view. It is not, Aristotle had contended, a separate and transcendent Form of the Good, but knowledge of *other* individual particulars and their relations that adequates natural knowledge. This, of course, was Thomas' view. However, he added that, though natural knowledge is adequate in its own right, it is "perfected" by knowledge of God.

In order to understand Duns's position and his relation to Thomas, it is important to see that, though the Franciscan Order of which Duns was a member clung to the Augustinian tradition, Duns himself minimized the role of divine illumination. That he should do so followed, of course, from his insistence on the univocity of being. In the following passage, drawn from Duns's discussion of this question, the reader should note that, though Duns adopted a generally Thomistic position, his approach to the problem, his method of reasoning, and his emphases were all his own. Since the argument is complex and since it is possible to quote only a portion of his discussion, it may be useful to give a brief synopsis of the discussion before quoting from it at length. The question to be discussed, then, is *"Whether any sure and pure truth can be known naturally by the understanding of the wayfarer without the special illumination of the uncreated light?"*[k]

Duns first gave the arguments for the negative answer (that is, that no sure and pure truth can be known without special illumination), which he held to be mistaken. These arguments consist chiefly in a whole battery of citations from Augustine's writings to the effect that divine illumination is necessary. But reason as well as authority seemed to some to support the negative thesis. Duns found no less than ten arguments by which thinkers arguing on rational grounds had sought to confirm authority by showing that a denial of illumination ends in scepticism.

Against this formidable array of evidence, Duns set a single sentence from Paul's letter to the Romans: "Ever since the creation of the world, [God's] invisible nature—his eternal power and divine character—have been clearly perceptible through what he has made.[9,1]

This, as Duns pointed out, is an unambiguous declaration, and, since it appears in Holy Scripture, he held that it must be true. Therefore it was essential for Duns (1) to show that the Augustinian texts did not really mean what they seemed to mean and (2) to rebut the claim that a denial of illumination ends in scepticism. The former task was a problem of textual exegesis that need not detain us; the latter involved an ingenious piece of reasoning by which Duns sought to turn the tables on his opponents and show that it was their position, not his, that led to scepticism.

> It must be seen how infallible certitude can be had naturally of . . . three kinds of knowables . . . , namely, of *principles known through themselves* and of *conclusions*, secondly of *things known by experience*, thirdly, of *our actions*.
>
> *The certitude of first principles is shown.*—With reference to certitude of *principles* I say this: that the terms of principles known through themselves have such an *identity*, that one term known *evidently* includes the other necessarily; and therefore the understanding compounding those terms, from the fact that it apprehends them, has in itself the *necessary* cause of the *conformity* of that act of compounding to the terms themselves of which the composition is and likewise the *evident* cause of that conformity; and therefore, that conformity is evident to it necessarily. The necessary and evident cause of that conformity it apprehends in the terms: therefore, the *apprehension* of terms and their *composition* can not be in the understanding, unless the *conformity* of that composition to the terms stands, just as whiteness and whiteness can not stand unless *likeness* stands. But this conformity of composition in terms is the *truth of composition:* therefore, the composition of such terms can not stand unless there is truth, and thus the perception of that composition and the perception of terms can not stand, unless the perception of conformity of composition to terms stands and thus the perception of truth, for the first percepts obviously include the perception of that truth.
>
> The Philosopher confirms this reasoning by likeness in book IV of the *Metaphysics*, where he insists that the opposite of a first principle, such as, *it is impossible that the same thing be and not be,* can not come into the understanding of any one, because then there would be contrary opinions in the mind at the same time. . . .
>
> *The certitude of conclusions is shown.*—When the evidence or the certitude

---

9 Paul was arguing that since it is easy to know God, his pagan contemporaries could not appeal to ignorance as an excuse for not worshiping Him. Once again, the way in which Paul's theological innocence came to cause medieval thinkers much trouble is apparent.

of first principles has been had, it is evident how certitude may be had of conclusions inferred from them, because of the evidence of the perfect form of the syllogism, since the certitude of the conclusion depends only on the certitude of the principles and on the evidence of the inference.

The understanding does not err, although the senses err.—But will not the understanding err in this knowledge of principles and conclusions, if the senses are deceived concerning all the terms?—I reply, that with respect to this knowledge the understanding does not have the senses for cause, but only for occasion, for the understanding can not have knowledge of simples unless it has received that knowledge from the senses; still, having received it, it can compound simples with each other by its own power; and if from the relation of such simples there is a combination which is evidently true, the understanding will assent to that combination by its own power and by the power of the terms, not by power of the sense by which it receives the terms from without.—Example: if the reason of whole and the reason of greater are received from sense, and the understanding compounds the following: *every whole is greater than its part,* the understanding by its own power and that of these terms assents indubitably to this combination, and not only because it sees the terms conjoined in the thing, as it assents to the following, *Socrates is white,* because it saw that the terms are united in the thing. —Moreover, . . . if the species of whiteness and blackness had been impressed miraculously in dreams on one blind from birth, and if they remained subsequently in waking, the understanding abstracting from them would compound the following proposition, *white is not black;* and the understanding would not be deceived concerning this, even though the terms be received from erring sense; for the formal relation of the terms, to which it has reached, is the necessary cause of this negative truth.

The certitude concerning things known by experience is shown.—Concerning the second type of knowables, . . . I say that although experience is not had of all singulars, but of a large number, and that although it is not always had, but in a great many cases, still one who knows by experience knows infallibly that it is thus, and that it is always thus, and that it is thus in all, and he knows this by the following proposition reposing in the soul, *whatever occurs as in a great many things from some cause which is not free, is the natural effect of that cause,* which proposition is known to the understanding, even though it had accepted the terms of it from erring senses; for *a cause which is not free* can not produce *as in a great many things* an effect to the opposite of which it is ordered, or to which it is not ordered by its form: but a casual cause is ordered to the producing of the opposite of the casual effect or to not producing it; therefore, nothing is the casual cause in respect to an effect produced frequently by it, and if it is not free, it is a natural cause.

That, however, this effect occurs by such a cause producing *as in a great many cases,* this must be learned through experience; for to discover such a nature at one time with such an accident, at another with such another accident, it must be discovered that, howsoever great might be the diversity of such accidents, such an effect always followed that nature; therefore, such an effect follows not through some accident accidentally of that nature, but through the very nature in itself. . . .

Certitude concerning our actions is shown.—Concerning the third type of knowable things, . . . I say there is certitude concerning many of [our actions] just as of principles known through themselves, as is obvious from book IV of the *Metaphysics*. . . . According to the same Philosopher in the same place, that we are awake is known through itself as is a principle of demonstration. . . .

And as there is certitude concerning waking as concerning something known through itself, so likewise of many other actions which are in our power, as that I understand, that I hear, and thus of others which are perfect acts; for although there is no certitude that I see white which is located without, either in such a subject or at such a distance, because an illusion can be caused in the medium or in the organ and in many other ways, nevertheless there is certitude that I see, even though an illusion be caused in the organ, which illusion in the organ seems to be the greatest of illusions, as for example, when an act is caused in the organ itself, not by a present object, but such as is made naturally by a present object. And thus the faculty would have its act, if such an illusion or passion were supposed, and that would truly be what is called vision there, whether it be action or passion, or both. But if the illusion were not caused in the organ itself, . . . still sight would see.[m]

It is evident that this analysis is much more rigorous than the corresponding section of the *Summa Theologica*.[10] Thomas' aims in treating this question were, characteristically, those of a mediator. He first emphasized that *either* view (illumination or no illumination), taken in isolation from the other, is unsatisfactory. He next showed how—by the doctrine of double causality—both views are true and, in fact, supplement each other. Since every finite effect is produced both by other finite natures *and* by God, we need to know both God and the other finite natures in order to obtain an adequate knowledge of any finite effect. His conception of the problem that needed solution was determined by his metaphysical interests and, especially, by his conception of the larger purpose of the *Summa*—to effect a synthesis of all points of view. Indeed, Thomas' discussion of this topic is evidence of his capacity to appreciate widely different points of view and his talent for compromise.

Duns, in contrast, was less interested in the larger metaphysical connotations of the matter than in the straightforward epistemological problem: Is there or is there not adequate knowledge without illumination? Thus he began by distinguishing (as it had not occurred to Thomas to do) various fields in which natural knowledge is possible—various kinds of judgments, that is, that attain to certainty. It will be noted that Duns assumed general agreement that certainty is possible in these fields. His attention was directed to ascertaining, by means of a masterly

10 See pp. 234–37.

analysis of the nature of evidence, why such certain judgments are possible. In this respect Duns's inquiry was in the spirit of Kant's "critical" method, though, of course, his conclusions differed from Kant's because the development of modern science after Duns's time radically altered philosophers' conceptions of the nature of empirical certainty.

What, then, did Duns's analysis show to be the roots of certainty in the three classes of certain propositions that he distinguished? There is no special problem about propositions concerning our actions, but about both the other types a word may be said. Propositions of the first type, that is, those that are apodeictically certain, are certain because "one term includes the other." Hence it is impossible to assert the one and deny the other without contradicting oneself—without, that is, "holding contrary opinions in the mind at the same time." For instance, the proposition, "All points on the circumference of a circle are equidistant from the center," is apodeictically certain. Because equidistance from the center is a property of circles by definition, we would contradict ourselves if we asserted that some object was a circle but that the points on its circumference were not equidistant from its center.

Also interesting is Duns's attempt to justify induction in his account of the second type of certainty, namely, the certainty of things known by experience. The problem, as Duns saw it, is that we often do not have experience of all the singulars of which we want to assert some property. Because we have seen some stones fall, we can assert that these stones have fallen. But we have not seen *all* stones fall. How, then, are we justified in asserting that all stones necessarily fall? What, that is, is the basis of our inference from an observed some to an unobserved all? Duns's answer was that the basis for such inferences is the proposition, "Whatever occurs as in a great many things from some cause which is not free, is the natural effect of that cause." We may agree that if this proposition is true, inferences of the kind in question are warranted. But what is the evidence for the proposition? According to Duns, the proposition is "known to the understanding" in virtue of the following consideration: "A cause which is not free cannot produce as in a great many things an effect to the opposite of which it is ordered," that is, nature is a regular order of uniformly operating secondary causes.

It is much to Duns's credit that he saw that inductive inferences need justification. Unfortunately, the justification he proposed is inadequate: How do we know that nature is uniform? If our knowledge of the uniformity of nature is derived from our experience of nature, then it rests on an inductive inference, and we are caught in a vicious circle. We have used induction in attempting to justify induction. Nevertheless, Duns's account compares very favorably with that given by Thomas, whose overly facile assumptions about the naturalness of nature have already been noted.[11] If Duns did not solve the problem of induction, he at least

11 See pp. 238–39.

saw that there was a problem to be solved. What is more, his analysis helped to fix the problem with precision.

One more point in connection with Duns's account of induction may be mentioned. This is his conviction that nature is uniform, that is, that God operates through a regular order of secondary causes. Here, of course, he agreed with Thomas.[12] This conviction, passed down from generation to generation and sanctioned by the Church, was of great importance for the development of modern science. One must believe there is an order before one starts to look for it, and if the earliest modern scientists had not been brought up in this climate of opinion, they would never have sought ways of ascertaining exactly what the order of secondary causes is. Thomas and Duns did not themselves contribute to the development of scientific method for a number of reasons—because they were not much interested in the order of secondary causes and because, insofar as they thought about this order at all, they conceived it to be teleological. But the weight of their authority, detrimental in so many respects to the rise of free inquiry, at least preserved the notion that nature is a possible object of knowledge and so a suitable field for free inquiry.

So far various aspects of Duns's theory of knowledge have been discussed and contrasted with Thomas' views. So much attention has been devoted to this subject both because the attempt to validate the objectivity of human knowledge seems to have been Duns's central philosophical concern and because his conception of the nature and limitations of human knowledge so largely determined his views on other important points, to which we may now turn.

(2) PRINCIPLE OF INDIVIDUATION

It is often said, and rightly so, that Duns was more concerned with the individual than was Thomas. Yet it would never have entered Duns's head to assume, as many modern philosophers have, that the individual is the supreme object of moral and political value. For him, as for Thomas, nothing finite had intrinsic value; man was not valuable as man, but as God's creature and the object of His providential care. The most that can be said is that, in emphasizing the individual's reality, Duns provided a metaphysical base from which it was possible for later philosophers to assert the individual's value. In any case, it was characteristic of Duns's primarily epistemological orientation that he approached the whole question of individuality from the side of cognition rather than from the side of value.

It has been said more than once that Duns's primary interest was to validate the claims of the human intellect to real knowledge. Now, singulars are among the objects the intellect claims to know. The question Duns asked was "Can this claim be justified on the Aristotelian-Thomistic theory of knowledge?" According

12 See p. 232.

to this view, what individualizes is matter; but matter, being by definition merely potential, is unknowable. Hence it would seem that we can know only the generic properties of things, not their innermost individuality. Thomas was, of course, aware of this difficulty. But he thought it could be met by asserting that, though it is true that we cannot *know* the individuality of a singular (for knowledge, by definition, is knowledge of forms), we can *sense* its individuality. Our knowledge of a singular is therefore a kind of synthesis of our cognition of the singular's form (its whatness) and our sensuous awareness of its particularity (its thisness).

But even if this is accepted as an adequate reply (Duns, of course, rejected it), other difficulties are involved in adopting the Aristotelian-Thomistic conception of matter as the principle of individuation. Thomas' view seems to undermine the dogma of personal immortality. For if matter individuates, what survives death and the corruption of the body is not *this* man. Moreover, the notions that matter individuates and that angels are immaterial lead to the odd conclusion that individual angels differ only as species differ.[13]

Hence Duns held it desirable to find something other than matter—something more real, something more positive—to serve as the principle of individuation. What could this be? Duns approached this question, once again, from a consideration of the criteria for objective knowledge. Since he accepted the basic Aristotelian doctrine that what we know is form, it seemed to him obvious that, if we know individuality, it must be form. Form, that is to say, must give not only the whatness of singulars but also their thisness. Every form is *this* form, is (to use Duns's technical term) "contracted" into this, that, or the other singular. There is not merely a form "man," which is individualized as Plato, Socrates, and Aristotle by being embedded in different bits of matter. There is a form "Platoneity" (which is the form of Plato and the knowable aspect of Plato); there is a form "Socrateity" (which is the knowable aspect of Socrates); there is a form "Aristotleity" (which is the knowable aspect of Aristotle).

But did this not take Duns too far in the direction of nominalism? In making Plato, Socrates, and Aristotle knowable as individuals (by giving each an individual form), did he not make an objective knowledge of "man" impossible? No; for, according to Duns, there is also a form "man" distinct enough to be a real object of knowledge but not distinct enough to be a separate entity.[14] In a word, the distinction between the form "man" and the form "Platoneity" is neither a "real" distinction (as the realists maintained) nor a "rational" distinction (as the nominalists maintained), but a "formal" distinction.

So far in this presentation of Duns's view, the form "man" and the form "Platoneity" have been spoken of, but this language is inexact. It is the kind of language that would be appropriate if the distinction were real instead of formal. Hence it is better to use Duns's own terminology and to refer to "man" and "Platoneity" as two contractions, at different levels of generality, of a single

13 See pp. 239–41.
14 See pp. 302–03.

form. Contraction is not, of course, a process in time that has for its end product individuality. Genera do not exist independently and subsequently contract to become species, nor do species exist independently and then contract to become individuals. Only individuals—Plato, Socrates, Aristotle—exist. But in each of them, by logical analysis, various elements can be distinguished. For instance, in the individual Plato, "animal" and "man" (the contraction of animal) and "Platoneity" (the contraction of man) can all be distinguished.

Thus Duns replaced the old distinction between universal and particular with a distinction between two contractions. But is this only a verbal distinction? What, exactly, is the difference between the kind of contraction he called a universal and the kind of contraction he called an individual? Duns's answer was that a universal is capable of division into "parts" of which it can be predicated, whereas an individual is not. Thus the genus "man" is divisible into various "parts" (or species)—Greek, Persian, and so on—of which "man," the genus, is predicable. But in this process we eventually come to a "part" that cannot be so divided; *this* part is by definition an individual. Socrates can, of course, be divided into limbs, head, body; but "Socrates" cannot be predicated of these parts as "man" can be predicated of its parts.

Duns's name for this individual contraction, the terminus of the process of logical division, was *haecceitas,* or, as we would say, "thisness" as opposed to "whatness" (*quidditas*). The *haecceitas* of any singular is not mere potentiality, not mere matter. It is a positive element, formally distinct from the other positive elements (such as species and genus) and precisely as real—no more, no less—as they are. This conception of *haecceitas* bears on Duns's account of the relation between essence and existence in finite beings. It is not necessary for a finite essence to become embedded in some bit of matter in order for it to achieve individual particularity and exist. *Qua* essence, it is already individualized.

(3) RELATIVE PRIMACY OF WILL AND INTELLECT

This brings us to another major issue on which Duns and Thomas were divided, one on which Duns put himself definitely in the Augustinian camp. A central feature of Thomism is its emphasis on intellect—on the primacy of intellect in God and man, and, generally, on the rational structure of the created universe. Duns, on the contrary, assigned primacy to will, in both God and man, and introduced some important restrictions on the extent to which the universe can be said to be thoroughly rational.

First, as regards man, Duns had to allow, of course, that we can will only what we know about and that, in this sense, will depends on intellect. But he was more impressed by the fact that will moves intellect (we choose, for instance, to think about such-and-such). He defined this distinction in the following terms. Cognition of the object is only "accidentally" the cause of our willing it; will, on the other hand, is "properly and really" the cause of cognition. Intellect has causes other than itself—will, insofar as willing causes us to think; the object thought about, insofar as it determines what we think about it. But will has no cause other than itself. Like God's will, ours is completely free to choose—whatever it will. It follows that, in Duns's view, Thomas was mistaken in holding that we necessarily will what we see to be good. Our will is always contingent; we can *always* choose something different from what we do choose. Quite apart from whatever may be thought about this doctrine as psychological theory, it obviously took Duns dangerously far down the path to Pelagianism.

Further, Duns held that will is primary in God. This caused equally grave difficulties for him. If will is primary, there is no reason, it would appear, for God to act as He does. If there is no reason for God's acts, they are completely arbitrary. Murder, for instance, is wrong only because God happened to decree it to be wrong. Had He chosen (and, since there was no reason for choosing as He did, He might just as well have chosen otherwise) to command us to commit murder, it would be wrong to protect human life. And how do we know that God may not, tomorrow or the next day, change His decrees? If there is no *rational* basis for a distinction between virtue and vice, the distinction rests entirely on what can only be described as divine whim. A science of ethics becomes utterly impossible, and the possibility of acting morally comes to depend on our ability to guess what God's orders are going to be.

It was to avoid these dangerous conclusions that Thomas argued that God works according to eternal exemplars. But Duns saw that this Thomistic solution is involved in grave difficulties of its own. If God works by exemplars (even if these are held to be ideas in God's mind rather than independent, Platonic archetypes), God's freedom is limited. He is no longer omnipotent; He can no longer will *anything*, but only what is consistent with the eternal exemplars. It would seem, then, that Christian philosophy faces a major dilemma. Either God is free and the world is the irrational product of an arbitrary will, or the world is rational and God's will is limited.

Duns refused to choose between these distressing alternatives and, as usual, sought to escape the dilemma by more rigorously analyzing the alternatives. His argument at this point is extremely complex; it is possible to do no more here than suggest its main points. To begin with, as might be expected, he denied that the distinction between divine intellect and divine will is real. God's will could not possibly be subordinate to His intellect in the way in which, for instance, one individual man may be subordinate to another man. Thus, in men, even though will is free, it waits on the findings of intellect; without intellect's "advice," men would often will wrongly. But the divine will is not similarly fallible; even without the divine intellect it would never will mistakenly. Though the divine intellect does indeed provide the reasons why the divine will should will what it wills (reasons that would move the divine will if it were not divine), these reasons do not actually move the will. It freely moves itself. Though it moves in conformity with what the divine intellect advises, it does not move *because* intellect advises. Thus Duns held that, in God, there are, as it were, two operations—which, because they have identical results, appear to be causally dependent. But, he immediately added, in saying this we must not exaggerate the distinctness of the two operations; they are "formally" distinct, not "really" separate.

Though this is an ingenious formula, it did not save Duns from having to allow that the only reason for many moral laws is the fact that God happened to choose them. Duns appears, indeed, to have drawn the line only at the Ten Commandments. These, he held, God wills because they are good; lesser laws are good because He wills them. The distinction here was based on Duns's conviction that an attempt to deny any one of the Ten Commandments involves a logical contradiction (like denying that the whole is greater than the part). Since even God cannot will or think a contradiction, this validates the Ten Commandments. Any lesser law that cannot be validated in this way is, however, arbitrary in the sense that it depends on God's will alone.

Though Duns thus sought to avoid an ethic based exclusively on will and power, his emphasis on the primacy of will inevitably led in that direction. This amounts to saying that he did not succeed in resolving the dilemma; since he chose the volitional "horn," the consequences it entails followed in spite of all his efforts. Consider, for instance, the distinction just pointed out between major moral laws like the Ten Commandments and lesser moral rules. Suppose this distinction could not be maintained. Suppose, as has been held, no logical contradiction is involved in asserting that murder and dishonoring parents are right. In this event, Duns would have to allow that the major laws, like the minor ones, are dependent on God's will.

(4) LIMITATIONS OF NATURAL THEOLOGY

Finally, in this survey of Duns's differences from Thomas, we come to the question of the limits of natural theology. Thomas, of course, held that the spheres of theology and philosophy overlap to a considerable extent; he called this overlapping area of knowledge *natural theology*—"theology," because the subject matter of this science is the divine nature; "natural," because knowledge of the divine nature is attainable by natural means, that is, by the natural light of reason. Though Duns agreed with Thomas that theology and philosophy overlap to some extent and that a science of the divine nature is possible, he significantly reduced the area of this science's domain.

This may seem paradoxical in view of Duns's emphasis on the univocity of being and his insistence on the possibility of a natural knowledge of God. But, though he insisted on man's natural capacity to know God, he also held that in our present state, as a punishment for Adam's sin, we lack this capacity. Hence, as we have seen, Duns agreed with Thomas about the fact of limitation. That *some* limitation exists was, of course, essential from the point of view of medieval churchmen, intent on justifying the Church as an institution. To allow that man in his present state is capable of knowing God adequately would have been to open the way to mysticism and private religion—to Protestantism, in a word.

On the other hand, in avoiding this danger, it was important not to go so far in the other direction as to land in a sceptical denial of the possibility of any human knowledge of God. Duns believed that his formula—"a natural capacity but a present limitation of that capacity"—steered a safe middle course.

These considerations explain why Duns did not extend the domain of natural theology beyond the points fixed by Thomas, but they throw no light on why he actually limited it more severely. This is explained by the fact that Duns set much more rigorous criteria for demonstration than did Thomas. This, in its turn, was connected with Duns's interest in the certainty and objectivity of human knowledge. Because he set a higher standard for objectivity than did Thomas, Duns ended with less objective knowledge. Thus he made two major criticisms of Thomas' position. First, though Thomas himself did not realize it, his denial of univocity made it impossible for him to prove anything at all about God's nature. Second, because of Thomas' failure to understand the nature of evidence, he thought he had proved much more than can be proved about God. In a word, whereas it is possible to prove more about God than Thomas *actually* proved, it is not possible to prove as much about God as Thomas *thought* he had proved.

These points are illustrated in Duns's attitude toward the problem of proving God's existence. Though he agreed with Thomas that proofs of God's existence have to rest on an inference from effects to their cause,[15] he denied that such proofs can be absolutely conclusive. Here, surely, he was more correct than Thomas. Again, as regards specific Thomistic proofs, he was not impressed by the first-mover argument. The cause of movement, he realized, need not be the cause of being. Hence the argument did not prove the existence of the Christian God, but only that of Aristotle's unmoved mover.

Duns believed the argument from contingent being to be more effective. That contingent beings exist is, he thought, an obvious fact of experience. Since a contingent being cannot have caused itself, it must have been produced either by some other contingent being or by a necessary being. If its cause was a necessary being, the desired conclusion follows immediately—there is a necessary being. If its cause was another contingent being, this being in its turn must have been produced either by a necessary being or by a contingent being. Since Duns agreed with Thomas that there cannot be an infinite series of contingent causes, he held that ultimately we must come to a necessary being.

Necessity is not the only attribute of God that Duns believed capable of proof. It is also possible, he thought, to prove that God is one (for only one necessary being can exist, he maintained), that He is perfect and that He is good. On the other hand, he thought it impossible to prove much that Thomas thought could be proved—that God is omnipotent, that He is providential, that He has many

15 Unlike Thomas, Duns did not totally reject Anselm's ontological proof, but he thought it had to be "colored" before it could be accepted. Even so corrected, however, it did not yield a demonstrable conclusion. Unfortunately, the question of what Duns thought could be proved about God's nature and how he thought it could be proved is much complicated by uncertainty about the authorship of certain texts.

other of the theologically essential attributes. Consider, for instance, omnipotence. It can be proved, Duns held, that God is the ultimate cause of everything that happens. This follows, of course, from the argument about necessity and contingency. But the proof involves the introduction of intermediate causes, and it is not possible (Duns believed) to prove that God could produce everything *directly*, without intermediate causes. Hence it is not possible to prove that God is omnipotent in the full theological sense of that term.

Duns not only reduced the sphere of natural theology; he also, as compared with Thomas, emphasized its practical intent. Both these divergencies from Thomas were, of course, connected with Duns's voluntarism and his insistence on the primacy of will. To just the extent that God acts arbitrarily, it is impossible for man to give a rational account of His nature; we have to depend on His revelation of Himself to us instead of on our reason. To just the extent that will is primary in man, God's intent is to move our wills, not to enlighten our intellects. Of course, the difference between Thomas and Duns here is more a difference of degree than of kind. But there *is* a difference in emphasis. This is reflected in Duns's feeling that it would be well to call theology "wisdom" instead of "science." That is, theology, he held, is basically a matter of revelation, not of proof. And God's intent, in what He reveals to us and what He withholds from us, is to modify our conduct. His concern is less with what we know than with what we do. "Holy Scripture is a kind of knowledge divinely given in order to direct men to a supernatural end."

From this emphasis on Holy Scripture as the revealed word of God, one might suppose that Duns held the final authority to be the Bible. But he was too good a churchman for that. He argued that the grounds for belief in the Bible rest on the still higher authority of the Church, conceived of as a divine institution. This ultimate authority is not the bare scriptural account but the accumulation of comment on and interpretation of it made by the Church over the centuries. Thus, in contrast to Thomas, Duns insistently affirmed the Immaculate Conception of the Virgin Mary, though the Bible says nothing of this doctrine. The Church has sided with Duns on this point. This relegation of the Bible to a relatively subordinate position was characteristic of the later Scholastics and became one of the points of attack for the Protestant reformers, whose historical sense led them back to the "purity" of the Bible and the earliest fathers.

SUMMARY

To the historian of philosophy, Duns is a very interesting thinker. He is far more representative of the last phase of medieval thought than Roger Bacon. Indeed, he represents about all that thought *could* do within the limitations orthodoxy had set for itself. What philosophy could do was to refine and refine, distinguish and distinguish, interpret and interpret. Since the main positions had been irrevocably established, one could only hope, as it were, to remove every minor blemish by repeated polishing of the surface. In this process, Duns developed extremely efficient tools of analysis. Modern thinkers with a pragmatic bent are inclined to regret that he expended his obviously fine intellect on abstract metaphysical and theological problems. How much more profitable it would have been, such philosophers feel, had he given the same attention to the numerous social and political questions that desperately needed rigorous analysis. But this criticism overlooks the fact that the questions Duns discussed were important to him and to the society of his time—far more important than the social and political problems that seem so important to pragmatic philosophers.

These questions all centered around the crucial medieval problem of fixing the relation between faith and reason. This was a crucial problem precisely because men of the Middle Ages found they needed both; until they could show the two to be in thoroughgoing harmony, the medieval world view lacked stability. To demonstrate the rationality of Christian faith was the task Thomas had set for himself. But though Duns agreed that Thomas' program for working out this demonstration (that is, the Aristotelian metaphysics) was basically correct, he did not believe that Thomas had entirely succeeded. He therefore proposed to do better than Thomas what Thomas himself had tried to do. Thus, in intent, Scotism was systematic, positive, and rational. But, partly because Duns used a sharper instrument than Thomas had used, the net result was otherwise. By reducing the domain of natural theology, Duns upset the delicate balance Thomas had established between reason and revelation and so prepared the way for the thesis that reason is strictly a secular instrument. The final result of trying to save theology by excluding it from the field of rational inquiry was, ironically enough, its relegation to an increasingly inconsequential role in the coming "Age of Reason." By initiating this policy, by upsetting the Thomistic balance, by emphasizing the role of revelation, Duns helped to produce precisely the state of affairs that he would have most deplored—the isolation of religion.

William of Occam

If Duns shows the maximum that could be done inside the orthodox Scholastic framework, William shows what happens when those limits are pressed too strongly. For he developed those tendencies in Scotism that were deviations from Thomism to a point at which the Thomistic compromise was destroyed.

LIFE

Like Duns and Roger Bacon, Occam was a Franciscan; like them, he began his studies at Oxford and later moved to Paris. By 1323 Occam's reputation had spread sufficiently for his teachings to be viewed with suspicion by the Church, and he was summoned to defend himself against the charge of teaching heretical views. His case moved slowly, and meanwhile he became involved in other difficulties. Another case being adjudicated before the papal court was concerned with a dispute over how literally St. Francis' vow of poverty should be interpreted by the order he had founded, of which Occam was a member. In the bitter dispute that ensued, Occam sided against the pope and with those who insisted that true Christianity implied literal poverty. He and the other leaders of the opposition were excommunicated in 1328 but took refuge with the emperor Louis of Bavaria. Since this was a moment at which the old feud between empire and papacy flared up again, Occam was welcomed by the emperor. "Do you defend me with your sword; I will defend you with my pen," Occam said to him on his arrival. Occam's belief that St. Francis was correct naturally disposed him to oppose the pope's claim to temporal authority. His role as a publicist and propagandist for the emperor led him to more and more extreme positions, and eventually he formulated a political theory that was prophetic of the coming secular age. Here, however, we must confine ourselves to considering how his thought fits into the pattern of declining Scholasticism.

THE SEPARATE SPHERES OF FAITH AND REASON

As a young man at Paris, William had studied Duns's views, and though he was critical of some aspects of Scotism, many of his conclusions were but the logical development of Duns's own position. Thus he carried to the limit the process, which Duns had begun, of narrowing the domain of natural theology. He held that neither God's existence nor His unity nor His infinity can be proved. Not only is it impossible to prove these basic theological propositions, but, according to William, faith does not supplement and perfect reason. The spheres of faith and reason are so distinct that reason may on occasion contradict faith, that is, it may be possible to prove the contradictory of certain dogmas. When this happens, we must follow faith even though we see it to be irrational. For in theology faith is supreme and reason is irrelevant.

These radical conclusions about the irrationality of theology seemed to William to be entailed by the doctrine of God's omnipotence. If we take seriously the affirmation of the creed, "I believe in God the Father Almighty . . ." we have to conclude, Occam held, that God can do literally anything. He could, had He so chosen, have become incarnate as ox or ass instead of as man. If God's election to assume the body of a man was merely an arbitrary act of will rather than a decision based on a rational plan, it is obviously idle for us to try to *understand* the incarnation. Similar considerations apply to all the other Christian mysteries.

Again, Occam argued, the doctrine of God's omnipotence means that the validity of cognition is severely limited. When I perceive my desk, I assume that my desk exists and is the cause of the perception. But God, being omnipotent, could destroy the desk and nevertheless, by an act of will, cause me to have exactly the perception of it that I have in its actual presence. In other words, bearing in mind Duns's definition of omnipotence,[16] one can say that it is just as possible for God to produce any effect (for example, my perception of my desk) directly, by a special act of will, as it is for Him to produce it by means of secondary causes (for example, by means of the physical desk and the normal series of changes it causes in my sense organs). The former would, of course, be a miracle. But God can produce any miracle He chooses, and we can never be sure whether any particular occurrence is or is not a miracle.

> Intuitive cognition . . . can exist concerning a non-existent thing. And I prove this conclusion . . . as follows: Every absolute thing distinct in place and subject from another absolute thing can exist without the latter in virtue of divine power; since it does not seem likely that if God wishes to destroy [one] absolute thing . . . , He is necessitated to destroy another absolute thing. . . . But since . . . vision is an absolute thing distinct in place and subject from the object . . . , that vision can remain in existence, the [object] having been destroyed [that is, my perception of the desk and the desk itself are distinct things; God can destroy one without destroying the other].[n]

A virtually complete scepticism about natural knowledge would seem to be the only possible conclusion to this argument. Occam appears, somewhat inconsistently, to have drawn back a little from this extreme position, but others went on to draw the logical conclusion. Thus one of William's pupils, Nicholaus of Autrecourt, maintained that we can be sure only of (1) the immediate data of consciousness (that I am now seeing a mahogany-colored sense datum, but not that it is a desk) and (2) the purely formal relationships that can be derived from the principle of contradiction (such as, "If what I am sensing is red, it is not not-red"). It follows, as Nicholaus pointed out, that we cannot be certain of the existence of any substance, not even that of our own soul;[17] nor can we be certain of causality.

These conclusions result from the following considerations. Substance never appears in perception. I perceive a mahogany-colored, rectangular-shaped datum —not the substance having these attributes. I perceive anger, fear, hunger—not the soul experiencing these states. If substance itself is not in the perceptual field, it must be an inference from that field. But is the inference valid? Obviously not, on Occam's premise. For the principle of contradiction is the only certain principle, and it merely states that a given object cannot have contradictory properties (A and not-A) at the same time. There is nothing, of course, that prevents different things from having the contradictory properties. Hence, since substance and attribute, however closely connected they may be in some respects, are not identical, there is nothing contradictory about one's being present and

16 See pp. 312–13.
17 J. R. Weinberg's arguments that Nicholaus held the existence of the soul to be suspect seem conclusive (*Nicholaus of Autrecourt,* pp. 41 ff.).

the other's being absent. It follows that it is never possible to infer from the presence of one the existence of any other. "From the fact that one thing is known to exist, it cannot be inferred that another thing exists." This is but the logical terminus of Occam's thesis (which Occam himself had inherited from Duns) that there is only one exception to God's arbitrary will—the principle of contradiction. That this line of reasoning operates as effectively against cause as against substance is easily seen. To say that A causes B is to make an inference (we never *see* A causing B). But since A and B are distinct, the inference is invalid.[18]

So much for the sceptical conclusions about the possibility of a natural knowledge that can be (that were, in fact) drawn from Occam's views. To say now that one of Occam's major concerns was to establish natural science on a firm footing may seem strange. But it is possible that Occam himself did not realize the full implications of his theological views, and even if he had, he would presumably have felt that the sharp distinctions he drew between theology and science prevented any communication, let alone any contradiction, between the two realms. After all, the sceptical conclusions just described follow from a purely theological premise, the omnipotence of God. Conclusions reached in this field could have no more bearing on scientific truth than reason in its turn could have on revelation and faith. Occam was well on his way to the double-truth doctrine of the Averroists,[19] which held theological truth and rational truth, like Kipling's East and West, to be twain that can never meet.

OCCAM'S THEORY OF KNOWLEDGE

Excluding, then, any theological considerations from his natural science, as he had excluded rational considerations from his theology, Occam proceeded to reexamine the basis of scientific knowledge. His starting point was the conviction that the views of both Thomas and Duns were too deeply infected with Augustinian Neoplatonism to be adequate. Though they both believed they had safeguarded the adequacy of natural knowledge, they had both allowed the existence (in some sense) of universals. William, for his part, wished to go back to what he took to be the pure Aristotle, untainted with any suggestion of Platonic "realism," for he saw that the doctrine that universals are real had always been associated with the proposition that the sense world is mere appearance. The more real the realm of universals, the less real is this world in comparison and, correspondingly, the more men must rely for real knowledge on some kind of extranatural illumination. For, according to the realists' view, our dealings with sense objects can at best give only fragmentary suggestions of reality, incomplete and only partially true. Final knowledge, the complete truth, resides in the Form

18 It is hardly necessary to add that Nicholaus' views were condemned (in 1346) by the Papal Curia. He was obliged to make a public retraction, his books were burned, and he was deprived of his academic degrees.
19 See pp. 326–27.

of the Good, which, being suprasensible, can easily be interpreted as supranatural. Thus this type of view always hovers on the brink of mysticism, if it does not descend into it. The real is something beyond sense that comes to men as a gift, through illumination, rather than something that, because it is *of* sense, men find *in* sense.

It is easy today to understand, and to sympathize with, William's desire to work out a theory of knowledge that validates the thinking of finite minds, that begins with, and completes itself in, the particulars of sense perception. As we have seen, Thomas and Duns, each in his own way, sympathized with this point of view. But they, indeed, most medieval thinkers, also held that to abandon universals altogether is to surrender the possibility of scientific knowledge. For science aims at general, not at particular, assertions, and if there are no universals, what are general assertions about? Therefore it seemed to them necessary to hold on to universals, though Duns attempted to reduce the threat they posed to the independent validity of natural knowledge by asserting that they have only a formal, not a real, existence.

But this, William believed, was a wholly unnecessary concession to realism. He thought he could save scientific knowledge without Duns's complicated apparatus of forms and their various contractions. He began by pointing out that what we think *about* are the individual particulars of sense perception. What we think about them *with* are universals. Universals are the tools with which we think; except in the science of logic, they are not themselves objects of thought. In order to fix this distinction, Occam called the sciences (physics, psychology, and so on) that are concerned with the world of things "real" sciences. Logic, however, he called a "rational" science; it does not deal with real objects but with the "signs" by means of which the mind knows real objects. It is not concerned with these signs as having meanings (that is, as being true or false); that is the business of physics. It is not concerned with how they arise in the mind; that is the business of psychology. It is concerned simply with the various ways in which we may combine these signs so as to express what we want to express. Its purpose, in other words, is to reveal how the real sciences use signs significantly.[20]

If the objects of study in logic are not things but signs, it is necessary to ask what a sign is. In the most general sense, a sign is simply something that stands for or represents something else. Thus smoke is a sign of fire; tears are a sign of sorrow. In the realm of discourse, however, we are concerned with those signs that stand for the particular individuals of sense perception. Such signs may be either natural or conventional. The concept that the mind forms in the act of understanding or perceiving is the natural sign of the thing understood or perceived; the written or spoken word by which the object is indicated is its conventional sign. The same conventional sign may be used in quite different

20 This account of Occam's logic follows E. A. Moody, *The Logic of William of Ockham* (Sheed and Ward, London, 1935).

ways in different contexts. For instance, in the sentence, "Man is an animal," the sign "man" stands for certain existent things—Plato, Socrates, Aristotle; in the sentence, "'Man' is a three-letter word," it stands for itself. In the second sentence something is being said about the sign (that is why it is enclosed in quotes). In the first sentence something is being said about the things the sign is the sign of. William's way of describing this difference was to say that in the first sentence the term is used "significantly" and that in the second it is used "nonsignificantly."

Next, Occam distinguished between what he called "terms of first intention" and "terms of second intention." The former are terms that stand for (are signs of) real things—"cow," "horse," and "man" all stand for individual existents. The latter are terms that stand for other terms—"noun," "verb," "universal," for instance. It is obvious that these two distinctions cut across each other. A second intention term (for example, "genus") can be used either significantly (as in the sentence, "A genus is predicable of the species under it") or nonsignificantly (as in the sentence, "'Genus' is a five-letter word").

It is now possible to redefine with precision the nature of logic, as William conceived of it. The objects of study in logic are terms of second intention used significantly. Though William's logic is interesting in its own right, we are concerned here only with the question of how he used the distinctions just described to solve the puzzle about the status of universals and to fix the nature of the objects of scientific knowledge. Some terms, he said, are signs of individuals—the term "Plato," for instance, or "Socrates." Other terms are signs of many individuals—the term "man," for instance. All natural knowledge is knowledge of individuals, but since science aims at general knowledge, it attempts to make general statements that are true of many individuals. Because this is the aim of science, scientific statements are made up of universal terms rather than individual terms. But to say, "Man is mortal," is only a shorthand way of saying, "Socrates is mortal and Plato is mortal and Aristotle is mortal and so on."

This is all there is to a universal. Accordingly, there is no "problem" of universals at all. A universal is an immense convenience, a great time-saver, but it is only a term—a tool used in reasoning scientifically. It is not a thing, and not an object of thought except in logic, in which, of course, it is simply a term of second intention. The realists supposed that universals are things (objects of thought) because they failed to see the elementary distinction between terms of first intention and terms of second intention.

One point remains to be cleared up. A universal, in Occam's view, is nothing more than a tool—a sign of many. But besides the obviously conventional sign (the written or spoken word "man"), is there a natural sign? It seemed clear to Occam that there is indeed a natural sign; it is what was loosely called, a moment ago, the concept that the mind forms as it understands or perceives.[21]

---

21 This distinguishes Occam's view from the extreme nominalism of Roscelin and his school. They would have allowed only conventional signs. It might be better, therefore, not to call Occam a "nominalist," as many have done, but to call him a "terminist."

Is it possible to say more definitely what sort of status this concept, or natural sign, has in the mind? According to Occam, there are three possibilities:

> But what, in the soul, is this thing which is a sign? It must be said that with regard to this there are various opinions. For some say that it is nothing but a certain fiction produced by the soul. Others say that it is a certain quality existing subjectively in the soul, distinct from the act of understanding. Others say that it is the act of understanding. And in favor of these there is this to be said: what can be explained on fewer principles is explained needlessly by more. Everything, however, which is explained through positing something distinct from the act of understanding can be explained without positing such a distinct thing. For to stand for something and to signify something can belong just as well to the act of understanding as to this fictive entity; therefore one ought not to posit anything else beyond the act of understanding.[o]

Thus Occam rejected as an unnecessary complication the view that a universal (as a natural sign) is some sort of entity thought by the mind; it is nothing but the act of thinking itself.

Occam's argument here contains one of the guiding principles of his thought: "What can be explained on fewer principles is explained needlessly by more." This maxim, which came to be known as "Occam's razor," is a most important methodological principle: "Do not multiply entities beyond necessity"—that is, avoid postulating entities to account for what can be explained without them. Or alternatively, when presented with two hypotheses, both of which account for a given fact, give preference to the simpler. This is a rule that has guided, and is still guiding, the development of modern scientific thought. The reason, for instance, that Copernicus and everyone since his day has preferred the heliocentric to the geocentric hypothesis is not that the latter breaks down (for it is quite possible to work out a consistent description of the movements of the planets on the hypothesis that the earth is stationary and at the center of the system), but that the former is much simpler.

Occam's attitude of mind has sometimes been called "empirical." It was empirical in the sense that, for Occam, knowledge was of the sense world. But it was not empirical in the sense of being opposed to rationalism. Occam's science was still deductive and demonstrative, altogether different from the inductive and experimental method at which Bacon had vaguely hinted, the method that was actually to be developed one hundred and fifty years later. A better way to describe Occam's attitude is to say that, as far as the sciences go, it was secular. Occam wanted to get on without divine assistance in the way of special illuminations. This point of view really follows from his determination to separate the spheres of reason and revelation. If they are separate, reason must be able to operate without recourse to extranatural aids. It must be able to reach its own kind of truth in its own kind of way.

BACON AND OCCAM

It is not easy to assess exactly the roles Bacon and Occam played in the decline of Scholasticism or the impact they had on the development of the thought that was to dominate the coming centuries. Neither, certainly, was as unorthodox as some modern commentators have supposed. Such as their rebellion was, it was still confined—at least in intent—within the framework of a basically medieval view. Neither for a moment questioned the authority of the Church in spiritual matters, nor the supremacy of theology. Nevertheless, Occam's Aristotelianism, with its emphasis on a knowledge that is true and complete in this world, was in fact disruptive of the Scholastic position insofar as it encouraged men to explore the sensible world and to track down the finite truths it contains. So, too, his "razor," if used more ruthlessly than he employed it, was capable of destroying the whole teleological and metaphysical basis of medieval science, which Occam himself accepted. One might indeed say that the empirical and descriptive science that was eventually worked out, the science that Occam himself did not dream of, came to be preferred on what amount to Occamist grounds. The new science gave a *simpler* account of natural occurrences than could be derived from the hidden purposes, occult forces, and divine love that had dominated earlier explanations of nature. It came to be preferred, too, on Baconian grounds: It was more *useful*. It resulted in immense technological improvements and inventions of the kind Bacon himself had dimly prophesied. All this, of course, was yet far in the future. The point is that Occam and Bacon, though still Scholastics in many respects, expressed a view that later flowered into the modern scientific spirit.

But this does not answer the question of the extent of these thinkers' "influence" on later thought. Although Bacon had his pupils, whom, presumably, he imbued with his views, he was too much of an individualist to have founded an actual school. With Occam, however, the situation is different. There was an active school of "nominalist" logicians who looked to him as master. Even more significant for future developments, a number of his pupils turned their attention to the study of natural science with the new secular and empirical point of view that he had enunciated.

Nicholas of Oresme (1320–82), one of Occam's pupils, held that the observed movements of the planets might be better accounted for on the assumption that the outer sphere of the fixed stars is stationary and the earth is in motion than (as in the standard view of the day) on the assumption that the earth is stationary and the sphere of the fixed stars is moving around it.

John Buridan (about 1300–about 1358), another student of Occam's, argued, in accordance with the latter's "razor," that the celestial bodies must be composed of the same matter as the earth. There is no reason, he held, to assume two kinds of matter when one will serve. Buridan also maintained that the motion imparted by any body to another body is proportional to the velocity of the first body and the quantity of matter in the second. Motions once begun continue indefinitely unless interfered with. Hence, if God launched the planets with a certain quantity of motion, they will continue in their courses naturally; there will be no need for further intervention. Accordingly, the Aristotelian hypothesis that the planets are continuously moved by "intelligences" is unnecessary and may be discarded in accordance with the methodology of the "razor."

The last point was brought out by Buridan in an interesting discussion of the acceleration of freely falling bodies. A few extracts from this discussion will illustrate the critical and empirical quality of Buridan's thought as contrasted with the old wives' tales recounted by Bartholomew and Vincent.[22] But note that Buridan's experiments were not used to test hypotheses; they were introduced to convince the reader of the truth of conclusions that Buridan himself had already reached by deductive reasoning.

> Whether natural motion ought to be swifter in the end than the beginning . . . . With respect to this question it ought to be said that it is a conclusion not to be doubted factually, for, as it has been said, all people perceive that the motion of a heavy body downward is continually accelerated, it having been posited that it falls through a uniform medium. For everybody perceives that by the amount that a stone descends over a greater distance and falls on a man, by that amount does it more seriously injure him.
>
> But the great difficulty in this question is why this [acceleration] is so. Concerning this matter there have been many different opinions. The Commentator [Averroes] in the second book [of his commentary on the *De Caelo*] ventures some obscure statements on it, declaring that a heavy body approaching the end is moved more swiftly because of a great desire for the end and because of the heating action of its motion. From these statements two opinions have sprouted.
>
> The first opinion was that motion produces heat, as it is said in the second book of this [work, the *De Caelo*], and, therefore, a heavy body descending swiftly through the air makes that air hot, and consequently it [the air] becomes rarefied. The air, thus rarefied, is more easily divisible and less resistant. Now, if the resistance is diminished, it is reasonable that the movement becomes swifter.
>
> But this argument is insufficient. In the first place, because the air in the summer is noticeably hotter than in the winter, and yet the same stone falling an equal distance in the summer and in the winter is not moved with appreciably greater speed in the summer than in the winter; nor does it strike harder. Furthermore, . . . a man moves his hand just as swiftly as a stone falls toward the beginning of its movement. This is apparent, because striking another person hurts him more than the falling stone, even if the stone is harder. And yet a man so moving his hand does not heat the air sensibly, since he would perceive that heating. . . .
>
> The other opinion which originated from the statements of the Commentator is this: Place is related to the thing placed as a final cause, as Aristotle

22 See pp. 166–70.

implies and the Commentator explains in the fourth book of the *Physics*.
. . . It seems reasonable that the heavy body is moved more swiftly by the
same amount that it is nearer to its natural place. This is because, if place
is the moving cause, then it can move that body more strongly when the
body is nearer to it, for an agent acts more strongly on something near to
it than on something far away from it. And if place were nothing but the
final cause which the heavy body seeks naturally and for the attainment of
which the body is moved, then it seems reasonable that the natural appetite
for that end is increased more from it as that end is nearer. And so it seems
in every way reasonable that a heavy body is moved more swiftly by the
amount that is nearer to [its] downward place. But in descending continually
it ought to be moved more and more swiftly.

But this opinion . . . is against manifest experience, for you can lift the
same stone near the earth just as easily as you can in a high place if that
stone were there, for example, at the top of a tower. . . .

Again, let a stone begin to fall from a high place to the earth and another
similar stone begin to fall from a low place to the earth. Then these stones,
when they should be at a distance of one foot from the earth, ought to be
moved equally fast and one ought not to be swifter than the other if the
greater velocity should arise only from nearness to [their] natural place, because they should be equally near to [their] natural place. Yet it is manifest
to the senses that the body which should fall from the high point would be
moved much more quickly than that which should fall from the low point,
and it would kill a man while the other stone [falling from the low point]
would not hurt him. . . .

I conclude, therefore, that the accelerated natural movements of heavy
and light bodies do not arise from greater proximity to [their] natural place,
but from something else that is either near or far, but which is varied by
reason of the length of the motion. . . .

With the [foregoing] methods of solving this question set aside, there remains, it seems to me, one necessary solution. It is my supposition that the
natural gravity of the stone remains always the same and similar before the
movement, after the movement, and during the movement. Hence the stone
is found to be equally heavy after the movement as it was before it. I suppose
also that the resistance which arises from the medium remains the same or
is similar, since, as I have said, it does not appear to me that the air lower
and nearer to the earth should be less resistant than the superior air. Rather
the superior air perhaps ought to be less resistant because it is more subtle.
Third, I suppose that if the moving body is the same, the total mover is the
same, and the resistance also is the same or similar, the movement will remain
equally swift, since the proportion of mover to moving body and to the resistance will remain [the same]. Then I add that in the movement downward
of the heavy body the movement does not remain equally fast but continually
becomes swifter.

From these [suppositions] it is concluded that another moving force concurs
in that movement beyond the natural gravity which was moving [the body]
from the beginning and which remains always the same. Then finally I say
that this other mover is not the place which attracts the heavy body as the

magnet does the iron; nor is it some force existing in the place and arising either from the heavens or from something else, because it would immediately follow that the same heavy body would begin to be moved more swiftly from a low place than from a high one, and we experience the contrary of this conclusion. . . .

From these [reasons] it follows that one must imagine that a heavy body not only acquires motion unto itself from its principal mover, i.e., its gravity, but that it also acquires unto itself a certain impetus with that motion. This impetus has the power of moving the heavy body in conjunction with the permanent natural gravity. And because that impetus is acquired in common with motion, hence the swifter the motion is, the greater and stronger the impetus is. So, therefore, from the beginning the heavy body is moved by its natural gravity only; hence it is moved slowly. Afterwards it is moved by that same gravity and by the impetus acquired at the same time; consequently, it is moved more swiftly. And because the movement becomes swifter, therefore the impetus also becomes greater and stronger, and thus the heavy body is moved by its natural gravity and by that greater impetus simultaneously, and so it will again be moved faster; and thus it will always and continually be accelerated to the end. And just as the impetus is acquired in common with motion, so it is decreased or becomes deficient in common with the decrease and deficiency of the motion.

And you have an experiment [to support this position]: If you cause a large and very heavy smith's mill [that is, a wheel] to rotate and you then cease to move it, it will still move a while longer by this impetus it has acquired. Nay, you cannot immediately bring it to rest, but on account of the resistance from the gravity of the mill, the impetus would be continually diminished until the mill would cease to move. And if the mill would last forever without some diminution or alteration of it, and there were no resistance corrupting the impetus, perhaps the mill would be moved perpetually by that impetus.

And thus one could imagine that it is unnecessary to posit intelligences as the movers of celestial bodies since the Holy Scriptures do not inform us that intelligences must be posited. For it could be said that when God created the celestial spheres, He began to move each of them as He wished, and they are still moved by the impetus which He gave to them because, there being no resistance, the impetus is neither corrupted nor diminished.ᴾ

The Averroists

Occam's brand of Aristotelianism was not the only version of Aristotle's thought that came into vogue during this period. It will be recalled that the Aristotelian writings came to be known in the West through Arabian translations and commentaries. Of these, the most influential in the West were those by Averroes (1126–98), who denied personal immortality and affirmed the eternity of the world. Despite the Church's intense opposition to Averroes' views, they have continued to this day to exercise great influence on thought. The only way the

Christian Averroists could maintain their position was to go even further than Duns and Occam in separating theology and philosophy and to adopt a doctrine of double truth. What is true in philosophy (no personal immortality) is false in theology, and vice versa.

The importance of these views in the history of philosophy is that, like Occam's views, they helped to secularize science and philosophy and to free them, insofar as the Averroists were successful in maintaining their position against a deeply suspicious Church, from the restraints of dogma. The convenient concept of a double truth thus created an opportunity for independent investigation within the bounds of orthodoxy, which otherwise could not have occurred until the authority of the Church had been shattered. Moreover, Averroism revived that interest in the empirical sense world that, as we have seen, Occam himself had found in Aristotle. This interest was less noticeable in Paris, where the Averroists were embroiled in theological arguments, than in Padua, where, because the Venetians did not tolerate papal interference, the theologians had much less weight. In northern Italy, then, especially at Padua, there developed schools of medicine and surgery that were vigorous, enterprising, and empirically oriented.[23]

There is little profit in trying to distinguish the Occamist, Averroist, and Baconian influences at work in creating this new secular and empirical point of view. More important than attempting to trace the influence of this or that particular philosopher is seeing that these thinkers—Bacon and Occam, for instance—were not isolated phenomena. Rather, they were signs of a new climate of opinion that was beginning to emerge. When it developed far enough, when it spread widely enough, the Middle Ages came to an end. If the theories of Occam and Bacon were among the causes of this new climate of opinion, it is just as true that they were among its chief effects. Therefore, instead of trying to assess the causal roles of Occam and Bacon in this unfolding process, one should see them as two representatives, unusual by reason of their penetration and brilliance but otherwise typical, of an age of transition.

23 See, for instance, L. Thorndike, *Science and Thought in the Fifteenth Century* (Columbia University Press, 1929), pp. 59–80, for an account of a work on surgery by a Paduan scholar and doctor, Leonard of Bertipaglia.

Notes

Chapter 1 / The New Religious Orientation

a Prudentius, *Peristephanon*, X, 1011, quoted in F. Cumont, *The Oriental Religions in Roman Paganism* (Open Court, Chicago, 1911), p. 66.
b Cyprian, *Ad Demetr.* 3, quoted in W. R. Inge, *The Philosophy of Plotinus* (Longmans, New York, 1929), Vol. I, pp. 25–26.
c *The Republic*, translated by B. Jowett, in *The Dialogues of Plato* (Random House, New York, 1937), Vol. I, 509.
d *Enneads*, translated by G. H. Turnbull, in *The Essence of Plotinus* (Oxford, New York, 1934), V, iii, 12–17; V, v, 4–9; VI, ix, 5–6.
e *Ibid.*, I, iii, 4–5.
f *Ibid.*, V, iii, 12; V, v, 10–11; VI, vii, 16; III, viii, 10; IV, iv, 9; VI, iv, 2; III, viii, 4.
g *Ibid.*, III, ii, 4; III, iv, 5, 2, and 3.
h *Ibid.*, V, i, 4.
i *Ibid.*, V, i, 2.

j   *Ibid.*, III, viii, 9; V, iii, 9.
k   *Ibid.*, III, vi, 5.
l   Inge, *The Philosophy of Plotinus, op. cit.*, Vol. II, p. 152.
m   Quoted in W. E. H. Lecky, *History of European Morals* (Appleton, New York, 1869), Vol. I, p. 417.
n   Isa. 10:5 ff., in *The Complete Bible*, translated by J. M. P. Smith and E. J. Goodspeed (University of Chicago Press, 1939).
o   I Kings 21:28–29.
p   I Kings 19:11–13.
q   Amos 6:1 ff.
r   Amos 2:6–7.
s   Amos 5:21–24.
t   Hos. 6:6.
u   Mic. 6:6–8.
v   Ps. 119:97, 72, and 45; 1:2.
w   Matt. 5:28.
x   Mark 7:5, 9, 18, and 20–23.
y   Matt. 7:11.
z   Matt. 11:20–21 and 23–24.
a   Matt. 6:19–21; Mark 8:35–36.
b   Acts 2:45–47.
c   Luke 12:33; Matt. 19:21.

Chapter 2   /   Christianity: The Formative Years

a   See, for instance, Phil. 3:5, in *The Complete Bible*, translated by J. M. P. Smith and E. J. Goodspeed (University of Chicago Press, 1939).
b   See, for instance, Gal. 1:13–14.
c   Rom. 1:13 and 15–17; 2:17–18 and 25–29; 3:9–11, 20–25, and 28–31; 5:1–3 and 5–7.
d   Rom. 5:12, 14, and 18–19.
e   Rom. 7:5–6.
f   Rom. 7:14–25.
g   Rom. 8:1–10, 28–35, and 38–39.
h   Rom. 6:4 and 10–11.
i   Gal. 3:25–28.
j   Gal. 5:13, 16–23, and 25.
k   Rom. 12:4–9.
l   Phil. 2:6 and 9.
m   I Cor. 15:24 and 28.
n   Phil. 2:6–8.
o   John 1:1–15 and 18.
p   John 14:13–18 and 23.
q   I Cor. 14:2, 5, 18–19, 23, 27–32, and 40.
r   *Gnosticism: A Source Book of Heretical Writings from the Early Christian Period*, edited by R. M. Grant (Harper & Row, New York, 1961), pp. 24–25.
s   Quoted in H. A. Wolfson, *The Philosophy of the Church Fathers* (Harvard University Press, 1956), Vol. I, p. 103.
t   Letter to Demetrias, quoted in A. C. McGiffert, *A History of Christian Thought* (Scribner's, New York, 1933), Vol. II, pp. 125–26.

Chapter 3   /   Augustine: God the Creator

a   Lactantius, *De Mortibus Persecutorum*, Ch. 48, quoted in P. Gardner-Smith, *The Church in the Roman Empire* (Cambridge University Press, 1932), p. 31.
b   Quoted in Gardner-Smith, *op. cit.*, p. 100.
c   *Confessions*, translated by J. G. Pilkington (Liveright, New York, 1943), II, i, 1; I, xviii, 30; II, iv, 9.
d   *Ibid.*, III, i, 1; III, ii, 2; IV, i, 1.
e   *Ibid.*, III, vii, 12; IV, xv, 24 and 26; V, x, 18 and 20.
f   *Ibid.*, VII, v, 7; VII, vii, 11.
g   *Ibid.*, VII, v, 7; VI, v, 7.
h   Rom. 7:18–19 and 24, in *The Complete Bible*, translated by J. M. P. Smith and E. J. Goodspeed (University of Chicago Press, 1939).
i   *Confessions*, translated by Pilkington, *op. cit.*, VIII, i, 1 and 2.
j   *Ibid.*, VIII, v, 10 and 12.
k   *Ibid.*, VIII, vi, 15; VIII, vii, 16 and 17; VIII, xi, 25–26; VIII, xii, 28–29.
l   *Ibid.*, I, i, 1 and 2; I, iv, 4.
m   F. H. Bradley, in *Appearance and Reality* (Clarendon Press, Oxford, 1930), p. 5.
n   *Confessions*, translated by Pilkington, *op. cit.*, XI, v, 7.
o   *City of God*, translated by M. Dods (T. & T. Clark, Edinburgh, 1872), xi, 26.
p   *Confessions*, translated by Pilkington, *op. cit.*, XI, xi, 13 ff.
q   *City of God*, translated by Dods, *op. cit.*, xi, 27.
r   *Ibid.*, x, 3; xi, 13; xix, 11.
s   *Confessions*, translated by Pilkington, *op. cit.*, I, vi, 7.
t   *Ibid.*, V, viii, 14 and 15.
u   *City of God*, translated by Dods, *op. cit.*, xi, 22.
v   *Ibid.*, xii, 1; xxii, 1.
w   *Ibid.*, v, 9–10.

Chapter 4   /   Augustine: The Created Universe

a   *City of God*, translated by M. Dods (T. & T. Clark, Edinburgh, 1872), xv, 1.
b   See, for instance, *ibid.*, xxi, 9–13.
c   *Ibid.*, xxii, 30.
d   *Ibid.*, xix, 7.
e   *Confessions*, translated by J. G. Pilkington (Liveright, New York, 1943), VIII, vii, 16.
f   *Ibid.*, VII, xvi, 22.
g   *City of God*, translated by Dods, *op. cit.*, xxii, 1; xii, 1, 6–8, and 21.
h   *Ibid.*, xiv, 13.
i   *Ibid.*, xiv, 14; xxii, 22.
j   *Ibid.*, xix, 25.
k   See Rom. 7:15–25; and *Confessions*, translated by Pilkington, *op. cit.*, VIII, vii, 17.
l   *Confessions*, translated by Pilkington, *op. cit.*, VIII, x, 22.
m   *City of God*, translated by Dods, *op. cit.*, xii, 3; xiv, 5 and 3.
n   Sermon 101, quoted in J. McCabe, *St. Augustine and His Age* (Putnam's, New York, 1902), p. 212.
o   *Confessions*, translated by Pilkington, *op. cit.*, X, xxxi, 44 and 47.
p   *Ibid.*, X, xxxiv, 51; X, xxxv, 54.
q   *City of God*, translated by Dods, *op. cit.*, xxii, 22.
r   *Ibid.*, v, 21.

s   *Ibid.,* xix, 15.
t   *Ibid.,* iv, 3.
u   *Ibid.,* i, 16.
v   *Ibid.,* xix, 25.
w   *Confessions,* translated by Pilkington, *op. cit.,* X, xxxix, 64.
x   *Ibid.,* X, xxxii, 48.
y   *City of God,* translated by Dods, *op. cit.,* xxii, 22.
z   *Confessions,* translated by Pilkington, *op. cit.,* IV, xii, 19.
a   *City of God,* translated by Dods, *op. cit.,* xiv, 27.
b   *Ibid.,* xiv, 26.
c   Letter 93, quoted in E. M. Pickman, *The Mind of Latin Christendom* (Oxford, New York, 1937), p. 570.
d   *De Baptismo,* II, 3 (4), quoted in A. C. McGiffert, *A History of Christian Thought* (Scribner's, New York, 1933), Vol. II, p. 116.
e   *Confessions,* translated by Pilkington, *op. cit.,* X, iii, 4.
f   *City of God,* translated by Dods, *op. cit.,* xxi, 4 and 5.
g   *Ibid.,* x, 12.
h   *Ibid.,* xxi, 8.
i   *Ibid.,* x, 21.

Chapter 5   /   The Medieval Interval

a   Letter from Charlemagne to the Abbot of Fulda, quoted in F. A. Ogg, *A Source Book of Mediaeval History* (American Book, New York, 1907), pp. 147–48.
b   Quoted in O. J. Thatcher and E. H. McNeal, *A Source Book for Medieval History* (Scribner's, New York, 1905), pp. 85–86.
c   Quoted in M. B. Foster, *Masters of Political Thought* (Houghton Mifflin, Boston, 1941), p. 234.
d   Quoted in Foster, *op. cit.,* p. 235.
e   Quoted in E. F. Henderson, *Select Historical Documents* (George Bell, London, 1896), pp. 325 and 328.
f   Quoted in Thatcher and McNeal, *op. cit.,* p. 156.
g   *Rule of St. Benedict,* in Thatcher and McNeal, *op. cit.,* pp. 435 ff.
h   St. Bonaventura, *Life of St. Francis,* translated by E. G. Salter (J. M. Dent and Sons, London, 1910), pp. 307–09, 314, 316–17, 322, 329–31, 353, 378, and 384–85.
i   *Joinville's Chronicle of the Crusade of St. Louis,* in *Memoirs of the Crusades,* translated by F. T. Marzials (Everyman, E. P. Dutton, New York, 1908), p. 142.
j   *Ibid.,* p. 276.
k   *Ibid.,* pp. 140–41, 148, and 145.
l   *Ibid.,* p. 144.
m   *Ibid.,* pp. 159–60.
n   *Ibid.,* p. 151.
o   *Ibid.,* pp. 321–23.
p   Quotations in this section are from *Aucassin and Nicolete,* translated by A. Lang (Nutt, London, 1887), pp. 3 and 56; and from *The Romance of the Rose,* translated by F. S. Ellis (J. M. Dent and Sons, London, 1903), ll. 1673 ff., 1707 ff., and 1965 ff.
q   Translated by D. G. Rossetti.
r   *The Purgatorio,* translated by J. Ciardi (Mentor Books, New York, 1957), Canto XXX, ll. 31 and 34–39.
s   *Mediaeval Lore from Bartholomew Anglicus,* edited by R. Steele (Chatto and Windus, London, 1924), pp. 21–22, 31–32, 36–37, 23–24, 42, 45–46, and 69–70.
t   Quoted in G. G. Coulton, *Life in the Middle Ages* (Macmillan, New York, 1931), Vol. II, pp. 1–2.

u *On the Division of Nature,* translated by C. Schwartz (St. John's College Bookstore, Annapolis, 1940), I, 6.

v *Ibid.,* I, 14.

w *Ibid.,* I, 15.

x *Ibid.,* I, 72 and 74.

y *Ibid.,* I, 7.

z *Ibid.,* I, 9 and 10.

a *Ibid.,* I, 11.

b Boethius, *Commentary on Porphyry's Introduction,* translated by R. McKeon, in *Selections from Medieval Philosophers* (Scribner's, New York, 1920), Vol. I, p. 91.

c *On the Division of Nature,* translated by Schwartz, *op. cit.,* I, 5.

d *On the Division of Nature,* translated by R. McKeon, in *Selections from Medieval Philosophers, op. cit.,* Vol. I, p. 129.

e *The Glosses of Peter Abailard on Porphyry,* translated by R. McKeon, in *Selections from Medieval Philosophers, op. cit.,* Vol. I, pp. 218–21.

f *Ibid.,* pp. 222–27.

g *Ibid.,* p. 232.

h *Ibid.,* p. 241.

i *Ibid.,* pp. 245–47 and 249–54.

j *On the Division of Nature,* translated by Schwartz, *op. cit.,* I, 66 and 69.

k *Ibid.,* I, 63 and 69.

l Sermon 74, quoted in A. C. McGiffert, *A History of Christian Thought* (Scribner's, New York, 1933), Vol. II, pp. 228–29.

m *De Fide Trinitatis,* quoted in McGiffert, *op. cit.,* Vol. II, p. 186.

n St. Anselm, *Proslogium,* translated by S. N. Deane (Open Court, Chicago, 1903), Chs. 1–4, pp. 6–10.

o Gaunilo, *In Behalf of the Fool,* translated by S. N. Deane (Open Court, Chicago, 1903), p. 151.

Chapter 6 / Thomas: Metaphysics

a *Summa Theologica,* edited by A. C. Pegis, in *Basic Writings of Saint Thomas Aquinas* (Random House, New York, 1945), Pt. I, Ques. 1, Art. 8.

b *Ibid.,* Art. 8.

c *Ibid.,* Pt. I, Ques. 2, Art. 3.

d *Ibid.,* Pt. I, Ques. 2, Art. 1, Reply Obj. 1.

e *Ibid.,* Pt. I, Ques. 2, Art. 1, Reply Obj. 2.

f See *ibid.,* Pt. I, Ques. 3, Art. 1; and *Summa Contra Gentiles,* translated by the English Dominican Fathers (Burns Oates, London, 1924), I, xx.

g See *Summa Theologica,* Pt. I, Ques. 3, Art. 2; and *Summa Contra Gentiles,* I, xvii.

h See *Summa Theologica,* Pt. I, Ques. 3, Art. 7; and *Summa Contra Gentiles,* I, xviii.

i See *Summa Theologica,* Pt. I, Ques. 3, Art. 3; and *Summa Contra Gentiles,* I, xvi.

j *Summa Theologica,* Pt. I, Ques. 4, Art. 1.

k *Ibid.,* Pt. I, Ques. 5, Art. 1, Ans.

l *Summa Contra Gentiles,* I, xliv.

m *Summa Theologica,* Pt. I, Ques. 14, Art. 1, Ans.

n *Summa Contra Gentiles,* I, xlix.

o *Ibid.,* I, lxv.

p *Summa Theologica,* Pt. I, Ques. 19, Art. 1, Ans.

q *Summa Contra Gentiles,* I, lxxv.

r *Summa Theologica,* Pt. I, Ques. 66, Art. 1, Reply Obj. 1; Ques. 68, Art. 3, Ans.

s See *ibid.,* Pt. I, Ques. 19, Art. 2, Ans.

t *Ibid.,* Pt. I, Ques. 22, Art. 1, Ans.

u *Ibid.*, Pt. I, Ques. 22, Art. 2, Reply Obj. 1.
v See *ibid.*, Pt. I, Ques. 19, Art. 5, Reply Obj. 2.
w See *Summa Contra Gentiles*, III, ci.
x *Summa Theologica*, Pt. I, Ques. 22, Art. 4, Ans.
y *Ibid.*, Pt. I, Ques. 68, Art. 2, Reply Objs. 1 and 2.
z *Ibid.*, Pt. I, Ques. 68, Art. 1, Ans.; Art. 2, Ans.
a *Summa Contra Gentiles*, III, lxix, lxx, and lxxvii.

Chapter 7 / Thomas: Psychology, Ethics, Politics

a See *Summa Theologica*, edited by A. C. Pegis, in *Basic Writings of Saint Thomas Aquinas* (Random House, New York, 1945), Pt. I, Ques. 63, Art. 2.
b *Ibid.*, Pt. I, Ques. 78, Art. 4, Ans.
c *Ibid.*
d *Ibid.*, Pt. I, Ques. 79, Art. 3, Ans.
e See *Summa Contra Gentiles*, translated by the English Dominican Fathers (Burns Oates, London, 1924), II, lxxvi–lxxviii; and *Summa Theologica*, Pt. I, Ques. 79, Arts. 4 and 5.
f See *Summa Contra Gentiles*, II, lv.
g See *Summa Theologica*, Pt. I, Ques. 82, Art. 1.
h See *ibid.*, Pt. I–II, Ques. 14, Art. 1.
i See *ibid.*, Pt. I–II, Ques. 10, Art. 2.
j *Ibid.*, Pt. I, Ques. 83, Art. 1, Reply Obj. 5.
k *Ibid.*, Pt. I–II, Ques. 17, Art. 9, Reply Obj. 3.
l *Ibid.*, Pt. I–II, Ques. 17, Art. 7, Ans.
m *Ibid.*, Pt. I, Ques. 81, Art. 3, Reply Obj. 2; Pt. I–II, Ques. 9, Art. 2, Ans.
n *Ibid.*, Pt. I, Ques. 83, Art. 1, Reply Obj. 3.
o G. Murphy, *Personality* (Harper & Row, New York, 1947), p. 290.
p *Ibid.*, p. 917.
q *Summa Contra Gentiles*, III, xxv.
r *Ibid.*, III, xxxviii.
s *Ibid.*, III, xxxvii–xxxviii.
t *Ibid.*, III, lxi–lxii.
u *Summa Theologica*, Pt. I–II, Ques. 18, Art. 4, Ans.
v *Ibid.*, Pt. I–II, Ques. 20, Art. 5, Ans.
w See *ibid.*, Pt. I–II, Ques. 8, Art. 1.
x *Ibid.*, Pt. I–II, Ques. 93, Art. 1, Ans.
y See *ibid.*, Pt. I–II, Ques. 91, Art. 2, Ans.
z *Ibid.*, Pt. I–II, Ques. 57, Art. 2, Ans.; Ques. 59, Art. 4, Ans.
a *Summa Contra Gentiles*, III, cxxxiii and cxxxv.
b *Ibid.*, III, cxxxvi.
c *Summa Theologica*, Pt. I–II, Ques. 62, Art. 1, Ans.; Art. 3, Ans.
d See II Cor. 13:13.
e *Summa Theologica*, Pt. I–II, Ques. 64, Art. 4.
f *Ibid.*, Pt. I–II, Ques. 95, Art. 1, Ans.
g *Ibid.*, Pt. I–II, Ques. 90, Art. 4, Ans.
h *De Regimine Principum*, translated by G. B. Phelan (published for the Institute of Mediaeval Studies by Sheed and Ward, London, 1938), I, 1.
i *Ibid.*
j *Ibid.*, I, 2.
k *Ibid.*, I, 14.
l *Summa Theologica*, Pt. I–II, Ques. 90, Art. 3, Ans.

m *De Regimine Principum,* translated by G. B. Phelan, *op. cit.,* I, 6.
n *Summa Theologica,* Pt. I–II, Ques. 97, Art. 3, Ans.
o *Summa Contra Gentiles,* III, lxxiii; and *Summa Theologica,* Pt. I, Ques. 83, Art. 1, Ans.
p See *Summa Theologica,* Pt. I, Ques. 23, Arts. 1 and 3.
q *Ibid.,* Pt. I, Ques. 23, Art. 5, Reply Obj. 3.
r *Ibid.,* Pt. I, Ques. 23, Art. 2, Ans.; Art. 5, Reply Obj. 3.
s *Ibid.,* Pt. I–II, Ques. 109, Art. 3, Ans.
t *Ibid.,* Pt. I–II, Ques. 111, Art. 3, Ans.
u *Ibid.,* Pt. I–II, Ques. 109, Art. 6, Ans.; Ques. 112, Art. 2, Ans.
v *Ibid.,* Pt. I, Ques. 23, Art. 3, Reply Obj. 3; Pt. I–II, Ques. 109, Art. 6, Reply Objs. 1 and 4; Ques. 112, Arts. 2 and 3, Ans.

Chapter 8 / The End of the Middle Ages

a Quoted in *Cambridge Modern History* (Macmillan, New York, 1903–52), Vol. I (1930), p. 585.
b Quoted in H. O. Taylor, *The Mediaeval Mind* (Macmillan, New York, 1927), Vol. II, p. 519.
c Quoted in J. H. Bridges, *The Life and Work of Roger Bacon* (Williams and Norgate, London, 1914), p. 30.
d See, for instance, *Opus Majus,* translated by R. B. Burke (University of Pennsylvania Press, 1928), Vol. II, pp. 580–82.
e *Ibid.,* Vol. I, pp. 3 and 36.
f *Ibid.,* Vol. II, pp. 419–20, 430–32, and 576–78.
g *Ibid.,* Vol. II, pp. 583–90, 593, 599, and 601.
h *Ibid.,* Vol. I, pp. 4–5 and 23.
i *Ibid.,* Vol. I, pp. 44 and 48.
j *Ibid.,* Vol. I, pp. 64–65.
k *The Oxford Commentary on the Four Books of the Master of the Sentences,* translated by R. McKeon, in *Selections from Medieval Philosophers* (Scribner's, New York, 1920), Vol. II, p. 313.
l Rom. 1:19–20, in *The Complete Bible,* translated by J. M. P. Smith and E. J. Goodspeed (University of Chicago Press, 1939).
m *Oxford Commentary,* translated by McKeon, in *Selections from Medieval Philosophers, op. cit.,* Vol. II, pp. 324–26 and 329–30.
n Quoted in J. R. Weinberg, *Nicholaus of Autrecourt* (Princeton University Press, 1948), pp. 88–89.
o *Sum of All Logic,* I, 12, 6R, quoted in E. A. Moody, *The Logic of William of Ockham* (Sheed and Ward, London, 1935), pp. 49–50.
p John Buridan, *Questions on the Four Books on the Heavens and the World of Aristotle,* in M. Clagett, *The Science of Mechanism in the Middle Ages* (University of Wisconsin Press, 1959), pp. 557–61.

Suggestions for Further Reading

The best course to pursue is to turn directly to the various great texts from which the selections in this volume have been drawn. Thus, instead of being content with the extracts given here, read more deeply in Augustine's *City of God* and in Thomas' *Summa Theologica*. Information concerning translations and editions will be found in the bibliographical notes section.

Beyond the masters themselves, here is a short list of books about them and their times that should help to make their theories more intelligible.

AUGUSTINE

R. W. Battenhouse (editor): *A Companion to the Study of Augustine* (New York, 1955). Essays by sixteen scholars, covering Augustine's life and major works and a number of special topics.

H. A. Deane: *The Political and Social Ideas of St. Augustine* (New York, 1963). Since

Augustine's views on politics are scattered in many different works, this study includes extensive excerpts as well as comment and criticism.

E. Portalie: *A Guide to the Thought of Saint Augustine,* translated by R. J. Bastion, with an introduction by V. J. Bourke (Chicago, 1960). Though this study is almost seventy years old, it has only recently become available in English. The introduction contains detailed bibliographical information regarding recent scholarship.

THOMAS

F. Copleston: *Aquinas* (Baltimore, 1955). A useful study by a distinguished historian of philosophy.

M. C. D'Arcy: *Thomas Aquinas* (Boston, 1930). An able exposition by an English Catholic.

E. Gilson: *The Philosophy of St. Thomas Aquinas* (Cambridge, 1929). One of the ablest expositions available to the general reader.

M. Grabmann: *Thomas Aquinas, His Personality and Thought* (New York, 1928). A detailed and sympathetic account of Thomas' life and personality.

J. Maritain: *St. Thomas Aquinas,* translated by J. F. Scanlan (London, 1946). Holds Thomism to be the correct antidote for the vices of the "anti-Christian revolution" of contemporary culture.

GENERAL

C. N. Cochrane: *Christianity and Classical Culture* (New York, 1944). A scholarly study of the Augustan ideal and of its criticism by Christian apologists. "The theme of this work is the revolution in thought and action which came about through the impact of Christianity upon the Graeco-Roman world."

M. de Wulf: *History of Medieval Philosophy* (New York, 1935–38). A detailed and encyclopedic study; the standard history of the period.

E. R. Dodds: *Pagan and Christian in an Age of Anxiety* (Cambridge, 1965). Concentrates on the period from Marcus Aurelius to the conversion of Constantine. Written from the point of view of one who is "interested less in the issues that separated the combatants than in the attitudes and experiences which bound them together."

E. Gilson: *The Spirit of Mediaeval Philosophy* (New York, 1936). One of the best introductions to the philosophy of the period.

W. R. Inge: *The Philosophy of Plotinus* (London, 1929). A detailed and useful study by a sympathetic theologian.

A. C. McGiffert: *A History of Christian Thought* (New York, 1932). A temperate and very useful handbook.

P. Merlan: *From Platonism to Neoplatonism* (The Hague, 1960). A detailed and learned study that minimizes the differences between Platonism and Neoplatonism.

E. A. Moody: *The Logic of William of Ockham* (New York, 1965). Holds that Occam's logical theories are surprisingly "modern" and free from the kinds of theological presuppositions that dominated most medieval philosophical inquiry.

E. M. Pickman: *The Mind of Latin Christendom* (New York, 1937). Especially good on Augustine.

H. Pirenne: *Medieval Cities* (New York, 1956). Stimulating lectures for the general public, emphasizing the role of "the middle class in the development of the modern economic system and modern culture."

H. Rashdall: *The Universities of Europe in the Middle Ages* (Oxford, 1936). One of the classic works on this subject.

A. Schweitzer: *The Quest of the Historical Jesus* (New York, 1955). A good summary of nineteenth- and twentieth-century scholarship in this field.

J. G. Sikes: *Peter Abailard* (New York, 1965). Emphasizes Abelard's intellectualism, his interest in ethical theory, and his method of applying logic to theological questions.

H. O. Taylor: *The Mediaeval Mind* (Cambridge, Mass., 1959). Discusses "the various strains that entered into the Mediaeval character" and analyzes some of the representative personalities in which it was displayed.

Glossary

Short, dictionary-type definitions of philosophical terms are likely to be misleading, for philosophers use terms in many different ways and with little regard to common usage (on which, of course, dictionary definitions are based). Accordingly, many of the definitions given in this Glossary are accompanied by references to places in the text where the terms in question appear in a concrete context. For terms not defined in the Glossary, consult the Index; for fuller treatment of them and of other philosophical terms, see *The Encyclopedia of Philosophy*, edited by P. Edwards (Free Press, New York, 1967). Also available are the *Dictionary of Philosophy*, edited by D. D. Runes (Philosophical Library, New York, 1942), and *Dictionary of Philosophy and Psychology*, edited by J. M. Baldwin (Macmillan, New York, 1925). The *Encyclopaedia Britannica* (eleventh edition) contains excellent articles on many philosophical terms, including some of those in this Glossary.

Abstraction: The power of separating, in thought, one part of a complex from the other parts and attending to it separately. Thus to consider the color of an apple in isolation from the apple's other qualities would be to abstract this quality for attention.

A priori: What is known independently of sense perception and for this reason held to be indubitable. The doctrine of innate ideas (see definition) was an attempt to account for the alleged existence of a priori knowledge.

Attribute: See **Substance**.

Axiom: A proposition held to be self-evidently true and so neither requiring nor indeed capable of proof. Hence a first principle from which all proofs start. Those who deny the self-evident truth of axioms hold them to be simply postulates from which such-and-such theorems can be deduced. Thus, according to this view, the axioms of one deductive system may be deduced from another set of postulates in some other deductive system.

Conceptualism: The view that universals are neither independently existing entities nor mere names, but are concepts formed in the mind. See **Realism, Nominalism,** and **Universal**.

Contingent: That which may be and also may not be. Hence an event whose occurrence is not necessarily determined (see **Determinism**) by other events.

Cosmology: The study of the universal world process. Distinguished from ontology (see definition) chiefly by the fact that, whereas the latter asks what reality *is*, cosmology asks how reality unfolds and develops in successive stages.

Deduction: A type of inference (see definition) that yields necessary conclusions. In deduction, one or more propositions (called "premises") being assumed, another proposition (the conclusion) is seen to be entailed or implied. It is usually held that in deduction the movement of thought is from premises of greater generality to a conclusion of lesser generality (from the premises "All men are mortal" and "All Greeks are men," we deduce that "All Greeks are mortal"), but the chief mark of deduction is the necessity with which the conclusion follows from the premises.

Determinism: The theory that denies contingency (see **Contingent**) and claims that everything that happens happens necessarily and in accordance with some regular pattern or law. There are three main types, or versions, of determinism: (1) a *scientific determinism* (in which all events are determined by antecedent events in time), (2) a *logical determinism* (as with Spinoza), and (3) a *teleological determinism* (as with Augustine, who held that all events are determined in accordance with God's plan [see pp. 129–30]).

Dialectic: A term used to designate the process by which (as, for instance, in Plotinus' view) we pass from the hypothetical starting points of the various special sciences to the unconditioned first principle, or the Form of the Good (see pp. 8–12).

Discursive: The characteristic of the human intelligence that limits it, in the main, to a step-by-step reasoning—from premises to conclusion, from this conclusion to another, and so on. Hence to be contrasted with the all-inclusive vision of the mystic (see pp. 199–201), with the possible operation of a suprahuman intellect (see pp. 178–79), and with the way in which, according to Aristotle and other writers, axioms (see **Axiom**) and other self-evident principles are comprehended by the mind.

Dualism: Any view that holds two ultimate and irreducible principles to be necessary to explain the world. Manicheism (see pp. 67–69), a type of dualism, was a recurrent danger for Christian thinkers, since to introduce a second irreducible explanatory principle is to limit God (see pp. 94–100).

Empiricism: The view that holds sense perception to be the sole source of human knowledge.

Epistemology: From the Greek terms *episteme* (knowledge) and *logos* (theory, account). Hence the study of the origins, nature, and limitations of knowledge.

Essence: The that-about-a-thing-that-makes-it-what-it-is, in contrast to those properties that the thing may happen to possess but need not possess in order to be itself. Thus it is held (1) that we have to distinguish between those properties of Socrates that are "accidental" and so nonessential (for example, dying by hemlock) and those properties that are essential (for example, those traits of character and personality that made him the man he was). Further, it is held (2) that we have to distinguish between essence and existence (see definition): It is possible (according to this view) to define Socrates' essence exhaustively; yet when we have done so, the question still remains whether any such being exists. Holders of this view would maintain that there is only one object in which essence and existence are inseparable; this object is God (For Thomas' discussion of this point, see pp. 223–25).

Eudaemonism: From the Greek term *eudaimonia*, usually translated as "happiness." Hence the view that the end of life consists in happiness, conceived of as an all-round, balanced, long-range type of well-being, in distinction from pleasure. Contrasted with hedonism (see definition).

Existence: Actuality or factuality. Contrasted with essence (see definition).

Experiment: A situation arranged to test an hypothesis. Contrasted with "mere" observation.

Free will: The doctrine of contingency (see **Contingent**) applied specifically to human behavior; the denial that men's acts are completely determined (see **Determinism**). The question of free will is important because many philosophers hold that "ought" implies "can"—that moral judgments of approbation and disapprobation are meaningless unless the acts judged about are free, that is, under the control of the agent, who, had he so chosen, might have done otherwise. The main problems connected with free will are (1) what meaning, if any, can be attached to the notion of a free choice and (2) how the possibility of being otherwise is compatible with either (a) belief in an omnipotent and omniscient Deity or (b) the doctrine of universal causal determinism. See Index.

Hedonism: The view that pleasure is man's good. Contrasted with eudaemonism (see definition). *Ethical hedonism* holds either (1) that a man's own pleasure is the sole end worth aiming at or (2) that other people's pleasure is to be taken into account. *Psychological hedonism* holds that, whatever men ought to aim at, they do in fact aim at pleasure.

Humanism: A variously used term. Employed (1) to describe the type of view that distinguishes man from animals on the ground that man has certain moral obligations. Also used (2) to contrast a secular type of ethics with a religious ethics. Thus Plato's and Aristotle's ethics could be called "humanistic," in contrast with the ethics of Augustine, on the ground that they hold man himself, rather than God, to be the supreme value. Also used (3) to designate a particular historical movement, beginning in the fourteenth century, that emphasized the study of classical literature and the revival of classical ideals.

Idealism: In general, any view that holds reality to be mental or "spiritual," or mind-dependent. *Subjective idealism* emphasizes the ultimate reality of the knowing subject and may either admit the existence of a plurality of such subjects or deny the existence of all save one (in which case the view is called solipsism [see definition]).

Objective idealism denies that the distinction between subject and object, between knower and known, is ultimate and maintains that all finite knowers and their thoughts are included in an Absolute Thought.

Induction: A type of inference (see definition) in which (in contrast to deduction [see definition]) the movement of thought is from lesser to greater generality. Thus induction begins, not from premises, but from observed particulars (for example, the observation that A, B, and C all have the property x) and seeks to establish some generalization about them (for example, that all members of the class y, of which A, B, and C are members, have the property x). The main problem connected with induction is the difficulty of determining the conditions under which we are warranted in moving from an observed "Some so-and-so's have such-and-such" to the unobserved "All so-and-so's probably have such-and-such."

Inference: The movement of thought by which we reach a conclusion from premises. Thus we speak of inductive and of deductive inference.

Innate ideas: According to the doctrine of innate ideas, we must distinguish between (1) ideas that we acquire in the course of our experience and (2) ideas that we possess antecedently to all experience. Holders of this view would allow that some experience may be the occasion of our becoming consciously aware of an innate idea, but they would argue that the idea itself (for example, the idea of absolute equality) can never be found in experience.

Intuition: Direct and immediate knowledge. To be contrasted with discursive (see definition) knowledge.

Judgment: The movement of thought by which, for example, we assert (or deny) some predicate of a subject, or, more generally, by which we connect two terms by some relation. Thus, when we say "This rose is red" or "New York is east of Chicago," we judge. Following Kant, most philosophers distinguish between (1) *analytical judgments,* in which the predicate concept is contained in the subject concept, and (2) *synthetical judgments,* in which the predicate concept is not so contained; and also between (3) *a priori judgments,* which are universal and necessary, and (4) *a posteriori judgments,* which are not universal and necessary.

Law of nature: See **Natural law.**

Materialism: The doctrine that reality is matter. Whereas idealism (see definition) holds that matter is "really" the thought of some mind or other, materialism holds that minds and all other apparently nonmaterial things (for example, gods) are reducible to the complex motions of material particles.

Metaphysics: The study of the ultimate nature of reality, or, as some philosophers would say, the study of "being as such." To be contrasted, therefore, with physics, which studies the "being" of physical nature; with astronomy, which studies the "being" of the solar system; with biology, which studies the "being" of animate nature; and so on. By "being as such," these philosophers mean, not the special characteristics of special kinds of things (for example, living things), but the most general and pervasive characteristics of all things.

Monism: The view that everything is reducible to one kind of thing, or that one principle of explanation is sufficient to explain everything. No Christian philosopher could be a monist, for the Christian must insist on an ultimate and irreducible distinction between God the Creator and the universe He created.

Mysticism: The view that reality is ineffable and transcendent; that it is known, therefore, by some special, nonrational means; that knowledge of it is incommunicable in any precise conceptual scheme; and that it is communicable, if at all, only in poetic imagery and metaphor (see, for instance, pp. 12–13).

Naturalism: Another variously used term. (1) In one meaning, naturalism is a view that excludes any reference to supernatural principles and holds the world to be explicable in terms of scientifically verifiable concepts. In this meaning, naturalism is roughly equivalent to secularism and, like humanism (see definition), can be contrasted with a religiously oriented theory like Neoplatonism. (2) In another meaning, the emphasis is on the unity of behavior; any difference in kind between men and animals is denied, and human conduct and human institutions are held to be simply more complex instances of behavior patterns occurring among lower organisms. In this sense, naturalism is to be contrasted with humanism.

Natural law: This term may designate (1) a pattern of regularity that holds in physical nature. Thus people talk about the "law" of gravity and hold it to be a law of nature (or a natural law) that bodies attract each other directly with their masses and inversely with the square of their distance. Those who affirm the existence of natural laws in this sense hold that these laws are necessary and universal (not merely empirical generalizations concerning observable sequences) and that they are discoverable by reason. Or the term may designate (2) a moral imperative—not a description of what actually happens in the physical world, but a description of what *ought* to happen in men's relations to one another. In this sense, too, these laws would be regarded by those who affirm their existence as being of universal application and discoverable by reason. (For a typical medieval version of natural law, see pp. 264–65).

Nominalism: The view that only particulars are real and that universals (see **Universal**) are but observable likenesses among the particulars of sense experience. (For an example of medieval nominalism, see p. 189.)

Objective: To say that anything is "objective" is to say that it is real, that it has a public nature independent of us and of our judgments about it. Thus the question of whether or not values are objective turns on whether or not values are more than private preferences. If they are private preferences, our value judgments are subjective, and there is no more disputing about them than there is about judgments of taste: My good is what *I* prefer; yours is what *you* prefer. On the other hand, if values are objective, it follows that when we differ about them, at least one of us is mistaken.

Ontological argument: An argument for the existence of God, first formulated by St. Anselm (see pp. 201–06). According to this argument, since perfection implies existence, God necessarily exists.

Ontology: From the Greek terms *ontos* (being) and *logos* (theory, account). About equivalent in meaning to metaphysics (see definition). When we inquire about the "ontological status" of something, say, perception, we ask whether the objects of perception are real or illusory, and, if real, what sort of reality they possess (for example, whether they are mind-dependent or whether they exist independently of minds), and so on.

Pantheism: From the Greek terms *pan* (all) and *theos* (god). Hence the view that all things share in the divine nature, or that all things are parts of god. Pantheism represented a danger that Christian thinkers, who were committed to a transcendent God, had at all costs to avoid (see, for instance, pp. 182–84).

Phenomenalism: A type of view that, like idealism (see definition), holds that what we know is mind-dependent, but that, unlike idealism, holds that reality itself is not mind-dependent. Usually, phenomenalism does not attempt to inquire into the possible underlying causes of events, but limits itself to generalizing about empirically observable sequences.

Primary qualities: Those qualities thought to belong to bodies. To be distinguished from secondary qualities, which are held to be products of the interaction between our sense organs and the primary qualities of bodies.

Rationalism: (1) As contrasted with empiricism (see definition), rationalism means reliance on reason (that is, on deduction, on the criterion of logical consistency). (2) As contrasted with authoritarianism or mysticism (see definition), rationalism means reliance on our human powers.

Realism: (1) As contrasted with nominalism (see definition), realism holds that universals are real, and more real than the particulars of sense experience. (For a medieval version of this form of realism, see pp. 187–88.) (2) As contrasted with idealism (see definition), realism holds that the objects of our knowledge are not mind-dependent but are independently existing entities. (3) As contrasted with idealism in still another sense, realism is the point of view that interests itself in men and institutions as they are, rather than as they ought to be. In this sense, realism is almost equivalent to naturalism (see definition).

Relativism: The view that maintains our judgments to be relative to (that is, conditioned upon) certain factors such as cultural milieu or individual bias. Hence the view that we do not possess any absolute, objective (see definition) truth. The relativist need not hold that all judgments are relative; it is possible, for instance, to hold that the physical sciences yield absolute truth while maintaining that in other fields (for example, ethics and religion) there is no absolute truth.

Scepticism: The position that denies the possibility of knowledge. Here, as with relativism (see definition), it is possible either to have a total scepticism or to limit one's scepticism to certain fields. Thus it is possible (as with Plato) to be sceptical of sense perception while holding that we can reach the truth by means of reason, or (as with St. Bernard) to be sceptical of reason while holding that we can reach the truth in a mystical experience (see **Mysticism**).

Scholasticism: The philosophical method in vogue during much of the Middle Ages. First worked out by Abelard and given its classic form by Thomas Aquinas.

Solipsism: From the Latin terms *solus* (alone) and *ipse* (self). Hence the view that everything other than oneself is a state of oneself.

Subjectivism: See **Objective, Relativism,** and **Scepticism**.

Substance: Another variously used term. (1) In one meaning, substance is simply that which is real. Thus Aristotle called those amalgams of matter and form that he took reality to consist of "substances." (2) In another meaning, substance is about equivalent to essence (see definition). Also, (3) substance is contrasted with attribute (or property, or quality) as that which *has* the attributes. Thus substance is the underlying (and unknown) ground in which properties are thought to inhere; it is that about which we are judging when we assert properties of a subject, for example, when we say "The rose is red." Hence (4) substance is that which, unlike an attribute or property, exists in its own right and depends on nothing else. See Index.

Teleology: From the Greek terms *telos* (end, goal) and *logos* (theory, account). Hence the view that affirms the reality of purpose and holds the universe either to be consciously designed (as with the Christian doctrine of a providential God) or (as with Aristotle) to be the working out of partly conscious, partly unconscious purposes that are immanent in the developing organisms.

Theology: From the Greek terms *theos* (god) and *logos* (theory, account). Hence the study of the divine nature and its properties. *Natural theology* is that part of theology held to be accessible to men by means of rational inquiry. *Revealed theology* is that part of theology held to be inaccessible to men unless they are aided by revelation.

Universal: A universal is that which is predicable of many. Thus "man" is a universal because it is predicable of Washington, Jefferson, Hamilton, and all other individual men. The main problem about universals concerns their ontological status (see **Ontology**). Are they (1) separate entities distinct from the individuals of which they are predicable, (2) real but not separable, or (3) not real at all, but merely the names of likenesses shared by certain particulars? See **Nominalism, Realism,** and Index.

Voluntarism: The theory that asserts the primacy of will over intellect as an explanatory principle of human behavior, of God's nature, and of the universe as a whole. (For an example of medieval voluntarism, see pp. 311–13).

Index

This is primarily an index of proper names. Thus titles and principal topics of discussion are indexed under the authors. Topics that recur in the work of several philosophers are also indexed as main entries. Page numbers in *italics* refer to quotations; those in **boldface** refer to major discussions.